MARTYRDOM IN THE SIKH TRADITION

The notion of martyrdom and the role of martyrs in religious and political history constitutes a major component in discourse among Sikh throughout the world. This book examines how and why Sikhs began to represent their history as a history of persecutions and martyrdoms and how these understandings continue to play such a vital role in the Sikh community today. It explores the different approaches to the martyrdom of Guru Arjan, Guru Tegh Bahadur, and other prominent Sikhs. Through an analysis of Sikh scriptures and eighteenth and nineteenth century Sikh literature it demonstrates how the Singh Sabha 'reform' movement and the heroism of the Akalis in the 1920s shaped historical facts and interpretations.

Fenech's interdisciplinary study is invaluable for all those interested in nineteenth-century Indian religious history and in the history of the Sikh people as well as for scholars of history, sociology, religion, anthropology, politics, and culture.

Louis E. Fenech is Associate Professor of South Asian History, University of Northern Iowa.

MARTYRDOM IN THE SIKH TRADITION

Playing the 'Game of Love'

Louis E. Fenech

OXFORD
UNIVERSITY PRESS

OXFORD
UNIVERSITY PRESS

Oxford University Press is a department of the University of Oxford.
It furthers the University's objective of excellence in research, scholarship,
and education by publishing worldwide. Oxford is a registered trademark of
Oxford University Press in the UK and in certain other countries

Published in India by
Oxford University Press
YMCA Library Building, 1 Jai Singh Road, New Delhi 110 001, India

First Edition published in 2000
Oxford India Paperbacks 2005
Third impression 2015

ISBN-13: 978-0-19-567901-4
ISBN-10: 0-19-567901-6

Typeset in Times New Roman
by Wordsmiths, Delhi 110 034

jau tau prem khelaṇ kā chāu
siru dharī talī gali merī āu
itu māragi pair dharījai
siru dījai kāṇi na kījai

If you want to play the game of love approach me with your head on the palm of your hand. Place your feet on this path and give your head without regard to the opinion of others.

Guru Nanak, *Slok vārān te vadhik* 20, Adi Granth, p. 1412.

To
PROFESSOR W.H. McLEOD
in gratitude

Be-mai sajjādah rangīn kon garat pīr-i moghān guyad
Kah sālik be-khabr na-bovad za rāh o rasam manzilhā
Ḥafez

Contents

Illustrations

Preface

> I counted twenty-three 1979 calendars in that room. No-one cared
> what day it was, but calendars were cheap and decorative. All
> depicted religious scenes and included, in a generous and hospitable
> way, the Hindu god Krishna flirting with the milkmaids, the mosque
> at Mecca and Christ nailed to the cross. The Sikh pictures portrayed
> their Gurus and gruesome excerpts from their history: gory battle-
> scenes, babies being spiked on spears, severed heads and limbs and
> men boiling in cauldrons of oil or being sawn in half vertically. I
> tried to pretend the calendars weren't there but Jungli was always
> drawing my attention to one or other horrendous scene, recounting
> their stoic exploits with pride.[1]

There is perhaps no more inauspicious way to begin a book on the
Sikh tradition than to quote from Sarah Lloyd's *An Indian Attachment*, the account of her one-year affair in 1979 with a Sikh named
Jungli. Two particular points make this clear. The first is that this
work is a typical example of the 'personal' orientalism that Edward
Said decries in his celebrated book, *Orientalism*, a discourse in which
European and American authors '[find] in the Orient a locale sympathetic to their private myths, obsessions and requirements'.[2] The
second is that Jungli is a Nihang Sikh. Although a minuscule segment
of the entire Sikh Panth at best, Nihangs are easily the most flamboyant and martial type of Sikh identity (or so they claim).
Appropriating his words as authoritative makes it appear as if Jungli
is, indeed, representative of Sikhs and Sikhism in general.[3]

Having said this, however, we should also point out the particular
benefits of this citation. The quotation, for example, allows one to
infer the reverence for martyrs and for martyrdom within the Sikh
tradition—Jungli's Nihang background notwithstanding. No doubt
even a casual observer of today's Sikh tradition cannot avoid noting

such respect and reverence as it permeates virtually every facet of contemporary Punjabi Sikh culture. But what, to my mind, adds a substantial emphasis to this point is that Jungli is quoted as having said these words in 1979, five years before the situation in Punjab took the drastic turn which made the theme of martyrdom amongst the Sikhs so memorable to many journalists and scholars of India.[4] It was in June 1984 that Operation Bluestar commenced, in which the then Prime Minister of India, Indira Gandhi, sent the Indian Army into the Golden Temple to flush out entrenched Sikh militants led by Jarnail Singh Bhindranwale and Major-General Shahbeg Singh. The Prime Minister's decision to storm (or liberate) Harimandir eventually resulted in her assassination by two of her trusted Sikh bodyguards on 31 October 1984 and the widespread killing of Sikhs, especially in Delhi, the day after her death. It was this tragic humiliation which played a fundamental role in convincing many Sikhs to take to a life of militancy. This decision eventually led to the organization of militant Sikh cells in which the martyr's appeal was paramount.[5] A letter sent to the President of India in 1987 and attributed to the celebrated slayers of General Vaidya, Sukhjinder 'Sukha' Singh and Harijinder 'Jinda' Singh, makes this abundantly clear:

The elimination of Mr. Vaidya ... was a holy act on our difficult path of martyrdom. By performing our historic task we have reminded you that our heroes like Sukha Singh, Mehtab Singh, Udham Singh are shadowing you tyrants...We accept with great joy the penalty of death pronounced by your court of law ... by touching the sharp edge of death we are moving towards fullness. Without martyrdom the magnificent fare of life cannot come into full swing ... [the] Guru Granth Sahib instills tremendous self-confidence in us. Inspired [by this sacred text], our heroes like Sukha Singh and Mehtab Singh [were able to kill] a tyrant like Massa Ranghar and bring [his] head as an offering to the [Sikh] community. Our inspiration also stems from the same Guru Granth Sahib... Our Beant Singh and Satwant Singh [Mrs. Gandhi's assassins] were also inspired by the light of the same Guru Granth Sahib and they went for a great deed. After them, we too had the privilege of being inspired by a ray of the same divine light and we struck General Vaidya in Pune.[6]

In this brief excerpt employing the Sikh rhetoric of martyrdom, there are many themes which we will touch upon in this book.

In 1984 as well, some eight hundred and fifty kilometres southeast of Amritsar, another explosive affair was commencing. The Vishva

Hindu Parishad (VHP, World Council of Hindus), a Hindu nationalist movement, launched a campaign to liberate the so-called birthplace of the Hindu god Rama in Ayodhya, the Ramjanambhumi. This decision would eventually result in the destruction of the Babri mosque on 6 December 1992 by a Hindu mob and, subsequently, riots throughout the subcontinent between Hindus and Muslims, in which thousands, especially Muslims, lost their lives.[7]

It was principally the Ayodhya controversy and the events surrounding it which precipitated the numerous books and monographs dealing with religious nationalism in South Asia. For these scholars, the Ayodhya events as well as those in Amritsar were symbolic of the rise of religious nationalism. More often than not, therefore, the happenings in Punjab over the last two decades have found a place in their texts, sometimes forming substantial chapters within such monographs. All these texts, relying completely on secondary sources, note the reverence that contemporary Sikhs have for martyrs and martyrdom and how this has allegedly figured in the current drive (amongst some Sikhs anyway) for a separate Sikh state known as Khalistan. Indeed, there can be no doubt that the allure of martyrdom has played a major role in this effort.[8]

Yet what is the history and origin of this tradition within Sikhism that so enraptured a large number of present-day Sikhs to end their lives in what appears to be, in retrospect, so fruitless a task? Clearly, the reference to martyrs had and continues to have an extraordinary appeal. How this developed and how it is sustained is the subject of the present book.

This book represents a revised version of my dissertation, 'Playing the "Game of Love": The Sikh Tradition of Martyrdom', submitted for the Ph.D. degree to the Centre for South Asian Studies at the University of Toronto in 1995. It was here as an undergraduate in the early 1980s that I cultivated my interest in the Punjab and the Sikh people. I was ironically first attracted to the Sikh tradition in 1984 not because of the events in Punjab at this time (of which I knew very little), but as a result of sitting in on what would be the last class that the great Indologist; A.L. Basham, ever taught. The next year, Professor W.H. McLeod, a student of Basham in the early 1960s, was appointed as a visiting Commonwealth Scholar to the University of Toronto, a fact that allowed me to further enrich my fascination for the Sikh tradition. It was in this class that I first became aware of the profound Sikh reverence for martyrdom and here that I was fortunate enough to first encounter the stirring narrative of Baba Dip Singh, the great Sikh martyr of Amritsar.

It was this narrative which especially attracted me and I chose initially to write a paper on it for McLeod's class. I abandoned the project at first because of the paucity of material on the subject. Little did I know at the time, however, that I would again take up this endeavour, which would take the better part of twelve years and numerous trips to the Punjab to complete.

In the process of completing it, I have accumulated, as most scholars do, a large number of debts. The most rewarding experience has been having Hew McLeod as my supervisor and mentor. He led me through the dissertation with a sensitive and guiding hand, demonstrating an insightfulness and compassion that I have rarely encountered. As the dissertation was being transformed into a book, he was always there to offer helpful critiques and suggestions. To him I owe the greatest thanks and it is to him that I dedicate this book as a token of my appreciation and affection. Warmest thanks are also due to Margaret McLeod for her unfailing patience. I am also grateful to three others who, unbeknownst to them, had a significant impact on my understanding of the Sikh tradition. My discussions with Surjit Hans during the many lunches we shared and the wonderful evening walks we took through the fields adjoining Guru Nanak Dev University were considerable in shaping my opinions. To him I owe a particular debt of gratitude, which I warmly acknowledge here. Also, to my tutor of Punjabi and Braj, Prem Singh of the Linguistics Department at Delhi University. For the honour of his company, his wisdom and his limitless patience, I am profoundly grateful. I also send my thanks to his wonderful family, who allowed us to work in their kitchen unperturbed. Finally, there is Harish Puri and his family. Our stimulating conversations made contemporary events and Punjab politics much more lucid to me. Their hospitality and encouragement, moreover, made the heat of Amritsar in June barely noticeable.

Numerous others also deserve a special note of gratitude. My good friend and colleague, Pashaura Singh, was always only a phone call away to offer suggestions and help with difficult translations. His enthusiastic (and at times critical) comments were very much appreciated. My thanks to Van Dusenbery, Harjot Oberoi and Jerry Barrier as well, whose valued comments on various drafts of this work made my task far less difficult. I also wish to acknowledge the thought-provoking remarks I received from J.T. O'Connell, Maria

Subtelny, W.G. Oxtoby, Stella Sandahl, Beth Davies, Darshan Singh of Panjab University, J.S. Grewal, J.S. Rahi, Gurdharam Singh Khalsa, Greg Kozolowski, N.K. Wagle, Milton Israel, Ranjit Singh Bajwa and Ken Bliele. A special note of thanks to Professor Indu Banga who made my stay at Panjab University in Chandigarh a very comfortable and fruitful one. Also, thanks are due to my colleagues at the University of Northern Iowa, particularly Greg Bruess, Chuck Holcombe, Reinier H. Hesselink, and John Johnson, who helped provide a very comfortable and stimulating atmosphere in which to work. I must note that the responsibility for the opinions expressed in this book are mine alone.

I am also grateful to those institutions which aided me in my research. To Guru Nanak Dev University, in particular Professor Virk of the Physics Department, and all my friends' at the Faculty House and in the Department of History who made me feel welcome. I also acknowledge with thanks the librarians and personnel at the Sikh History Research Department at Khalsa College, particularly the director Kulvinder Singh Bajwa, who allowed me access to rare manuscripts and to the various Sikh newspapers published during the Gurdwara Reform Movement. I appreciate the help of the staff of the Bhai Vir Singh Sahitya Sadan of New Delhi, especially its chief librarian, Navneet Kaur, and its director, Mohinder Singh. Also, the staff at the Delhi University Guest House who made my stay in India's capital a pleasant one has my thanks. I acknowledge with thanks the assistance of the Shastri Indo-Canadian Institute, which funded a prolonged stay in India during 1990–91; the Social Sciences and Research Council of Canada, which contributed funds for a return trip to Punjab in 1993; and the University of Northern Iowa, whose faculty fellowship allowed me to complete my research in Amritsar in June 1997. Thanks also to Tim O'Connor and David Walker for their financial assistance. Moreover, I thank the British Library, which granted me permission to use the photograph of Jathedar Santa Singh of Sargodha (who led the third *Sahīdī jathā* to Jaito in 1924) which appears on the front cover of this book. For this photo, I thank Amandeep Singh Madra as well. Thanks also to the Secretary of the SGPC, Bhai Surjit Singh, who allowed me to reproduce the various paintings of Kirpal Singh which appear in this book.

Friends and relatives in England and Canada deserve a special note of recognition. My parents, of course, deserve great thanks for allowing me to pursue studies at the University of Toronto in what clearly seemed to them an esoteric subject. My in-laws in Cornwall, Reg and Peggy Edwards, provided a very relaxed atmosphere after months of fieldwork in the Punjab. The late Shirley Uldall, secretary of the Centre for South Asian Studies at the University of Toronto, along with my professors and colleagues at the Centre deserve a measure of gratitude, which I note here. Shirley's encouragement and warmth made my last year at Toronto an especially pleasant one. My friends, Peter Ribeiro and Tom Newton, also deserve special mention for their various contributions to the present work.

Finally, my deepest gratitude to my wife, Christine, and my children, Hanno and Agatha. They have indeed suffered during my absences, a fact which they will not acknowledge. My wife was both a challenging and enthusiastic listener during the various stages of the book. Her keen insight and support has helped sustain me throughout the years.

Notes

1. Sarah Lloyd, *An Indian Attachment* (New York, 1984), p. 24.

2. Edward W. Said, *Orientalism* (New York, 1979), p. 170.

3. One can be easily misled that this is the case as recent books have indirectly cast the Nihang as the typical Sikh.

4. It is uncertain whether Jungli was aware of the clash between the Damdami Taksal and the Sant Nirankaris at the Golden Temple on the first day of Baisakhi 1978. The thirteen Sikhs who were killed in this skirmish are considered martyrs.

5. Mark Tully and Satish Jacob, *Amritsar: Mrs. Gandhi's Last Battle* (London, 1986) deal with Operation Bluestar. For the martyr's appeal in the Sikh struggle, see Joyce Pettigrew, *The Sikhs of the Punjab: Unheard Voices of State and Guerilla Violence* (London, 1995). Of course, a young Sikh's decision to take to militancy was based on far more factors than the perceived humiliation of the Sikhs. Joyce Pettigrew's 'The State and Local Groupings in the Sikh Rural Areas, Post-1984', in Gurharpal Singh et al. (ed.), *Punjabi Identity: Continuity and Change* (Delhi, 1996), pp. 139–58 demonstrates some of the complexities involved in joining the guerrilla struggle.

6. It is well known that Sukha and Jinda did not write this letter.

7. See, for example, Peter van der Veer, *Religious Nationalism: Hindus and Muslims in India* (Berkeley, 1994).

8. Significant texts include van der Veer's *Religious Nationalism*; Stanley Tambiah, *Leveling Crowds: Ethnonationalist Conflicts and Collective Violence in South Asia* (Berkeley, 1996), pp. 101–62; G.J. Larson's *India's Agony over Religion* (Albany, 1995), pp. 234–44; Mark Juergensmeyer, *The New Cold War: Religious Nationalism Confronts the Secular State* (Berkeley, 1993); and Paul Brass, *Ethnicity and Nationalism: Theory and Comparison* (Delhi, 1991), pp. 167–237.

Note on Orthography

This book makes considerable use of Indian-language words. Often, only a word's first appearance is italicized. In most cases, I have retained the original Punjabi/Gurmukhi spellings rather than their more popular Hindi/Devanagri constructs. Nasalization is indicated with a *n*. I have also retained the Punjabi/Gurmukhi spellings for common Persian-loan words. The final *he-havvaz* in Persian is transliterated as *-ah,* while the Persian *izāfat* is transcribed as *-i.* Finally, most words are pluralized after the English standard, by adding an 's' at the end of the word.

Except where otherwise noted, the translations from Punjabi, Braj and Persian are my own, with some editorial assistance from W.H. McLeod and Pashaura Singh. In scriptural translations, I have relied on two translated versions of the Sikh scripture, the Adi Granth: Sahib Singh's *Srī Gurū Granth Sāhib Darpan,* 10 vols. (Jullundhur, 1962–4) and G.S. Talib, *Sri Guru Granth Sahib,* 4 vols. (Patiala, 1988). The standard text from which all quotations have been taken is Teja Singh's *Śabadārath Srī Gurū Granth Sāhib Jī,* 4 vols. (Patiala, 1985), which follows the standard Adi Granth pagination of 1,430 pages. For the Dasam Granth, I have relied principally on the three volumes of Randhir Singh (ed.), *Śabadārath Dasam Granth Sāhib Jī* (Patiala, 1985).

Abbreviations

AG	Ādi Granth
Ar.	Arabic
approx.	approximately
b.	born in
B40	W.H. McLeod (ed. and trans.), *The B40 Janam-Sakhi* (Amritsar, 1980)
BG	Vir Singh (ed.), *Vārān Bhāī Gurdās Satīk* (Delhi, 1997)
BLSA	Ganda Singh (ed.), *Bhagat Lakshman Singh Autobiography* (Calcutta, 1966)
CCOHP	Chief Commissioner's Office Home Proceedings
CE	Common era
CSL	The Central Sikh League
CKD	The Chief Khalsa Diwan
CSRn	W.H. McLeod (ed. and trans.), *The Chaupa Singh Rahit-Nama* (Dunedin, 1987)
d.	died in
DG	Chatar Singh, et al. (ed.), *Srī Dasam Granth Sāhib Jī* (Amritsar, 1988)
EEAS	Ganda Singh (ed.), *Early European Accounts of the Sikhs and History of Origin and Progress of the Sikhs* (New Delhi, 1974).
EoS	Harbans Singh (ed.), *The Encyclopaedia of Sikhism*, I (Patiala, 1992)
ESC	W.H. McLeod, *Evolution of the Sikh Community* (Oxford, 1975)
esp.	especially
EST	W.H. McLeod, *Early Sikh Tradition: A Study of the Janam-Sākhis* (Oxford, 1980)
Glossary	Denzil Ibbetson, E. Maclagan and H.A. Rose, *A Glossary of the Tribes and Castes of the Punjab and North-West Frontier Province*, 3 vols. (first published, 1919; Patiala, 1990)

GNDU	Guru Nanak Dev University, Amritsar
GNSR	W.H. McLeod, *Gurū Nānak and the Sikh Religion* (Oxford, 1968)
GRM	Teja Singh, *The Gurdwara Reform Movement and the Sikh Awakening* (Jullundhur, 1922)
H.	Hijra. The date according to the Islamic calendar
Hi.	Hindi
JAOS	*Journal of the American Oriental Society*
JRH	*Journal of Regional History* (Amritsar)
JSS	*Journal of Sikh Studies* (Amritsar)
KCF	Khalistan Commando Force
KTS	Khalsa Tract Society
lit.	literally
MK	Kahn Singh Nabha, *Gur-śabad Ratanākar Mahān Koś* (4th edn, Patiala, 1981)
n.	note
n.d.	no date
Nk.	The year according to the *Nānak-śāhī* calendar. Begins in 1469 CE with the birth of Guru Nanak
n.p.	no place
Pun.	Punjabi
pbd.	published
PnP	Gian Singh, *Panth Prakāś* (Patiala, 1987)
PPHC	*Proceedings of the Punjab History Conference* (Patiala)
PPP	*Punjab, Past and Present* (Patiala)
PrPP	Rattan Singh Bhangu, *Prāchīn Panth Prakāś* (5th edn, Delhi, 1982), Vir Singh (ed.)
S.	*sammat*. The year according to the Bikramajit calendar. Approximately 57 years ahead of the Common era calendar
SGPC	The Shiromani Gurdwara Prabandhak Committee
Sk.	Sanskrit
SP	Santokh Singh, *Srī Gur-pratāp Sūraj Granth,* 15 vols. (Patiala, 1989–92), Vir Singh (ed.)
TGK	Gian Singh, *Tavārīkh Gurū Khālsā,* 2 vols. (Patiala, 1987, 1993)
TSSS	W.H. McLeod (ed.), *Textual Sources for the Study of Sikhism* (Manchester, 1984)
WhS	W.H. McLeod, *Who is a Sikh? The Problem of Sikh Identity* (Oxford, 1989)

ONE

Introduction

Many speak of courage, speaking cannot give it, it's in the face of
death we must live it. When things are down and darkest, that's
when we'll stand the tallest. Until the last star falls, we won't give
an inch at all. Stand as Khalsa! Strong as steel, steady as stone; give
our lives to God and Guru, mind and soul, breath and bone.

Guru Arjun gave his life, to stand for what was right. He was
burned and tortured five long days and nights. He could have stopped
it any time just by giving in. His strength a solid wall; he never gave
an inch at all!

Sons of the Khalsa, remember those who died; stood their ground
until their last breath so we who live now might live free lives.[1]

To many contemporary Sikhs the concept of martyrdom is a
fundamental feature of the Sikh tradition, representing a
doctrine which has been in place for the last five centuries.
According to present-day Sikh tradition, the idea was first consciously
emphasized by the Sikh Gurus, in particular Guru Nanak, and exemplified by two Guru-martyrs and countless brave Sikhs who had
suffered death while opposing the tyranny of an overwhelming
enemy.[2] The significance of martyrdom is often noticed by those
outside the Sikh tradition who chance to visit Sikh places of worship
or *gurdwārās*. Most gurdwaras, for example, will have on display at
least one painting of past Sikh martyrs (and possibly of present-day
Sikhs believed to have been martyred) within their precincts in all
its gory detail. Schools for Sikh children, moreover, both within and
outside India, will also exhibit such pictures.[3]

In the vast majority of contemporary Sikh history books, the
importance of martyrdom is underscored as the two events which

are held to have fundamentally changed the nature of the community were believed to be martyrdoms. According to this version of history, the martyrdom of Guru Arjan, the fifth Guru, led to the militarization of the community in 1606, while the martyrdom of his grandson, the ninth Sikh Master, Guru Tegh Bahadur, in 1675 was the event which precipitated the creation of the Khalsa, the elite, militant order formed in 1699 by the tenth and last Guru of the Sikhs, Guru Gobind Singh (1666–1708). Tradition maintains that the resistance to oppression which these two heroic deaths enshrined was embodied by the Sikhs of the eighteenth century who had followed the tenth Guru and adopted the standard or Rahit he had prescribed prior to his death in 1708. It was the adherence to such high ideals and the desire to die for these that allowed the Khalsa to thrive in this age of fierce persecution and which, the history continues, made inevitable the victory of the Panth. The result was that in 1799, a proud Ranjit Singh along with his large band of Khalsa Sikhs had made his way into Lahore as its conqueror, thus initiating a glorious forty-year reign. The Khalsa's fearless resistance to tyranny, the moral and tactical victories it scored against its Mughal and Afghan opponents in battle and in its spectacular martyrdoms, had borne fruit. For many Sikh historians, to allude to a well-worn phrase, the blood of the martyr was the seed of the Panth.[4]

There are few words in the English language which evoke as emotive a response as 'martyr' and 'martyrdom'. Despite the fact that these words can be easily devalued, such as in describing a sufferer as a 'martyr' to backache or some other such malady, there is still nothing quite like martyrdom. The view that a person of flesh and blood, someone like us, can suffer intense pain and agony in support of some cause, ideology or religion and thus procure a glorious and honourable death, has inspired many an unlettered and cultured person alike to fervently rush into the hereafter. Martyrdom, of course, does not depend upon the way one dies or the agonies to which one is subjected, but, to allude to the famous Augustinian dictum, upon the cause for which one undergoes the supreme sacrifice.[5] The difference between 'to die' and 'to die a martyr', therefore, is a substantial one. Although martyrdoms today are hardly so common in the so-called western world as they were, for example, during the first centuries of the nascent Christian church, martyrdom remains 'a powerful force at the intersection of religion and politics'.[6] It is perhaps for this reason that martyrdom is so particularly well suited to the Sikh tradition, one in which, we are often told, religion and politics coalesce. Sikhs, however, do not use the English word 'martyr' to signify their valiantly dead.

Śahīd and *Śahīdī*

The term that Sikhs have adopted to describe their martyrs is the Arabic word *shāhīd* (pl. *shuhadā*). The primary meaning of this term in the Qur'ān is as 'witness', the one who testifies for Allah and the Prophet Muhammad. As 'witness', the word *shāhīd* has a pre-Quranic history as a part of the legal language in Arabic, being used to designate all kinds of attestation, testimony and observation.[7] It was only after the Islamic conquest of Palestine in the seventh century that Arabs (like the Syrians before them) translated the Graeco-Christian term as 'witness' into Arabic. It was such translation which arrived at the term *shāhīd,* designating Muslims who fell in battle before unbelievers, or martyrs. The word became understood in its general sense as the one who witnesses to his faith by the sacrifice of his life, therefore, through Christian influence. As Bowersock notes, the concept as well as the word was absorbed 'directly from Greek during those early centuries of Islam when Christian churches still flourished in Palestine and Greek was still spoken'.[8]

Why did the followers of an Indian religion choose an Arabic term intimately associated with Islam to describe their martyrs? Contemporary Sikh scholars argue that Sikhs of the fifteenth, sixteenth and seventeenth centuries utilized this particular Islamic term (and others) in order to 'chalk out a line of orientation for itself [Sikhism] away from Brahmanical orthodoxy and other ... religious idea[s] ... rooted in Hinduism'.[9] This statement is misleading, implying that Sikhs had adopted the noun to bring their faith more in line with Muslim understanding. This is a suggestion with which the vast majority of scholars of the Sikh tradition would disagree. Clearly, both these interpretations are concerned with identity and thus mirror late nineteenth- and early twentieth-century anxieties rather than sixteenth- or seventeenth-century ones. It is now well known that it was only after the 1870s that the boundaries of categories such as 'Hindu', 'Muslim' and 'Sikh' were established.[10]

One problem that G.S. Talib's argument entails is that it ignores the fact that by the time of Guru Nanak's birth (1469 CE), the noun 'shahid' had been used in the Indian subcontinent for well over 500 years and had, over this time, become a part of the cultural taxonomy of northern India. Although the shahid was still associated with Islam and the large majority of martyrs in the Punjab had come from the Muslim community, this association, especially until the end of the seventeenth century, was by no means a rigid one. As in Arabian, Persian and Central Asian cultures, the shahid in popular north Indian culture had its place in the vast pantheon of benign and malevolent beings whose beneficial and curative powers were sought out by all people, irrespective of the religious tradition or traditions to which they may have adhered. With this in mind, one may assume that shahids (as entities within this pantheon) could belong to any of the religious traditions of northern India. Men and women we would today loosely identify as Sikh or Hindu would venerate shahids such as the Prophet Muhammad's son-in-law, 'Ali; the sons of 'Ali, Hasan and Husayn; the Baghdadi Sufi Mansur al-Hallaj, and the Islamic warrior-martyr Ghazi Miyan of Bahraich with as much reverence as they directed towards Shiva, the Devi, or the Sikh Gurus. We can assume, moreover, that they would propitiate the shahids of their respective traditions as well. The term 'shahid' was thus used by all peoples of sixteenth-century South Asia whose religious loyalties, we can say retrospectively, 'promiscuously' overlapped. As the first Sikh Guru refers to the Muslim shahid in one of his *śabads* or hymns, it is likely that he was aware of the reverence in which the shahid was held by all north Indians and the pilgrimages that the pious undertook to the various *mash-hads* or martyries scattered across the Punjab.[11]

Another problem we find in the argument that the Sikhs adopted the term 'shahid' to buttress a non-Hindu identity is its failure to realize the significance of the fact that there is no corresponding term for shahid or *śahādat* (martyrdom) which is indigenous to India.[12] To this day, moreover, there is no Indian-language noun for the witness as signifying one who dies for his or her faith. This seems to imply that the concept of martyrdom was not a cultural form to ancient, classical and medieval north Indians as it lacked concordance in an overt category of language.[13] One may assume then that Sikhs eventually adopted the word 'shahid' to describe Sikh martyrs because it was readily available and already signified what Sikh authors understood by heroic death before oppressors and unjust magistrates. As we will see, however, this adoption occurred far later than contemporary accounts of the Sikh tradition of martyrdom claim.[14] Therefore, when scholars of Sikhism posit the belief that ancient and classical Indians voluntarily suffered and died to overthrow a tyrant, this is an obvious attempt to read present-day values back into history (indeed, for many, a temptation too hard to resist).[15] The same can be said for the first Europeans who undertook the study of Sanskrit. In nineteenth- and twentieth-century English-Sanskrit dictionaries, terms to express the idea of martyr exist, but these appear to have been coined either for the sake of the dictionaries themselves or because the compilers were searching for Sanskrit words to translate English concepts which they already had in mind. Furthermore, these words are derived from terms for features particular to the Indian environment. Elements such as the asceticism or renunciation (*tyāga* or *samnyāsa*) so common to the classical, fourfold *āśrama* arrangement[16] and sacrifice or offerings to the gods (*balidāna*) are at the heart of Sanskrit and Hindi words coined to mean martyr.[17] Indeed, it is not until the Indian nationalist struggle in the late nineteenth and early to mid-twentieth century that the semantic range of words such as balidan begin to incorporate the concept of martyr as one who dies for a cause. This was especially so amongst nascent Hindu nationalists such as V.D. Savarkar, author of the famous tract, *Hindutva,* and president of the Hindu Mahasabha (Great Assembly of Hindus) for seven consecutive years.[18] Although such terminology has come into the Punjabi language and is often found in Sikh martyrologies, the situation of the statements in which this terminology appears (idioms like *prān denā,* literally 'to give up one's breath', for example) never suggests the type of ascetic practices that such language may evoke in the Hindu context. The meaning to be inferred from these idioms is clearly martyrdom or to die the death of a martyr.[19] One may assume that for many Sikhs today, therefore, the 'Hindu' ideas behind such terms would be unacceptable as the themes these words elicit in a 'Hindu' context are features of Indian tradition and culture against which the Sikh Gurus and the other poets whose hymns are included within the Sikh scripture, the Adi Granth, often spoke. The infrequency of all terms but shahid to describe the martyr in contemporary popular Sikh literature, *kathā* (homily) and song support such a conclusion.[20]

The terms coined in Sanskrit which emphasize sacrifice, however, do allow us to speculate as to how the concept of martyrdom was understood by the non-Muslim culture in north India and why the notion was successfully transplanted. The association between the shahid and the sacrificial animal victim, for example, certainly existed in the Arab world prior to Islam's political dominance in the Indian subcontinent (*circa* 1200). One may speculate that it was this association which facilitated the easy transition of the concept of martyr from its original West Asian to its new South Asian soil. According to a tradition that refers to the Arabs and which occurs as cited in the Book of Law revealed to Moses, the Arabs seek to bring themselves 'near unto Allah' by shedding their blood in fighting for the cause of religion.[21] This was, continues the tradition, unlike those people preceding the Arabs who had attempted to acquire such proximity to the divine by offering up to the Supreme Lord the blood of oxen or cows, sheep or goats, and camels.[22] The Arabic term that designates both these offerings is *qurbān* (pl. *qarābān*). The contemporary word means 'sacrifice' or 'sacrificial victim' and indeed, is found to designate such as far back as the Qur'ān.[23] The word seems to have come directly from the Arabic *q-r-b* 'to be near' and thus, the meaning implied by qurban or 'sacrifice' is that which brings one into greater proximity to the divine, closer to God in both a physical and metaphorical way. Logically, the greater the sacrifice, the more closely one approaches the divine.

The association between the shahid and qurban is certainly implied in the above tradition. By the late thirteenth century CE (seventh century H.), the Arabic lexicographer, Muhammad ibn Manzur, in his famous *Lisān al-'Arab* (completed 689 H./1290 CE) could write in his heading for the term 'qurbān' that a characteristic of the Muslim community is that 'their qurbān is their blood', indicating that it is their own blood which Muslim martyrs offer to God rather than that of the sacrificial animal.[24] As this is the greatest of all offerings one can make (namely, one's life), the martyr's position in paradise is assured. According to popular Islamic tradition, the shahid receives (among numerous special privileges) the highest rank in paradise, occupying the place nearest the throne of God.[25]

Although this association is clearly present, the idea of the sacrificial offering is by no means central to the concept of shahid as we have it today in the Punjab.[26] What is indeed fundamental to the idea, as the word 'shahid' or witness denotes, is resistance (to oppression) and defiance (of tyranny). The shahid, like his Greek counterpart, the μάρτυς, is a witness after all, and according to G.W.H. Lampe, 'as a witness he [the martyr] is, as it were, on the offensive against the persecuting power.'[27] Implicit in the present-day idea of shahid, in other words, is that which is testified against, namely oppression. The shahid is one who dies heroically, testifying to his or her faith on the path of God.²ˣ It is this emphasis which is undeniably at the very core of the contemporary Sikh understanding of the shahid.

For Sikhs the shahid is a highly revered figure, an unambiguous exemplar of virtue, truth and moral justification. Sikh shahids give their lives to uphold righteousness (*dharam*) under the most painful and chilling circumstances, providing testimony (*śahādat*) to their faith with their blood. As with Christian and Muslim 'witnesses to the truth', the unsought-for reward Sikh martyrs receive for such stalwart and courageous behaviour in the face of torture and imminent death is liberation from the cycle of existence, union with God (Akal Purakh, 'The One Beyond Time'). Shahids thus become the ideal Sikh athletes of piety, offering a glorious example of resistance to tyrannical authority while paying the ultimate price for their powerful commitment to the Sikh faith, its doctrines, symbols and Gurus.²⁹ Every heroic Sikh martyrdom, then, is portrayed as an active testament to the faith whose essential theme is the testimony to injustice and oppression.

The Term *Śahīd* in Early Sikh History

Yet this exclusive emphasis on the resistance to oppression inherent in the present-day Punjabi term 'shahid' in Sikhism is remarkably contemporary. Its first sustained appearance is in the late nineteenth-century writings of Gian Singh and Ditt Singh. This should elicit less surprise when we note that the term 'shahid' itself does not occur in Sikh literature in reference to specifically Sikh martyrs until the beginning of the nineteenth century, that is, in Seva Singh Kaushish's *Sahīd-bilās* (around 1802), a hagiography of the celebrated companion of the tenth Guru and compiler of the Dasam Granth, Mani Singh.³⁰ This is not to suggest that the idea of martyrdom is absent from eighteenth-century Sikh tradition. Indeed, it is not. The absence of specific terminology notwithstanding, the concept of the martyr is easily discernible in the fifth canto of the *Bachitar Nāṭak* (The Wonderful Drama), the so-called autobiography of Guru Gobind Singh believed to have been composed between 1688–99.³¹ We also find the concept in an early eighteenth-century gur-bilas work, *Srī Gur-sobhā* (Radiance of the Guru). Sainipati, the author of this text, believed to be a contemporary of the tenth Guru, states the following in reference to two of the four sons of Guru Gobind Singh, the *chār sāhib-zāde*, to each of whom Sikh tradition accords the status of martyr:

They left this world protecting their religion [an act for which] they have received praise and honour. It was the destiny of Fateh Singh and Jujhar Singh to sacrifice their lives (*taje prān*) [for the benefit of the Panth]. Throughout the entire world their sacrifice is well known.[32]

As our poet has the tenth Guru himself state, Sikhs who died in this way truly earned an honoured place in the 'Court' of Akal Purakh:

At that time [Guru] Gobind [Singh] contemplated [the fact that the Khalsa saw him] as its refuge: 'Today [dying in battle as] Khalsa [Sikhs] they have achieved elect status in the court of the True Guru.'[33]

Such statements are representative of eighteenth-century Sikh literature in general, and the gur-bilas literature in particular, regarding a courageous demise. Poets like the author of the *Bachitar Nāṭak* and Kavi Sainipati demonstrate that the heroic death we today associate with shahadat and shahidi, as well as the instant passage to heaven noted by Guru Gobind Singh above, were apparently much ·appreciated and sought after in this period. But these authors, like almost all eighteenth-century Sikh poets, choose not to appropriate the word shahid to describe those Sikhs who died while protecting the oppressed or testifying to the truth, nor do we find the terms 'shahadat' or 'shahidi' in their accounts. The general lack of specific terms to designate the concept of martyr and martyrdom seems to indicate that these ideas were not remarkable features of the nascent Khalsa Sikh tradition, their presence notwithstanding. Nevertheless, an examination of the reasons for the exclusion of these words from the Sikh literature of the eighteenth century allows us to recognize why the term 'shahid' is first understood exclusively as the witness only in the literature of the late nineteenth century. To do this, however, we must begin by examining the use of the word in seventeenth-century Sikh literature.

It is true that we find the word 'shahid' twice in the Adi Granth (whose compilation was completed in 1604) and four times in the *vārs* (odes) of Bhai Gurdas (d. *circa* 1637), an eminent seventeenth-century Sikh theologian.[34] Such findings would indicate that the idea of martyrdom does have a long history in the Sikh tradition. This does not appear to be the case, however, for in all but one of these instances the word is used in its Islamic sense, specifically signifying the Muslim shahid rather than what we would come to identify as the Sikh martyr. Note the following hymns of Guru Nanak and Bhagat Ravi Das:

Pirs, prophets, seekers, devotees, martyrs *(śuhde)* and others witnessing to the truth *(śahīd)* along with shaikhs, Sufi saints *(maśāik)*, qazis, mullas, dervishes and others who have the divine portal within sight, all of these people are blessed by God, all utter his praises.[35]

He in whose family were observed the '*Īd* [*ul-fiṭr* commemorating the end of the fast of Ramadan] and the '*Īd* [*ul-qurbān*] on which goats were ritually slaughtered. He whose people slaughtered cows, and venerated shaikhs, shahids and pirs. [Bhagat Kabir's] father did all this, yet Kabir himself, who became famous throughout the world, acted differently.[36]

In describing the practices of Bhagat Kabir's family, Ravi Das' hymn clearly alludes to the Muslim shahid whom pious Muslims would have honoured and propitiated, while in Guru Nanak's shabad above, we recognize the first Master's characteristic appropriation of Islamic terminology: it is the 'true' Muslim and the 'true' shahid who have access to liberation.[37] To imply, as some scholars do in their attempt to trace the concept of martyrdom back to the origins of Sikhism, that the shahid here is not specifically Muslim but rather typically Sikh is to assert that the pir, qazi, shaikh and other Islamic religious personnel within the first Guru's hymn are also not Muslims but Sikhs.[38] To these hymns we may add three of the *śloks* (verses) in which Bhai Gurdas uses the term 'shahid'.

There are lakhs of witnesses to the truth and lakhs of martyrs. There are lakhs of devotees, ecstatic ascetics, and maulanas.[39]

They hold fairs *(zārat)* at [the burial places of] numerous martyrs and other witnesses to the truth.[40]

There are several shaikhs, Sufi saints, devotees, witnesses to the truth and martyrs.[41]

Again, the shahid in these hymns can only be the Muslim variety as the term appears amongst categories that would have been identified as clearly Islamic in the period in which our theologian was composing his hymns. There is a significant deviation from this trend, however, one which appears in the third *vār* of Bhai Gurdas:

The *śahīd* cultivates truthfulness and patience. This person eradicates both doubt and fear.[42]

Even this novel exception should not be understood to indicate the Sikh shahid as we know it today, an error that often crops up in accounts dealing with the tradition of martyrdom in Sikhism.[43] In this one case, the context of the entire *pauṛi* clearly indicates that the term 'shahid' is used as a synonym for the *jīvan-mukt*, the one who is liberated from the cycle of existence while yet physically alive. In this verse, the notion of bearing witness to the truth with one's life is nowhere present.

With these examples at our disposal we may postulate that it is the term's intimate association with Islam that may have prompted eighteenth-century Sikh authors to preclude the words 'shahid' and 'shahadat' from their particular brand of Sikh hagiography. After all, the early eighteenth century was, by all contemporary Persian and later European accounts dealing with the Sikhs, a period when Khalsa Sikhs faced vicious persecution by their Mughal and Afghan enemies, antagonists who were invariably described as Muslim.[44] Sikh tradition often notes that the Mughal emperor, Farrukh Siyar (r. 1713–19), would pay twenty-five rupees for every severed Sikh head and one hundred rupees for every live Sikh captive in order to capture the rebel Sikh leader, Banda Bahadur. Although Banda and his followers were finally captured and executed in Delhi in 1716, Mughal policy regarding the extermination of Khalsa Sikhs continued well into the eighteenth century.[45] As it was in this period that our gur-bilas authors were composing their works, it comes as no surprise that their literature characterizes Islam as base and corrupt and the struggle against its adherents as righteous and sacred.[46] This anti-Islamic theme, moreover, was also characteristic of the eighteenth-century *rahit-nāmā* literature as well as the *janam-sākhī* literature of this era, albeit to a much lesser extent.[47]

With the return to Kabul in 1765 of Ahmad Shah Abdali, premier antagonist of the Khalsa, the tide of Khalsa Sikh fortunes slowly began to rise. It was during this year that the Sikh misls gained a firm foothold in Lahore, a control that eventually resulted in their virtual dominance of the Punjab under the leader of the Shukarchakia misl, Ranjit Singh, in 1799. With the Khalsa Sikh displacement of Muslim rule in the Punjab, the apparent threat that Muslims presented the Sikhs dramatically, if not completely, subsided. The ferocious character of Islam that our eighteenth-century Sikh authors perceived was perhaps softened, making it possible for nineteenth-century Sikh writers to appropriate a terminology that was earlier considered Islamic. We find, furthermore, that the anti-Muslim bias characteristic of eighteenth-century Sikh literature was not as pronounced in the literature of the nineteenth. Indeed, as Surjit Hans notes, the conciliatory tone towards Muslims one finds in the nineteenth-century gur-bilas work attributed to Koer Singh, the *Gurbilās Pātsāhī 10,* is highly significant in this regard.⁴⁸ Clearly, Koer Singh and other Sikh authors of the Lahore Darbar were writing in a period in which Sikhs had assumed a position of substantial political power.

It was during the first decade of the nineteenth century, the initial rule of Ranjit Singh, that Seva Singh Kaushish wrote his *Śahīd-bilās*. Assuming that Seva Singh can be trusted to know what would attract his audience and engage their interest, the title itself, 'The Pleasure of the Martyr', seems to illustrate the reverence that Sikhs of this era accorded the martyr. As it echoes the title of the gur-bilas works, one may assume that for Seva Singh, Sikh martyrs like Mani Singh were on a footing equal to that of the Gurus. Evidently, the piety of the *Śahīd-bilās* is of the same quality as that which we discover in the gur-bilas works, emphasizing the bravery and heroic quality of its protagonists.

Garja Singh claims that Seva Singh was a *bhaṭṭ* or bard, the son of one Kesar Singh Kaushish, who was a descendant through six generations of Bhai Kirat Shahid, one of the four sons of *Bhaṭṭ* Bhikkhan, whose hymns are included within the Adi Granth.⁴⁹ Like his father, Kirat Shahid was also a bhatt whose panegyrics (along with those of three of his brothers) are found within the Sikh scripture.⁵⁰ Kirat Shahid, as the name suggests, is also remembered as a martyr today as he was allegedly killed in the famous Battle of Amritsar in April 1634⁵¹ along with the paternal grandfather of Mani Singh, Ballu Panwar, who was also a retainer of the sixth Sikh Master, Guru Hargobind.⁵² It appears that Seva Singh's family knew of their connection to Mani Singh since, as Garja Singh maintains, Seva Singh wrote this martyrology on the basis of oral information passed down through the generations of his family.⁵³ Such a text, one may assume, may have been produced not only to glorify the martyr, Mani Singh, but also in order to further enhance the prestige of Seva Singh's household.

An examination of Seva Singh's text plainly demonstrates that he understands the shahid to be a martyr who provides testimony to injustice, heroically witnessing to the truth with his blood. In reference to the family of Mani Singh, for instance, Seva Singh states the following:

[Bhai Mani Singh's] entire family, his father, all his ancestors, sons and brothers died splendid deaths as martyrs (*hoe śahīd*) for the sake of righteousness. [Such sacrifice demonstrated that] they were the supreme disciples of the Sikh Gurus.[54]

According to tradition, whole generations of Mani Singh's extended family lost their lives in the service of the Guru.[55] In regard to a pitched battle fought between the Khalsa and Mughal forces on 15 Basaikhi S. 1766 (12 April 1709), furthermore, Seva Singh contends that

Joining battle [they fought] as Singhs and died glorious deaths as martyrs (*śahīd hoe*). They sacrificed their lives by the sword near the tank of Ramsar [modern-day Amritsar]. So were heard the shouts of triumph, resounding for the Singhs on every side. None [of their oppressors] dared raise his head, for the evil deeds of the scoundrels were recognised by all.[56]

Such examples allow us to conjecture that when the terms 'shahid' and 'shahadat' enter the realm of Sikh literature in the early nineteenth century, they are initially grafted upon the understanding of the martyr we find originally in the *Bachitar Nāṭak* and in *Gur-sobhā*. This new terminology, of course, already intended the ideal deaths noted in these early eighteenth-century works. Yet it also signified far more.

This leads us to the query posed earlier. How is it that the exclusion of the term 'shahid' from eighteenth-century Sikh literature allows us to observe why it first comes to mean the witness exclusively only in the late nineteenth? To be sure, the answer does lie in the terminology's close association with Islam. We have already implied above that the word *shahīd* in Arabic connotes far more than a pious Muslim's heroic death on the battlefield against unbelievers or a person killed for his beliefs. According to T.W. Arnold, for example, 'The term *shahid* is given a wide interpretation in Muslim India.'[57] No doubt this is the case in both Hindu and Sikh India as well (as if the three can be differentiated!). In fact, as we will note in the fifth chapter, there were a large number of deaths that merited the status of shahid, deaths which were in many ways similar to those that produced the malevolent ghosts known in Punjabi folk culture as *bīr, bhūt, pret, baitāl* or *churel*—in particular, untimely and often violent, bloody deaths. In connection with this Islamic affiliation, we may speculate further, therefore, that the term was also excluded from the gur-bilas literature of the eighteenth century because it did not signify what our gur-bilas authors wished their audience to understand in regard to heroic death in battle or painful death meted out by dishonest judges. If the eighteenth-century gur-bilas authors were not just composing their works as a pious activity but indeed, as an attempt to enthuse Khalsa Sikhs (and perhaps recruit future warriors) during this period of Khalsa Sikh persecution, then they could not allow their terminology to be misinterpreted.[58] As we see in *Gursobhā*, entities such as the bhut and baital were fearsome and negative ones, often appearing on the battle scene after a slaughter, a conventional image in contemporary descriptions of battles.[59]

With [fiendish] glee ghosts (*bhūt*), goblins (*baitāl*) and Shiv [himself] dance on the field of battle; vultures hover [above].[60]

We may assume that for our gur-bilas authors, heroic death in battle, with the anticipated reward of paradise or liberation (that is the fate of the martyr), is very different from 'living' as a mischievous ghost or object of propitiation (or the fate of the shahid as understood in the eighteenth century).

As Harjot Oberoi has noted, all aspects of pre-colonial Sikh tradition were firmly rooted in 'Indic cultural thinking'[61] and the shahid was no exception. Like a bhut, bir, baital or churel, the shahid was also one of the many supernatural entities who were sought out and propitiated by members of all Punjabi communities. In this light, it is clear that the contemporary Punjabi term 'shahid' signifies far less today than it did one hundred and fifty years ago. One can assume that Seva Singh appropriates the word 'shahid' to signify the martyr in a new, less hostile and relatively relaxed atmosphere. This may have appeared as natural to our author as the word intended the heroic deaths and the meanings associated with such deaths which he desired to convey. Of course, by no means would Seva Singh wish the status of Mani Singh or other heroic Sikhs mentioned in his text to be misconstrued as this could perhaps curtail his own family's distinction.[62] Nevertheless, it seems unlikely that his audience would have perceived the shahid exclusively as the witness to truth. For the vast majority of rural Sikhs who formed the bulk of the Sikh Panth in this period, the shahid signified far more than a pious Sikh (or Muslim or Hindu) killed for his or her beliefs. When the term is brought into Sikh literature in the early nineteenth century, one can assume that with it come the many characteristics it traditionally possesses in the Islamic tradition. From the time of Seva Singh onward, therefore, the other meanings of the term gradually begin to assert themselves. We will observe in the fifth chapter how later nineteenth-century works, such as the *Sau Sakhīān* (1834), attributed to Guru Gobind Singh, and even Ratan Singh Bhangu's renowned *Prachīn Panth Prakās* (1841), understand the shahid to mean more than the witness to truth, as more than Seva Singh did. The definition posited earlier for the Sikh shahid, in other words, was by no means the exclusive definition of the term in the eighteenth or early to mid-nineteenth century.

We may now ask how it is that the word 'shahid' by the early twentieth century, came to denote solely the Sikh martyr who sacrifices his or her life in the protection of dharam. For this answer we must look to the late nineteenth-century Sikh reform movement, known as the Singh Sabha or Singh Society, among whose more prominent members were Gian Singh and Ditt Singh. It was under the auspices of this group that the many understandings of the Punjabi concept 'shahid' were marginalized. As the Singh Sabha sought to rid the late nineteenth-century Sikh tradition of features it felt were not aligned to their interpretation of the Sikh scripture and to their understanding of Sikhism, the figure of the martyr began to align itself more closely to the concept of the shahid as the witness to truth through the sacrifice of one's life. To wit, it is by means of Singh Sabha efforts that the shahid became the witness and the martyr, as Professor Lampe notes above, to the exclusion of all other definitions. No longer would the shahid be the supernatural entity common to Sikh and Punjabi understandings prior to the mid-nineteenth century.

Support for the shift in meaning of the term 'shahid' may be found in the development of the Sikh conception of the *zindā śahīd* or the 'living martyr', a term one often encounters in today's Punjabi Sikh literature. Although there is no formal Sikh statement or doctrine in regard to the zinda shahid, the term appears in the late nineteenth century and was bestowed upon those Sikhs who were believed to heroically defy authority and resist oppression in the pursuit of noble Panthic goals. The idea is that these men and women suffered oppression as harsh as that endured by past Sikh martyrs, but continued to live to defy authority and face further harsh treatment.[63] It seems logical to assume that the title develops out of the emphasis on witnessing against persecution, noted above.[64] If the stress on the term 'shahid' as resisting oppressors and suffering in the process were as prevalent prior to the British annexation of the Punjab in 1849, the title of zinda shahid would have been surely given to some pious Sikh. Certainly there were many Sikhs deserving of this status during the Guru period (1469–1708), the heroic eighteenth century, or the time of the Anglo–Sikh wars (1845–9). Yet the term 'zinda shahid' is absent from all pre-annexation Sikh literature. This absence allows us to infer that the zinda shahid is a contemporary phenomenon, one which developed as the element of witnessing to oppression became paramount in the term shahid. Indeed, the first Sikh to become a living-martyr was Bhai Takht Singh of Ferozepur (1860–1933), a pioneer in Sikh female education whose school, the Sikh Kanya Mahavidyala, is today legendary.[65] The problems he faced in establishing and running the school were vast and forced Takht Singh to often undertake arduous journeys the world over to raise funds to continue the institution's existence. In pursuing his goal to educate Sikh women, Takht Singh was clearly aware of the immense difficulties he would suffer. When asked about these, Takht Singh is alleged to have replied, 'I am ready to suffer any trouble while walking the path of righteousness. Jail, death, even dishonour, would not keep me back from the true course.'[66] This suggests that the exclusive emphasis in the noun 'shahid' on resisting oppression, out of which the concept of 'zinda shahid' originated, is also contemporary. One could assume that the term 'zinda shahid' was perhaps formulated by the Singh Sabha in order to emphasize the new understanding of the shahid. After all, men initially labelled zinda shahid, such as Takht Singh and Kharak Singh (1868–1963),[67] all followed a Singh Sabha agenda, one in which the martyr played an eminent role.

Rhetorical Strategy and the Singh Sabha Project

In the task of understanding how the Singh Sabha fulfilled that agenda and came to dominate the Sikh imagination, we must keep in mind what, on the surface, is a rather obvious point: that the Singh Sabha communicated its vision through language. Although much has been written on the Singh Sabha project to date, the specific language employed by its members, their rhetorical approaches in particular, has not yet secured the attention it deserves.[68] A critical examination of various tracts, handbills, books, and especially newspapers published under the agency of the Singh Sabha or by those influenced by the group's interpretations, as well as homilies delivered by exegetes (*giānis*), preachers (*prachāraks*) and missionaries (*updesaks*) who were members of the Singh Sabha, demonstrates that the Sabha utilized a number of rhetorical strategies in perpetuating amongst its Sikh and non-Sikh audiences the understanding that Sikhism is a distinct revelation, a unique tradition whose premier identity is that of the Khalsa variety. The most powerful and profound of these strategies is what I term the 'rhetoric of martyrdom'. This is a rhetorical scheme, incidentally, which continues to act as a chart, formula, or guide which Sikhs the world over consult when trying to decide on various courses of action to adopt in the search for the better life—a fact that contemporary events no doubt underscore, as does the epigraph with which this chapter begins. I contend that it is principally through this rhetoric, as well as the actions it engenders (actions which themselves are a form of non-verbal rhetoric) that martyrs and martyrdom begin to occupy such a prominent place in the Sikh religious tradition and that the term 'shahid' comes to solely signify the martyr as it is understood today.

Of course, as we have demonstrated, martyrdom was not something new to those within the Sikh Panth. But this feature of the tradition received a strength and a coherence that it had not known previously, thanks to Singh Sabha efforts. One can also argue that it is through the rhetoric of martyrdom, moreover, that the Singh Sabha achieved the dramatic success that it did. Indeed, the historical and literary evidence suggests that in the late nineteenth and early twentieth centuries, the rhetoric of martyrdom became a form of stylistic medicine that Singh Sabha writers and exegetes administered to themselves and to their audience—in this case, those who identified themselves as Sikh—which allowed both groups (author and audience) to adjust to life in this period and help determine what action to take toward it.[69] That action was invariably one dictated by the precepts of the Singh Sabha and its various offspring organizations, the Chief Khalsa Diwan, the Central Sikh League, the Shiromani Gurdwara Prabandhak Committee and the Akali Dal.

A discussion of rhetoric as a strategy or guide in matters of human welfare and as stylistic medicine are some of the key points in the concept of rhetoric as effectively developed by the literary critic, Kenneth Burke.[70] I have found it useful to draw upon his ideas in comprehending the Singh Sabha project and its phenomenal achievement. Burke defines rhetoric as

the use of words by human agents to form attitudes or induce action in other human agents...Whatever form rhetoric takes, it is rooted in an essential function of language itself ... the use of language as a symbolic means of inducing cooperation in beings, that by nature respond to symbols.[71]

According to Burke, '[Rhetorical] works are answers to questions posed by the situation in which they arose.' Not only are these mere answers, he attests, but they are strategic and stylized ones: 'there is,' Burke tells us, 'a difference in style or strategy, if one says "yes" in tonalities that imply "thank God!" or in tonalities that imply "alas!" '[72] He maintains that one should, therefore, think of the function of rhetoric as 'the adopting of various strategies for the encompassing of situations'. Such strategies, Burke continues,

size up the situations, name their structure and outstanding ingredients, and name them in a way that contains an attitude towards them.[73]

Rhetoric thus provides not only a name or attitude for the situation, but a creative tactic for dealing with that situation or solving the problems inherent in it. Burke notes that rhetoric functions as 'instruction', helping people manoeuver through life in order to feel more at home in the chaos of the modern world.[74] As a guide or strategy, moreover, language in general and rhetoric in particular are not merely sounds devoid of content, but are a part of what Burke terms 'symbolic action'. To underscore the nature of language as symbolic action, Burke defines his system of thought as 'dramatism'. The key word here, of course, is drama. According to Burke, language is like drama in its ability to span both reality and representation, at times confounding the two. Moreover, drama, like language, is symbolic in that it represents something that may well have occurred in 'real life'. To paraphrase one of Burke's many followers: on the one hand, Shakespeare's *Macbeth* seems to be about something that may be happening in 'real life'. On the other hand, drama is its own reality, enacted on stage. Macbeth and his cohorts need never have existed for a play about him to do its work with an audience, motivating them and shaping their attitudes.[75] So, too, the tales narrated in the martyrologies of the Singh Sabha need not have occurred in order to inspire and alter the attitudes of late nineteenth- and early twentieth-century Sikhs.[76]

The predicaments faced by the Singh Sabha in the late nineteenth and early twentieth centuries, of course, were ones principally concerned with evolving Sikh identity. The situation which the Singh Sabha's rhetoric encompassed was, therefore, a situation of persuasion, that is, the attempt to influence those who styled themselves Sikh to understand the Singh Sabha interpretation of Sikh tradition and identity, as against other definitions offered by opponents of the Sabha (such as members of the Arya Samaj and those whom Oberoi

styles 'Sanatan' or traditional Sikhs[77]), as the only rendition of their
faith. The rhetoric of martyrdom was a particularly effective tool, a
significant strategic device, to use Burke's terminology, in establishing the limits of this identity.

By its very character, when used as strategy, rhetoric assumes
opposing views, or in this specific case different interpretations of
Sikh identity. Burke's notion of 'identification', his major addition to
the definition of rhetoric, is helpful here. In his analysis of Aristotle's
Rhetoric, Burke likens 'persuasion' to 'identification' since he holds
that persuasion is the result of identification: 'You persuade a man
only insofar as you can talk his language by speech, gesture, tonality,
order, image, attitude, idea, *identifying* your ways with his.' This is,
he notes, 'perhaps the simplest form of persuasion'.[78] Drawing upon
this point, Sandra Sizer argues in her examination of nineteenth-
century American gospel hymns and social religion that:

Since the situation which rhetoric seeks to encompass is a situation ... of
debate and argument, we cannot view its definitions of the world merely
as abstract systems. Rather, we must see them as strategic definitions
proposed over against other definitions offered by opponents.

She continues,

The rhetor's world is ... one of conflicting claims and avid argumentation.
In adopting a particular strategy, one attempts to stake out territory and
persuade others to join. Thus rhetoric involves that aspect of the human
condition whereby people express and recognize their mutual affinities,
their belonging to the same group, and especially, to *this* group and not *that.*
Rhetoric recognizes the divisions among people into various classes of
beings; rhetorical criticism seeks to make clear what the 'identifications' are,
and how the 'belonging' is conceived.[79]

The idea of identity is here unmistakable. An analysis of the Singh
Sabha's rhetoric (i.e. rhetorical criticism) makes clear what the
category 'Sikh' connoted in the twentieth century and how one could
belong.

One should note that the theme of martyrdom is also particularly
well suited to the situation in which the Singh Sabha found itself,
for by its very nature, martyrdom also deals with identity, and
dramatically so. In the hands of the Singh Sabha, the martyr became
the symbol of corporate Sikh identity *par excellence.* In his horrific
death the Sikh martyr was made to resolutely proclaim the separate
identity of the Sikh Panth to the entire world in a particularly moving

fashion, whether scalped, broken on the wheel, boiled alive, or sawn asunder. For the Singh Sabha, these heroic men died in order to protect the Sikh faith, a faith clearly identified with the religious tradition that the Singh Sabha advocated. The rhetoric of martyrdom constantly implied or made explicit this point: that Sikhs in the past sacrificed their lives in order to uphold the version of the Sikh religious tradition (the Singh Sabha rendition) to which contemporary Sikhs were not adhering.

The adoption of an analysis of the Singh Sabha's rhetoric and thus the techniques the group adopted to persuade its audience seems to imply that members of this Sabha were using rhetoric in a calculating manner, cognizant of their choice of language and free to manipulate words and symbols as they chose. We cannot assume, however, that Singh Sabha ideologues were always fully conscious of their choice of techniques and why these were successful. Burke alludes to this point by noting that the speaker may also be an audience: 'A man can be his own audience, insofar as he, even in his secret thoughts, cultivates certain ideas or images for the effect he hopes they may have upon him.' It is this notion, Burke argues, which places socialization under the rubric of rhetoric.[80] As Douglas Haynes notes in his path-breaking study of rhetoric and ritual in the west Indian city of Surat during the nineteenth century:

In the process of attempting to persuade others, humans constantly generate the cultural meanings by which they themselves understand reality and perceive their own interests. As people present their cases to their potential followers and as they defend their formulations against the claims of their rivals, they develop commitments to principles they have espoused; they come to see alternative principles as threatening, illogical, or hopelessly utopian. The understandings that they generate may thus create new limitations for themselves in future formulations... Logic employed repeatedly can assume the authority of 'common sense', so that individuals and groups find it difficult to formulate and conceive of their own self interests outside its limits.[81]

What I wish to point out is that Singh Sabha ideologues did not adopt a rhetorical scheme which intimately involved the theme of martyrdom simply as a problem-solving tool for the situation at hand, self-consciously employing a strategy that constantly alluded to themes with which the vast majority of Sikhs in the late nineteenth century—Khalsa, Sahajdhari, Namdhari, Nirankari, Seva Panthi or otherwise—would have been familiar. The evidence clearly suggests that these ideologues were convinced beyond doubt that martyrs and martyrdom had played a fundamental role in shaping the Sikh people and their tradition prior to its so-called period of corruption, the time of the Lahore Darbar (1799–1849). They were also convinced that contemporary Sikhs, through their practice of 'non-Sikh' rites, were failing to honour the precious sacrifice of past Sikh martyrs. For the Singh Sabha, all this was 'common sense'. We can, therefore, say that the rhetoric of martyrdom the Singh Sabha employed for many decades was not an explicit or conscious strategy. Rather, it appears to be an unconscious structure akin to grammar, a form available to members of a society which people learn to manipulate in particular ways for particular effects. One learns this rhetorical structure in the same way that one acquires the rules of grammar, by imitation and by being corrected, without in many cases acquiring the ability to explicate upon its rules.[82] At this point in our discussion, we can say that what the Singh Sabha drew upon in its construction of this strategy was the traditional model of the martyr which we noted in the various *gur-bilās* and *śahīd-bilās* literature predating the Singh Sabha which it, perhaps unknowingly, refined and amplified in the light of its particular context and situation. We will note in later chapters that it was a common feature of pre-Singh Sabha Sikh tradition and that it was a relatively simple matter for the Singh Sabha and later, the CKD and Akali Dal, to interpret these heroic acts in the light of their late nineteenth-century understanding of Sikhism.

It is Singh Sabha rhetoric in general and the rhetoric of martyrdom in particular which provided a vocabulary of thoughts, actions, emotions and attitudes for codifying and thus interpreting the late nineteenth- and early twentieth-century situations. In the light of the concept of rhetoric, we find that 'form and metaphor articulate a structure of the world and simultaneously create a community with its own specific identity'.[83] As the Singh Sabha's interpretation of the Sikh tradition gradually comes to the forefront, the rhetoric of martyrdom which was appropriated to dramatically put that message forward made martyrs and martyrdom seem far more intimately associated with the Sikh tradition and the Sikh people, and, as well, with Sikh history than ever before.

Here we can employ the notion of 'imagined community' made famous by Benedict Anderson.[84] Although Anderson deals specific- ally with the origins and spread of nationalism, his idea of the imagined community fits very well into this analysis of the Singh Sabha project. Anderson maintains that the imagined community is composed of members of a collectivity who rarely, if ever, share interpersonal relations and face-to-face familiarity, yet who are persuaded by the dissemination of literary publications and media messages produced and transmitted by ideologues that they are indeed a people sharing origins, traditions, hopes and aspirations. A key feature of this construction, according to Anderson, is the rise of vernacular publishing ('print-as-commodity'), particularly newspapers. Implicit in this reasoning is the rhetorical strategies that ideologues appropriate. It is these strategies which help in creating the boundaries of the community and shaping its world-view.[85]

N. Gerald Barrier was the first scholar to underscore the fact that the Singh Sabha project coincided with the rise of vernacular newspapers and publications in northern India, as well as with other methods of communication, including the telegraph and rail travel technologies of which the Sabha made very good use.[86] For the most part, the newspapers and tracts, disseminated throughout the Punjab and beyond, not only brought Sikhs together physically in town and village gurdwaras where such newspapers were often read aloud to illiterate Sikhs, but aided in the creation of a community of believers who gradually began to see themselves defined in terms of both the rhetoric that the Singh Sabha had appropriated to disseminate its message and the identity couched within that rhetoric. As scholars are just beginning to discover, it is principally through language that human beings engage in the social construction of reality.[87] Indeed, newspapers expressing Sikh concerns were somewhat aware of their role in broadcasting Singh Sabha ideas and bringing the community together, both in a physical and imaginative setting. As the *Sikh Sipāhī* (the Sikh Soldier) notes in its article on Sikh newspapers ('*Sikh Akhbār*') of 28 March 1919,

Disseminating worthwhile sentiments, [Sikh newspapers] attune the public to the notion of a single community.[88]

The rhetoric of martyrdom clearly equated present-day Sikhs with their pious and heroic brethren of the past in order to persuade contemporary Sikhs to adopt Singh Sabha standards and thus establish a single community. By late 1921, during the famous Keys Agitation of the Gurdwara Reform Movement,[89] for example, an article in the very influential Sikh newspaper, the *Akālī*, could call upon Sikhs in

the following fashion and have all readers understand that it was the
Sikhs, especially Khalsa Sikhs, to whom the proposal was directed:

O Khalsa which has been broken on the wheel! [O Khalsa] which has
been torn limb from limb! [O Khalsa] which has been wrapped alive in
cotton wool and then set ablaze! O Khalsa which [has suffered all this]
but has not suffered in reputation [nor lost its] self-respect [and honour]!...O
sons of martyrs!...Today we must follow the sacred, exemplary achievement
of Guru Tegh Bahadur and become martyrs.[90]

Here, the connection between contemporary Sikhs and martyrdom
is beyond doubt as the tortures mentioned in the text of the summons
are those which seventeenth- and eighteenth-century Sikhs are
popularly believed to have undergone in the early 1920s (a belief
which persists to this day). Such a call describes the Sikhs of the
present in terms signifying the ideal Sikhs of the (supposed) past,
creating a symbolic bond between the two groups and thus implying
.the existence of a single ('imagined') community that transcends
both time and space. In the words of Kenneth Burke, such equations
(which one often finds in Sikh newspapers of the period) are established through 'associational clusters' which allow us to determine
'what goes with what'.[91] In this light, we can say that by the 1920s
(and before), the kind of act and image that go with the constructs
'Sikh' and 'Sikh Panth'—what the 'essence' of the Sikh becomes, in
other words—is sacrifice, heroism and ultimately martyrdom.

In closing, we can extend Joyce Pettigrew's observation regarding
contemporary Sikhs killed in the recent period of strife to the Sikhs
who offered themselves for martyrdom during the Gurdwara Reform
Movement: 'By their concrete acts of heroism, individuals do not
merely commemorate a long and honourable tradition [of martyr-
dom], they also give substance to the insubstantial entity of the
Panth.'[92] In other words, the Sikh community comes together symbolically in the martyr and is substantiated and made public through
martyrdom.[93] It is thanks principally to the Singh Sabha's sustained
use of the rhetoric of martyrdom that the Sikh community begins to
see itself in this way, as a community 'through whose veins flows
the blood of martyrdom'. Yet there should be one qualification in
Pettigrew's maxim in the context of the Gurdwara Reform Movement, and this regards the term 'commemorate'. In dealing with the
early 1920s, 'commemorate' is not the appropriate word to use.
Rather, drawing upon Burke's insights on the concept of rhetoric, I

would argue that 'persuade' or 'influence' are better terms. Brave Akali Sikhs, through their heroic acts which were simultaneously rhetorical actions,[94] persuaded Sikhs and others not only to see theirs as a community of heroic warrior-martyrs but also to understand Sikh history according to the interpretations of that history posed by the Singh Sabha, one in which martyrdom plays a fundamental role. To read back into Sikh history, in other words, the values that Akalis underscored during the agitation, values broadcast by Singh Sabha ideologues for well over forty years prior to the movement to liberate Sikh gurdwaras from their traditional custodians, values which had become a part of 'everyday life' for a large number of Sikhs.

One can, therefore, assume that the concept of martyrdom has not always been as fundamental to Sikhism and the Sikh people as popular histories suggest. The notion is rather fundamental to the type of history these texts narrate,[95] a history aligned with one of the many versions of the Sikh religious tradition and its history that were available in the late nineteenth and early twentieth centuries. This particular rendition was developed and nurtured by the Singh Sabha. The fact that this interpretation is indeed viewed by the vast majority of Sikhs as the only reading of the faith makes it seem that martyrdom is fundamental to Sikhism. The power of the Singh Sabha's understanding is underscored by the fact that many scholars outside the Sikh tradition also contend that martyrdom has been a principal feature of the faith since its beginnings, tracing the idea of martyrdom to the first Guru. There is, of course, no historical or scriptural evidence in support of this claim.[96]

What these authors seem to ignore is the fact that there are categories of Sikhs whose thinking is not aligned with that of the Singh Sabha. For Sikhs of the Udasi or ascetic tradition, for example, it is highly unlikely that martyrdom figures at all in their understanding of Gurmat. With the hegemony of the Singh Sabha understanding of Sikhism, groups such as the Udasis were gradually seen as insignificant and were eventually consigned to the margins of the community.[97]

I should note at the outset that the term 'martyr' is very much a subjective one, communicating a strong Sikh value judgement. As we noted earlier, those Sikhs called martyrs are believed to have bravely witnessed to their faith despite the imminent mutilation and death they would suffer. For this reason, these Sikhs, especially under the Singh Sabha, became a cultural ideal to which preceding generations of the pious would be compared. These past valiant members of the Panth, moreover, would provide the model contemporary Sikhs were asked to emulate in the early twentieth century and are still asked to follow today.[98] Since I wish to understand the prominence of martyrdom throughout the Sikh tradition, I have chosen to style these people the way Sikhs and their martyrologists have since at least the early nineteenth century. I am, I should note, well aware that one person's heroic defiance is another's criminal insurrection.[99]

Let me note the structure this book will follow. Including this introduction, the book comprises seven chapters. Chapter Two will deal with the way the tradition of martyrdom has been passed down to generations of Sikhs. The third examines the popular tradition itself, while the fourth will critically examine Sikh, Persian and English sources implying the existence of a concept of martyrdom amongst late seventeenth- and early eighteenth-century Sikhs. Chapter Five will composite a picture of how the shahid was understood prior to the annexation of the Punjab in the mid-nineteenth century. Chapter Six deals with the Singh Sabha and how it appropriated and used the popular reverence for martyrs to secure its own aims and ensure that its interpretation of the Sikh tradition would come to dominate the Sikh imagination. The seventh chapter deals with the Gurdwara Reform Movement of the early to mid-1920s. The subversive potential of the numerous martyrologies written and issued under the auspices of the Singh Sabha, as well as the rhetoric of martyrdom that members of this society had constantly used for forty years prior to 1920, provided a discourse of martyrdom for those Sikhs who wanted to resist the authority of the British Government, which had an indirect control over sacred Sikh institutions. The final chapter provides a summary, which maintains that it is this legacy that contemporary Sikhs have inherited.

Finally, it should be noted that in Chapters Five and Six, in particular, I have made use of Michel Foucault's influential writings on the nature of punishment.[100] Foucault's discussion on the spectacle of public execution as political ritual in France, by which the power of authority is inscribed on the body of the criminal and sovereignty reaffirmed, has, however, provided only limited help in understanding the process I have described above.[101] Although the process of public torture Foucault narrates can certainly be applied to the Akalis who were publicly beaten and killed in their attempt to liberate the gurdwaras from their hereditary custodians, we must note some significant differences. John Knott has already pointed out one of these qualifications, which is that 'Foucault's model of punishment does not address the kind of *agon* [struggle; contest] one finds in the accounts of religious suffering.'[102] To this may be added the fact that the criminals undergoing public execution in seventeenth-century France really had no choice in the matter. These men and women were condemned criminals upon whom the king was exacting revenge for their allegedly horrendous acts. The martyrs in popular Sikh martyrologies as well as the Akalis of this century, however, had the option to have all punishment cease by choosing either to abjure their faith or not engage in the struggle to free the gurdwaras. This is a choice, I must add, of which all spectators would have been clearly aware. It was this sustained spectacle of the heroic acts of these contemporary Sikh martyrs, I believe, that assured the hegemony of the Singh Sabha interpretation of Sikh tradition.

Notes

1. This passage begins the 'Song of the Khalsa' of Sikh Dharma for the Western Hemisphere. S.S.S.K. Khalsa, *The History of Sikh Dharma in the Western Hemisphere* (Española, 1995), p. 127.

2. For example, Kharak Singh's editorial 'Martyrdom in Sikhism', in *Abstracts of Sikh Studies* (January, 1994), pp. 1–10.

3. Ric Dolphin, 'The Struggles of the Sikhs', in *Equinox* 76 (August 1994), p. 38.

4. In particular, Harbans Singh, *Heritage of the Sikhs* (Delhi, 1984), pp. 50–5; 68–87; 116–43.

5. *Martyrum non facit poena, sed causa* [*Epistle* 89.2]: 'It is not the punishment that makes one a martyr, but the cause.'

6. G.W. Bowersock, *Martyrdom & Rome* (Cambridge, 1995), p. 4.

7. Jennette Wakin (ed.), *The Function of Documents in Islamic Law: The Chapter on Sales from Tahāwi's* Kitāb Al-Shurūṭ Al-Kabir (Albany, 1972), pp. 6–8, 65–70.

8. G.W. Bowersock, *Martyrdom & Rome*, pp. 19–20 and Ignaz Goldziher, *Muhammedanishce Studien* [trans. S. Stern, *Muslim Studies* II (London, 1971), pp. 350–2.] An analysis of the Arabic term and the close relationship to its Greek counterpart is provided in A.J. Wensinck's 'The Oriental Doctrine of the Martyrs', in *Mededeelingen der koninklijke akademie van wetenschappen* 53, A, 2 (Amsterdam, 1920), pp. 147–74.

9. G.S. Talib, 'The Concept and Tradition of Martyrdom in Sikhism', in G.S. Talib (ed.), *Guru Tegh Bahadur: Background and Supreme Sacrifice* (Patiala, 1976), p. 188.

10. How this was accomplished is the basis of Harjot Oberoi's recent *The*

Construction of Religious Boundaries: Culture, Identity and Diversity in the Sikh Tradition (New Delhi, 1994). Oberoi deals primarily with the Sikh tradition, but his findings can certainly be carried over to the other religious traditions of late nineteenth-century Punjab. Islam is perhaps the exception here though, as nascent reform movements which attempted to distance Muslims from Hindus can be traced back to at least the sixteenth and seventeenth centuries (and possibly before) with figures such as Shaikh Ahmad Sirhindi (1564–1624) and Shah Wali-ullah (1703–62). Oberoi's views may be contrasted with those found in Dipankar Gupta's *The Context of Ethnicity: Sikh Identity in a Comparative Perspective* (Delhi, 1996), pp. 141, 143, 173.

11. Guru Nanak's *Siri rāg aṣṭapadī* 1 (2), *AG*, p. 53.

12. G.S. Talib, 'Martyrdom in Sikhism', p. 180, does note the absence of 'an adequate term' for either martyr or martyrdom. But he claims,

[s]uch absence ... should not be supposed to imply that the spiritual attitude accompanying martyrdom was unknown to the people of India in ancient times.

13. Oberoi makes this point in regard to the absence of the term 'religion'. *Construction*, pp. 12 ff.

14. We will observe that the concept was adopted before the word itself.

15. G.S. Talib, 'Martyrdom in Sikhism', p. 181:

... in the absence of proper historiography in ancient India, it is difficult to establish the facts of martyrdom. All that can be speculated is that ... the Aryans *must* have had their martyrs (my emphasis).

16. Background in Patrick Olivelle, 'The Notion of Asramas in the Dharma-sūtras', in *Weiner Zeitschrift für die Kunde Südasiens* XVIII (1974), pp. 27–35; and his 'Contributions to the Semantic History of *Samnyāsa*', in *JAOS* 101 (1978), pp. 265–74.

17. Monier-Williams provides a number of Sanskrit terms under the English heading 'martyr'. Some of these are *sākṣi; svadharmmāratham prāṇatyāgi; dehatyāgi; jīvinatyāgi;* and *nyastadehah.* M. Monier-Williams, *A Dictionary, English and Sanskrit* (London, 1851), p. 484. A contemporary Hindi term for martyr is *hutātmā*. R.S. McGregor, *The Oxford Hindi-English Dictionary* (Delhi, 1995), p. 1077. When one examines the English definitions of these terms in Sanskrit-English dictionaries, the English word 'martyr' does not appear.

18. See Surjit Hans, 'The Metaphysics of Militant Nationalism', in *JSS* XIII:2 (1985), pp. 85–131.

19. Within the eighteenth-century literature of the *gur-bilās* (pleasure of the Guru) genre, for example, terms which evoke such 'Hindu' understandings (for example, *prān tajaṇā* or 'to renounce breath') are often used as idioms for 'death' and 'sacrifice'. Although the literature of this genre is clearly one which underwrites the multifaceted Sikh tradition of the eighteenth century, in which one finds numerous 'Hindu' elements, the context of statements concerning sacrifice in this literature does not suggest the ascetic practices we associate with Hindu renouncers. The meaning to be inferred, clearly, is martyr. This is also, unequivocally, the case today. See, for example, Ganda Singh (ed.), *Kavi Saināpati Rachit Sri Gur-sobhā* (Patiala, 1988), pp. 108, 131 (hereafter *Gur-sobhā*).

20. I have never found such words as *prāndenvālā* or *prāntyagī* as synonyms for 'martyr' in Sikh martyrologies.

21. E.W. Lane's *Arabic-English Lexicon* I:7 (1st pbd. 1885. New York, 1956), p. 2507.

22. Ibid.

23. Within the Qur'ān, there are three occurrences of the term *qurbān* in all: 3:179; 5:30; 46:27. For background see A.J. Wensinck, 'Kurbān', in *The Encyclopaedia of Islam* V:1 (new edn, Leiden, 1979), pp. 436–7.

24. Wensinck, 'Kurbān', pp. 436–7.

25. There are various degrees of proximity but all traditional accounts narrate that the position of martyrs is very close to the Divine. Wensinck, 'Oriental Doctrine', pp. 2–4; and W. Bjorkman, Shahīd', in *The Encyclopaedia of Islam* 4:1 (Leiden, 1934), pp. 259–61. Other privileges martyrs receive are the freedom from all past sins, the right to intercede on behalf of the Muslim community, and the right to return to earth so that they may be once again killed *fī sabīl allāh* or 'on the path of God'.

26. The term *qurbānī* is perhaps the most popular of all terms for sacrifice in Punjabi (*kurbānī*).

27. G.W.H. Lampe, 'Martyrdom and Inspiration', in William Horbury and Brian McNeil (ed.), *Suffering and Martyrdom in the New Testament: Studies Presented to G.M. Styler by the Cambridge New Testament Seminar* (Cambridge, 1981), p. 118. It is for this reason, incidentally, that the ascetic, the sati, the Jain monk who undergoes *sallekhana* or religious death through fasting, as well as the various past lives of the Buddha as noted in the Jataka tales do not classify as martyrs.

28. As Wensinck points out, 'Oriental Doctrine', p. 7, '[the shahid] is one who fights in order that Allāh's Word may be prevalent.' Björkman, 'Shahīd', p. 260, also notes that anyone who dies 'in defending the right against injustice ... against the *zalim* [or tyrant]' is a shahid; and A.A. Dihkhuda's *Lughat Nāmah* no. 171 (Tehran, 1325 H./1947 CE), p. 131, claims that shahadat is *koshtah shodah dar rāh-i khodā* or 'to be killed on the path of God.'

29. From this point onwards, I have drawn freely from my article 'Martyrdom and the Sikh Tradition', in *JAOS* 117.4 (1997), pp. 623–42.

30. Garja Singh (ed.), *Shahīd-bilās (Bhāī Manī Singh) krit Sevā Singh* (Ludhiana, 1961). There are a number of early uses of the term shahid that should be here noted. According to John Malcolm's *Sketch of the Sikhs* (London, 1812), p. 195, 'The tribe of Acalís (immortals) ... and the Nirmala and Shahid ... read the sacred writings ...' We may assume, therefore, that the word shahid was probably adopted by a group of Sikhs in the late eighteenth or early nineteenth century. This group may perhaps trace its lineage to the Shahid *misl* (confederacy) and possibly to Baba Dip Singh the misl's legendary founder. The word shahid also appears in one *bait* or couplet found in the Persian *Divān-i Goyā* attributed to Nand Lal Goya, an eminent Sikh poet:

With one gesture of [the Beloved's] eyebrow we are martyred. There is no cure now as the arrow is shot from its bow. [7:3

It is unlikely here that the reference is to Sikh martyrdom as being a 'martyr to love' is a common topos in Persian ghazal poetry. Finally the word appears as part of the compound terms *shahid-ganj* and *pāk-shahīd* respectively found in both the Chaupa Singh Rahit-nama and the *Triya Charitr* of the Dasam Granth:

Anyplace where Sikhs have given their heads will be known as a *shahīd-ganj*, a 'martyr-treasury'.   *CSRn* 474 [p. 110]

During the battle many fell as 'pure martyrs' in the field (*hūe pāk-shāhīd jangāh mayānai*)   *Triya Charitr* 102:30 [*DG*, p. 948]

In both cases these is ambiguity. While Chaupa Singh references the spot on which a slain Sikh falls rather than the Sikh him or herself the *Triya Charitr* modifies the shahid with the term *pāk* or 'pure' implying that there were many 'impure' eighteenth-century understandings of the shahid. Such 'impure' or inclusivist understandings will be the subject of Chapter Five. Further reading is found in Annemarie Schimmel, *Mystical Dimensions of Islam* (Chapel Hill, 1975), pp. 11, 65, 76, 90. For Nand Lal's *Divān* see Lou Fenech, 'Persian Sikh Scripture: The Ghazals of Bhāī Nand Lal Goyā,' in the *International Journal of Punjab Studies* I:1 (1994), pp. 49–70.

31. See Chapter Five for the *Bachitar Nāṭak*.

32. *Gur-sobhā*, p. 131. Today's standard version of the *chhoṭe sāhib-zāde* story replaces Jujhar Singh with Zorawar Singh, another of the tenth Guru's sons. In the introduction to *Gur-Sobhā*, Ganga Singh explains Sainipati's 'mistake' (*bhulekhā*) regarding the sahib-zade, pp. 33–4.

33. Ibid., p. 128.

34. If we include its plural form, *suhade*, the number of total occurrences rises to ten.

35. Guru Nanak, *Sirī rāg aṣṭapadī* (2), AG, p. 53. Although terms in the Adi Granth may sometimes be doubled for emphasis, the conjunction *aur* ('and') between *śuhade* and *śahīd* may indicate that the first Guru did not understand *śahīd* and *śuhade* to mean 'martyr' and 'martyrs', respectively. The question then is how does one define these words? In modern Urdu, the term *śuhadā* means a 'bad or loose character', but it seems unlikely that the context of the above hymn will support such a definition here. Rather, Guru Nanak may understand the term *śahīd* to mean something other than the term 'martyr' with which we are familiar today.

36. Ravi Das, *Rāg malār* 3:2, AG, p. 1293.

37. For Guru Nanak's use of Islamic terminology see W.H. McLeod, *The Sikhs: History, Religion, and Society* (Columbia, 1989), pp. 28–9.

38. Mona Kang, 'The Concept of Martyrdom in Sikhism and Sikh Martyrs upto Eighteenth Century', (unpublished Ph.D. dissertation, Punjab University, Chandigarh, 1990), p. 46.

39. *BG*, *vār* 8, *pauri* 8, *śalok* 3, p. 68.

40. *BG*, 21:13:2, p. 335. Also see Note 35 above.

41. *BG*, 40:8:2, p. 625.

42. *BG*, 3:18:2, p. 68.

43. Bhajan Singh, *Sāde Śahīd* (Amritsar, 1997), p. 10.

44. The following edict was issued to the *faujdārs* (commanders) of Shahjahanabad on 10 December 1710 by Bahadur Shah:

The disciples of Nanak (*nānak-parastān*) are to be slaughtered in every place that they are found.

EEAS, p. 193, n. 11.

45. *TGK* II, pp. 78–88. Compare this with Muzaffar Alam, *The Crisis of*

Empire in Mughal North India: Awadh and Punjab 1707-1748 (New Delhi, 1986), pp. 134-75.

46. Sukkha Singh claims, for example,

Justice becomes injustice in the sight of the Muslims, anguish rules all. Gone are the virtues of all the Kshatriyas (warriors), contemplation, charity, gifts without number.

and

The burden of the Muslims has brought suffering to all. No Kshatriya can be seen abroad.

G.K. Jaggi (ed.), *Gur-bilās Pātśāhī 10 Bhāī Sukkhā Siṅgh* (Patiala, 1989), pp. 30, 58.

47. See, for example, P.S. Padam, *Rahit-nāme* (Amritsar, 1991) as well as *CSRn*, p. 42. The anti-Islamic theme of the janam-sakhis is the motif of Guru Nanak's 'Triumph over Islam'. *EST*, p. 102.

48. Surjit Hans, *A Reconstruction of Sikh History from Sikh Literature* (Jalandhar, 1988), p. 269. That Sikhs were favoured in early nineteenth-century Sikh literature is clear in S.S. Sagar, *Historical Analysis of Nanak Prakash Bhai Santokh Singh* (Amritsar, 1993), p. 91.

49. This Bhikkhan should not be confused with the Sufi Baba Bhikhan (1480-1573), whose hymns are also included in the Adi Granth (*Rāg soraṭh*, AG, p. 659). Bhatt Bhikkhan's songs appear as *Savaie* 19, AG, p. 1395. Initially, bhatts were brahman bards before joining Sikh ranks. Seva Singh's surname, Kaushish, for example, is probably derived from the name *kauśik*, a brahman caste.

50. Bhatt Kirat, *Savaie* 55, AG, p. 1405. Garja Singh fails to mention this point about Kirat Shahid.

51. The battle is noted in *TGK* I, pp. 482-3. Here the battle took place in 1628.

52. It is according to the *Bhaṭṭ Vahī Multānī Sindhī* that Ballu is noted as Guru Hargobind's companion. See 'Ballū', in *EoS* I, p. 268.

53. *Śahīd-bilās*, pp. 5-6. This brief biography of Seva Singh is all that Garja Singh supplies in his introduction.

54. *Śahīd-bilās*, p. 71. See also pp. 68, 84, 89, 92, 93. It is based in part on the language used in *Śahīd-bilās* that Garja Singh argues the text's early nineteenth-century date. See his introduction, p. 6. We should note that Seva Singh does not completely displace the earlier formulations of the gur-bilas literature regarding martyrdom. For example,

[Mani Singh] was torn limb from limb but not a sigh escaped his mouth. For the sake of righteousness he sacrificed his life (*die prān*). To become a sacrifice for the sake of the Guru is the [true] service (*sevā*) of God.

Śahīd-bilās, p. 54.

55. Garja Singh provides an extended genealogy of Mani Singh (based on the *Bhaṭṭ Vahīs* and *Paṇḍā Vahīs*), noting the numerous members of the latter's family who became martyrs (twenty-eight in all). *Śahīd-bilās*, pp. 105-6.

56. Ibid., p. 80. Apparently, the battle's date is mentioned in the *Bhaṭṭ Vahī Talaudā Pargaṇā Jīnd*. *Śahīd-bilās*, p. 79.

57. T.W. Arnold, 'Saints and Martyrs (Muhammadan in India)', in *The Encyclopaedia of Religion and Ethics* XI (New York, 1921), p. 72.

58. See Chapter Four. According to Sikh tradition, Guru Gobind Singh composed a large segment of his Dasam Granth in order to enthuse Sikhs to martial action. Surjit Hans also shares this view. *Reconstruction*, p. 246.

59. Hans, *Reconstruction*, p. 246.

60. *Gur-sobhā*, p. 70. See also verse 3:339, p. 108.

61. *Construction*, pp. 47-8.

62. Among other martyrs mentioned in the text are Guru Tegh Bahadur, Bhai Gulzar Singh (a companion of Mani Singh), the martyred sons of Guru Gobind Singh, Tara Singh, Sahib Singh (the brother of Mata Sahib Kaur), and the adopted son of Mata Sundari, Ajit Singh. *Sahīd-bilās*, pp. 59, 84, 92.

63. It should be noted that there are also 'living martyrs' in the Sufi (or Islamic mystic) tradition, men who have, according to E. Kohlberg, 'joined the "greater *djihād*", successfully fight[ing] their *nafs* [one's base instincts].' See his 'Shahīd' in C.E. Bosworth, et al. (ed.), *The Encyclopaedia of Islam* IX, fascs. 149-50 (Leiden, 1995), p. 206.

64. It also appears that Singh Sabha writers may have developed the idea of the *zindā śahīd* in order to come to terms with what clearly appeared to be the end of martyrdom in the Sikh tradition. In the late nineteenth and early twentieth centuries, the possibility of procuring the traditional death of the martyr as narrated in the numerous Singh Sabha martyrologies was remote, to say the least.

65. Background in Attar Singh's *Jindā śahīd nūn moran lai vichār te tajwiz* (Lahore, 1916).

66. S.S. Caveeshar, *The Sikh Studies* (Lahore, 1937), p. 145.

67. Baba Kharak Singh helped found the CSL in 1919. See Sukhmani Bal, *Politics of the Central Sikh League* (Delhi, 1990), p. 31.

68. See, for example, the numerous articles and books. written by W.H. McLeod, N.G. Barrier and Harjot Oberoi, noted throughout this monograph. Although Oberoi does not focus specifically on the Singh Sabha use of rhetoric, one should point out that he does imply the Singh Sabha's use of language and rhetoric in his focus on the *episteme*. The episteme is the precursor to the 'discursive formation' in Michel Foucault's thought. Like the discursive formation, the episteme is a unit of discourse, discourse being the total of practices, utterances, speech acts and interactions which combined, frame a shared space of public behaviour for a collectivity of people. See Oberoi's *Construction*, pp. 1-35.

69. S.K. Foss, et al. (ed.), *Contemporary Perspectives on Rhetoric* (Prospect Heights, Ill., 1991), p. 177.

70. Kenneth Burke, 'Literature as Equipment for Living', in his *The Philosophy of Literary Form: Studies in Symbolic Action* (Baton Rouge, 1966), pp. 293-304. Also pp. 60-6.

71. Kenneth Burke, *A Rhetoric of Motives* (New York, 1950), pp. 41, 43.

72. Burke, *The Philosophy of Literary Form*, p. 1.

73. Ibid.

74. Ibid., pp. 1, 109, 283, 289.

75. Barry Brummett (ed.), *Landmark Essays on Kenneth Burke* (Anaheim, 1993), pp. xiii-xv.

76. Amongst the many books that appropriate Burke's ideas is Victor Turner's

Dramas, Fields and Metaphors: Symbolic Action in Human Society (Ithaca, 1973). Turner's understanding of 'structure', 'anti-structure' and *communitas* will be drawn upon in discussing the Gurdwara Reform Movement.

77. For Sanatan Sikhism see Oberoi, *Construction*, p. 92–138. The Arya Samaj in Punjab is analysed in Kenneth Jones, *Arya Dharam: Hindu Consciousness in 19th Century Punjab* (Berkeley, 1976).

78. Burke, *A Rhetoric of Motives*, p. 55; also pp. 21, 24, 46. Burke further discusses the concept of identification in his *Language as Symbolic Action: Essays on Life, Literature and Method* (Berkeley, 1966), p. 301. In his *Permanence and Change* (New York, 1935), p. 71, Burke likens identification to 'ingratiation' or an attempt to 'gain favor by the hypnotic or suggestive process of "saying the right thing" '.

79. S.S. Sizer, *Gospel Hymns and Social Religion: The Rhetoric of Nineteenth-century Revivalism* (Philadelphia, 1978), p. 17. Sizer uses the term 'rhetorical criticism' to refer to the activity of the discipline which studies rhetoric (p. 183).

80. Burke notes, for example:

The individual person, striving to form himself in accordance with the communicative norms that match the cooperative ways of his society, is by the same token concerned with the rhetoric of identification. To act upon himself persuasively, he must variously resort to images and ideas that are formative.

Burke, *A Rhetoric of Motives*, pp. 38–9; and *Language as Symbolic Action*, p. 301.

81. Douglas Haynes, *Rhetoric and Ritual in Colonial India: The Shaping of a Public Culture in Surat City, 1852–1928* (Berkeley, 1991), p. 24.

82. My thinking in this regard follows that of Sandra Sizer. See her *Gospel Hymns*, pp. 14–16.

83. Ibid., pp. 18–19.

84. Benedict Anderson, *Imagined Communities: Reflections on the Origin and Spread of Nationalism* (London, 1992).

85. Ibid., pp. 37–46.

86. See. N.G. Barrier, *The Sikhs and Their Literature: A Guide to Books, Tracts & Periodicals (1849–1919)* (Delhi, 1970), pp. xvii–xlv.

87. Burke's logology, for example, is a linguistic ontology. Burke, *The Rhetoric of Religion* (Berkeley, 1970), chapter 1.

88. As quoted in Amarjit Kaur, 'The Nascent Sikh Politics: 1919–1921', I (unpublished Ph.D. dissertation, GNDU, 1992), p. 333.

89. See Chapter Seven.

90. *Akālī*, 4 December 1921, p. 2.

91. Burke, *The Philosophy of Literary Form*, p. 20.

92. Joyce Pettigrew, 'Betrayal and Nation-building Among the Sikhs', in *Journal of Commonwealth & Comparative Politics* XXIX:1 (London, 1991), p. 37.

93. See Miri Rubin, 'Choosing Death? Experiences of Martyrdom in Late Medieval Europe', in Diana Wood (ed.), *Martyrs and Martyrologies* (Oxford, 1993), p. 153.

94. According to Burke, 'Persuasion cannot be confined to the strictly verbal; it is a mixture of symbolism and definite empirical operations.' *A Rhetoric of Motives*, pp. 161, and 171–3.

95. See Chapter Two.

96. Joyce Pettigrew's 'Martyrdom and Guerrilla Organisation in Punjab', *Journal of Commonwealth & Comparative Politics* 30:3 (November 1992), pp. 389–90; her *The Sikhs of the Punjab: Unheard Voices of State and Guerrilla Violence* (London, 1995); and C.K. Mahmood, *Fighting for Faith and Nation: Dialogues with Sikh Militants* (Philadelphia, 1997), pp. 32–4 for example.

97. Perhaps Udasi indifference towards Sikh martyrs may have led to their marginalization.

98. For example, Kuldip Singh, 'Restoring the Khalsa Image: A Blueprint for 21st Century', in *The Sikh Review* 42:2:482 (1994), pp. 52 ff.

99. Within Muslim accounts, for example, Muslims killed in battle with the Khalsa are referred to as shahids, especially the famous Sayyid Ahmad Barelvi, leader of the *mujāhidīn* movement, who declared a jihad against the Sikhs of Ranjit Singh's domains and was killed by them in Balakot in 1831. For background on Barelvi see Aziz Ahmad, *Studies in Islamic Culture in the Indian Environment* (Oxford, 1964), pp. 209–17. The famous eighteenth-century Urdu poet, Mir Taqi Mir, moreover, mentions how offensive Sikhs appeared to those people of Delhi whose city they often raided in the mid- to late eighteenth century:

Thieves, pickpockets, Sikhs, Marathas, beggars, kings—all prey on us. Happy is he who has no wealth; this is the one true wealth today.

Ralph Russell and Khurshidal Islam, *Three Mughal Poets: Mir, Sauda, Mir Hasan* (Harvard, 1969), p. 221.

100. Michel Foucault, *Surveiller et Punir; Naissance de la Prison* [trans. Alan Sheridan, *Discipline & Punish: The Birth of the Prison* (New York, 1979), pp. 43ff.].

101. I follow here the discussion in J.R. Knott's *Discourses of Martyrdom in English Literature, 1563–1694* (Cambridge, 1992), p. 9. Also see David Potter, 'Martyrdom as Spectacle', in Ruth Scodel (ed.), *Theater and Society in the Classical World* (Ann Arbor, 1993), pp. 53–88. For criticism of Foucault's *Surveiller et Punir* see P. Spierenburg, *The Spectacle of Suffering* (Cambridge, 1984), pp. viii–ix.

102. John Knott, *Discourses of Martyrdom*, p. 9.

TWO

The Tradition and its Transmission

Sikh history is a tale of sacrifices, persecutions and martyrdoms
invited by the Sikhs in the service of their mission. It is for this
mission that the Gurus had inspired, prepared and led them.[1]

In November 1990, during the day-long celebration of the birth
anniversary of Guru Nanak, I had the distinct pleasure of attending
a number of singing performances in the precincts of Gurdwara
Rakabganj in New Delhi. Along with the anticipated *rāgīs*, profes-
sional musicians who sing hymns from the Sikh scriptures, there
were groups of singers present known as *dhādhī jathās*. Although
these groups are more associated with rural Punjab, they occasionally
venture to famous urban gurdwaras, both in India and abroad, to
give concerts. The repertoire of these musicians, unlike that of ragis,
does not usually include the hymns of the Adi Granth or those of
Bhai Gurdas, both of which convey the theological tenets of Sikhism.
Rather, dhadhis sing the martial anecdotes associated with Gurus
Hargobind and Gobind Singh, with the Sikh heroes of the seventeenth
century and with the subsequent Sikh struggle after the tenth Guru's
death in 1708. Since many of these heroes were also martyrs, martyrdom no doubt figures prominently in their ballads.

The fact that Gurdwara Rakabganj is associated with the martyrdom of the ninth Sikh Master, Guru Tegh Bahadur, indicates that
dhadhi concerts are a regular feature in the gurdwara's list of events,
and this is undoubtedly the case.[2] Nevertheless, on that day, the
distinctive sound of the *saraṅgī* (a violin-like instrument) and *dhādh*
(a small drum) seemed quite out of place since Guru Nanak is
generally characterized as a quietistic religious teacher who preached
a doctrine of liberation based upon *nām simraṇ*, meditation on the

nām of Akal Purakh.[3] The strains of a music considered martial would thus be the last thing one would expect to hear during this occasion. Why, I asked myself, were these singers present?

The concern which engendered this question was in no way shared by the tens of thousands of Sikhs and non-Sikhs enjoying the festivities. To the Sikhs, it was obvious that such heroic tunes should be associated with the life and message of Guru Nanak. As the quote above from Jagjit Singh's *The Sikh Revolution* implies, the history of the Sikhs is one in which the adherents of Gurmat (Sikhism) personify the ideals which the Gurus enshrined in their compositions, undergoing persecution and martyrdom so that these ideals could be instituted and/or upheld. This is indeed an interpretation of Sikh history which the vast majority of contemporary Sikhs would accept as absolutely inviolable. It is to the influence of the Gurus, therefore, that Sikhs attribute the martyr's ability to such selfless action. As we will see, one of the most influential Gurus in this regard is the founder of the faith, Guru Nanak. The invigorating sound of the militant music of the dhadhi jathas then, particularly on this Gurpurab (a celebration in connection with the life of one of the Sikh Gurus), was natural, eliciting not a curious response from the Sikhs present but a highly pleasurable one.

Since one must either attend a gurdwara on a specially designated day in order to listen to dhadhis or be fortunate enough to reside in a Punjabi village during one of their visits, their music is one facet of Punjabi Sikh culture with which very few non-Punjabis are familiar. This is truly unfortunate because dhadhis continue to form an important element in Punjabi Sikh society. Considered 'traditional Sikh intellectuals',[4] dhadhis transmit to rural Sikhs, particularly, what is considered to be the history of the heroic period of the Panth (the Sikh community), the eighteenth century. As the commander of the KCF, Beant Singh (d. 1990), noted in an interview a few months before his death:

In the early days of my life I heard much about Shahid Bhagat Singh and Baba Dip Singh in *dhadhi* gatherings. Wherever there were such gatherings I used to attend. I've always listened to their [dhadhi] songs. Listening to them gave me a lot of strength. Listening to our people's history is important to us.[5]

For many Sikhs, dhadhis are the historians of the Panth and without doubt, dhadhis see themselves as such.[6] Today, their ballads are almost exclusively devoted to narrating the battles of the seventeenth and eighteenth centuries, battles in which it is believed that Sikhs like Baba Dip Singh distinguished themselves through their courage, selflessness and martyrdom. Dhadhis thus bring the Sikh pantheon of heroes and martyrs to life. Recently, dhadhis have also incorporated what are popularly considered modern Sikh struggles into their stock of regularly performed pieces. Despite such odes being banned by the Government of India in 1984, one would often hear a composition about Operation Bluestar in the months after June of that year, detailing the heroism of both Shahbeg Singh and Jarnail Singh Bhindranwale, men who are considered modern-day Sikh martyrs by a large number of Sikhs.[7]

Dhadhi performances generate a zeal which is indeed breathtaking. Their inspirational concerts are almost always punctuated by numerous, intermittent shouts of the popular Sikh *jaikārā* or battle-cry *Sat Srī Akāl!* (True is the Timeless [One]) from the gathered crowd.[8] Songs within the dhadhi tradition are themselves enormously enthusiastic, reflecting a spirit of optimism and defiance that is today believed to be very much a part of the Sikh tradition.[9] One would not have to search for long to find dhadhi audio cassettes. A number of shops alongside virtually any gurdwara in Amritsar district, in particular, sell these items. Titles such as *Rākhe mazlūmān de: prasaṅg bhāī tārū siṅgh jī* (The protector of the oppressed: the story of Bhai Taru Singh Ji), *Aṅkhī yodhe* (Self-respecting warriors), *Sikh yodhā: bhāī bachchitar siṅgh* (A Sikh warrior: Bhai Bachittar Singh[10]); and *Jīvaṇī bābā dīp siṅgh paraupkārī sūrmā* (The biography of Baba Dip Singh, the benevolent warrior) from popular dhadhi audio tapes help capture the type of message that their ballads communicate.[11] Such messages have also broken out of the dhadhi genre and entered today's popular Punjabi music, one example being Sukhvinder Panchi's *Sahīdīān: sikh qaum de lahū raṅge itihās dī dāstān* (Martyrdoms: the tragic story of the blood-soaked history of the Sikh people). In all these, the warriors are extreme in their bravery, prowess and determination. Equally extreme are their opponents, though the latter exercise this zeal in barbarity, cruelty and treachery.

The vast majority of dhadhi songs narrate the exceptionally powerful myth of the eighteenth-century Khalsa, a golden age in which Sikh warriors braved hazards beyond description, willing to become martyrs so that all people may have the right to worship freely in an age of the most despicable intolerance.[12] These provide an interpretation of Sikh history that pits dauntless courage against vile deception, truth and justice against tyranny and oppression. On one side, we have heroes and martyrs, on the other, tyrants and despots. Despite the moving tragedies that these songs narrate, their intent is never to invoke pessimism. Rather, these seek to uplift and inspire, to produce in Sikhs a sense of optimism (*charhdi kalā*, 'raised spirits') and to strengthen their courage so that they may bear their daily tribulations and fight against perceived injustice with uncommon bravery, particularly in times of crisis. The music of the dhadhis is, then, a key feature in the process that Veena Das describes in her analysis of Sikh militant discourse as it is this which '[i]mput[es] an identity of events and the return of certain key constellations in Sikh history, [establishing] contemporaneity ... between non-contemporaneous events'. In other words, dhadhis help in representing the current Sikh struggle as 'a continuation of a series of struggles that Sikhs have had to historically wage in order to preserve their identity'.[13]

Whether these struggles were as historical as Das claims is open to argument. What is not is the fact that the accounts which dhadhis sing are clearly about martyrs, and like written martyrologies, these songs present victory in the midst of the most bitter defeats. It is through a death met serenely, fearlessly and courageously that their protagonists defeat their slayers. The fact that dhadhis have been performing throughout the Punjab since the time of Guru Nanak and earlier is alone testament to their sustained popularity and the strength of the themes about which they sing.[14] Of course, prior to the Sikh and Mughal enmity, dhadhis drew their stock of characters from other sources. To specifically determine what dhadhis sang about in the fifteenth and sixteenth centuries is very difficult. Yet if Guru Nanak's *Vār Āsā* 11:2 does allude to dhadhis, we may surmise that heroes and battles certainly formed a significant part of their collective themes.[15] In the late seventeenth and eighteenth centuries, however, characters from Punjabi and Rajasthani folklore were incorporated into their ballads. Within famous folk tales, such as Hir-Ranjha, Sassi-Pannu, Mirza-Sahiban, Jaimal-Fatta and a host of others, are intertwined themes of honour, courage, love and sacrifice, themes very similar to those which permeate the martyrologies and battle accounts of present dhadhi compositions.[16] Courage, defiance, endurance, fearlessness, loyalty, altruism and martyrdom—these are traditions within Sikhism which are today sung in the dhadhi tradition. For Sikhs, the appeal of dhadhi songs and the influence these generate is vast. So vast, in fact, that the Dharam Prachar Committee or missionary branch of the SGPC had in the early 1970s, and possibly before, employed four dhadhi jathas 'to sing ballads to villagers and impress religion upon them'.[17]

Tradition

The word 'tradition' has been used directly above in two different, though related, senses. In the first case, tradition designates the means by which Sikh belief and practice is transmitted. The dhadhi tradition is certainly one of the vehicles through which the ideal of martyrdom is handed down and expressed. Very closely connected with the vehicle of transmission is the transmitted knowledge, in this case martyrdom. The term 'tradition' is also applied to this transmitted ideal or 'norm' itself. Tradition also indicates, therefore, a particular belief or practice held to have been handed down from the past and implicitly believed, for which there is little or no documented historical evidence. Such traditions stress that they embody an unchanging truth from a source that is authoritative. Because of their relative antiquity, these command a strong respect, an esteem which is also applied to its transmitters. Listeners assume that the transmitters are reliable and communicate traditions without substantial change.[18]

In this discussion, the term 'tradition' is also used descriptively, amounting to little more than a way of naming the Sikh religion. When we speak of 'the Sikh tradition', therefore, we simply mean what is commonly called 'Sikhism'. In the modern study of religion, this way of speaking about religions is quite commonplace, despite the fact that such an application seems to single out traditionality as the most basic characteristic of a religion.[19]

From the general we move on to the specific. When one speaks of the tradition of martyrdom in Sikhism, one acknowledges three closely intertwined meanings. The first is a reference to the popular history of the Panth's martyrs, the oral and written martyrologies which are believed to document the lives of martyrs such as Guru Tegh Bahadur, Taru Singh and Mani Singh, to name a few. The accounts that dhadhis narrate often fall into this category. As we have seen, these narratives are quite fervent, very different from the caution and meticulousness which has come to be associated with the academic historian. In fact, this chapter began with a discussion of dhadhi ballads for precisely this reason. Within the present discussion, the concern is not with events as these occurred but with history as it is popularly understood by the vast majority of Sikhs today. In such martyrologies, there is implied a belief that within the very life-blood of these and all Sikhs, particularly those of the Khalsa variety, there is some mystical substance which provides the ability to undergo such a trial as martyrdom, an element which captures what is felt to be the 'essence' of Sikhism.[20] This popular belief, then, provides the second of our three interrelated meanings.

In this case, belief is meant to engender practice. The third meaning maintains that whenever a situation arises which is perceived as similar to those within popular accounts, the Sikh reaction to the current problem must also be similar to the type of response encountered in the martyrologies.[21] The tradition of martyrdom offers the possibility of a variety of responses without emphasizing the virtues of any particular one over another.[22] A Sikh may, therefore, respond to injustice non-violently, as did Guru Arjan, or by drawing the sword, as did the elder sons of the tenth Guru. One must, however, respond. If a tyrant raises his head once again, Sikhs must take action and be willing to die in the attempt to put an end to the persecution such an oppressor encourages. They must, in other words, provide 'testimony' (*śahādat*) to prevailing injustice, as their eighteenth-century brothers and sisters are believed to have done, showing solidarity with those who suffer under such injustice and joy in sacrificing one's life alongside them.[23] Not to do so is a violation of values which Sikhs hold most dear.[24]

Of course, this is the ideal, but it is an ideal which has been proven to inspire Sikhs to acts of rare courage and daring. Examples of Sikhs taking such action are many. During the Gurdwara Reform Movement, both the Akalis and the Babbar Akalis responded to British policies which they considered tyrannical in a way which reflected the ideals found in many popular martyr accounts.[25] So, too, did Mewa Singh respond. A Sikh immigrant who was executed by the government of Canada on 11 January 1915 for shooting a Canadian immigration inspector, Mewa Singh, is believed to have taken revenge against what he considered insults to the Sikh religion by Canadian authorities.[26] The Sikhs belonging to the Ghadr Movement of the early twentieth century; the members of the Akali Dal who acted on behalf of the Punjabi Suba in the 1950s and 1960s; Sikhs who joined the Punjabi Naxalite movement in the 1960s; those Akalis who courted arrest, imprisonment and death during the

Emergency imposed by Indira Gandhi from 1975 to 1977; and the many Sikhs who have recently died in the years prior to and after June 1984 felt that they acted in accordance with Sikh traditions of heroism, defiance and martyrdom.[27]

Implied above is the fact that there are themes within the tradition of martyrdom which are in themselves Sikh traditions. It has been noted elsewhere that martyrdom, along with heroism, endurance, defiance, loyalty and altruism, emerges as one of the most powerful of the many intertwined themes in the 'myth of the rise and ultimate victory of the Khalsa'.[28] The isolation here, however, as McLeod implies, is strictly academic, one that does not mirror reality as it is understood by Sikhs. Nevertheless, one may isolate the tradition of martyrdom for the purpose of the present discussion, noting that in the Sikh martyr, all other themes in the myth meet. The martyr displays his courage, altruism and defiance to the last breath, to a point beyond which one cannot go. This human inability to progress beyond death makes the tradition of martyrdom the 'supreme' expression of the other traditions in question. In other words, the martyr tradition takes the traditions within it to their furthest extent. More precisely, however, the traditions of heroism, defiance and so on, taken to their furthest end, form the martyr tradition. For Sikhs, a reference to Sikh martyrs is, therefore, a reference to the ultimate embodiment of heroism, defiance, endurance, loyalty, fearlessness and altruism.

From these traditions, one may certainly detach martyrdom without much being lost on the former's part. Both Bidhi Chand Chhina and Jassa Singh Ahluvalia, for example, are known for their courage, defiance and loyalty, characteristics which are by no means diminished because of the fact that they were not martyred.[29] Yet where men like Bidhi Chand exhibited a willingness to die, Sikhs hailed as martyrs, such as Tara Singh or Dip Singh, have actually succeeded in dying for Sikh ideals.[30] It is significant to note that the intention to die in the defence of righteousness is not enough to make one a martyr in Sikhism.[31]

This fact is clearly brought forth in the traditional story of the creation of the Khalsa. According to tradition, on the first day of Baisakh, 1699 (sc. 1756), Guru Gobind Singh addressed a large gathering of Sikhs at Kesgarh, requesting the heads of five Sikhs as a sacrifice to Akal Purakh. The five Sikhs to come forward did so with the intention of offering their heads to the tenth Guru. These *pañj piāre*, or Five Cherished Ones as they were later called, were convinced that on this day, their lives would end as a sacrifice at the request of their Guru. The tenth Guru, however, did not end their lives. Following the apparent slaying of the last of the five inside a tent, he brought all of them out unharmed. On presenting these Sikhs to the gathered Panth, he stated that this exercise was devised to test the loyalty and courage of his Sikhs since his Khalsa would require members to always be prepared to offer their heads for righteousness and for their Guru.[32] Despite their intention, the first five members of the Khalsa are never referred to as martyrs.[33] The tradition of martyrdom, therefore, implies that it is one's actual death for righteousness which places the martyr on a much higher pedestal than Sikh heroes like Bidhi Chand or Hari Singh Nalwa, whether the only difference between the two was simply an accident of history or not.[34] One cannot speak about Sikh martyrs, therefore, without alluding to the powerful themes and traditions mentioned above, nor can one disentangle these themes from the concept of martyrdom. Should one attempt to do so, the term 'martyrdom' will, of course, be no longer applicable. In this case, we simply describe a death, in many cases the death of a hero, yet nevertheless one devoid of the meaning which martyrdom implies as a witness to injustice with one's life.[35] This is a very simple difference, but a fundamental one. In today's popular Sikh martyr tradition, there is no martyr who is not heroic, altruistic, fearless and defiant.

Transmission

The introduction to dhadhis indicates to those of us who rely on the written word that the majority of Sikhs derive their understanding of the faith and its traditions from other sources. Writings are indeed important and their influence in the Punjab is certainly on the rise. The sight of popular histories, pamphlets, magazines and even comic-books dealing with the tradition of martyrdom in Sikhism is not altogether rare in Punjabi cities.[36] With these, one may include the martyr stories found in children's school-readers, story-books and the various charms which are written on the top of lorries, on the back of bicycle rickshaws, or just below the windshields of the ubiquitous three-wheeled motorized rickshaws.[37]

For now, however, both English and Punjabi writings are still secondary. In the countryside, where the majority of Sikhs dwell, such writings are not so commonplace. Dhadhis, very much a feature of rural Punjab, transmit the tradition of martyrdom within Sikhism to succeeding generations of Sikhs through oral communication, the principal mediator of the tradition. In daily life, the notion of martyrdom is deployed through metaphor and metonymy. The Sikh soldiers who fell in battle during both the two world wars and the Indo-Pakistani conflicts are termed martyrs.[38] Within the last century, the Panth has been conferring the title zinda shahid or 'living martyr' on those Sikhs who are believed to have confronted oppression as fierce as that encountered by classical Sikh martyrs in their attempt to pursue what are deemed noble goals. Rather than die, however, these Sikhs continue living, striving to realize their ideals.[39]

When Sikh historians describe the events of the eighteenth century, they invoke a popular phrase believed to have been composed in this period which is still recited today with vigour in both towns and villages:

Mir Mannu is our sickle and we the fodder for him to mow. The more Mir Mannu harvests, the more the Sikhs will grow.[40]

For the many Sikh murders for which he is directly responsible, Mir Mannu has carved a special niche in Sikh demonology. This brief ditty alludes to this fact while glorifying the Sikh contempt for death and the belief in their ability to cheerfully embrace martyrdom. That suffering and dying for one's faith is a fructifying act is a metaphor that one often encounters in Sikh martyrologies. Indeed, for the authors of these works, as for the famous Christian martyrologist, Tertullian, the blood of the martyr is the seed of the Church.[41]

In the Punjabi language, the type of talk we encounter in the Mir Mannu quip is termed *bol bālā* (lit., 'superior talk'), a phrase which captures the Sikh spirit of belittling misfortune.[42] Not only do we find bol bala in many martyrological accounts of the Sikhs—the man appointed as executioner of eighteenth-century Sikhs, for example, is referred to reverently as Mukt, the deliverer[43]—but in the contemporary crisis, bol bala is appropriated by Sikh militants to describe the tortures to which they were allegedly subjected while in police custody. As Pettigrew notes, for example, one of the people she interviewed used the term *ṭāhuṇī* (a mild thrashing one may give a disobedient child) to describe a particularly vicious torture he had undergone, while another guerrilla simply stated that his torturers were 'just needling me'.[44] Other examples of bol bala incorporate martyrdom into popular idioms and jokes.[45] A joke which probably originated during British rule and is still recited today alludes to the famous eighteenth-century Sikh martyr, Baba Dip Singh (without actually mentioning him), to highlight the belief in the Sikhs' innate ability as soldiers, particularly their endurance on the field of battle:

An English officer was conducting an interview with Rajputs, Marathas and Sikhs. He wanted to examine their bravery. The first he questioned was one of the Rajputs, 'What is that innate virtue that Rajputs possess which you shall all bring into the army?' The Rajput responded, 'Sahib! We are Rajputs. And for the sake of honour we always remain prepared to die.'

After the Rajput, in answer to the same question a Maratha said, 'We are Marathas! In battle we show our backs only after we have died.'

Finally, the Sikh's time to respond came and he said, 'Sahib! We are Sikhs, and in battle we continue to fight even after having died!'[46]

In the Sikh response, the allusion to Baba Dip Singh is clear. The Dip Singh narrative maintains that this exemplary Khalsa Sikh continued to battle through the Afghan hordes for hours even after having been decapitated.

There are a number of more mundane uses of the notion of martyrdom. One such usage is brought forth in the unwritten 'code' of Punjabi dacoits (armed robbers) who continued to work in the Punjab even after Independence. A dacoit who was killed in a police encounter, especially if prior to his death he managed to kill a constable, is considered a martyr.[47] Moreover, we see the term 'martyr' applied to both Sucha Singh Surma and Jiuna Maur, folk bandits whose death anniversaries are observed by many Punjabis,[48] as well as to men such as Bhagat Singh and Udham Singh, both of whom were executed by the British Government as political terrorists.[49] Incidentally, although both these men are claimed as Sikh martyrs, they had actually renounced their Sikh identity many years before their deaths. The martyr narrative is also incorporated into some of the more colourful activities which illustrate Punjabi Sikh life. Not only are there gurdwaras erected as *mashahīd* (sing. *mash-had*) or martyries and numerous children's schools dedicated to Sikh martyrs throughout Punjab, but there are also anniversaries marking the deaths of prominent Sikh martyrs that are celebrated with much eclat.[50] From religious processions (*jalūs*) and pilgrimages (*yātrā* or *jātrā*) to political rallies which invoke the tradition through the inevitable shouting of slogans, all play their part in keeping alive and perpetuating the Sikh tradition of martyrdom.

For the most part, rural Sikhs begin their introduction to the faith at home through the stories from Sikh history which they are told as children by their parents. This introduction is supplemented and reinforced with the preaching delivered in the local gurdwara. Here, the Sikh tradition of martyrdom, among many other Sikh traditions, is often invoked, particularly in *katha*, a form of scriptural exegesis or homily. What makes this such an effective means of transmission is that the giani (Sikh preacher) will punctuate a point from tradition with a hymn from the scripture (or vice versa), thus inculcating in many Sikhs a way of understanding and interpreting the Adi Granth and possibly the Dasam Granth.[51] Yet the most effective means of transmission within the gurdwara seems to be the constant recitation of prayer. The Sikh prayer, Ardas (Petition),[52] is recited by the *sangat* (congregation) at the end of most Sikh rituals. Consisting of three parts, the second portion of Ardas enjoins Sikhs to call to mind the sacrifices their brethren are believed to have made in the past, and for this reason, we may assume that its words are firmly lodged in the minds and understanding of its reciters and listeners.[53] The relevant portion of Ardas appears below.

Those male and female Singhs who gave their heads for the faith; who were torn limb from limb, scalped, broken on the wheel and sawn asunder; who sacrificed their lives for the protection of the sacred gurdwaras, never abandoning their faith; and who zealously guarded the sacred kes of the true Sikh: O valiant Khalsa, keep your attention on their merits and call on God saying Vahiguru![54]

Indeed, one Khalistani militant maintains that it was the contemplation of this portion of Ardas which sustained him during a particularly trying episode of torture.[55] The cataloguing of bodily tortures we note in Ardas has become a standard feature in both Sikh literature on martyrdom and oral tradition.[56] Such features are, of course, intended to magnify the heroism of those who stoically died these deaths. Indeed, the more abuses martyrs suffer without disavowing their faith, the more exalted their victory over the oppressor.[57]

Yet this inscription of tortures is also featured in another vehicle through which the Sikh tradition of martyrdom is communicated to pious Sikhs: Sikh art, both popular and respectable; and the guardian of orthodoxy in which the latter are housed, the museum or *ajaibghar* (lit. House of Astonishment). One must not underestimate the power of the mass-produced popular bazaar print as a vehicle for Sikh tradition. Although the pictures which are commonly found in this genre are those depicting the first and tenth Guru, the most popular print by far is the horrific depiction of the decapitated eighteenth-century Sikh warrior-martyr, Baba Dip Singh. The fact that Sikhs can come face-to-face with such stirring narratives and have *darśan* (sacred viewing) of past Sikh martyrs for only a very few rupees ensures the notable influence these prints possess in perpetuating the tradition of martyrdom in Sikhism. In many cases, moreover, such art may be procured free of charge as companies owned by Sikhs (in India and abroad) often advertise their wares by regularly giving away calendars in which such prints are featured.[58]

Most of the mass-produced prints one finds are an inheritance from the 'respectable' depictions lodged in Sikh museums. Throughout the Sikh world there are two museums, in particular, that are easily accessible and display numerous paintings in which Sikh martyrdoms are featured. These are the Baba Bhagel Singh Museum, adjoining Gurdwara Bangla Sahib in New Delhi, and the Central Sikh Museum, found in the Clock Tower on the precincts of Harimandir Sahib.[59] Clearly, the curators of these museums are aware of the museum's importance in the transmission of tradition. As one ascends the stairs of the Clock Tower at Harimandir, for example, a placard comes into view which notes the year of the museum's debut (1958), that it was established by the SGPC, and the various artefacts it initially housed. It then names the artists whose paintings have been placed within the museum since its inception, works which 'accurately capture Sikh history' (*sikh itihās di pūran jhalak dinde han*). The final paragraph is worth quoting in full:

Through the [various] paintings in this museum the artist Sardar Kirpal Singh has effectively captured the distinctive behaviour [of the Sikhs] and the manners of the Singhs and the Singhnis who gave their heads for the faith, who were torn limb from limb, were scalped, broken on the wheel, who had their bodies sawn asunder, who were boiled in cauldrons, sacrificed for the upkeep and service of the sacred gurdwaras, and who protected to their last breaths the sacred hair of Sikhism. Thanks to these paintings we possess knowledge regarding the courage and tolerant nature of the Singhs. In this museum the endeavour is to make widely known through these paintings Sikh history, culture, traditions and the martyrdoms the Sikhs contributed in the struggle for the country's freedom.

The pattern in this paragraph is clearly reminiscent of Ardas, and one may postulate that a tour through this and other museums in which such visual martyrologies are vividly portrayed is, indeed,

Reproduction of Kirpal Singh's *Bhāī Manī Siṅghjī [dī Śahīdī]* (The Martyrdom of Bhai Mani Singh)
[From Satbir Singh, *Ailbum Kendrī Sikh Ajāibghar* (Amritsar, 1992), p. 53]

akin to reciting the prayer.[60] But it is more than this. The museum provides a space to stop and contemplate the Ardas, thus bringing to it an intensity which its repetition in a gurdwara may not. It is a place, in other words, which provides Sikhs a space to take darshan of their Gurus, heroic martyrs and the various artefacts with which they were associated. As such, one can assume that its impact would be profound and lasting.

The quotation above notes the art of Kirpal Singh, the founder of the Central Sikh Museum. Kirpal Singh's paintings, depicting scenes from the martyr tradition, appear very frequently in this and other museums, and have been reproduced in the popular bazaar print. Throughout the gruesome scenes this artist depicts are a number of messages that the viewer can easily extract. Note, for example, the more obvious elements in Kirpal Singh's 1957 painting of Bhai Mani Singh's martyrdom. Here, one sees Mani Singh just off centre, seated on the ground. Before him kneels the executioner. Mani Singh is painted very fair (so fair, in fact, that he seems to glow—an indication of the presence of God's light), with handsome features and an expression on his face denoting stoic calm in the face of imminent mutilation and death. The executioner, on the other hand, is painted with dark skin and grotesque facial features, made more prominent due to the expression of bewilderment on his face.[61] The qazi (a Muslim judge appointed by the government to enforce Islamic law) facing the back of the executioner, holding what seems to be the Qur'ān or perhaps a copy of Hannafi's *shari'a* (Islamic law) in his left hand, is also depicted in a macabre fashion, a grotesque representation of Muslims which is common in Kirpal Singh's art and in that of his legion of imitators.[62] Common also is the portrayal of Khalsa fearlessness, bravery, loyalty and endurance one finds in the person of Mani Singh. One need only spend an hour observing the numerous Sikh families which filter through the museums to acknowledge their awe at, and keen familiarity with, the narratives. To the delight of their young children, every Sikh parent becomes a historian at this time, ever dwelling on the Khalsa's ability to bear all the punishment meted out to it by its treacherous Mughal and Afghan adversaries, and its eventual triumph over these merciless oppressors.

So influential are these paintings that many Sikhs often describe eighteenth-century Sikh struggles by unknowingly alluding to the scenes depicted in them (particularly those episodes depicted in the paintings of Kirpal Singh) rather than to historical texts. The paintings become more than just representations, or an author's interpretation of events; therefore, they become valid reconstructions of the past, invested with historical accuracy and potency. In an interview with Cynthia Mahmood, an unnamed Sikh woman gives her understanding of this period of Sikh history:

When some Sikh women were in the custody of the Mughal emperor in Lahore[63] their small sons were put to death right in front of their eyes. They were thrown onto swords and their bodies were chopped up and made into garlands, and the Sikh women had to wear these necklaces made of the chopped bodies of their children. With folded hands they thanked God that their children had stood the test of their faith and had died bravely.

With this terrifying scene in mind, she concludes in the present:

I have only two sons, and if they get sacrificed, it will be the great grace of the Guru that we will be able to give back what was the gift of God to us.[64]

Portions of the horrific episode this the woman depicts above do appear in Gian Singh's *Panth Prakās*, as well as in Vir Singh's novels,

Reproduction of Kirpal Singh's *Sidak ton Santān Sadke* (Sacrificing Family before Faith)
   [From Satbir Singh, *Ailbum Kendrī Sikh Ajāibghar* (Amritsar, 1992), p. 52]

Sundarī and *Bijai Siṅgh*.[65] One may nevertheless assume that it is the scene from Kirpal Singh's 1959 painting, which the Central Sikh Museum guide titles 'Sacrificing Family before Faith' (*Sidak ton Santān Sadake*), that our informant has in mind. It is this painting alone which depicts all the tortures our informant notes with an intensity that the textual example obviously lacked.[66]

   Although its influence among Sikhs is secondary, literature merits serious study for those of us outside of the tradition. We note, of course, that it is not as powerful as the oral or visual variety of transmission, nor is its idiom as fluent (particularly in English). However, the majority of sources we shall be examining are written by Sikhs who have been raised in environments in which dhadhi music, katha and various other activities in Punjabi life which reinforce the martyr tradition are encountered on an almost daily basis. Their perceptions are, therefore, inevitably coloured by oral tradition, a factor which deeply figures in their narratives. We shall begin with the way in which historians have portrayed the tradition since Bhagat Lakshman Singh published his *Sikh Martyrs*.

The choice of Lakshman Singh's narrative is by no means an arbitrary one. Apart from the fact that this work is one to which later writers often refer, a number of reasons make it the ideal departure point. *Sikh Martyrs*, published in 1923, was the first sustained Singh Sabha popular account in English which dealt with Sikh martyrdom and Sikh martyrs alone. That it came out when it did was surely not coincidental. The year of its publication saw the height of one of the most critical periods in Sikh history, the Gurdwara Reform Movement (1920–5). This was a period in which a number of Sikhs 'courted martyrdom'[67] in their attempt to liberate Sikh gurdwaras from their traditional custodians, the *mahants*, a group characterized in a manner similar to that appropriated for eighteenth-century Sikh opponents. It was a time, moreover, when the use of what I have termed 'the rhetoric of martyrdom' was very well established, thanks to the initial efforts of the Singh Sabha and subsequently, those of its heirs, the CKD and the Akali Dal.[68] No doubt, an account of past Sikh martyrs would have found a receptive audience at this time of Sikh sacrifices. Surprisingly, however, there is very little mention of contemporary events in the monograph.

It seems that the accounts which deal solely with martyrdom in the Sikh tradition are not as many as one would expect. This should not, however, be a cause of concern. Since the early twentieth century, martyrdom has become such an integral part of the Sikh tradition that virtually any book which deals with the history of Sikhism will either include lengthy chapters on the topic or will allude, directly or indirectly, to this most popular of Sikh traditions. These, of course, are not martyrologies in the specific sense. Within the Sikh tradition, for example, there is no account which can compare to John Foxe's masterpiece, the *Acts and Monuments* (first compiled in 1563), which was based on the letters written by the many Christian martyrs whose stories are recounted within the text and the personal observations of Foxe and his two editors.[69] However, the Sikh accounts may be considered martyrologies because they do contain sections devoted to Sikh martyrs. As we have indicated above, these accounts are written as histories but, in fact, embody a faithful devotee's testament to the glory of his community's heroic dead. On the basis of this criterion, then, the number of books which deal at length with the persecutions of the seventeenth and eighteenth centuries and the Sikh martyrs these produced are vast. We began this chapter with a citation from Jagjit Singh's *The Sikh Revolution* and have subsequently mentioned *Sikh Martyrs* by Lakshman Singh. As the title implies, *Sikh Martyrs* is not a treatise devoted to the theme of martyrdom in Sikh theology, but rather, a group of anecdotes brought together whose sole unifying theme is the belief that each protagonist was killed in the attempt to uphold that righteousness of which the Gurus spoke, choosing death over abandoning their faith in the Guru. This work is, in other words, an encomium or a high-flown expression of praise in honour of past Sikh martyrs. It is an *acta martyrum*.

One of the only theological foundations for martyrdom that Lakshman Singh provides is the statement that Sikhs were willing and able to die for their ideals simply because the first Guru taught them 'right thinking and right living and made them self-respecting and self-reliant'.[70] As such, *Sikh Martyrs* is by no means a sophisticated account. This should not, however, imply that the value of the work is negligible. In fact, it is this account which sets the narrative pattern that the vast majority of preceding texts in both Punjabi and English follow. The book locates the origin of the Sikh tradition of martyrdom in the hymns and life of Guru Nanak, demonstrating how these ideals were pursued in their entirety by his successors (in particular, the Guru-martyrs and Guru Gobind Singh) and their disciples, and indicates that this innate Sikh ability to offer one's life for the destruction of tyranny and bear tremendous suffering is the factor which granted the Khalsa its eventual sovereignty.[71]

Jagjit Singh follows this pattern. However, he views martyrdom as an essential component in his detailed theory of revolution. This provides an overall reading of Sikh history with which, for the most part, many other works will disagree. These authors, among whom are included Ganda Singh, Harbans Singh and Teja Singh, will nevertheless acknowledge that many of Jagjit Singh's specific interpretations are correct. Among these accepted interpretations are included the idea that Guru Nanak, through a divine foresight, was cognizant of his Panth's potential future conflict with the Mughal empire, consciously embedding within his hymns injunctions to encourage sacrificing oneself for the sake of truth. It also assumes that the Panth which the Gurus led was 'the progressive development of a single sustained ideal'.[72] Such interpretations, moreover, have gained a much firmer foothold since the events of 1984.[73]

Both Lakshman Singh's and Jagjit Singh's works may be cited as examples. To these can be added Harbans Singh's *The Heritage of the Sikhs;* Teja Singh and Ganda Singh's brief *A Short History of the Sikhs;* Hari Ram Gupta's *History of the Sikhs;* G.S. Chhabra's *Advanced History of the Punjab;* and *A History of the Sikh People, 1469–1978* by Gopal Singh.[74] More recent contributions, based in large part on those mentioned above, are Sunita Puri, *Advent of Sikh Religion: A Socio-Political Perspective* published in 1993, but this is based primarily upon her 1986 doctoral thesis; and Mona Kang's unpublished 1990 doctoral dissertation on Sikh martyrdom.[75] What makes these accounts worthy of separate mention is that like *Sikh Martyrs,* they were produced in a period in which both Sikhs and Hindus in the Punjab and Delhi suffered terrible tragedy as a result of the post–June 1984 events. Although it is not specifically mentioned in their respective texts, the significant facts are that Sunita Puri was writing her dissertation during the Sikh pogroms of November 1984, and that Beant Singh, the assassin of Indira Gandhi (believed to be a modern-day Sikh martyr), resided very close to (and was at one point a student at) Panjab University, Chandigarh, where Mona Kang's thesis was produced.[76] Along lines similar to those found in the music of the dhadhis, these dissertations strike a resounding note of optimism in a dark period. Despite their intention to present the history of the Sikhs in an objective fashion, these works are an attempt, albeit an unconscious one, at *charhdi kalā,* to uplift and inspire Sikhs in this current time of crisis. The rhetoric that permeates their narratives clearly demonstrates this conclusion.

The list above is by no means exhaustive, but it does provide a sample of titles in English widely perceived as authoritative among the majority of Sikhs. Though they claim to be scholarly, these texts are, in fact, popular, all sharing an interpretation of the Sikh tradition which was forged in the late nineteenth and early twentieth centuries by the most influential Sikh movement to date, the Singh Sabha.

Formed to bring an end to what was perceived as a threat to the Sikh way of life, the Singh Sabha developed an interpretation of Sikh history and tradition so persuasive that today, 125 years after the movement's inception, it is the standard against which all other interpretations are judged and often dismissed. In fact, for many Sikhs this is not an interpretation at all. It is the actual description of the history of the Panth.[77] In the late nineteenth and early twentieth centuries, wherever a group of Sikhs would gather, be it concerned Sikhs in the small towns of the Punjab, Sikh immigrants and workers in Vancouver and East Africa, or Sikh soldiers posted in Hong Kong, Malaysia, or Singapore, a Singh Sabha would most likely develop to discuss religious matters and promote Sikh interests.[78] These groups would usually ally themselves intellectually to one of the two main bodies, the Singh Sabha of Amritsar or the Singh Sabha of Lahore.

The Singh Sabha and Martyrdom

Begun in 1873 and made up of upper-class aristocrats, the Amritsar Singh Sabha sought to advocate an interpretation of the Sikh tradition that would not only maintain the privileges which their status as descendants of the Gurus and members of the Punjabi princely lineages allowed them in the community, but would also enjoin Sikhs to view the Panth as simply one (albeit an important one) among the many panths which make up the Hindu mosaic. The Amritsar Sabha strongly emphasized the maintenance of 'traditional' or *sanātan* Sikh culture, which included retaining the multifarious nineteenth-century understanding of Sikhism that allowed for numerous Sikh traditions and identities—Nanakpanthi, Sangatshahi, Udasi, Jitmali, Khalsa, Sahajdhari and many others—without emphasizing the authority of any one over the others, and which contained many features that we would today identify as Hindu, such as for example, the reverence for idols.

Though bearing the same name and, initially, a similar charter, the Singh Sabha of Lahore was radically different from its Amritsar counterpart. Created six years after the Amritsar group, the Lahore chapter drew its membership from lower and outcaste Sikhs. Reflecting this background in its policies, this sabha championed the social and economic uplift of poor Sikhs, as well as the abolition of all caste status, and strongly supported as the principal Sikh identity an *amrit-dhārī* or initiated Khalsa identity which stood well outside anything even remotely Hindu. The contemporary nineteenth-century understanding of Sikhism with its plurality of identities supported by the Amritsar Singh Sabha was, as a result, viewed suspiciously by members of the Lahore chapter. The Lahore Singh Sabha eventually became known as the 'Tat Khalsa' (the true Khalsa) because it was this body which believed that its fervently Khalsa interpretation of the Sikh tradition truly reflected the intentions of the Gurus, a fact to which the original Tat Khalsa of the early eighteenth century is believed to have adhered.[79] Today, whenever a reference is made to the Singh Sabha, it is usually in regard to the more zealous members of the Lahore society. When the Singh

Sabha's ideas concerning historiography, doctrine, or social policy are described, this is invariably the case.[80]

In the attempt to throw the frontiers of Sikhism into a focus much sharper than had ever before been achieved, the Tat Khalsa utilized a series of techniques to eliminate what it perceived as 'Hindu elements' from contemporary Sikh practice and interpretations.[81] Of these techniques, one of the most potent we will examine is the use made of the strong pre–Singh Sabha tradition of martyrdom. A number of reasons demonstrate that it was only logical that the Tat Khalsa would adopt this approach. First, the tradition of martyrdom was very well known to the vast majority of those who considered themselves Sikh in the late nineteenth century, due in part to the dhadhi jathas which roamed from village to village.[82] This was so, regardless of the type of Sikhism to which they subscribed. As we have seen, itinerant dhadhis spread the ideals enunciated in their narratives throughout the land of the five rivers. Secondly, the status of martyr is awarded by the leadership of a community to those who offer their lives voluntarily in solidarity with their group in conflict with another ideologically contrasting group.[83] As mentioned in the introduction, there is thus inherent in the concept of martyrdom an emphasis on identity. The martyr chooses death rather than renouncing his or her faith. This may be interpreted symbolically as an extreme statement which makes clear that the group to which the martyr belongs is unlike any other. In such a spectacular death, the martyr loudly announces the distinct identity of his or her group to the world.

A further implication here is that the martyr's death is a message which deters future deviance within the group itself. When we become aware of the number of Sikh identities which the Tat Khalsa wished to dispel in the nineteenth and twentieth centuries, such a choice of tactics elicits no surprise.[84] These messages were, of course, present in the martyr narratives (both oral and written) prior to the Singh Sabha.[85] Yet such messages do not seem to have attracted as much focus as those features of the martyr's death which underscore the courage, endurance and sacrifice of the martyr.[86] It was the Singh Sabha which exploited the inherent element of identity in martyrdom in the attempt to subjugate the popular devotion to martyrs to their particular interests. The blood of the martyr provided the Tat Khalsa with the almost limitless potential to recast Sikhism into a form congenial to their own interpretation of the tradition and to ensure that this interpretation would become standard. As we have noted, the Tat Khalsa interpretation of the Sikh tradition placed the Khalsa Sikh identity above all others.

Before progressing, we should be well aware of the fierce fidelity that all literature aligned with the Singh Sabha interpretation exhibits concerning Sikh martyrs and the tradition of martyrdom in Sikhism. One would certainly be wise not to underestimate its power. This is a tradition which commands the militant allegiance of the majority of today's Sikhs, a violation of which will cause the most vehement opposition.[87] Due to the Tat Khalsa's aggressive campaign, the pre–Singh Sabha connection between Khalsa Sikhs and the ability to become a martyr was much more strongly expressed and emphasized. Despite the fact that there are believed to have been Sikh martyrs prior to the inauguration of the Khalsa in 1699, the martyr tradition became intimately connected with this militant order.[88] Of the post-1699 Sikh martyrs, all but one were Khalsa Sikhs. Even in regard to this individual, however, Khalsa overtones are definitely present in modern accounts.[89] Implied is the belief that the resolve to become a martyr flows directly from the water of initiation (*amrit*) stirred by the double-edged sword (*khaṇḍā*), an initiation ceremony (*pāhul*) believed to have originated with the tenth Guru.[90] According to Lakshman Singh,

The membership of this Church [that is the Khalsa] was confined only to men who swore at baptism to go through all ordeals for their faith, to make all imaginable sacrifices for the emancipation of their fellow-beings and for their all-around uplift, and to start a regular crusade against all vested interests.[91]

As we have implied, there is in our sources a standard Tat Khalsa narrative beyond which none will venture. Within the pattern, however, there are varying degrees of emphasis on specific characters and particular incidents. Throughout the range of texts there is, for example, a differing degree of emphasis on Guru Nanak's role in the Sikh martyr tradition. All, however, concur that it was Guru Nanak who was responsible for initiating it.[92] In examining the martyrdom of Guru Arjan, moreover, many accounts will discount the role of Chandu Shah and/or Guru Arjan's aid to Prince Khusrau, while others will highlight these. Although there are some vehement disagreements, as long as each text maintains that Guru Arjan died the death of a martyr, it is within the pattern. We also find that some texts will deal with the martyr-Gurus alone, thereby ignoring the supposed role that the first three successors of Guru Nanak played in the tradition. Other sources will not. The next chapter attempts, in part, not only to draw together all the anecdotes that are within this narrative pattern, but also to present the Sikh theology of martyrdom which is implied in our accounts, through rarely, if ever, set down systematically.

Conclusion

Let us conclude this chapter by noting that it has dealt with defining the Sikh martyr tradition in relation to other Sikh traditions, as well as explaining the various ways in which the tradition is communicated to Sikhs both within the Punjab and abroad. Indeed, we have attempted to demonstrate that the martyr tradition permeates numerous facets of Punjabi Sikh oral and written culture. In some cases, the Punjabi town or city is itself a stage on which the props of martyrdom are displayed.

Amritsar is by far the best example of this. In this city, one finds many of its numerous civic and religious features named in honour of those believed to be Sikh martyrs. There is, for example, Udham Singh Chauk (crossing) on Queen's Road, half a kilometre or so east of Vir Singh's orphanage, as well as Gurdwara Shahidganj, adjoining the Shahidganj Khalsa Memorial School in Railway Colony, erected in memory of the thirteen Sikhs who were killed in the 1978 disturbances in Amritsar.[93] There is the Kot (city-wall), named after Baba Dip Singh, close to Gurdwara Shahidganj Baba Dip Singh. Passing through Ram Bagh to reach Dip Singh's gurdwara, one comes across Gurdwara Manji Sahib, dedicated to the martyr, Akali Phoola Singh. Further back in Ram Bagh, close to the Maharaja Ranjit Singh Museum and behind the Guru Tegh Bahadur Hospital, is the *Nāmdhārī Śahīdī Samārak,* a memorial to the four Namdhari Sikh 'martyrs' who were hung in Amritsar in 1871.[94] Near Harimandir Sahib, moreover, there is Gurdwara Saragarhi Sahib, erected in honour of those Sikhs killed during the Battle of Saragarhi in 1897 (all of whom are considered martyrs), and before Gandhi Gate stands a statue of Udham Singh, bearded, turbaned and with pistol in hand, which was unveiled on 26 December 1990 to celebrate the fiftieth anniversary of his 'martyrdom'. The plaque over which the statue of this *aṇkhīla mahān śahīd* (great self-respecting martyr) stands begins with the refrain to Guru Nanak's *Rāg vaḍahansu alāhanīān* 2:3:

Blessed is the death of heroic men if their dying is approved of [by the immortal Lord].[95]

It is the tradition that these civic features signify which shall be noted in the following chapter, a tradition which, as we have made clear, is aligned with the Singh Sabha/Tat Khalsa interpretation of Sikh tradition.

Notes

1. Jagjit Singh, *The Sikh Revolution* (New Delhi, 1981), p. 101.

2. According to tradition, it was on the spot that is today occupied by Gurdwara Rakabganj that Guru Tegh Bahadur's decapitated corpse was cremated in S. 1732 (1675). *TGK* I, pp. 756–8.

3. For example, Khushwant Singh, *A History of the Sikhs* I (Princeton, 1963), pp. 29-48. For *nām simraṇ* see *GNSR*, pp. 214–19.

4. Harjot Oberoi, 'Bhais, Babas and Gyanis: Traditional Intellectuals in Nineteenth-Century Punjab', in *Studies in History* II: 2 (1980), pp. 33–62.

5. Joyce Pettigrew, *The Sikhs of the Punjab: Unheard Voices of State and Guerrilla Violence* (London, 1995), pp. 177; 167, 181. The KCF was considered the main guerrilla group during the turbulent years after Operation Bluestar. Dhadhis not only spread 'Panthic ideals' to militants, as Pettigrew notes, but to rural Sikhs generally. 'Martyrdom and Guerrilla Organisation in Punjab', in *The Journal of Commonwealth & Comparative Politics* XXX: 3 (1992), p. 396 quotes a 'Panthic Committee' spokesman:

When young boys hear the *dhadhis* singing at *melas* [festivals] about our heroes in the past, they say, 'This is how we want to die since we have to die anyway.'

6. 'When I was young I learnt much about the Singhs from the *dhadhi darbars*. I fell in love with the Singhs', says R.S. Bhola, a lieutenant-general in the KCF. According to Wasan Singh Zaffarwal, leader of the KCF, moreover, the accounts that dhadhis narrate provide an 'alternative education' from the government-(i.e. Hindu-)controlled education in Punjab's secondary schools. Pettigrew, *Sikhs of the Punjab*, pp. 146; 177.

7. Song 6 in Pettigrew, 'Songs of the Sikh Resistance Movement', in *Asian Music* (Fall/Winter, 1991-92), pp. 108-11. The specific dhadhi songs Pettigrew notes were recorded in England, a fact that indicates the sensitive issue to which they allude. A brief account of the characters in song 6 appears in Mark Tully and Satish Jacob, *Amritsar: Mrs. Gandhi's Last Battle* (London, 1985). After Bluestar, the Government of India banned dhadhi music specifically and the playing of *vār* music in general. Despite this ban, however, Sikh bus drivers in Punjab had dhadhi tapes playing continually in their buses while driving from town to town. Music shops along Amritsar's Hall Bazaar, moreover, are alleged to have defiantly displayed dhadhi cassettes. (Harish Puri, personal communication, 1993.)

8. Today, the phrase *Sat Srī Akāl* is the common Sikh greeting.

9. See 'The Right to Resist' in P.S. Gill, *Trinity of Sikhism: Philosophy, Religion and State* (Jullundur, 1973), pp. 248–59.

10. For Bachittar Singh see S.S. Ashok (ed.), *Gurbilās Pātśāhī 10 krit Kuir Singh* (Patiala, 1968), pp. 167, 312; and *MK*, p. 1098.

11. Each of these audio cassettes was purchased from the shops across the front entrance to Harimandir Sahib.

12. W.H. McLeod, 'The Sikh Struggle in the Eighteenth Century and its Relevance for Today', in *History of Religions* 31: 4 (1992), pp. 344–62.

13. Veena Das, 'Time, Self and Community: Features of the Sikh Militant Discourse', in her *Critical Events: An Anthropological Perspective on Contemporary India* (New Delhi, 1995), pp. 118–36.

14. Pettigrew, 'Songs of the Sikh Resistance Movement', p. 86, indicates that the dhadhi tradition arose in the time of Guru Hargobind. She bases this conclusion on the statements found in Madanjit Kaur, *The Golden Temple Past and Present* (Amritsar, 1983), pp. 21–2. It is clear, however, that Guru Nanak refers to himself as a dhadhi in *Vār mājh* 27, AG, p. 150:

I, a useless dhadhi, was set to task. In the time before time I was commanded to praise him night and day. This dhadhi was summoned by the Lord to the palace of truth.

15. In *Vār Āsā* 11: 2, AG, pp. 468–9, Guru Nanak seems to refer to dhadhis:

[those] who loudly sing of heroes and battles.

16. Before the early nineteenth century, dhadhis sang about the heroes of Punjabi folklore, such as Jaimal and Fatta, Dulla Bhatti and Mirza Sahiban. D.S. Johal, 'Punjabi Literature (Late 18th–Early 19th Century)', in *JRH* IV (1983), pp. 20–42; Sukhpal Singh, *Pañjābī Lok-gāthā* (Jalandhar, 1987), pp. 47–53. Books on Punjabi folklore are many. For example, R.C. Temple, *The Legends of the Punjab*, 3 vols. (Patiala, 1988). There is also a tradition which maintains that dhadhis sang the *Āsā dī vār* every morning within the Akal Takht during the period of Guru Hargobind. G.S. Chhabra, *Advanced History of the Punjab* I (Jullundur, 1971), p. 203.

17. Narinderjit Singh, 'Shiromani Gurdwara Prabhandak Committee, Amritsar', in John Webster (ed.), *Popular Religion in the Punjab Today* (Delhi, 1974), p. 11.

18. Background in Edward Shils, *Tradition* (Chicago, 1981), pp. 91 ff.

19. For the problems associated with this classification see Paul Valliere's 'Tradition', in Mircea Eliade (ed.), *The Encyclopedia of Religion* XIV (New York, 1987), pp. 1–16.

20. Note the words of P.S. Gill: 'The spirit of martyrdom for faith flows in the veins of Sikhs and when transferred to other fields, it works with equal zeal and fervour.' *Guru Tegh Bahadur: The Unique Martyr* (Jullundur, 1975), p. 1.

21. Shils' *Tradition*, p. 24:

Most traditions of belief are normative in the sense that they are intended to influence the conduct of the audience to which they are addressed, beyond the limits of assent to their factual correctness.

22. Ibid., pp. 44 ff.

23. Pettigrew, 'Martyrdom and Guerrilla Organisation', p. 389.

24. Jagjit Singh states that within Sikhism, 'armed resistance to tyranny is a

religious duty'. *The Sikh Revolution*, p. 95. Also Mona Kang, 'Concept of Martyrdom in Sikhism and Sikh Martyrs up to the Eighteenth Century' (unpub. Ph.D. thesis, Panjab University, Chandigarh, 1990), p. 178.

25. Discussed in Chapter Six.

26. The anniversary of Mewa Singh's 'martyrdom' is celebrated by the Sikh community of Vancouver every January. For details regarding Mewa Singh see Hugh Johnston, *The Voyage of the Komagata Maru: The Sikh Challenge to Canada's Colour Bar* (Delhi, 1979), 129–33. There are only two other Sikhs who are believed to have secured a martyr's death outside of India. These are Bhai Maharaj Singh, who died in 1856 while in a Singapore jail, and Udham Singh, who was executed in London in 1941. For Maharaj Singh see Choor Singh, *Bhai Maharaj Singh: Saint-Soldier* (Singapore, 1991). I am indebted to Van Dusenbury, who provided me with a copy of this pamphlet. An exhaustive account of Udham Singh can be found in Roger Perkins, *The Amritsar Legacy: Golden Temple to Caxton Hall, the Story of a Killing* (Chippenham, 1989).

27. Harish Puri, *Ghadr Movement: Ideology, Organisation and Strategy* (Amritsar, 1993), pp. 211, 248, 276, explains the romantic stories of Sikh martyrs and Ghadr recruitment. Sikh Naxalites are discussed in P.S. Judge, *Insurrection to Agitation: The Naxalite Movement in Punjab* (Bombay, 1992), pp. 77, 107. For the contemporary period see Pettigrew, *The Sikhs of Punjab;* and W.H. McLeod, 'The Role of Sikh Doctrine and Tradition in the Current Punjab Crisis', in B.L. Smith (ed.), *Boeings and Bullock-carts: Studies in Change and Continuity in Indian Civilization*, IV (Delhi, 1990), pp. 95–116.

28. McLeod, 'The Sikh Struggle in the Eighteenth Century', pp. 356–7.

29. For Jassa Singh Ahluvalia see M.L. Ahluwalia, *Life and Times of Jassa Singh Ahluwalia* (Patiala, 1989). For Bidhi Chand see *MK*, pp. 870–1.

30. Tara Singh Shahid is noted in Lakshman Singh, *Sikh Martyrs* (Ludhiana, 1989), pp. 95–102.

31. I would, therefore, strongly disagree with Mahmood's claim that the Khalsa Sikh is 'a martyr from the moment of initiation'. *Fighting for Faith and Nation*, p. 191.

32. *TGK* I, pp. 857–61. Three members of the five beloved ones would, however, die the deaths of martyrs during the siege of Chamkaur. See Chapter Three.

33. The exception that I have seen to this rule is an article reproduced in *The Khalsa Advocate*, 23 January 1908, p. 6.

34. For Nalwa consult the various essays in P.S. Kapur (ed.), *Perspectives on Hari Singh Nalwa* (Jalandhar, 1993).

35. See Chapter One.

36. Over the last ten years, I have amassed a large collection of such martyrologies, including the comic-book martyrologies of Satbir Singh. All of these publications may be found throughout the Punjab. The 72nd anniversary of the Nankana Sahib massacre of 21 February 1921 saw a large number of posters put up all over Amritsar City dealing with the tradition of martyrdom in Sikhism and how the Sikhs killed on this day embodied that tradition. There was also a series of posters commemorating 'Martyrdom Day' (23 March 1993) in honour of Bhagat Singh (d. 1931) and his companions.

37. In Amritsar City and its outlying districts, the most common charm is

'Great is the glory of the martyr Baba Dip Singh Ji'. Other examples of written charms appear in *Glossary*, pp. 236–7. In the eight-volume *Amardip Pañjābi Paṭh Mālā* (Jalandhar, 1977–90), children's readers which are taught throughout the schools in Punjab, one will come across the stories of popular Sikh martyrs. Finally, one should also take note of the famous novels of Vir Singh. Although historical fiction, many Sikhs understand stories such as *Sundari* and *Bijai Siṅgh* to actually reflect real events.

38. Delhi Sikh Gurdwara Prabandhak Committee, *The Sikhs: Portrait of Courage* (Delhi, 1966), pp. 135–61.

39. As mentioned in the introduction, the bestowing of such a title is very rare indeed.

40. This jingle appears in many books dealing with eighteenth-century Sikh history. For example, Teja Singh and Ganda Singh, *A Short History of the Sikhs* (Patiala, 1989), p. 140.

41. In the *Khalsa Advocate*, 18 March 1910, p. 4, for example, Sujan Singh declared that 'the blood of so many martyrs has been the seed of their [the Sikhs'] church'. Also see Lakshman Singh, *Sikh Martyrs*, p. 8.

42. Teja Singh, *The Growth of Responsibility in Sikhism* (Lahore, 1942), pp. 55–6, describes many terms that demonstrate *bol bālā*. In a dictionary of Punjabi idioms, *bol bālā honā* is defined as *charhdi kalā vich honā* or 'to be in high spirits'. See *Puñjābi Muhāvarā Koś* (Patiala, 1987), p. 243. It should be noted that the term *bol bālā* has also been recently used to describe decrees passed by various Sikh militant organizations in the Punjab. See Dipankar Gupta, *The Context of Ethnicity: Sikh Identity in a Comparative Perspective* (Delhi, 1996), chapter 6.

43. Teja Singh and Ganda Singh, *A Short History*, p. 96.

44. Pettigrew, *Sikhs of the Punjab*, p. 141.

45. There are many Punjabi idioms which allude to the Sikh martyr tradition, the most popular being *sir denā* and *sis vārṇā* both meaning to 'offer [one's] head' or 'sacrifice one's life'. *Puñjābi Muhāvarā Koś*, pp. 32, 34.

46. I am indebted to Pashaura Singh who recited this joke for me in December 1993.

47. The life of the dacoit was considered romantic by many Punjabi as well as by many English children in the early twentieth century.

48. P.S. Judge, *Insurrection to Agitation*, p. 57. It is around Bhatinda in particular that Sucha Singh is revered. For his story see the popular folk tales by Daulat Ram, *Suchchā Siṅgh Sūrmā* (Amritsar, n.d.); and Rita Din, *Suchchā Siṅgh Sūrmā* (Amritsar, n.d.). Also R.S. Bajwa, 'The Structures of Violence in a Panjabi Legend: Sucha Singh Surma (Sucha Singh the Valiant)'. Paper seen through the author's courtesy. There are a number of audio cassettes which eulogize the heroic deeds of these folk bandits.

49. There are two paintings of Udham Singh in the *Śahīdi Chitarśālā* or 'Martyr's Gallery' within the precincts of Jallianwala Bagh, one across the other. One shows him as a Khalsa Sikh while the other has him shaved! For Udham Singh see J.S. Grewal and Harish Puri (ed.), *Letters of Udham Singh* (Amritsar, 1974). Note also that a small plaque at the bottom of the painting of Bhagat Singh in the Central Sikh Museum states that he was a kes-dhari Sikh and shows him as such. According to popular belief, Bhagat Singh took amrit after having

met with Sant Randhir Singh prior to his execution in 1931, a point that Randhir Singh notes in his autobiography. See Randhir Singh, *'Bhagat Singh nāl mulākāt'*, in his *Jelh Chiṭṭhiān* (Ludhiana, 1992), pp. 447–57. This painting, however, is taken from a photograph taken during Bhagat Singh's first incarceration at the age of nineteen. Compare Satbir Singh (ed.), *Ailbam Kendri Sikh Ajāibghar* (Amritsar, 1992), p. 70, with K.K. Khullar, *Shaheed Bhagat Singh* (New Delhi, 1981), the second illustration across page 80. Of course, through the incorporation of such well-known 'freedom fighters' into its own roster of martyrs, the tradition attempts to demonstrate how faithfully the Panth adhered to the nationalist agenda.

50. Two black-and-white photographs of the procession in honour of the tercentenary of Guru Tegh Bahadur's martyrdom may be found in G.R. Thursby, *The Sikhs* (Leiden, 1992), plates xxvi–xxvii. On the 6th, 7th, and 8th day of Poh (usually late December), a three-day *Śahīdī joṛ melā* is held around Gurdwara Qatalgarh at Chamkaur Sahib to commemorate the martyrs of the Battle of Chamkaur, particularly the *vaḍḍe sāhib-zāde*. See *EoS*, pp. 431–2. At Gurdwara Shahidganj at Muktsar in Faridkot, moreover, lakhs of devotees gather to honour the forty liberated ones. Finally, the anniversary of Baba Dip Singh's martyrdom is celebrated in Amritsar every January and the death of Bhagat Singh and his companions is commemorated on 23 March throughout the subcontinent. See G.S. Randhir, *Sikh Shrines in India* (New Delhi, 1990), pp. 28–9; and W.O. Cole and P.S. Sambhi, *The Sikhs: Their Religious Beliefs and Practices* (London, 1978), p. 133.

51. See the very telling words of Ranjit Dhaliwal as quoted in Harold Coward, *Sacred Word and Sacred Text* (New York, 1988), p. 134.

52. Persian *'arz dāsht*, 'written petition from an inferior to a superior'.

53. Here, I follow the insightful observations of W.H. McLeod, 'The Sikh Struggle in the Eighteenth Century', pp. 348–9.

54. *Sikh Rahit Maryādā* (16th edn, Amritsar, 1983), p. 9. A footnote here states that all portions of Ardas apart from the initial invocation to the sword and the verses beginning with *nānak nām* may be modified in congregational settings. There are also references to other martyrs in the printed Ardas. See J.S. Neki, *Ardās: Darśan Rūp Abhiās* (Jalandhar, 1991), pp. 144–60.

55. Mahmood, *Fighting for Faith and Nation*, p. 37:

In our daily prayers we remember all our Sikh martyrs during the Mughal period, those who went through terrible hardship. They were cut to pieces, made to survive on a small loaf of bread, and they withstood all those tortures. I used to think, 'What type of people were they?' and while I was in the movement, there was sometimes a little thought in the back of my mind that if the time came, would I be able to behave as those brave Sikhs, my ancestors, did? But finally when I went through it, it was not me but those other Sikhs who were sustaining that. It seemed they were taking the pain with me. I felt, then, the satisfaction of knowing that with Guru's grace I was able to pass the test of being a Sikh.

56. For example, Teja Singh and Ganda Singh, *A Short History*, pp. 96–8. Such cataloguing is also evident in newspaper accounts of the early twentieth century and particularly in contemporary katha. See Chapters Six and Seven.

57. John Knott, *Discourses of Martyrdom in English Literature, 1563–1694* (Cambridge, 1993), p. 37.

58. For the concept of *darśan* in Indian religions generally see Diana Eck's *Darśan: Seeing the Divine Image in India* (Chambersburg, 1981), pp. 9–12. See W.H. McLeod, *Popular Sikh Art* (New Delhi, 1995) for the bazaar print.

59. The Central Sikh Museum also houses weapons believed to have been used by Sikh martyrs. These are also objects of veneration and may sustain the martyr tradition. *Sikh Ajāibghar,* pp. 102–3.

60. A comic-book version of Ardas does just this. Superimposed over copies of the paintings in the Central Sikh Museum are the verses of the prayer. See *Ardās* (Amritsar, 1993).

61. According to tradition, the Mughal governor of Lahore had ordered that Mani Singh's body be chopped joint by joint on his refusal to accept Islam. As the execution began, the executioner grasped Mani Singh's arm in order to begin with the wrist. Mani Singh, however, asked the executioner to uphold the precise wording of the order and begin with the first joint of his thumb. This is probably the reason for the executioner's surprise. Tradition also notes that Mani Singh was tortured in this way to fulfil a prophecy enunciated by the gathered Khalsa. This would be his punishment for his attempt to rearrange the hymns of the Adi Granth (or to metaphorically dismember the scripture joint by joint) in accordance with their authors rather than their poetic measures. See P.S. Padam (ed.), *Bhaī Kesar Singh Chhibbar krit: Bansāvalī-nāmā Dasān Pātśāhīan kā* (Amritsar, 1997), pp. 159–61; and Garja Singh (ed.), *Śahīd-bilās (Bhāī Manī Singh) krit Sevā Singh* (Ludhiana, 1961), pp. 86–93.

62. See, for example, *Sikh Ajāibghar,* pp. 34, 41, 46, 48. For another artist's rendition of Kirpal Singh's representations see the various drawings in Satbir Singh's *Illustrated Martyrdom Tradition* (New Delhi, 1983).

63. According to tradition, it was not the Mughal emperor but Mir Mannu who was present in Lahore during these executions.

64. Mahmood, *Fighting for Faith and Nation,* pp. 105–6. Later (p. 226), Mahmood calls this anecdote a 'historical episode'! The art of Kirpal Singh may also be included in what Mahmood refers to as 'massacre art' (p. 189), though she applies the term specifically to the paintings produced after Operation Bluestar, in which broken corpses are depicted around the demolished Akal Takht.

65. *PnP,* p. 828; Vir Singh, *Sundarī* (Delhi, 1989), p. 112 and his *Bijai Singh* (Delhi, 1989), pp. 92–3.

66. *Sikh Ajāibghar,* p. 52. With this in mind, it is no surprise that the third chapter in McLeod's *Popular Sikh Art,* pp. 50–79, deals with Sikh history through bazaar prints. We may extend his argument to the museum paintings on which many of these prints are based.

67. The metaphor of 'marrying death' is a popular one. See, for example, *PrPP,* p. 417.

68. Lakshman Singh, *Sikh Martyrs.* The narratives in this work are primarily based on those found in Gian Singh's *PnP* and *TGK.* These provide what is the standard Tat Khalsa interpretation of Sikh history. This was despite the fact that Gian Singh was himself a Nirmala Sikh, associated with the more conservative Sanatan Singh Sabha of Amritsar.

69. Susan Wabuda, 'Henry Bull, Miles Coverdale, and the Making of Foxe's Book of Martyrs', in Diana Wood (ed.), *Martyrs and Martyrologies* (Oxford, 1993), pp. 245–58.

70. Lakshman Singh, *Sikh Martyrs*, p. 42.

71. We note, however, that the text does not enunciate this pattern as clearly as above (see *Sikh Martyrs*, pp. 27-8, 181, 199, 214-23). The most recent example of this narrative pattern appears in Mahmood, *Fighting for Faith and Nation*, pp. 26-49.

72. See McLeod's analysis of Jagjit Singh's overall thesis, *The Sikhs: History, Religion and Society* (New York, 1989), pp. 39-40. Many other authors will not acknowledge, as does Jagjit Singh, that the ideal of the Gurus was one of revolution. The sustained ideal which the Gurus constantly kept in mind, they hold, is one that emphasizes the destruction of tyranny and the establishment of righteousness.

73. Also Jagjit Singh's *Perspectives on Sikh Studies* (New Delhi, 1985); and his *In the Caravans of Revolution: Another Perspective View of the Sikh Revolution* (Sirhind, 1988).

74. Harbans Singh, *The Heritage of the Sikhs* (Delhi, 1983); Teja Singh and Ganda Singh, *A Short History*; H.R. Gupta, *History of the Sikhs*, 5 vols. (New Delhi, 1978); G.S. Chhabra, *Advanced History* I; and Gopal Singh, A *History of the Sikh People, 1469-1978* (New Delhi, 1979).

75. Sunita Puri, *Advent of Sikh Religion: A Socio-political Perspective* (New Delhi, 1993), pp. xviii-xix; and Kang, 'Concept of Martyrdom'.

76. The views found in Jagjit Singh's writings are clearly echoed in Puri and Kang. Significant is the fact that Mona Kang does not carry her conclusions through to the present day (conversation with Darshan Singh of Panjab University, February 1993).

77. Harbans Singh, 'The Origin of the Singh Sabha', in *PPP* VII: 1 (1973), pp. 23-33. The definitive Tat Khalsa interpretation of Sikh history in English is M.A. Macauliffe's *The Sikh Religion: Its Gurus, Sacred Writings and Authors*, 6 vols. (Oxford, 1909).

78. N.G. Barrier, *The Sikhs and Their Literature: A Guide to Books, Tracts & Periodicals (1849-1919)* (Delhi, 1970), pp. xvii-xlv; and his 'Sikh Emigrants and Their Homeland: The Transmission of Information, Resources and Values in the Early Twentieth Century', in N.G. Barrier and V.A. Dusenbery (ed.), *The Sikh Diaspora: Migration and Experience Beyond Punjab* (Delhi, 1989), pp. 49-89.

79. The early eighteenth-century Tat Khalsa was formed, so tradition states, to distinguish itself from the followers of Banda Bahadur, the Bandai Khalsa, whose leader was excommunicated by the tenth Guru's wife. H.R. Gupta, *History of the Sikhs* II, p. 25.

80. Harjot Oberoi's 'A Historical and Bibliographical Reconstruction of the Singh Sabha in Nineteenth-century Punjab', in *JSS* X:3 (1983), pp. 108-30, highlights the major differences between Sanatan and Tat Khalsa Sikhs.

81. These techniques are discussed in the following chapters and in Harjot Oberoi, *The Construction of Religious Boundaries: Culture, Identity and Diversity in the Sikh Tradition* (New Delhi and Chicago, 1994), chapters 4-7.

82. D.S. Johal states that the sixteenth-century author of *Qissa Hīr Rañjhā*, Damodar Gulati, mentions that on 'festive occasions the rural people delighted in hearing *vārs*, or martial ballads, from hired *dhaḍis* [*sic*] or minstrels'. See his 'Heroic Literature in Punjabi (1800-1850')', in *JRH* II (1981), p. 58.

83. S.Z. Klausner, 'Martyrdom', in *The Encyclopedia of Religion* IX, p. 230.

84. For a description of these identities see H.S. Oberoi, 'From Ritual to Counter, Rethinking the Hindu-Sikh Question, 1884–1915' in J.T. O'Connell, et al. (ed.), *Sikh History and Religion in the Twentieth Century* (Toronto, 1988), pp. 136–58. How the Tat Khalsa utilized martyrdom rhetoric will be discussed in Chapter Six.

85. Bhangu, for example, maintains that Taru Singh opted to die rather than have his *kesas* cut. *PrPP*, pp. 289–93.

86. For the seemingly popular perception of and devotion to martyrs prior to the Singh Sabha, consult *Glossary* III, pp. 398–9. The specific martyrs mentioned are Baba Dip Singh and his disciple, Sada Singh.

87. In the February 1974 issue of the *JSS*, for example, the editors expunged Fauja Singh's article, 'Execution of Guru Tegh Bahadur—A New Look'. This article was deemed controversial because it focused upon Mughal-biased Persian accounts. Its expulsion initiated a literal war of words which continued in the pages of the *JSS* for two years. For criticisms and counter-criticisms of Fauja Singh's article see *JSS* I:2 (1974), pp. 122–6; J.S. Grewal, 'Freedom of Responsibility in Historical Scholarship', in *JSS* II:1 (1975), pp. 124–34; Kapur Singh, 'Who Killed Guru Tegh Bahadur?' in *JSS* II:2 (1975), pp. 153–66; and Fauja Singh's counter-criticisms, 'Execution of Guru Tegh Bahadur', in *JSS* III:1 (1976), pp. 183–97. Moreover, in recent times the Sikh scholar, Pashaura Singh, has come under serious criticism from various Sikh groups in North America and the SGPC for stating in his doctoral thesis that Guru Arjan was murdered while in Mughal custody rather than martyred. See Pashaura Singh's rejoinder in Chandigarh's *The Tribune*, 8 March 1993, p. 8.

88. Examples of pre-Khalsa Sikh martyrs are Guru Arjan, Guru Tegh Bahadur, Mati Das, Sati Das and Dayal Das. See D.S Dhillon and B.S. Cheema, 'Martyrdom of Three Companions of Guru Tegh Bahadur', in *PPHC* 19 (1985) pp. 170–6, and Lakshman Singh, *Sikh Martyrs*, pp. 48, 51–5. The pictures depicting the martyrdom of Bhai Dayala painted by Gurdit Singh (1968) and that depicting Mati Das' execution, painted by Kirpal Singh (1957), portray these pre-Khalsa Sikhs as Khalsa Sikhs. *Sikh Ajāibghar*, pp. 45, 46.

89. The Sikh in question is Haqiqat Rai. Although he is today acknowledged as a non-Khalsa Sikh, it is often mentioned that his wife belonged to a family of initiated or amrit-dhari Sikhs, thereby establishing his connection to the Khalsa. Lakshman Singh, *Sikh Martyrs*, p. 122.

90. The belief in this preparation's ability to effect an actual physical transformation in the novitiate is mentioned in Teja Singh and Ganda Singh, *A Short History*, p. 68.

91. Lakshman Singh, *Sikh Martyrs*, p. 74.

92. Compare the views of Jagjit Singh in *The Sikh Revolution*, p. 97, with those of Mona Kang, 'Concept of Martyrdom', p. 47.

93. See *A Memorial of Martyrs of Baisakhi 1978* (n.a; n.d.) 'exclusively devoted to the 13 Martyrs'.

94. Ganda Singh, *Kūkiān dī Vithiā* (Patiala, 1990), pp. 66–71.

95. Guru Nanak, *Rāg vaḍahansu alāhaṇīān* 2:3, AG, pp. 579–80.

THREE

Theology and Personnel

You cannot have courage without reading gurbani. Only the bani-reader can suffer torture and be capable of feats of strength.

Jarnail Singh Bhindranwale[1]

Nānak siru de chhūṭiai daragah pati pāe[2]

Nanak, by surrendering one's head one obtains honour in the court [of Akal Purakh].

It is with a rather enigmatic statement that Mona Kang concludes the fifth chapter of her dissertation: 'One can say that Sikh history is the history of martyrs.'[3] Such an understanding of Sikh history, especially over the last twenty years, is by no means uncommon. According to the pamphlet *Sahīdī*, produced by the All-India Pingalwara Society, for example:

The people of the world know that Sikh history is the history of martyrs, whose most glorious examples were Guru Arjan Dev ji and Guru Tegh Bahadur ji.[4]

Within his numerous speeches, moreover, Jarnail Singh Bhindranwale often described the Sikh Panth as a 'race whose history is written in the blood of martyrs'.[5] These are, of course, exaggerations at best as even a cursory glance at popular Sikh accounts will invalidate these claims. At any stage in its diachronic development, there was far more to Sikhism than martyrs and martyrdom. Despite this fact, however, one must not dismiss these contentions outright.

During the early 1980s, prior to the rise of full-scale militancy in the Punjab, a series of interviews were conducted amongst Sikhs throughout the villages around Batala by Clarence McMullen of the

Baring Institute.[6] Although the majority of Sikhs interviewed were illiterate, these respondents reported that they were quite familiar with the history of the Sikh Panth. The history with which these Sikhs were well acquainted is very telling. According to the opinions expressed in the interviews, the struggles the Panth underwent and the persecutions to which its members were subjected since the seventeenth century were much more important than the births of either Gurus Nanak or Gobind Singh, and even more significant than the foundation of the Khalsa.[7] The numerous martyrs these persecutions are believed to have produced strongly figured in this Sikh assessment as almost 35 per cent of those interviewed mentioned the martyrdom of Guru Arjan or Guru Tegh Bahadur as the single most important event in Sikh history.[8] Not only was theirs a history considered one of 'extreme' persecution, but it is also a history that, according to the villagers, must always be remembered.[9] As persecution and martyrdom are the most memorable themes in all of Sikh history for these respondents (a group depicting most rural Punjabi Sikhs[10]), the statements which begin this chapter are more representative of Sikh perceptions than one would at first assume.

McMullen maintains that this history is reinforced by Ardas, katha and Punjabi folklore, thus engendering within the Sikhs a 'psychology of persecution'.[11] This is only a partial explanation, however. Alongside such persecution is the victory over oppression and the eventual triumph of all Sikhs that the tradition of martyrdom makes explicit. It is this history which provided much-needed comfort and inspiration during the period of militancy. Indeed, one Sikh makes this point lucidly:

It was ... our tradition that [the] Sikh Gurus had sacrificed their own sons, their own children, and Sikh martyrs went through all kinds of difficulties but still upheld their values. This Sikh history was my only strength during the time I spent under torture.[12]

It is this strength and its accompanying victory which makes the theme of persecution so memorable. And it is this which the accounts we mentioned in the last chapter narrate.

The Martyrological Interpretation of Guru Nanak's History and Theology

The Tat Khalsa–aligned accounts we noted earlier begin by characterizing the late fifteenth and early sixteenth centuries as a period in which oppression and tyranny had free reign. This common description is, they maintain, based on the many compositions of the first Guru himself.[13] The verse to which they often refer in this regard is Guru Nanak's *Āsā dī vār* 11:2.

Together, greed and sin are the king and village accountant. The finance officer is falsehood, and the deputy summoned for counsel is lust. All three sit and plan together. The common people are blind, and bereft of knowledge they pay out bribes.[14]

Despite the continual assertions of W.H. McLeod and J.S. Grewal that what Guru Nanak left behind for the benefit of posterity was his theology and not a description of his period,[15] the vast majority of texts continue to subscribe to the above interpretation of the first Guru's age, and strongly so.[16] For them, this is indeed a palpable *kaliyug*, vividly manifest in the contemporary governing bodies of Guru Nanak's epoch. This understanding is essential to the Sikh martyr tradition. The next step taken, to set up a simplistic binary opposition in which the Guru strongly reacts to the actions of the administration, resoundingly condemning it through his hymns, characterizes Guru Nanak in a way which is very relevant within this tradition.

As Grewal has stated, such an emphasis on the hymns as reactions to political turmoil minimizes the strength of the Guru's 'moral fibre'.[17] It must be underlined that the texts in no way intend this deliberately. The Guru's 'moral fibre' is sacrificed so that other aspects of the Guru's character may be highlighted. In Sikh martyr tradition, the first Master's severe response to a regime described as draconian underscores his courage and defiance far more than a response to the abstract, cosmic age of degeneracy does. Harsh criticism directed towards the regime would have certainly put the Guru's very life in danger from authorities, the like of who had executed the Brahman Budhan for simply claiming that both Islam and Hinduism revealed Truth.[18] The texts which we singled out in the last chapter imply that the Guru was well aware of this danger.[19] It was probably this image of Guru Nanak that the Sikhs who gathered together for the dhadhi recital at Gurdwara Rakabganj, mentioned earlier, had in mind.

We should note that where in the martyr tradition's interpretation of hymns such as the *Bābur-vāṇī*, the focus rests upon the courage of Guru Nanak, many texts which do not deal specifically with this tradition, although unwilling to dismiss the notion emphasized in it, will rather highlight the Guru's sensitivity and anguish at the wanton destruction wrought by the invading hordes, placing such hymns within a recognizably theological context. The primary message in these hymns is straightforward. Humanity must look to Akal Purakh for protection, submitting itself to his will (*hukam*) and devoutly remembering his name (*nām*).[20] Of course, within the martyr tradition this message is not discounted. For it, however, Guru Nanak becomes imbued with the many characteristics that all martyrs possess: defiance, resistance, courage and fearlessness.[21] It is these virtues, moreover, that his hymns extol and these that Guru Nanak enjoins his disciples to embody. And thus, according to Gopal Singh,

> with [Guru Nanak's] rise arises also a galaxy of Saints who are also warriors ... dedicated to [the] service of others... Foreign imperialism is ended ... [as is] the tyranny of one way of life upon another ... men grow not only in the soul, but become more broad of limb, more full of defiance against earthly odds, and fighting not for the self, or an exclusive group, but for values, and against tyranny, whether spiritual or social, from whatever quarter it comes.[22]

　　Again, it is worth reiterating that the authors do not knowingly mislead their readers, nor write that which they consider to be untrue. For them Guru Nanak was truly heroic.[23] Despite the fact that the Guru was not a martyr, he possessed all the characteristics of one. He was, one may say, a potential martyr.[24] This is an interpretation of Guru Nanak's life and teachings that saturates the society in which the majority of our texts were produced. It is due, in part, to the tradition of martyrdom in Sikhism that this is so. We noted above that katha was an effective means of handing down Sikh traditions for it also impressed on Sikhs a way of interpreting the scripture. In all faiths, it is tradition which supplies the general framework and the accepted rules of discourse that interpretation requires, something that scripture itself cannot provide. Scripture, in other words, has a practical dependence on tradition.[25] When we examine the martyr tradition specifically, we note that the relationship between scripture and tradition is dialectic. The martyr tradition provides a framework to interpret the Adi Granth (as well as other texts within the Sikh canon) which, in turn, provides the material for the martyr tradition. Each feeds into the other in a continuous and circular process. When our authors approach the hymns of the first Guru, therefore, an interpretative model is already in hand.

The specific interpretation that tradition engenders attempts to bring all the teachings of scripture within its boundaries. It is tradition, in other words, which supplies the pious with a conceivable means by which to gain access to and make sense of the vast contents of scripture. This is a basic fact, but one which must nevertheless be kept in mind. The tradition of martyrdom supplies an interpretation which presents the teachings of Guru Nanak as directed towards a single goal, the defence of truth. Guru Nanak declares this intention in his *Rāmkālī kī vār* 13: 2:

O Nanak, falsehood must be destroyed. In the end, truth will prevail.[26]

Our texts imply, moreover, that this goal is commensurate with both the martial piety so characteristic of seventeenth- and eighteenth-century Sikhism and Guru Nanak's theology of liberation. The affinity with the former is evident, so our texts state, in Guru Nanak's description of Akal Purakh as *asur sanghār*, the 'destroyer of demons', and in the heroic stories from Puranic and epic mythology, which the Guru notes in his hymns, that stress divine chastisement.[27] Our authors make it clear that the Khalsa itself was created to manifest just this purpose.[28] These imply, moreover, that such references on the part of the first Guru anticipate Guru Gobind Singh's deification of the sword, with which the *Bachitar Nātak* begins.[29]

The martyr tradition incorporates Guru Nanak's theology of liberation by maintaining that all martyrs cultivate those qualities on which emphasis is placed in the *bāṇī* of the first Master: selfless service, truth, patience, courage, self-surrender, humility and self-respect, to name a few.[30] These are, after all, virtues to which all martyrs in today's popular martyrologies ascribe. Unlike other Sikh traditions, however, the martyr tradition attempts to take all these virtues to their natural limit, the death of the individual. It, therefore, makes concrete the potential which is implied in other Sikh traditions. That is, the heroic tradition in Sikhism will refer to the Sikh hero's potential for dying in upholding Sikh ideals. The martyr tradition highlights the fact that the martyr has actually died for such ideals.[31]

The Guru's stress that liberation is not the monopoly of those people who renounce the world is unmistakable. Guru Nanak denounces these ascetics and the lifestyle they follow in strong terms, affirming in their place the reality of the world and a life of disciplined worldliness.[32] The martyr tradition qualifies this affirmation of abiding pure within an impure world. Guru Nanak's rejection of the ascetic lifestyle becomes the Guru's command that all people must accept the responsibilities that living within the world peacefully entails. These include sacrificing one's life to ensure that all people are allowed their rights and that none suffer oppression,[33] acts which are also noted as very profound forms of *sevā* or selfless service.[34] In the words of one modern account:

It is implied in the [teachings of] Guru Nanak that if in any field of life there is aggression or injustice, the religious man cannot remain neutral; he must react in a righteous way. For, once the householder's life was considered to be the medium of the religious growth of man, it became natural for him to accept responsibility in all fields of life... In the theology of Guru Nanak, man as an instrument of God has to carry out the 'Will of God' in helping the weak and destroying the oppressor.[35]

Two very important points emerge from this conclusion. The first is that the destruction of tyranny is an expression of the 'Will of God'. For texts dealing with the tradition of martyrdom, this is very much in accord with the thought of Guru Nanak, who foresaw divine retribution for those kings who acted oppressively.[36] The term for 'will' that the author of the quote directly above has in mind is doubtless *hukam* (order), a word that designates, along with *nām*, *śabad, gurū, sach* and *nadar,* the divine self-expression in the bani of Guru Nanak.[37] According to the theology of the first Master, one who devoutly practises nam simran cleanses the *man* of *haumai* or 'self-centredness', the root of all evil in Sikhism, and thus attunes oneself to the hukam.[38] Through this practice of nam simran and the grace (*nadar*) of Akal Purakh, the devout progress through a series of five stages or realms (*khaṇḍs*), the pinnacle of which is *sach khaṇḍ,* the Realm of Truth. It is in this realm that the pious end their journey for it is here that one is perfectly and absolutely in tune with the divine order.[39] It is here that one is 'God-realized', the perfect *gur-mukh* (lit. 'facing the [Eternal] Guru').

The belief that the gur-mukh is fully integrated with the hukam indicates that the gur-mukh comes to inherit this order and will thus act as the will of God dictates.[40] The gur-mukh becomes, in other words, the 'instrument of God' because in this state he is God-like.[41] This is the second point which may be extracted from the quote above. As Akal Purakh chastises those who oppress, so, too, is the gur-mukh unable to sit by idly in the face of oppression. Inactivity in such cases is the prerogative of those who have not realized the hukam, the *man-mukh* ('facing towards the [uncleansed] *man*').[42] It may be discerned, therefore, that only those who rid themselves of haumai, through both the sustained, devout practice of nam simran and the grace of Akal Purakh, can battle the forces of evil and achieve martyrdom,[43] acting selflessly in defence of others with no desire whatsoever of reward in the hereafter. The texts acknowledge that all Sikh martyrs are liberated from the cycle of existence, yet these also tacitly note that only the liberated can become martyrs.[44] In some cases this admission is explicit. Alluding to the third var of Bhai Gurdas, the tradition notes that one must first become a zinda shahid by dying 'to the self' (here used as a synonym for the jivan-mukt, the one who is liberated yet alive[45]), only after which one can become a 'true' martyr.[46] Where in other religious traditions martyrdom is an act which redeems, our texts imply that in Sikhism only the redeemed are capable of martyrdom. And thus, the realization of sach khand is not the end of one's spiritual journey according to the Sikh tradition of martyrdom.

The accounts, in keeping with the first Guru's emphasis on both a disciplined worldliness and selfless service, further imply that not only must these gur-mukhs cleanse themselves of haumai, but that they must also destroy the social and institutional manifestations of this evil if such an opportunity presents itself. This implication is made definite in the writings of Jagjit Singh, who states that such manifestations of haumai must be eradicated, especially when these take the form of 'social and political aggrandizement'.[47] The very idea of liberation or *mukti,* then, becomes intentionally transformed by Guru Nanak to mean liberation from fear, so that for Sikhs, 'to seek martyrdom in the battles fought for upholding a high or noble cause was Mukti'.[48] We should by all means note that although the liberated alone possess the ability to become martyrs in the Sikh tradition, the inverse of this, that only martyrs are liberated, is not acceptable. All gur-mukhs are potential martyrs, willing to sacrifice their lives if circumstances warrant such action. When death in this manner occurs, it seals the perfection which the gur-mukh has already attained. One can, therefore, assume that as liberation is a gift from Akal Purakh, so, too, is martyrdom.

The way in which the tradition of martyrdom interprets Guru Nanak's treatment of suffering (*dukhu*) reinforces these conclusions. It is mentioned that Guru Nanak acknowledges two levels of suffering: that suffering which is innate to all human beings by virtue of their entanglement in the cycle of existence (*samsāru*) and the suffering which is encountered in everyday life as a result of hunger, distress, tyranny and so on. To overcome the latter, one need, according to Guru Nanak, interpret all such occurrences as the will of the divine, and bear such suffering in a spirit of resignation.[49] Along the lines one finds in Indian philosophical discourse, Guru Nanak maintains that the suffering which is innate to all humans can be eradicated by ridding oneself of its root (desire, or in the specific Sikh sense, of haumai) by fixing one's heart, mind and soul on the Divine. According to Guru Nanak, the sustained and devout practice of this will transmute all suffering to bliss.[50]

The authors are unanimous in their claim that all martyrs have their souls fixed on God while either undergoing various tortures or battling for righteousness.[51] The texts further state that although these men and women do suffer physically, they do not suffer spiritually for they have eradicated the greatest of sufferings, detachment from Akal Purakh. By implication, therefore, these people are among the liberated.[52] In his bani the Guru makes it abundantly clear that this supreme suffering is very real and very poignant. He implies, moreover (as far as our texts are concerned), that this spiritual suffering is much worse than any type of physical punishment that can be inflicted by an oppressor.[53] For this reason, state the texts, the torment that martyrs suffer at the hands of tyrants is undergone cheerfully. First, it is the will of God and second, this form of physical torture is nowhere near as great as the agony of being absorbed in haumai.[54] And so in the time of Mir Mannu, as noted in a 1906 martyrology, every Sikh captured

went smilingly to the place of execution, and after reciting some shabads of the Gurus bowed his head before the executioner, a sight which simply astonished the beholders.[55]

The martyr tradition takes this ability to bear torment cheerfully and indicates that through such action, Sikh martyrs attempt to embody the Guru's teaching that suffering must be 'meaningful and creative'.[56] In other words, rather than physically suffer through the mortification of the flesh by fasting or sexual renunciation, as was commonly practised among Hindu sannyasis and renunciates for their own individual liberation (practices against which, as we have seen, Guru Nanak spoke), the martyr must suffer in public and bear it cheerfully, so that through example he demonstrates that the truth to which he is a witness (shahid) will prevail. Through the spectacle of martyrdom, he silently but forcefully indicates that evil can be resisted, that in suffering and in death he triumphs over his slayers.[57] For the tradition of martyrdom, this is a creative and meaningful suffering because it 'induce[s] in others the attitude of mind to do likewise.'[58] Indeed the physical suffering the martyr undergoes is a form of selfless service to the Panth. The demonstration that a person of flesh and blood can undergo a painful physical death for Sikh ideals facilitates the recruitment of those who would also be willing to dedicate their lives to ensure that the ideals for which the martyr died are implemented. Ideally, if required, these recruited *sevādārs* would also sacrifice their lives. For Teja Singh,

If, therefore, the Sikh character has made its mark in the history of the world, it is because its foundation was laid on suffering for the sake of Truth. It is suffering that has intensified the Sikh character; and it is in this sense that, in Sikh Scripture, pain has been called a medicine, and hunger and affliction a blessing.[59]

The virtue of fearlessness is among the most important themes in the teachings of Guru Nanak, with respect to the tradition of martyrdom. It is not fearlessness as itself that the Guru enjoined his followers to embody, but that fearlessness which results from the fear of God. The two are very strongly interconnected in Sikh theology and form a recurrent theme in the bani of Guru Nanak. In the martyr tradition, a hymn in *Rāg gauṛi* is often recited, elaborating the connection:

That person who is immersed in the fear of God becomes fearless.[60]

We mentioned above that our texts interpret liberation to mean an emancipation from fear. For these texts, the fear of God is one of the essential characteristics that Sikhs, particularly Sikh martyrs, must possess. Once one inculcates this fear nothing else is held in terror, particularly tyrants, and the painful death they can inflict. Once one becomes fearless, according to tradition, one is liberated.[61] Again, the martyr tradition takes this theme to what it considers the limit of fearlessness. 'Nanak's aim,' states Sunita Puri, 'was to inspire such practical fearlessness that would restore confidence and normalcy to man's facilities so that he could react against given situations.'[62] In other words, with no fear of death, the gur-sikh does not hesitate to act when matters of conscience are involved. For confirmation of this, one need only recognize the way in which the martyr tradition interprets the *Mūl mantra*, the basic creedal statement with which the

Adi Granth begins.[63] Puri comments on the implied meanings in Guru Nanak's description of Akal Purakh as *nirbhau*, 'fearless'. Here, according to her text,

Nanak was not only describing an attribute of [the] Divine Being, but also inculcating in the minds of his followers the spirit of fearlessness towards established political authority.[64]

One thing remains to be said. Because the interpretation the martyr tradition puts forth is just that, an interpretation, it does not necessarily mean that it is an incorrect view of the history and meaning of the Guru's hymns. There is no single 'correct' interpretation of scripture, despite the Singh Sabha's efforts to convince Sikhs to the contrary. There is rather a plurality of traditions and interpretations based on the fact that we can never really know what Guru Nanak was thinking as he sang his shabads out to posterity. From his hymns, we may assume that the Guru was very much concerned with life in the world, and that human joy and suffering evoked a deep emotional response from him. The *Bābur-vāṇi* verses seem to make this clear.[65] Yet, as the Gurus themselves note, the meaning contained in gurbani is limitless.[66] It is obvious that the meaning which a Khalsa Sikh will appropriate from the first Guru's hymns will be different from that which a Nirmala or an Udasi Sikh extracts.[67]

Those who read the hymns of the first Guru, from pious Sikhs to critical scholars outside the tradition, will bring to these preconceptions and pre-understandings, a context of expectations and beliefs through which the various features of the text will be assessed. It is evident, for example, that since the events of 1984, a literal or 'fundamentalist' interpretation of the Adi Granth has surfaced amongst many pious Khalsa Sikhs.[68] This indicates something worthy of note. Readers do not encounter texts in a vacuum. Their historical and social positioning is very much a factor in the way in which they interpret texts. It is this idea which permeates Grewal's examination of Guru Nanak's reaction to his political milieu. According to Grewal, the hymns of the Guru did not explicitly advocate rebellion in the face of oppression, but were capable of engendering revolt, depending upon the nature and extent of the oppression encountered by readers or listeners.[69]

Martyrdom and the Sikh Gurus in Popular History

We may now state what the texts generally assume. The implicit allusion to Bhai Gurdas is clear. We note that this fits into the general interpretation of Nanak's period and follows the assertions of the janam-sakhis. Akal Purakh, hearing the cries of a world overburdened by tyranny and ritualism, sent Baba Nanak down to earth to bring light to this all-enveloping darkness.[70] Preaching a radically new faith which denounced the traditional Indian path of asceticism and renunciation, Guru Nanak enjoined his followers to recognize God as one, do away with caste and rituals, view all humanity as equal, and to seek liberation while living within the world. With no small amount of courage and defiance, he fearlessly converted Muslims to the Sikh faith and criticized both contemporary politics and social conditions, commanding his disciples to be willing to sacrifice their lives for the betterment of humanity if such a sacrifice was required. Of course, Guru Nanak was not asking his followers to seek out death or to simply throw their lives away. For our texts, the Guru was quite concerned with the preservation of life, but only life lived with honour justice and self-respect.[71] It was when these values were threatened that his disciples were ordered to liberate people from their antagonists or die in the attempt, and this only as a last resort.[72] This is the mission for which Guru Nanak had inspired and prepared his disciples. The verse with which this chapter begins is representative of this attitude.[73] For our texts, this is much more than a stress on the need for the constant exertion to serve God in all humility. Rather, it is a clear statement that the spiritual path which Guru Nanak elaborates in his compositions was indeed plagued with the most harsh hazards, one that the Guru himself describes as

A path sharper than the edge of a double-edged sword.[74]

For our sources, it was only natural that the successors of Guru Nanak travelled along this same hazardous path. After all, it was the divine light of Nanak that was passed on to each of the Gurus who followed him. This belief has been incorporated into the Adi Granth as each Guru whose hymns are included in it has the sobriquet 'Nanak'.[75] It is this continuity, moreover, which finds expression in the vars of Bhai Gurdas, the works attributed to Guru Gobind Singh, and the seventeenth-century *Dabistān-i Mazāhib*.[76] Logically, therefore, that same courage, defiance and fearlessness manifested by Guru Nanak becomes embodied in his immediate successor, Guru Angad.

According to tradition, while residing in his ancestral village of

Khadur, Guru Angad was visited by the Mughal emperor, Humayun, who was on his way to Iran after having been defeated in 1540. When Humayun came to the Guru to seek his blessings, Guru Angad was unable to meet the emperor immediately. Enraged by this, the emperor grasped the hilt of his sword and attempted to draw it out of its scabbard. One version of the story maintains that through a miracle effected by the Guru, the sword would not come out of its sheath. The Guru then chastised Humayun, indicating that he should have drawn his sword against Sher Shah rather than against a defenceless man of God. A second version discards the miracle and holds that Humayun's temper abated, after which he apologized and sought the Guru's forgiveness.[77] For the tradition of martyrdom, both versions demonstrate the Guru's fearlessness and patience in the face of mortal danger:

Had Humayun himself been not in trouble and had the Guru not shown fearless patience and calmness at the time, the first martyrdom of the Sikhs should perhaps have occurred there and then.[78]

The tradition maintains, moreover, that it was Guru Angad who placed an emphasis on the physical development of his Sikhs through the preparation of a wrestling ground at Khadur. It was this which, according to Chhabra, 'laid the foundations of the martial spirit which the sixth and tenth Guru infused in the Sikhs'.[79]

The tradition continues that Guru Angad also emphasized the virtues of physical fitness in order to prepare his Sikhs to actively engage in truth.[80] Naturally, strength and endurance are critical for those who wish to travel along the hazardous path which Guru Nanak outlined above. In his famous composition, *Anandu,* Guru Angad's successor, Amar Das, also describes this spiritual path in terms that echo Guru Nanak's *Mārū solahe* 8 noted earlier. For the third Guru, this is a path

Sharper than a dagger's point and thinner than a hair.[81]

Within the tradition of martyrdom, this verse is more than just an echo of Nanak's description; it is an affirmation of Guru Nanak's ideals. As the first Nanak enjoined his disciples to act decisively when confronted with injustice, so, too, did the third Nanak demand a steadfast commitment from his Sikhs to be willing to accept death so that truth and justice prevail. He explicitly asserted that the true Sikh must live in the world and accept all the responsibilities this entails, including the destruction of evil.[82] It is with this in mind that Guru Amar Das, according to the standard narrative, directly opposed the state in its attempt to levy pilgrimage taxes from the Hindus of the Punjab, an act which the third Master considered unjust.[83]

The fourth Guru, Ram Das, also enjoined his followers to embody those virtues on which Guru Nanak spoke. In fact, for the tradition, an injunction representative of the Guru's teachings in this regard is extracted from within Guru Ram Das' famous *Sūhī chhant* 2, a hymn that is today recited as the couple circumambulate the sacred scripture during the Sikh wedding ceremony, *Anand Kāraj*. The Guru here emphasizes that the purpose of one's life is to do all that is possible to ensure that righteousness prevails.[84] Guru Ram Das fulfilled this injunction, so the tradition implies, in the creation of the *masand* system. Masands became more than just the Guru's authorized agents to distant sangats, Sikh preachers and the collectors of pious offerings. Rather, theirs was a status akin to that of the nobility and their creation was deemed a step towards the formation of a 'righteous government', a clear alternative to the Mughal administration and an act of open defiance.[85] This is the precursor to what Jagjit Singh terms the premeditated 'institution' of *sachchā pādsāh* (true king).

Sacha Padshah, as its very name implies, was to be a combination of spiritual and temporal authority in one. It was to be the embodiment of the values for which Sikhism stood, as opposed to all political authority based on injustice, oppression and exploitation. This ideal was not only set up, but was also institutionalized. It is widely held, for example, that Guru Arjan used to hold assemblies which seemed like royal Darbars (court).[86]

Before dealing with Guru Arjan, the first Sikh martyr, we should pause to examine some of the inconsistencies which are readily apparent in the martyr tradition's formula. Is it enough to say that Guru Nanak was a potential martyr? In an age characterized along lines similar to those that distinguish the eighteenth century in Sikh historiography, in which people were persecuted for their beliefs and observances, why did the first Guru not act upon his very own words? Within the tradition, he is shown to exhort his followers to sacrifice themselves for the truth, yet both he and his disciples seem to avoid such action.[87] How do the texts explain this apparent lapse? Was the infamous jizya tax so often mentioned in Sikh martyr tradition any less discriminatory in Guru Nanak's period? Were the authorities much less intolerant? Obviously, the texts emphasize that this was not the case. Why, then, did not such a harsh regime persecute the Guru for preaching activities that both violated the precepts of Islam and criticized the government? A.C. Banerjee, analysing the sakhi in which Guru Nanak laughs at the qazi during namaz, is well aware of this question when he attempts to explain just why the Guru was able to escape imprisonment for such intolerable behaviour:

It is almost certain that the little incident at Sultanpur did not reach the ears of the Sultan in Delhi and the point raised by the local Qazi was disposed of by the local governor in accordance with his own liberal views.[88]

Banerjee implies, in other words, that the state did not take up the challenge offered by the Guru, a conclusion which, as we have seen, is seconded by G.S. Talib.[89] These two opinions, however, are exceptional views which, we may infer from their absence in other accounts, are not readily conceded. The tradition which the vast majority of other texts narrate acknowledges that the Guru did not act as might be expected, but it does not accept any suggestion that this was due to fear or to an unwillingness to act on his part. Instead, the tradition emphasizes Guru Nanak's keen wisdom, rationalizing his apparent inaction with relative ease: Guru Nanak did not volunteer himself for martyrdom because he realized that he must first 'morally and spiritually uplift' the oppressed. Once they were elevated, political upheaval would automatically follow.[90] Rather than fight for political and social change with the sword, the Guru, therefore, chose to do so through his ideas. The essence of the response is similar to that of later Sikh martyrs; the means of responding, however, is not. Moreover, the texts allow us to infer that Guru Nanak was well aware of the fact that his Panth would be unable to expand if it was known for the death of its members. For his 'reforms' to take effect, the Panth required a much larger number of adherents. The texts thus offer another reason. The Guru was kept from acting because he had too few followers supporting him to bring about a serious change. The words of Teja Singh and Ganda Singh may be cited in this context:

What would [Guru Nanak] not have done ... had he been in the position of Guru Gobind Singh? He could then only utter a cry and wish that the cows should become lions, but what would he not have done, if he had a nation at his back? Alas! He had no nation at his back. He and his successors had yet to create it. Still he [did] not sit down in impotent rage and utter idle jeremiads. He did as much as was possible to do in the circumstances.[91]

What the rest of the world may regard as an unwillingness to put into practice the doctrines the Guru himself taught is transformed into a conscious, intermediary stage of preparation, one which aimed at destroying the entrenched caste system and its attendant notions of inequality, thus wakening people to their responsibilities towards the world and society. Once done, the active, altruistic response to repression which the Guru implied in his hymns (so the tradition continues) would come about.[92]

One may infer, as do our texts, that such was the case with Nanak's three successors.[93] Although none of these Gurus had to contend with as harsh a political regime as had the first Guru, due to the tolerant policies of the enlightened Mughal emperor, Akbar, on the one hand, and the Panth's relatively insignificant numbers on the other, their period was by no means hazard-free. According to Sikh tradition, these Gurus were forced to deal with treachery from a number of sides: the sons of the previous Gurus who would not acknowledge the choice of their fathers and the present Guru's claim, orthodox Brahmans who felt that both their prestige and income would suffer as a result of the Gurus' teachings on equality and interior religion, and petty Muslim and Hindu nobles 'blinded by authority'.[94] In some cases, the three combined to accuse the innocent Gurus with some form of transgression, thus bringing the latter into direct contact with the Mughal administration in Delhi. Tradition narrates, for example, that on one occasion while in Lahore, Akbar himself had summoned Guru Amar Das from Goindwal to address the false charges directly.[95]

Yet these Gurus, like Nanak, take no overt action in response to aggression. The same questions which were posed earlier in regard to Guru Nanak are, therefore, applicable here. As may be expected, the texts deal with the next three Gurus in a way reminiscent of their treatment of Guru Nanak. When the son of Guru Angad, Datu, kicked Guru Amar Das in the midst of the gathered sangat, for example, the tradition emphasizes the third Guru's humility and forbearance, rather than his inaction. This is again the case when Guru Amar Das responded to Sikh complaints against Muslim oppression.[96] In this case, the texts again stress that the period of the first four Gurus was one of preparation. According to Jagjit Singh, Guru Nanak and the next three Gurus took no overt action against the state because

[they] were not interested in making empty declarations or idle gestures.

They aimed at building a mass movement and had to avoid taking premature false steps which could unnecessarily jeopardize the [Sikh] movement in its nascent stage.[97]

Once again, the implication that there were insufficient Sikhs to cause a serious change is offered. We may now return to the narrative. Although our sources are by no means in agreement on the machinations involved in Guru Arjan's death, they all acknowledge that this death was a martyrdom.[98] This is despite the fact that Guru Arjan may have been tortured and met his death in private.[99] The tradition that this execution was kept from public view may well have contributed to the controversy which surrounds the death of Guru Arjan[100] and may, moreover, aid in explaining why Guru Arjan's martyrdom receives the least attention of all popular Sikh martyrdoms in the eighteenth- and nineteenth-century gur-bilas literature.[101] That the administration in Lahore purposefully chose this line of action is not implausible.[102]

It is, however, popular tradition with which we are dealing, and according to that tradition, the fact that Guru Arjan's death lacked the public spectacle seems to be irrelevant. What is significant here is that a number of factors came together to persuade the new, less tolerant emperor, Jahangir, to put a stop to the fifth Guru's work at Goindwal. Along with the dramatic expansion of the Panth's size and influence, Sikhs began to appropriate a terminology to describe the Guru's situation that was similar to that commonly used by the Mughals. Moreover, Guru Arjan received considerable amounts of money from his masands. Our authors suggest that this was indeed a government which was parallel to that of the Mughals, a state within a state.[103] Secondly, a Hindu official, Chandu Shah, whose daughter was rejected by the fifth Guru as an appropriate spouse for Arjan's only son, combined with Guru Ram Das' eldest son, Prithi Chand, who also harboured a strong dislike for the then present Guru, and complained to the emperor of Arjan's allegedly anti-Islamic activities. Third, the head of the orthodox Naqshbandiyya order, Shaikh Ahmad Sirhindi, was in a strong position to influence the emperor and did so in regard to Guru Arjan. Finally, when it was felt that the fifth Guru aided in the campaign of the emperor's disloyal son, Khusrau, Jahangir saw this as the perfect opportunity to act against him.[104]

In response to all this, the emperor initiated a violent change in Sikh fortunes, beginning the enmity between the Sikhs and the Mughal administration which was to occupy much of the Panth's energies in the seventeenth and eighteenth centuries. According to tradition, Jahangir ordered Guru Arjan to accept Islam as his faith and to include within the Adi Granth hymns in honour of the Prophet Muhammad or be killed.[105] The Guru refused and though horrifically tortured, he remained steadfast, reciting hymns while sitting on a red-hot iron plate in the scorching heat of the Indian summer. Although the Sufi saint, Mian Mir, asked the Guru to allow him to intercede with the authorities, the Guru refused, stating that he bore this torture to set an example for his Sikhs, an assertion that dramatically expresses confidence in the victory over tyranny and persecution.[106] For the tradition, the theme of self-sacrifice is brought out by the Guru's refusal to allow his suffering to be alleviated despite Mian Mir's ability to do so. The tradition interprets this as the precise adherence to Guru Nanak's command for self-sacrifice so that righteousness might prevail. According to Mona Kang, for example,

[The] very idea of sacrifice as preached by Guru Nanak Dev had assumed ... practical shape when [the] fifth Guru, Arjan Dev, laid down his life for Sikh faith and beliefs ... he refused to abandon his religion.[107]

This same view is echoed by J.P. S. Uberoi, who claims that '[t]he life, work and death of Guru Arjun perfectly represent all that Guru Nanak had founded and anticipated'.[108]

The tradition implies, moreover, that in the Guru's stoic response to Mian Mir, one detects an attitude towards suffering, which is similar to that of the first Guru. Indeed, Guru Arjan had physically suffered under his captors, but as tradition maintains, this extreme torment was bearable for the Guru interpreted it as the will of God. As he was being tortured, tradition continues, the fifth Guru was constantly reciting his own *Āsā* 93, a hymn which underscores the belief that all must accept the will of God with cheerful resignation:

Whatsoever your will ordains is sweetness to me. All I require is the wealth of God's name.[109]

In further support, the tradition alludes to Guru Arjan's *Rāg bilāwalu* 79:

Under the protection of Parbraham not even a hot wind will blow by me. Brother, within his protective ring suffering assails me not. It is the True Guru, incarnate perfection, whom we have met. To the One who offers the medicine of the divine name is our devotion directed. [Refrain]. The Divine Protector has protected us all and removed all disease. Says Nanak, through his own grace the Lord is our helper.[110]

With the eradication of the greatest suffering, physical torment poses no challenge. When the Guru finally died, his blistered body swept away in the currents of the Ravi River, Sikhism had its first martyr, one who embodied the truth of which Guru Nanak spoke.[111] It was this event, according to tradition, that changed forever the course of Sikh history, for it was the martyrdom of Guru Arjan which led to the transformation of the Sikh Panth. From mere farmers and shopkeepers to brave warriors, this new Panth had a *mālā* or garland in one hand and a sword in the other.

The tradition implies that by the time of the fifth Guru, the period of preparation was over. Not only were there Sikhs across the entire subcontinent, but they were also found outside India, as far west as Baghdad and as far south as Sri Lanka. Amritsar and Tarn Taran were thriving towns filled with many Sikhs of all castes. The villages surrounding these towns were populated by large numbers of Sikhs, particularly Jat Sikhs, who pursued agricultural occupations. These were a people who often resorted to violence to settle disputes over honour and land, a natural tendency, so the texts state, considering the fact that the Punjab was the gateway through which all would-be 'conquerors' of India had to pass.[112]

Due to the execution and the dying injunctions of his father, the sixth Guru, Hargobind, girded himself with two swords at his investiture, the swords of temporal and spiritual authority (*mīrī/pīrī*). This made manifest his decision to arm the Panth so that it would be able to defend itself and all others from the might of the oppressive Mughal empire. Although this new burden was by no means light, it was desperately required. According to one pious Sikh, in order for the Sikh orchard to continue to fructify, a protective edge of thorny kikkar trees was essential.[113] To build up this perimeter, the Guru, therefore, harnessed the militant nature of the Jats, infusing it with a new courage, a courage which stemmed from goals of which Baba Nanak would have certainly approved, the defence of truth and conscience.

This was the same for both those Sikhs who were not Jats and the highwaymen and robbers who had joined the Guru's army in pursuit of booty. Military exercises, physical training, the erection of Fort Lohgarh in Amritsar, and the continual sound of both *rāgs* from the Adi Granth and martial music within the precincts of Harimandir Sahib and before the newly erected Akal Takht ('the Eternal Throne', the Sikh seat of temporal authority) were all designed to instil in these Sikhs martial qualities, a desire to defend the helpless and to ensure with their lives, if need be, that truth always prevailed.[114] When the time came for battle with the empire, therefore, these Sikhs were more than prepared. They had been moulded by their charismatic Guru into a force which blended in a unique harmony the courage and loyalty of the soldier with the spirituality of the saint. They were, in other words, the embodiment of the Sikh ideal, the *sant-sipāhī* (saint-soldier), warriors who, out of love for Akal Purakh and fellow beings, battle and die to destroy tyranny, protect the poor and establish social harmony.

According to tradition, Guru Hargobind was the first of the Sikh Gurus to manifest in his dress and person the purpose clearly enunciated in the hymns of Guru Nanak, to ensure that righteousness prevailed.[115] Not only were the battles that the sixth Guru and his Sikhs fought against the emperor's troops devoted to this scheme (battles which produced numerous Sikh martyrs),[116] but such altruism is seen in the Guru's conduct off the battlefield as well. The contemporary tradition makes clear that it was not Islam against which the sixth Guru fought but the Mughal government. If this were otherwise, why would he have built a mosque for his Muslim brothers and sisters at Kiratpur?[117] Moreover, as Guru Nanak after his imprisonment by Babur's forces obtained the release of numerous fellow captives, so, too, did Guru Hargobind refuse to leave the fort of Gwalior until his incarcerated prison-mates were given their freedom. This poignantly demonstrated the Guru's ability to sacrifice his interests for those of others and to suffer for their rights. It was this act, states tradition, which bestowed on Guru Hargobind the title *bandīchhor*, liberator of captives.[118]

As in most of Sikh tradition, the seventh and the eighth Gurus, Hari Rai and Hari Krishan, figure only insofar as they pursue the ideas elaborated by their predecessors. Of these two Gurus, the seventh is, however, more prominent in the tradition of martyrdom. Although he did not engage in battles himself, he did keep a retinue of 2200 warriors, an injunction he was asked to honour by his grandfather, the sixth Guru, prior to the latter's demise. Despite the tradition which emphasizes the compassion of Guru Hari Rai, one so deep that he wept at the sight of a flower on which he had trampled, the seventh Guru was willing to assist with troops anyone who he felt was unjustly threatened, regardless of their caste and status. The military aid he bestowed upon the brothers Kala and Karam Chand, for example, as well as the offer of help to Shah Jahan's mystically inclined son, Dara Shikoh, against Aurangzeb are all viewed in this light. These were again attempts to restore righteousness.[119] According to one scholar:

Guru Har Rai was the most magnanimous of men; and yet we must not forget that he was a soldier, a strong, self-respecting man. By way of protesting against the tyrannies of Aurangzeb, he vowed never to see his face, and even when summoned, he totally refused to appear before him.[120]

Of all the martyrs the Sikh faith has produced, none has received the attention that is given to Guru Tegh Bahadur. One would assume that the reason for this is due to the fact that he was not just a martyr but also a Guru. This explanation, however, fails to take into account Guru Arjan, who is perhaps the Sikh martyr whose story has seen the least print. One need not search far for the reason behind the ninth Guru's popularity. Firstly, Tegh Bahadur's martyrdom is interpreted as one of the major events which led to the creation of the Khalsa in 1699, believed to be a watershed in Sikh history. Secondly, the majority of books and articles dealing with the Guru's death were produced around the mid-1970s, close to or after the three-hundredth anniversary of Guru Tegh Bahadur's slaying.[121]

Although there are sources which present slightly different versions of the Tegh Bahadur narrative, the standard history may be reconstructed as follows. Born in 1621 to the great warrior Guru, Hargobind, Tegh Bahadur, according to the poet Sohan, was destined to become a great warrior in his own right.[122] Following his destiny, the young Tegh Bahadur demonstrated a rare piety, while excelling in both horsemanship and the use of arms. His skill in the latter he displayed in 1635 during the skirmish between his father's Sikhs and the Mughal army, now referred to as the battle of Kartarpur. At this time, he was in his fourteenth year. In his later years, he is shown to embody that humility of which Guru Nanak spoke. Unlike other members of his family, notably Dhir Mal, Tegh Bahadur gracefully acknowledged his father's choice of Har Rai, Baba Gurditta's youngest son, as the seventh Guru (despite the protestations of Tegh Bahadur's own mother[123]) rather than bolster his own claims and torment the legitimate line of Gurus. After Guru Hargobind's death, he left for Bakala, where he spent the next twelve years engaged in nam simran.

The tradition is quite clear that Tegh Bahadur was not an ascetic

during his residence at Bakala. He fulfilled his duties as a householder
and occasionally enjoyed a hunt.[124] Although living some distance
from Guru Hari Rai's location, the future Guru was kept abreast of
events relating to the Panth by his brother-in-law, Kirpal Chand.
After twelve years, Tegh Bahadur visited his nephew, Guru Hari
Rai, at Kiratpur, after which he began his missionary tours. While
on these tours, he was made aware of Ram Rai's apostasy and the
latter's friendly relations with the empire, as well as the death of
Guru Hari Rai. The future Guru's humility was again displayed on
his acceptance of the seventh Guru's choice of successor, Tegh
Bahadur's very young grand-nephew, Hari Krishan. Yet a few years
later, Tegh Bahadur had returned to Bakala and soon heard news of
Guru Hari Krishan's death. The time for his guruship had dawned.
The accounts maintain that Tegh Bahadur's very acceptance of this
mantle was an act of tremendous courage for he knew full well that
it was bound to have repercussions, particularly within the Mughal
administration. Aurangzeb, who had summoned the two previous
Gurus to his court in Delhi, had decided that the right to arbitrate the
succession to the guruship was his.[125]

According to tradition, Tegh Bahadur's life as Guru was fraught
with tremendous difficulties, problems to which he gave expression
in his compositions. From the very day he became Guru, he was
harassed by both family and state. In Bakala, his cousin, Dhir Mal,
had attempted to assassinate the newly declared Guru by instructing
his loyal masand, Shinan, to fire a shot at Tegh Bahadur.[126] After this
attempt had failed, Dhir Mal and his followers then ransacked the
Guru's house. Moreover, the heretical Mina Guru, Harji, grandson of
the infamous Prithi Chand, denied the Guru access to Harimandir
on the latter's first visit.[127] Despite the incredible setbacks with which
he had to contend, Guru Tegh Bahadur travelled extensively, tirelessly
proclaiming his message of hope to scattered sangats, inspiring all
people and encouraging them to bear their daily tribulations.[128] The
extant hukam-namas make both this and the high regard in which he
was held by his followers all too clear.[129] According to J.S. Grewal,
these inspirational talks were the 'silent but sure protest against
Aurangzeb's aggressive policy of persecution'.[130]

Following the tradition, we note that this form of protest had given
him a reputation throughout the subcontinent as a protector of the
helpless and oppressed, as well as awarded the Guru a month-long
custody in Delhi in 1665. But in spite of this he carried on. It was

ten years later, while residing in his new centre of Makhowal, that a deputation of Brahmans visited the Guru from Kashmir. Before him they narrated their tale of the dreaded persecution which their co-religionists unwillingly entertained. Deeply concerned for many years with the state of the oppression in northern India, Guru Tegh Bahadur now decided finally to confront the authorities in Delhi and there defend the right of all people to practise their religious beliefs in freedom and good conscience. He had the Brahmans send word to the Mughal emperor that if the administration could succeed in converting him to Islam, then all the non-Muslims of India would follow. If not, Aurangzeb must desist from his policy of religious tyranny.[131]

Upon entering Delhi, the Guru and his companions were arrested and imprisoned. After the group had refused to adopt Islam and thus abandon their faith, they were brought to Chandni Chauk, the main market square near the Red Fort. The Guru was then placed in an iron cage and forced to watch as his three closest companions, Bhais Mati Das, Sati Das and Dayal Das, were tortured to death before him, an act designed to impress upon the Guru the consequences that one who remains a Sikh must suffer.[132] Unperturbed by this public display, the Guru again refused to abjure his faith and was subsequently beheaded in a large public spectacle on the morning of 11 November 1675.[133]

The sources are unanimous in their claim that the life and sacrifice of the ninth Guru made manifest many of the teachings found in the bani of Guru Nanak. From many sources Tegh Bahadur's life and death are interpreted as the culmination of the ideology enunciated by the founder of Sikhism.[134] One would expect that the narratives which deal with Guru Tegh Bahadur would often make reference to the first Sikh martyr, Guru Arjan, since in many ways the deaths of these two Gurus were under similar circumstances. According to the tradition, the recalcitrant sons of the previous Guru (Prithi Chand in Guru Arjan's case and Ram Rai in Tegh Bahadur's) had informed on the present Guru's anti-establishment activities. Both Gurus were executed by the Mughal emperor for their unwillingness to embrace Islam and both Gurus are believed to have followed the injunctions of Guru Nanak precisely, passively offering themselves for execution as a demonstration that righteousness will always prevail.[135] Although some sources will briefly mention the fifth Guru's sacrifice, the tradition places far more emphasis on the relationship between the first and the ninth Gurus in relating Tegh Bahadur's narrative. When the tradition interprets an act of the ninth Guru, for example, an allusion to either one of his hymns or a hymn of Guru Nanak is always applied, rather than a reference to a hymn from Guru Arjan's bani.[136]

In fact, a close analysis demonstrates that Tegh Bahadur is presented along lines similar to those we find applied to Guru Nanak. Since the tradition is clear that Guru Tegh Bahadur was the ninth Nanak, such a practice seems only logical. Within the narrative we find, for example, that upon being presented to his father, the infant Tegh Bahadur was described as the very incarnation of the spirit of Guru Nanak.[137] Moreover, as Guru Nanak had gone on numerous missionary tours, so, too, did Tegh Bahadur, the second longest in terms of distance after Guru Nanak, so the tradition reminds us. On these tours, both Gurus spread their message of hope and encouragement in an age of insecurity and oppression. The texts thus imply that Tegh Bahadur's tours were indicative of that same concern for humanity that Guru Nanak evinced by simply choosing to proclaim his message of liberation.

Although the texts draw on a considerable amount of material in their construction of the standard Tegh Bahadur narrative,[138] the pattern in which an emphasis is placed on the ideological relationship between the first Guru and the ninth may be traced to the account one finds in the *Bachitar Nātak*, probably the first source in which mention is made of the ninth Guru's sacrifice. This should elicit no surprise, for this text is believed to have been written by Guru Gobind Singh, the son and successor of Guru Tegh Bahadur. An exceptional degree of sanctity is thus attached to it.

The verses in question are numbers four to sixteen in the fifth canto.[139] Here, we note that the number of verses that Guru Nanak receives is surpassed only by those devoted to Tegh Bahadur. One can easily detect that for the author of this passage, there is a special relationship between Guru Nanak and his eighth successor which is denied to the other successors of the first Guru. In this passage, only Guru Nanak and Guru Tegh Bahadur act beyond the mere reception and subsequent transmission of the single mystical flame. The main importance of the other seven Gurus is that they serve as the transmitters of this essence or divine light between Nanak and Tegh Bahadur.

Of course, the passage does not detract from the importance of Gurus Angad to Hari Krishan. We are made very aware of the belief that all the Gurus are the single manifestation of the one divine light. Yet to understand the relationship between the first and the ninth Guru within this passage, it must be placed within the context of the entire *Bachitar Nāṭak*, a text which attempts to understand the legacy inherited by Guru Gobind Singh and his position within it.[140] As the next canto implies, after the death of the ninth Guru, the light of Nanak is passed on to the tenth Guru. It begins by stating that it was in his previous life that Gobind Singh was appointed by Akal Purakh to continue spreading that righteousness which Guru Nanak brought into the world, and for which his father had died.[141] In the description of the battles in which Guru Gobind Singh participated, it is evident that this righteousness was foremost in the Guru's mind, both upheld and employed in the fighting. For the author of the *Bachitar Nāṭak*, the two most important Gurus before the tenth Master are the first and ninth, and one may clearly infer the author's implication that it is these two Gurus who have had the greatest influence on Nanak's last human successor. In this case, however, the greatest influence on the tenth Guru is the martyrdom of his father. This is implied by both the presentation of Tegh Bahadur only in his capacity as martyr and the relatively lengthy account of the sacrifice.[142] Within the passage, the ability to sacrifice life to ensure the righteousness which the first Guru brought into the world would continue, belonged to the ninth Guru alone.[143]

Since the verses above, describing the sacrifice of the ninth Guru, are amongst the most celebrated in Sikh literature, it is only logical that the relationship between Guru Nanak and Tegh Bahadur implied here would figure in the Tegh Bahadur narrative, particularly when the verses are often directly embedded within our texts.[144] In fact, the way the martyrdom is understood today seems to be a direct result of this passage.[145] With this in mind, the tradition's attempt to demonstrate that Guru Tegh Bahadur followed the ideals of Guru Nanak precisely elicits no surprise. Within the compositions of the ninth Guru, the dominant theme is one which also permeates those of the first Master, the absolute certainty of Akal Purakh's protective embrace in the midst of the most trying circumstances. The strong belief that many of these hymns were composed just prior to his execution in 1675 is firmly buttressed by this theme.[146] It is Guru Tegh Bahadur's strong insistence on the conquest of fear that is often noted as a loud echo of that same concern in the bani of Guru Nanak. The ninth Guru's *Slok* 16 often appears in this capacity:

Nanak says, 'Listen O mind, that person who fears nothing nor gives anyone cause to fear has alone obtained [the] true knowledge [of the divine].'[147]

Hagiography presents many episodes that underscore the belief that the ninth Guru exemplified this maxim. According to tradition, Guru Tegh Bahadur miraculously caused the shackles binding those of his fellow Sikh prisoners, who were unable to go through the terrifying ordeal, to unfasten. That he chose to remain in spite of his power to escape is indicative of his fearlessness.[148] In this light are interpreted three other incidents commonly found within the martyrdom narrative of the ninth Guru: Tegh Bahadur's refusal to be released in exchange for a miracle, the stoic composure he exhibited during the slaying of his more stalwart companions, and the famous incident with the paper around his neck.[149] For the ninth Guru, the tradition continues, only Akal Purakh could annul fear within his devotees. Following Guru Tegh Bahadur's *Slok* 33, the tradition notes that only those in a state of fearlessness are liberated.[150]

In the martyrdom of Tegh Bahadur the tradition also notes that Guru Nanak's injunction that righteous people must defy and resist tyranny (an injunction based on the tradition's interpretation of Nanak's *Vār malār* 19[151]), is a command which the ninth Guru personified in his choice to take on the plight of the Kashmiri Brahmans. According to S.S. Chawla, this was the fulfilment of Guru Nanak's concept of a single humanity as expressed in his famous pronouncement, 'There is neither Hindu nor Muslim.'[152] Moreover, the theme of a disciplined worldliness and its corollary of social responsibility, which recurs throughout the hymns of the first Guru, is also applied to the ninth Master. According to Ganda Singh, for example, the ninth Guru could not turn the Brahmans away, for Guru Nanak himself had stated while confronted with the ravages wrought by Babur's hordes:

If a powerful person were to beat upon another powerful person it is no matter for anger. [Refrain]. But if a lion were to fall upon a herd of cows, it is their master who must answer for it.[153]

According to the tradition, the Brahmans from Kashmir were like a herd of cows set upon by the ferocious Mughal government, which was attempting to deny them their right to practise their faith and wear their religious symbols.[154]

As the martyrdom of Guru Arjan led to a drastic change in the Sikh Panth, so, too, was the martyrdom of Guru Tegh Bahadur responsible for a most dramatic shift. According to tradition, this event played a considerable role in the creation of the Khalsa. The tradition states that amongst the crowd which had gathered to view the ninth Guru's execution, there were many Sikhs present. Rather than step forward and publicly note their objections to the slaying of their Master, however, these men and women chose to blend into the crowd and pass as non-Sikhs for fear of their lives. It was in the light of this cowardly action that Tegh Bahadur's successor, Gobind Singh, had vowed to create a group of Sikhs who would be both unable and unwilling to hide in the face of similar circumstances.[155] No longer would Sikhs accept a baptismal amrit stirred by the toe of their Guru and take on names like Das ('slave'), both of which imply servitude.[156] To inspire these Sikhs to act in the face of injustice, a new name and a new preparation were required, ones which infused into the noviciate the sweetness that had come to be associated with the Sikhs of old and the vigour and courage that the harsh times had necessitated.

The name would be 'Singh' (lion) and the amrit would be one prepared with sugar and water, stirred with the double-edged sword, (*khande dā amrit*). According to tradition, those who accepted the invigorating nectar and the name Singh saw themselves transformed. Donning five symbols indicative of this transformation, these new Sikhs chose to dedicate their lives to establish the righteousness for which the marytr-Guru had given his life and for which the tenth Guru had been born. Swearing at initiation to be loyal to their Guru to the death, and to live and die if required to destroy tyranny, the new Khalsa would forcefully act in the face of injustice.

The notion of martyrdom that permeates all Khalsa narratives begins with the very story of the order's creation. As we noted earlier, the first five men who were initiated into the order intended to give their lives for the Guru on that very day. The tradition suggests that the men and women who would afterwards join would always be willing to give their heads to the Guru, fighting each battle to the death solely for the defence of those ideals which Guru Nanak had issued two hundred years before and which Guru Gobind Singh had continued. As the Sikhs of Guru Hargobind were loyal to their last breath, so, too, were the Khalsa Sikhs of Gobind Singh.[157] Numerous anecdotes emphasize the belief that these Sikh warriors would often argue amongst themselves in determining who would be the first to sacrifice his life for the Guru.[158] We must reiterate that the interpretation we are presenting is aligned with the Singh Sabha rendering of Sikh history, a view which strongly implies that the blood of martyrdom flows only through the veins of the Sikhs of the Khalsa. From this, one may assume that it is only these Sikhs who have access to liberation.[159]

The man who animated and enthused the Khalsa has as revered a role in the tradition of martyrdom as the elite order he created. We may now turn to Guru Gobind Singh. Though not himself a martyr, the tenth Guru figures very prominently in the tradition of martyrdom. Lakshman Singh provides what is the standard understanding of the Guru's role. Acknowledging the fact that the tenth Master's death is not interpreted as a martyrdom, Lakshman Singh states the reason for his decision to include Gobind Singh within his famous monograph.

[Guru Gobind Singh] was at once a leader and follower, a prophet and a seer, a poet and scholar, an intrepid soldier and an astute tactician—most heroic in times of danger, most amiable and lovable in the days of peace, most loving and sacrificing, and most selfless in all that he did. Hence this brief history would be incomplete if it did not contain a brief memoir of this *prince of martyrs*, whose example it was that preeminently inspired most of the Khalsa to seek the crown of martyrdom.[160]

Although there are accounts which present the Guru's death as a martyrdom at the hands of a Pathan assassin,[161] the majority of texts will not concede this status. Instead, they imply that like Guru Nanak and all liberated Sikhs, the tenth Guru was a potential martyr. The difference here is, of course, the fact that Guru Gobind Singh fought battles to defend Sikh ideals, tradition implying that it was his skill as commander, swordsman and archer, as well as his endurance on the field, which kept him from falling in battle. As we will see, the tradition's interpretation of the many compositions attributed to the tenth Master strongly support the belief that the Guru's ideal death would be that of the martyr. Within the tradition of martyrdom, Guru Gobind Singh is described as the exemplary sant-sipahi, embodying all those virtues that martyrs possess: courage, loyalty, endurance, defiance and altruism. The tenth Master had not only sacrificed all his belongings, among which were included his writings and those of the previous Gurus, in order to ensure that his mission to defend righteousness would continue, but his beloved family as well.[162] Could anything less be expected from the ninth man within whom the divine spirit of Nanak dwelled?

Sikh tradition maintains that the tenth Guru brought to a fulfilment the very ideals which began with Guru Nanak. Indeed, in the various battles that the tenth Guru fought and in his creation of the Khalsa, Guru Nanak's ideals were fully realized.[163] These are interpreted as the constant struggle to ensure that truth prevails and that all humanity realizes its duty to praise the one and only God. Tradition maintains, incidentally, that these violent battles in no way altered the religion of Nanak. The words of Khushwant Singh's popular *History of the Sikhs* are often mentioned in this regard:

The only change Gobind brought in religion was to expose the other side of the medal. Whereas Nanak had propagated goodness, Gobind Singh condemned evil. One preached the love of one's neighbour, the other the punishment of transgressors. Nanak's God loved his saints; Gobind's God destroyed his enemies.[164]

The religion of Gobind Singh was the religion of Nanak, and all the latter's battles were ones which attempted to restore the righteousness on which Nanak's bani elaborates.[165] According to Grewal and Bal, in the *Bachitar Nāṭak*

we find Guru Gobind Singh convinced of his providential role to fulfil, in his own way, the mission of Nanak, and also conscious that he could not do so without meeting obstruction and opposition. His problem was to defend the claims of conscience against external interference.[166]

Tradition also notes that although the Sikhs of the previous Gurus were indeed brave and willing to commit themselves to ensuring the victory of righteousness, they had yet some distance to proceed before they would be up to the requirements that the new, harsh situation demanded. It continues that Guru Gobind Singh was very aware of this predicament years before he had chosen to create the Khalsa. Even as a child, for example, he would inspire his young companions and followers to show an interest in martial activity. As a young man, the Guru was determined to transform his Sikhs into the bravest of warriors. To further instil in Sikhs a strong desire to defend righteousness, the tenth Guru composed a series of hymns and epics which were to be brought together in the early eighteenth century as the Dasam Granth, or the Book of the Tenth King, by his boyhood companion, Mani Singh. Tradition states that Guru Gobind Singh

discovered that from reading the Ad[i] Granth the Sikhs became feeble-hearted. Therefore [he said], I myself will prepare such a Granth that the Sikhs from reading it will learn the art of ruling, the use of weapons and other skills, so that they will become fit for warfare.[167]

Moreover, according to one contemporary scholar, both the epics and the hymns within this scripture were written to

rouse the spirit of crusading zeal and sacrifice among those whom the Guru wished to prepare to take the sword against oppressors of his own day.[168]

As the tradition implies, the creation of the Khalsa was the final step in the process.

Tradition also interprets that the wars detailed in the Dasam Granth were dharam yudhs (righteous wars).[169] Although these wars were glorious ones, the decision to engage in such battles was not meant to be capricious or unprovoked. Only as a last resort must such a war be declared. This is clearly indicated in a famous extract from the tenth Guru's *Zafar-nāmā*, the Epistle of Moral Victory, a letter which was apparently written for the Mughal emperor, Aurangzeb.

When all alternatives have failed it is lawful to draw the sword from its scabbard.[170]

Only when righteousness and truth have been attacked may the sword be drawn for their protection, and this only after all other manners and methods to resolve the situation have been explored. Tradition maintains that Sikhs must always be defenders, not aggressors. All Sikh martyrs, of course, fall into the former category.

It is no wonder, therefore, that for the tradition of martyrdom the Khalsa and the overwhelming majority of famous eighteenth-century Sikh martyrs drew their inspiration from both the character and hymns of this altruistic, saintly warrior. Sikhs of this period joined the Khalsa and were willing to undergo, and succeeded in undergoing, various privations, including death, to institute the tenth Guru's ideal of righteousness. In the words of one nineteenth-century observer, 'Guru Gobind Singh had made himself master of the imagination of his followers.'[171]

Tradition is clear that it was with the tenth Guru in mind that the vast number of Sikh martyrs went to their deaths. Many eighteenth-century Sikhs acquired the status of martyr in the battles the Guru and his Khalsa fought. These include Udai Singh (who was killed while attempting to delay the Mughal *gaśtī fauj* or irregular army which pursued Guru Gobind Singh after his evacuation of Anandpur in December 1705) and his younger brother Bachittar Singh.[172] The skirmish in which Udai Singh lost his life is termed in some accounts as the Battle of Bachchora Sahib, taking place on the bank of the river Sarsa, as the Guru's camp had divided into two, one to guard the entrance point to the river and the other crossing the raging stream under cover of night.[173] It was while crossing the river that the Guru's family was accidentally divided into two more groups, the Guru himself along with his two elder sons and some forty warriors, making their way to the village Chamkaur, and the tenth Guru's mother and his two younger sons, who were taken to village Saheri. The latter group, betrayed by their Brahman servant, Gangu, was captured by the troops of Vazir Khan and taken to Sirhind.[174] Tradition continues that mere hours after their arrival at Chamkaur, the Guru's entourage, which had taken up position in a *garhi* or fortified house, was besieged by the pursuing troops. It was during this battle that a number of Sikhs died deaths as martyrs. Among the most hallowed names appear those of the heroic elder sons of the Guru himself, Sahibzade Ajit Singh and Jhujar Singh, who had been struck down in the thick of battle. Although mere boys, tradition maintains that they acquitted themselves in the conflict as true warriors, fighting to the very death. To heighten the poignancy of their deaths, one often comes across many a tender account of Guru Gobind Singh lovingly clothing his sons in battle attire.[175] Warriors who died alongside the Sahibzade include three of the original Cherished Five,[176] Bhai Madan Singh, Kotha Singh and the famous Mazhabi Sikh, Bhai Jivan Singh, in whose memory was erected Gurdwara Shahid Burj at Chamkaur Sahib.[177] To ensure that Guru Gobind Singh escaped the battle unharmed, five Sikhs as Panj Piare commanded the Guru to evacuate, while Sangat Singh and Sant Singh remained behind to deter the opposing force. Furthermore, two weeks later, in order to enable the Guru to continue evading the Mughal forces, a group of forty Sikhs who had previously abandoned the Guru fought to the death with a tenacity so rare that the Guru himself had blessed them with the title *chali mukte* or the Forty Liberated Ones.[178] Both these groups joined the swelling ranks of Sikh martyrs.

Martyrdom and the Sikhs of the Eighteenth Century

Many of the martyrdoms which populate contemporary narratives of eighteenth-century Sikh history are variations on the themes one finds in the accounts of Chamkaur, basically a heroic death while fighting in a dharam yudh. The account of Banda Bahadur who, according to tradition, fought heroically in accordance with the command of the deceased Gobind Singh is of this sort. Although there are many problems associated with the life and death of Banda, he is still perceived as a martyr by the Panth, by today's Panth in particular.[179] Along with Banda are remembered his followers captured at Gurdas

Nagal in 1716 and executed in Delhi, among whom was Baz Singh; and the many eighteenth-century Sikh warrior-martyrs whose names today are often heard in Punjabi Sikh households: Bhais Tara Singh, Bota Singh, Garja Singh, Mehtab Singh, Sukha Singh, the famous Gurbakhsh Singh Nihang whose memorial stands right behind the Akal Takht, the spot on which he is believed to have fallen; and Baba Ram Singh Bedi.[180] Children are also prominent on this list. One account tells of a young Sikh captured along with Banda whose mother had implored the authorities to release her son on the grounds that he had been forced to become a follower of the Guru. When she had passed the release papers on to the executioner, the son stepped forward, denouncing his mother as a liar. Claiming that he was indeed the 'humblemost servant of the Guru', the young Sikh appealed to the executioner to hurry his business so that he might join his Sikh brothers. Surprisingly, the first source to mention this anecdote was a Persian chronicler attached to the Mughal darbar.[181]

The other themes one detects in accounts on the eighteenth century are those which we come across in the narratives of Guru Arjan and Tegh Bahadur, defending righteousness to the last breath without recourse to the sword. Here, the names one often hears are Bhais Mani Singh, Taru Singh, Subeg Singh and Shahbaz Singh.[182] A prominent example of this theme is the traditional account of the martyrdom of the younger sons of Gobind Singh. Although the two elder sons of the Guru have a very prominent place within Sikh martyrologies, this is surpassed by the reverence the Panth directs towards the younger sons, the chhote sahib-zade, Fateh Singh and Zorawar Singh. The narrative of these two child martyrs is amongst those best known. According to tradition, these young boys were captured by a Mughal force along with their grandmother, soon after they had been separated from the tenth Guru's group in the river Sarsa. Under orders from the notorious Vazir Khan, Mughal governor of Sirhind, the boys were bricked up to their waists and then offered the choice of Islam or death. Fearlessly they accepted the latter. According to one account, they continued a Sodhi tradition of defiance and bravery which stretched back to Bibi Bhani, the daughter of Guru Amar Das.[183] This episode and only one other in which children play a significant role are noted for the level of cruelty they report.[184] The torture of helpless children, the calm loyalty of innocents to the tenth Guru and his Panth, as well as the nobility of these stalwart boys in accepting a martyr's death makes it highly dramatic indeed, ensuring this narrative's popularity. The testimony of Lakshman Singh, who toured the site where these young children were allegedly executed, allows the reader a singular insight into the popular perception. The powerful passage appears as follows.

I have visited the scene of this heart-rending tragedy. All the while I was there, a heavy load seemed to weigh me down, I could say nothing and ask nothing, and followed my guide from monument to monument like a walking statue. At length we reached the roof of the dungeon, where the venerable Mother Gujri lay interned and where she expired. I bade my companion to retire. The ground seemed to give way under my feet, and it required no small effort on my part to compose myself and recline against the parapet to the north, just the spot made sacred by the touch of the Mother's feet. That sacred spot I washed with my tears, which flowed in an incessant stream. Where so much water had lain concealed I cannot say; nor can I say how long I should have remained transfixed to the spot, had I not been called to myself by the ekka-driver ...[185]

One finds similar observations in nineteenth-century British accounts on the Sikhs. Writing at the beginning of the Singh Sabha movement, General J. Gordon became privy to the popular perception of Sirhind and the chhote sahib-zade:

[When the Guru was made aware of his sons' brutal slaying he] said that the death of his sons would not be avenged by the destruction of the town, which had done no harm, but that for the future every true Sikh who passed that way should pull down two bricks and throw them into the river in detestation of the crime committed on innocent children. This act has been observed by the faithful Govindi Sikhs through the many years; but little remains now, as the railway contractor some years ago appeared on the scene and carried away the mass of old Sirhind as ballast on which to lay the iron track—the iron made sacred by the martial Guru, and which every true Singh was commanded always to wear in some shape, either as a sword, a small hatchet, or as a bangle. The Sikh now in the railway carriage has the satisfaction of crushing under the wheels the ruins of the cursed city of Sirhind.[186]

The theme of vengeance which permeates Gordon's observations also figures strongly in the accounts dealing with the destruction of Sirhind and murder of Vazir Khan, led by Banda Bahadur.[187]

We should note that within the martyr tradition, both forms of martyrdom, those in which violence is appropriated as a last resort and those in which the sword is withheld, are revered and that there seems to be no text attempting to discriminate between the two. In between these, we find the Khalsa Sikhs killed in the two infamous holocausts, the *chhoṭā ghalūghārā* and *vaḍḍā ghalūghārā* (the lesser and greater massacres). Although these Sikhs are believed to be martyrs, the tradition records neither the names nor the heroic deeds of these men and women. All posterity records is the belief that these Sikhs underwent 'mass martyrdom' in order to ensure that truth prevailed.[188] It is stated that over sixty thousand Sikhs were killed in the two massacres, yet the tradition in no way acknowledges this as even a minor setback. Indeed, it advocates the reverse. According to Sikh tradition, a Sikh who had survived the Vadda Ghalughara, but lost one leg in the melee, was passing through the heaps of dead bodies the evening after the massacre. As he was surrounded by his slain comrades, he paused for a moment and offered a prayer to Akal Purakh. It began with these famous words:

Now all the fruit that is unfit to eat has been shaken from the tree.[189]

In other words, this was a prayer of thanks to Akal Purakh, through whose grace the Khalsa was now purified of those who were unable to persevere in the midst of harsh oppression. From the very jaws of the most bitter defeat, the tradition brings forth victory, a victory which could only strengthen the Khalsa in both body and spirit.[190] The ability to sustain such a massive loss and continue to offer the lives of its members as a sacrifice to righteousness proved the mettle of the Khalsa.

The mettle of the Khalsa is best demonstrated in the tradition of martyrdom through the enormously popular Dip Singh narrative. This heroic martyr deserves special mention, for no other figure in Sikh history, apart from Gurus Nanak and Gobind Singh themselves, receives as honoured a position, including the younger sons of the tenth Guru. Himself initiated by Guru Gobind Singh, Dip Singh, according to tradition, fought in the battles of Banda Bahadur; and later founded and led the Shahid Misl, a group of exceptionally zealous Sikhs sworn to martyrdom in the defence of righteousness. He also began the Damdami *taksāl* (mint), the Sikh seminary, which continues to this day, and was led by Jarnail Singh Bhindranwale until his death in 1984.[191] Dip Singh's association with the misl and taksal—one stressing militancy, the other learning and preaching—are indicative of his status as a Sikh sant-sipahi extraordinaire, next only to the tenth Guru himself.

Although Dip Singh is known best for his skill with weapons, the account of this warrior's life often mentions him in his capacity as accomplished preacher and scribe, who was taught the art of exegesis by the revered Mani Singh. The narrative maintains that in 1732, Dip Singh had gone off to the rescue of Ala Singh. This occurred while Dip Singh was still in charge of the famous Damdama shrine in Bhatinda and copying out the scripture. Forming in 1748 the misl which he would command for the next nine years, Dip Singh earned a reputation as a Singh warrior second to none. In 1757, while with his fighting band, he had heard of Jahan Khan's desecration of the Darbar Sahib. He had then vowed to the Guru that he would fight his way to Amritsar in an attempt to dislodge the Afghan despoilers. While travelling to Amritsar to fulfil his vow, a number of like-minded zealous Sikhs joined his entourage. Near Tarn Taran, this group was assailed by an army of eight thousand men. The fighting was fierce and barely a Sikh survived. Dip Singh also fell in this conflict, his head severed from his body. Yet tradition maintains that not even this was enough to keep a Khalsa warrior from his objective. According to Gian Singh, in the midst of battle one Sikh stared down at the headless Dip Singh and tauntingly remarked:

O wonder, venerable Singh! You said that you would become a martyr only after having reached Amritsar. Have you now pitched up your tent right here?[192]

Hearing these words, Dip Singh stood up with a supernatural effort and retrieving his severed head, continued towards the city. He proceeded to cut his way through the Afghans for fifteen kilometres, until he reached the pool of Ramsar on the outskirts of Amritsar city. Having stood true to his oath, he now flung his head the remaining distance to Harimandir.[193] Of course, many accounts today play down the miracle, insisting that the legend grew around the determined resolve the warrior exhibited in his attempt to fulfil his pledge.[194] Miracle or not, however, there is no difficulty inferring the themes of the standard narrative: bravery, loyalty to the Khalsa, resistance to tyranny, protection of gurdwaras, the stress on fulfilling a vow taken before the eternal Guru, sacrifice and martyrdom.

Although Sikhs the world over revere Dip Singh, one cannot escape noticing the zeal which Sikhs in Amritsar district display to this most glorious of warriors. One detects that the intense piety directed to Dip Singh is simply unsurpassed elsewhere. While visiting the gurdwara believed to be the spot on which Dip Singh succumbed to his fatal injury in 1993 (that is, Gurdwara Shahid Ganj Baba Dip Singh Ji in Amritsar), I was made aware of this extraordinary level of piety. An act of great merit is to donate a new *nisān* or saffron flag, on which the Khalsa symbol is displayed, to this gurdwara. At a cost of approximately 500 rupees per flag, not all residents of the city can afford such a donation. Yet inquiring into this activity, I was told that the first available date was some time in 1997! In other words, every day from when I had visited in early 1993 until 1997 would see a new Nishan Sahib flying from the gurdwara's flagpole. This piety was reflected within the gurdwara itself. Here, I discovered a queue of Sikhs who paid their respects to a picture of Dip Singh, placed on the *palkī* or dais upon which the scripture rests. Surprisingly, the portrait was not only above the copy of the Adi Granth, but right in front of the picture, there was placed a burning lamp over whose flame (termed *jot*) the devout would pass their hands and then anoint their foreheads or eyes, a practice in which the Sikhs I witnessed were engaging.[195] Since the *Sikh Rahit Maryādā* enjoins Sikhs to cease such pious displays, the orthodox should certainly consider practices as these anathema.[196] This type of unorthodox piety is also witnessed in many gurdwaras on the outskirts of Amritsar. One in particular, the gurdwara in village Gaggo Buha, forty kilometres from the city on the Khemkeru Road, celebrates what can only be called Dip Singh Shahid *pūjā* or the worship of the martyr Dip Singh.[197]

One will not see such ritual action openly displayed at the symbol of Sikh orthodoxy, the Golden Temple, but even a brief visit will note the reverence to Dip Singh. Here, one often finds the pious bowing reverently in front of Baba Dip Singh's shrine, which is situated on the *parikarma*, the square walkway in the middle of which is situated Harimandir Sahib (the Golden Temple), or waiting in line for some refreshment at the *chhabīl* or drinking-water stand dedicated to this heroic martyr. Finally, the hexagonal block which is believed to be the spot upon which the warrior's head fell is often decorated with marigolds.[198] To the Golden Temple one can add the gurdwaras which dot the road between Amritsar and Tarn Taran. The *samādh* of Baba Naudh Singh, for example, approximately half-way between the two towns and believed to be the very spot on which Dip Singh received his fatal wound, is the stopping point for all vehicles despite the religious affiliation of their occupants. Here they pay their respects to the martyr. Three kilometres up the road to Amritsar, one finds Gurdwara Sri Talha Sahib Shahid Jang Baba

Dip Singh Ji, which is also believed to be the spot on which the warrior's head was severed.[199]

For groups of Nihang Sikhs, Dip Singh may be considered the closest Sikh example of the 'patron saint'.[200] For many initiated into the 'mysteries' of these original Akalis or immortals, there is an actual prayer which implores the aid of this most stalwart of soldiers. In 1978, while training to confront the Sant Nirankaris after the various disturbances in the Punjab and Delhi,[201] a group of Sikhs at Gurdwara Rakabganj were recited this prayer by a Nihang leader, Gurmukh Singh Tiranvala. The esoteric prayer which they heard runs as follows:

By the grace of the Eternal One, the True Guru, the Single Reality. The prayer of the most glorious martyr Baba Dip Singh, master of the sword. Great is the glory of Baba Dip Singh who wields the double-edged sword, before whom both tyrants and oppressors fall. His shouts of victory resound throughout the universe. Prepare me for the next world, for your flag flies throughout the cosmic ages. I implore you through the grace of both Baba Nanak and Guru Gobind Singh: convert my worst tragedy to a minor injury. *Vāhigurū*.[202]

Here, we note the intermediary stage between devotee and Gurus Nanak and Gobind Singh in which Dip Singh is placed. The connection between the tenth Guru and Dip Singh is often elaborated in the tradition, but there is a relationship between this martyr and the first Guru which is expressed far more often. Note, for example, the most recent bazaar print of this exemplary Jat Sikh. Here, we find Dip Singh clothed in saffron and blue (the traditional colours of the Khalsa) leading his horse through flat terrain. Painted with his head turned back, he is shown poised to strike an unseen adversary with his drawn, double-edged sword. What is significant in this print for our purposes is not the use of space, colour, or gesture, but its subtitle:

sis talī te dharke praṇ pūrā karan vālā sūrmā

The warrior who fulfilled his resolution and placed his head on the palm of his hand.

It is these words which link Baba Dip Singh to the first Guru, for this statement is an obvious paraphrase of Guru Nanak's famous *Slok vārān te vadhīk* 20:

If you want to play the game of love approach me with your head on the palm of your hand. Place your feet on this path and give your head without regard to the opinions of others.[203]

It is this shalok which is placed below the large, gold-lettered invocation to Baba Dip Singh that greets one upon entering Gurdwara Shahidganj Baba Dip Singh.

Theologically, this shalok is explained as one recommending the Sikh's mandatory, absolute surrender to Akal Purakh in a 'spirit of unquestioning obedience' and humility.[204] The Sikh martyr tradition effortlessly incorporates this interpretation. For this tradition, the shalok becomes the 'essence' of Guru Nanak's stress on self-sacrifice. A Sikh must be willing to sacrifice what one holds most dear, including life. In the contemporary political turmoil, exhortations which directly allude to this hymn are commonplace in both print and political speeches. Whenever a difficult task confronts the Panth, or any group within Punjabi society for that matter, it is to this hymn that they often allude. The Ghadr party, for example, usually printed this shalok on the top of the front page of their Punjabi-Gurmukhi publication, *Hindostān Ghadr*, and it was often recited during the campaign to liberate gurdwaras from their traditional custodians.[205]

Finally, we note that it was this ability to make such sacrifices as embodied in Dip Singh which eventually won power for the Sikhs in the mid-eighteenth century. In his footsteps followed the valorous Sikhs of this period who fought altruistically and fearlessly, protecting both their own Panth and that of their Hindu brothers and sisters. For these Sikhs, it was no mere reward in the next life which made them plot such a course of action. They offered their heads to their Guru, expecting nothing in return but that all possess the freedom to worship as they please. Guru Nanak would expect no less of his Sikhs. For the tradition of martyrdom, it is suffering that creates power, and it was the ability to suffer and sacrifice that made *rāj karegā khālsā* (the Khalsa shall rule!) a reality.

We end this chapter in the late eighteenth century as the Sikhs began to further stabilize their political position with the capture of Lahore. Although the production of martyrs usually ends as soon as a nascent society achieves political power, the tradition of martyrdom in Sikhism does indeed continue after the Panth's consolidation in 1799. Of the very few martyrs of the Lahore Darbar, the most prominent is Akali Phula Singh, who was killed in the Battle of Naushera. Surprisingly, these battles are not referred to as dharam yudhs, but as battles which were fought to preserve the honour of the Sikh empire. The historical evidence, however, clearly suggests that Phula Singh's death occurred during a war of expansion. It is particularly during the second decade of the twentieth century when a much weakened Sikh Panth, only recently ousted from its suzerain position in the Punjab, is again confronted with another all but intractable foe, this time the British government in India and their sycophants, that the allure of martyrs and martyrdom began to permeate the many facets of Punjabi Sikh culture. This was a time when, according to tradition, Sikhs added lines to the Ardas.[206] To understand this appeal we examine in Chapter Six the Singh Sabha's particular contribution to the discourse.

This chapter has attempted to present the standard martyrdom narrative one finds in the vast majority of Sikh texts, as well as to put together a Sikh theology of martyrdom which, although implied in numerous texts, has never been set down systematically. We find in these accounts a pattern that all martyrological narrative follows: selecting incidents from Sikh history which present the Panth in the best possible light, indicating its victory over oppression through its ability to suffer and to sustain the most unbearable of losses, and to happily bear death through torture by viewing all such occurrences as the will of God. Never are mentioned the Persian accounts that chronicle, albeit with a strong pro-Mughal bias, the number of Sikhs who had actually chosen Islam over death.[207] Although these Sikhs do live, they live firstly defeated and secondly, as non-Sikhs in both name and spirit. Moreover, the tradition is silent in regard to those Sikhs killed by other Sikhs during the internecine struggles of the misl period and about martyrs of Sikh groups not associated with the dominant Singh Sabha tradition, in particular the Namdhari Sikhs executed by the British administration in the Punjab in 1872. Of course, these martyrs are remembered by their respective groups.[208]

We end with Baba Dip Singh, for in his narrative we recognize the appropriation of idealist terminology, which runs throughout the entire martyr tradition. This is brought forth through tradition's insistence that Dip Singh had simply followed the dictates of Guru Nanak precisely. What such examples do, in effect, is present an interpretative circle. These trace a pure circle from the present to the past and back to the present, as if the notion of martyrdom never really changed. In other words, the texts assume two things. They assume that the definition of martyrdom emphasized by the Singh Sabha in the late nineteenth and early twentieth centuries is the same as the eighteenth-century conception, and that this earlier notion is exactly what Guru Nanak had in mind in the fifteenth and sixteenth centuries.

We have seen this assumption in reference to Bhai Gurdas' third var and it may be also witnessed in the attempt by some authors to emphasize this point by alluding to the one occurrence of the term 'shahid' in the bani of Guru Nanak. As we mentioned in the introduction, this hymn is not in reference to the Sikh martyr, but it clearly demonstrates Nanak's appropriation of Muslim terminology.[209] When all is said, however, the tradition maintains that it was Guru Nanak who brought the notion of martyrdom into Sikhism. Our texts thus congratulate eighteenth-century Sikhs and their present-day brothers and sisters on a job well done, on having strictly upheld the injunctions laid down by the first Guru.

We are not yet through with Baba Dip Singh. Another Dip Singh portrait raises an issue which merits brief but serious consideration. According to tradition, as soon as Dip Singh reached Tarn Taran, he drew a line on the ground with his two-edged sword and commanded those who wished to sacrifice themselves for the defence of Harimandir Sahib to cross over. The portrait in question depicts this scene.[210] Just above the scene is a shalok from Kabir's *Mārū*, to which frequent reference is made in Sikh martyr tradition:

The sky-resounding kettle-drum is beaten and the target has been hit. The warrior enters the battlefield. Now is the time to fight.

The second stanza of this shalok appears just above the entrance to the Prakash Asthan, the room in which the Guru Granth Sahib is housed, at Gurdwara Baba Dip Singh Shahidganj in Amritsar:

He is recognised as a hero who fights for the sake of the wretched. Though cut limb from limb he may die, yet he does not flee the field of battle.[211]

Although less popular than the hymn above, there are other hymns of Kabir and a hymn by Namdev which also find their way into Sikh martyr tradition.[212] The obvious question these raise is what makes Guru Nanak the necessary authority in Sikh martyr tradition, in all Sikh tradition for that matter? Although Kabir's authentic dates are unknown, it is highly likely that he lived before the first Guru's period.[213] We need not dwell on this question long since for Sikhs, Guru Nanak is the founder of their faith and there the matter ends. To ensure this as fact, the popular tradition simply advocates that Kabir and all the other bhagats whose works are included within the Adi Granth were the disciples of Guru Nanak, an interpretation for which they find ample support in the traditional narratives of the first

Guru's life, the janam-sakhis.[214] To be considered legitimate, features of the Sikh faith are usually traced back to the founder. The inscription found on the coin struck by Banda Bahadur may be cited in this context. For Banda, his newly-established rule—believed to have initially been the rule of the Khalsa—was one sanctified by both Guru Nanak and Guru Gobind Singh.[215] This procedure is by no means limited to Sikhs. It may be seen, for example, in Islam, particularly Sufism, which often labels the Prophet Muhammad as the first Sufi.[216]

Finally, we note that the reverence present-day Sikhs exhibit towards Dip Singh raises a question regarding the amalgamation of folk-beliefs and notions of martyrdom. In many of the practices mentioned above, we find a conspicuous number of activities which are reminiscent of folk elements in Punjabi culture: the propitiation of those who have died unnatural deaths to ensure that the appeased spirits are not manifested into harmful bhuts or spirits; the reverence towards Sants in exchange for particular boons; and the attempt to procure barakat or blessing at the shrine of a particular saint. It is these elements in the martyr tradition, elements which are often silenced within the martyrological narratives, with which Chapter Five is concerned. The next chapter will apply the historian's art to critically examine many of the claims made by popular Sikh martyr tradition.

Notes

1. Joyce Pettigrew, 'In Search of a New Kingdom of Lahore', in *Pacific Affairs* 60 (1987), p. 5.

2. Guru Nanak, *Āsā aṣṭapadī* 18 (8), AG, p. 421.

3. Mona Kang, 'The Concept of Martyrdom in Sikhism and Sikh Martyrs up to the Eighteenth Century' (Ph.D. thesis, Panjab University, Chandigarh, 1990), p. 187.

4. Narain Singh, *Śahīdī* (Amritsar, 1997), pp. 5–6. Also Bhajan Singh, *Sāḍe Śahīd* (Amritsar, 1994), p. 13:

The very blood of [our] martyrs is the everlasting foundation of the Sikhs.

5. As found in Veena Das, 'Time, Self and Community: Features of Sikh Militant Discourse', in her *Critical Events: An Anthropological Perspective on Contemporary India* (New Delhi, 1995), p. 126.

6. The results of these interviews and the questionnaire which was distributed to the respondents may be found in C.O. McMullen, *Religious Beliefs and Practices of the Sikhs in Rural Punjab* (Delhi, 1989).

7. McMullen, *Sikhs in Rural Punjab*, p. 52. Table 3.13 indicates the events considered important in the minds of Sikh villagers. McMullen notes that less

than two per cent of the villagers considered the compilation of the Adi Granth as among the more important events in Sikh history.

8. Ibid.

9. Ibid., pp. 52–4. Table 3.14 mentions the degree of persecution that eighteenth-century Sikhs are believed to have suffered (431 of 500 respondents felt that Sikhs in this period were 'extremely' persecuted); 3.15 the reasons for this persecution; and 3.16 the importance of remembering this history of the Panth. This history, according to McMullen, 'is both very real and very meaningful to [the Sikhs]'. See p. 53. Also consult Tables 4.10–4.11, p. 82; and Table 4.43, p. 98.

10. Radhasaomis, Namdharis, Nirankaris and Nihangs were included in the survey. According to McMullen, all of these people 'considered themselves Sikhs'. Ibid., p. 11.

11. Ibid., p. 52.

12. Cynthia Mahmood, *Fighting for Faith and Nation: Dialogues with Sikh Militants* (Philadelphia, 1997), p. 103.

13. A.C. Banerjee, *Guru Nanak and His Times* (Patiala, 1984), p. 1.

14. Guru Nanak, *Vār āsā*, 11:2, AG, pp. 468–69. Also Nanak's *Vār mājh* 16:1 and *Vār malār* 22:1, AG, pp. 145, 1288; and his four hymns known collectively as the *Bābur-vāṇī: Āsā* 39, *Āsā aṣṭapadī* 11, *Āsā aṣṭapadī* 12, and *Tilaṅg* 5, AG, pp. 360, 417, 417–18, 722–3.

15. *GNSR*, p. 162 and J.S. Grewal, *Guru Nanak in History* (Chandigarh, 1969), pp. 154–6.

16. Teja Singh, *The Growth of Responsibility in Sikhism* (Lahore, 1942), p. 2, for example. The latest example of this tenacious persistence is Sunita Puri's *Advent of Sikh Religion: A Socio-political Perspective* (Delhi, 1993), pp. 202–4. The terms 'texts' or 'sources' used throughout this chapter refer to accounts of Sikh history aligned with the Tat Khalsa interpretation of Sikh tradition in which both martyrs and martyrdom strongly figure.

17. J.S. Grewal, *Guru Nanak in History*, p. 155.

18. Compare ibid., pp. 13–14 with Macauliffe's introduction to *The Sikh Religion: Its Gurus, Sacred Writings And Authors* I (Oxford, 1909), p. xliv.

19. According to one account, Guru Nanak continued preaching his doctrine in Kabul despite the warning that such preaching was very dangerous in a Muslim country. Jagjit Singh, *The Sikh Revolution* (Delhi, 1984), p. 160. Narain Singh claims that the first Guru purposely put his life in jeopardy by shouting out a different call to prayer while in Baghdad. Narain Singh, 'It is the Man and His Cause that Make Him a Martyr', in *JSS* VII:1,2 (1982), pp. 81–4.

20. For example A.C. Banerjee, *Guru Nanak*, pp. 177, 193–4. The theological concepts above are explained in *GNSR*, pp. 195–6, 199–203.

21. Gupta observes that:

Nanak did not belong to a caste of preachers. He was a Kshatriya, [a] wielder of the sword. It was under Muslim rule [that] they took to trade as [a] soldier's life was completely denied to them.

H.R. Gupta, *History of the Sikhs* I (Delhi, 1973), p. 58. Jagjit Singh contends that Guru Nanak's conversion of Muslims to the Sikh faith was 'a deliberate defiance of the Shariatic concept of the Muslim state'. *The Sikh Revolution*, p. 160.

22. Gopal Singh, *A History of the Sikh People, 1469–1978* (Delhi, 1979),

pp. 140–1. G.S. Talib, *Guru Nanak: His Personality and Vision* (Delhi, 1969), p. 231 states that '[Guru Nanak] brought the idea of martyrdom [to India] which was more or less alien to Indian thought'.

23. Harbans Singh, *Degh Tegh Fateh: Socio-Economic & Religio-Political Fundamentals of Sikhism* (Chandigarh, 1986), p. 119, mentions that the janamsakhis contain many anecdotes which demonstrate that Guru Nanak always supported righteous causes.

24. G.S. Talib, *A Study of the Moral Core of Guru Nanak's Teaching* (Chandigarh, 1970), p. 40, states the following in this regard:

... in Guru Nanak's own life[time] a situation demanding his entering into active conflict with organised tyranny did not happen to arise... If he escaped martyrdom, it was perhaps because the rulers of the day did not awake to his full meaning, under the impression that he was, after all, a Sadhu [ascetic].

25. Edward Shils, *Tradition* (Chicago, 1981), pp. 95 ff; and Paul Valliere, 'Tradition' in M. Eliade (ed.), *The Encyclopedia of Religion* 14 (New York, 1987), p. 4.

26. Nanak's *Rāmakali kī vār* 13:2, AG, p. 953.

27. Nanak's *Siri rāg astapadī* 10 (3), AG, p. 59.

28. Often, allusions to *Bachitar Nāṭak* 6:41–43, *DG*, pp. 57–8 underscore this belief.

29. *Bachitar Nāṭak* 1:1, *DG*, p. 39.

30. Mona Kang, 'The Concept of Martyrdom', pp. 139–150, elaborates on eleven 'values' in the Guru's teachings 'for the attainment of which,' she states, 'the Sikh Gurus and their followers had to sacrifice their lives and achieve martyrdom' (p. 139).

31. Hew McLeod, *Sikhism* (London, 1997), pp. 128–31.

32. Guru Nanak, *Sūhī* 8, AG, p. 730:

The path of true yoga is found by dwelling in God while yet living in the midst of the world's temptations.

The translation appears in *GNSR*, p. 211.

33. Avtar Singh, *Ethics of the Sikhs* (Patiala, 1983), p. 99, refers to Guru Nanak's *Mājh kī vār* 7:2, AG, p. 141, to make this point:

To deprive others of their rights [O Nanak] ought to be avoided as scrupulously as the Muslims avoid pork and the Hindus consider beef taboo.

34. Guru Nanak, *Mārū chaupad* 10 (2), AG, p. 992. The connection between *sevā* and the martyr in Sikhism is made in G.S. Talib's *A Study of the Moral Core*, p. 39 and Avtar Singh, *Ethics of the Sikhs*, pp. 194–201.

35. Madanjit Kaur, 'Guru Nanak in Indian Religious Traditions and Universalism of His Teachings', in Madanjit Kaur (ed.), *Guru Nanak and His Teachings* (Amritsar, 1989), pp. 28–9.

36. Guru Nanak's *Āsā* 39 and *Āsā astapadī* 11 (4–5), AG, pp. 360, 417 is noted to this effect in Sunita Puri, *Advent*, pp. 225–6.

37. A description of *hukam* and other terms noted here is found in *GNSR*, pp. 189–207.

38. *Japjī* 2, AG, p. 1:

Nanak, that person who understands the hukam, destroys haumai.

39. *Japjī* 37, AG, p. 8. *GNSR*, pp. 221-4, describes the mystical ascent through the five *khaṇḍs*.
40. Nripinder Singh, *The Sikh Moral Tradition*, p. 263; and G.S. Talib, 'Hukam—The Divine Ordinance', in Taran Singh (ed.), *Teachings of Guru Nanak Dev* (Patiala, 1977), p. 73.
41. Guru Nanak, *Dakhṇī oaṅkāru* 44 in measure *rāmakalī*, AG, p. 936:

The virtuous are united to the Lord through their merit. How may I meet them with love? By constantly remembering God in my heart I shall become like them.

42. Jagjit Singh, *The Sikh Revolution*, p. 91, states, 'Inaction and sloth are sins,' while Lakshman Singh, *Sikh Martyrs*, p. 21, notes, 'To chastise evil-doers and to face danger is the work of heroes, of gods, not of the good people who float along like dead fish.'
43. A hymn which is quoted to this effect is Nanak's *Dakhṇī oaṅkāru* 10, AG, p. 931:

The one who contemplates Ram with loving devotion battles [against evil] with his mind in perfect control.

See Harbans Singh, *Guru Nanak and the Origins of the Sikh Faith* (Patiala, 1969), p. 205. Also A.C. Banerjee, *Guru Nanak*, p. 194:

submission to the Will of God and repetition of His *Name* ... would prepare the ground for moral regeneration which would stimulate man's capacity for self-assertion and self-defence.

44. For example Santokh Singh, *Philosophical Foundations of the Sikh Value System* (New Delhi, 1981), p. 63: 'No altruistic service or goodness can flow out of an egoistic person.' Also G.S. Talib, 'The Basis and Development of Ethical Thought in Sikhism', in L.M. Joshi (ed.), *Sikhism* (Patiala, 1980), pp. 123-4:

True heroism is envisioned as waging battle against the lower self. From victory over it arises the spirit to fight in the human world against evil.

45. Guru Nanak's opinion of the jivan-mukt appears in *Mārū aṣṭpadī* 2 (6), AG, p. 1010.
46. *BG* 3:18:2. Narain Singh, 'It is the Man and His Cause', p. 87, refers to Guru Nanak as a living martyr and Gurus Arjan and Tegh Bahadur as 'real' martyrs.
47. Jagjit Singh, *The Sikh Revolution*, p. 93.
48. Ibid., p. 94.
49. G.S. Talib, 'Hukam—The Divine Ordinance', p. 73.
50. Guru Nanak's *Āsā dī vār* 12:1, AG, p. 469:

Suffering is the medicine and pleasure is the malady. Where pleasure exists God is absent.

51. According to the narratives, the martyr's constant recitation of shabads while undergoing torture demonstrates this. In Sikh art, moreover, the martyr's expressionless face also indicates absorption in God.

52. As the following quote makes clear, some texts maintain that those about to be martyred do not even suffer physically.

The martyr makes himself insensitive to all these extreme pains of tortures by concentrating on the Almighty God. When the mind is under perfect control bodily pains are not felt. The Sikhs, when tortured, carried themselves into such a stage where they did not feel the pain; this they did by meditating on the name of God and becoming one with the Supreme Spirit.

Whether pain is felt or not, however, the one about to become a martyr is still liberated prior to his or her death. The quote is from P.S. Gill, *Guru Tegh Bahadur: The Unique Martyr* (Jullundur, 1975), p. 89 and is perhaps an allusion to Guru Nanak's *Japji* 13, AG, p. 2: 'By remembering the Name all pain and suffering comes to an end.'

53. Guru Nanak, *Vār mājh* 9:3, AG, p. 142, for example:

If my body was to suffer in [unending] agony and if I were to come under the gaze of the evil planets, if blood-thirsty kings were to stand over my head and rule and if I were to remain in this state, still I would continue to chant your praises.

54. G.S. Talib, *Guru Nanak*, p. 236.

55. *Stirring Stories of the Heroism of Sikh Women and the Martyrdom of a Sikh Youth* (Lahore, 1906), pp. 21–2.

56. That Guru Nanak emphasizes a 'meaningful and creative' approach to suffering is found in the writings of G.S. Talib. G.S. Talib, *Guru Nanak*, p. 232; 'Ethical Thought in Sikhism', pp. 115–16; and 'The Concept and Tradition of Martyrdom', pp. 196–7.

57. For an analysis of the spectacle of torture, see Michel Foucault, *Surveiller et Punir; Naissance de la Prison* [tr. Alan Sheridan, *Discipline & Punish: The Birth of the Prison* (New York, 1979)], pp. 3–69.

58. G.S. Talib, 'Ethical Thought in Sikhism', p. 115.

59. Teja Singh, *Responsibility*, p. 36. Also P.S. Gill, *Guru Tegh Bahadur*, p. 90, deals with martyrdom's ability to 'bear fruit'.

60. Guru Nanak, *Rāg gaurī* 7 (4), AG, p. 223. The terms used to indicate fear of God are *bhai, bhau* and *daru*. A sustained exposition of this is Nanak's *Asā dī vār* 4:1, AG, p. 464.

61. P.S. Gill, *Guru Tegh Bahadur*, p. 99.

62. Sunita Puri, *Advent*, p. 56.

63. *Mūl mantra*, AG, p. 1.

64. Sunita Puri, *Advent*, pp. 103; 199.

65. *GNSR*, p. 163.

66. For example Guru Ram Das' *Asā chhant* 1, AG, p. 442. I base this on Pashaura Singh, 'The Text and Meaning of the Adi Granth', (unpubd. Ph.D. dissertation, University of Toronto, 1991), pp. 207–8.

67. The Nirmala interpretation of Sikh tradition appears in Gian Singh, *Pustak Khālsā Dharam Patit Pāvan Bhāg* (Amritsar, 1903). For the Udasi interpretation see Nripinder Singh, *The Sikh Moral Tradition*, p. 244–8.

68. W.H. McLeod, 'Sikh Fundamentalism', in the *JAOS* 118.1 (1998), pp. 15–27; T.N. Madan, 'The Double-Edged Sword: Fundamentalism and the Sikh Religious Tradition', in M.E. Marty, et al. (ed.), *Fundamentalisms Observed*

(Chicago, 1991), pp. 594–627; and Harjot Oberoi, 'Sikh Fundamentalism: Translating History into Theory', in M.E. Marty, et al. (ed.), *Fundamentalisms and the State* (Chicago, 1991), pp. 256–85.
    69. J.S. Grewal, *Guru Nanak in History*, p. 166.
    70. *BG* 1:23, p. 18.
    71. Hymns to which our texts allude in this regard are Guru Nanak's *Vār mājh* 10:1, AG, p. 142:

That person is truly alive whose *man* dwells in God. Nanak says [that apart from this person] no other person truly lives. If there is one such person alive he lives in dishonour and all he eats is poisonous.

According to Harbans Singh's *Degh Tegh Fateh*, p. 119, this hymn stresses the values of self-respect and honour. He further states that it demonstrates Guru Nanak's belief that leading a life full of humiliation and insults is 'most disgraceful'. Sunita Puri's interpretation of Guru Nanak's *Rāg rāmakalī aṣṭapadī* 2(8), AG, p. 903, also stresses this point: '[Guru Nanak] had condemned cowardliness and applauded the qualities of self-respect, confidence and manliness [*sic*].' *Advent*, p. 222.
    72. H.R. Gupta notes that Guru Nanak's ideal man is one who 'should resist evil, injustice, tyranny and wickedness'. *History of the Sikhs* I, pp. 90–1. Bhajan Singh claims that the first Sikh to be martyred was a disciple of Guru Nanak named Bhai Tara ji. *Saḍe Śahīd*, pp. 15–19.
    73. Nanak, *Āsā aṣṭpadī* 18 (8), AG, p. 421. For other representative hymns see *Vār mājh*, 15:1; *Vaḍahansu* 3; *Vaḍahansu Alāhaniā̃* 2; *Mārū chaupad* 10 (4); and *Ślok vārā̃ te vadhīk* 20; AG, pp. 145, 558, 579–80, 992, 1412.
    74. Nanak, *Mārū solhe* 8 (10), AG, p. 1028.
    75. Within the scripture the Gurus are referred to as *mahalā* (body) 1–5, or 9, in the order of their guruships.
    76. Bhai Gurdas, *Vār* 1:45, 46, 48 in *BG*, pp. 37–9; and *Bachitar Nātak* 5: 4–14, *DG*, pp. 53–54. For the *Dabistān-i Mazāhib*, see K. Isfandyar (ed.), *Dabistān-i Mazāhib* I (Tehran, 1362 H./1983 CE), pp. 198–207, as well as Ganda Singh's translation, 'Nanak Panthis or the Sikhs and Sikhism of the Mid-Eighteenth Century [*sic*]', in *PPP* I:1 (1967), pp. 47–71. The traditional image is that of ten torches, the flame of the first igniting the second and so on up to the tenth, an image first found in Rai Balvand and Satta the Dum, *Rāmakalī kī vār* 2, AG, p. 966.
    77. *PnP*, pp. 80–1; and *MK*, p. 279.
    78. G.S. Chhabra, *Advanced History* I, pp. 166–7.
    79. Ibid., p. 127.
    80. H.R. Gupta, *History of the Sikhs* I, p. 117. Gupta extracts this conclusion from Guru Amar Das' *Rāg bilāwalu* 2 (1), AG, p. 842:

The body discovers tranquillity when it dwells in the Guru's teaching.

    81. Guru Amar Das, *Anandu* 14, AG, p. 918. Also see *BG*, pp. 142, 177.:

[The path of] *Gur-sikhī* is narrow, [it is as difficult as] eating a tasteless stone. It is sharper than a *khaṇḍā*'s edge and finer than a hair. [9:2:2–3]

[The path of] *Gur-sikhī* is narrow, sharper than a *khaṇḍā*'s edge. [11:5:1]

82. Sunita Puri, *Advent*, p. 200, claims that Guru Amar Das commanded his Sikhs to 'live in [the world], work in it, participate in its affairs, fight evil and endeavour to make it an ideal place to live in'.

83. Harbans Singh, *Degh Tegh Fateh*, pp. 120, 148, draws this conclusion on Guru Ram Das' *Tukhāri chhant* 4 (4), AG, p. 1116:

The tax-collectors could not even obtain half a cowrie for their money-boxes. In disgrace they were struck silent.

84. Guru Ram Das, *Sūhi chhant* 2 (1), AG, p. 773. Note particularly the second stanza:

Affirm righteousness and meditate on the Name of Hari, the Name that the sacred books prescribe.

The martyr tradition supplies the following interpretation of this verse: 'The purpose of an individual's life is to strive hard for the triumph of righteousness in the world.' Sunita Puri, *Advent*, p. 200. Also Sahib Singh, *Śri Gurū Granth Sāhib Darpaṇ* V, pp. 576–7.

85. Harbans Singh, *Degh Tegh Fateh*, p. 120. Chhabra's *Advanced History* I, p. 133, claims that

there is no doubt that these activities of the Guru did entail political consequences when a living contact with the Sikhs was established, through which not only the financial needs of the Gurus were satisfied, but through which also the Sikh propaganda against the Muslim tyranny could be carried, the weapons for the battles could be collected and the Sikh recruits into the Guru's forces procured, as was done in the times of Guru Hargobind and Guru Gobind Singh.

86. Jagjit Singh, *The Sikh Revolution*, p. 154.

87. The only conflict between the Guru and the state our sources narrate is the sakhi found in the *Purātan* collection, in which Guru Nanak along with Mardana was jailed during Babur's destruction of Saidpur. *GNSR*, p. 44.

88. A.C. Banerjee, *Guru Nanak to Guru Gobind Singh* (New Delhi, 1978), p. 100. The particular sakhi appears in *B40*, pp. 21–6.

89. See note 24.

90. This is a paraphrase of *Sikh Martyrs*, p. 6. The hymns of Guru Nanak which Teja Singh and Ganda Singh quote to underscore the 'moral degradation' of the inhabitants of India are in *Vār āsā* and *Basant*. See their *A Short History of the Sikhs* (Patiala, 1989), p. 13. Also Puri, *Advent*, p. 113, who interprets Nanak's *Dhanāsari* 3 (3), AG, p. 663, to this effect.

91. Teja Singh and Ganda Singh, *A Short History*, p. 13.

92. Teja Singh, *Responsibility*, pp. 4–5.

93. Harbans Singh, *Degh Tegh Fateh*, p. 121:

... the need to resort to arms on the part of the Sikh religion existed when this religion was established. But since no open and direct challenge was made by the 'State' till the martyrdom of the fifth Guru, no occasion arose for the earlier Sikh Gurus to take up arms actively.

94. G.S. Chhabra, *Advanced History* I, pp. 131, 135–6. Sikh tradition does narrate an incident where conflict with Akbar's government seemed inevitable.

Akbar's minister, Birbal, was about to punish Guru Amar Das after the Guru had refused to pay a tribute. The dire situation in Baluchistan, however, forced the commander to bypass Goindwal. See *SP* V, pp. 1491–8.

95. Khushwant Singh, *A History of the Sikhs* I, p. 54.

96. H.R. Gupta, *History of the Sikhs* I, p. 121.

97. Jagjit Singh, *The Sikh Revolution*, p. 160.

98. Compare, for example, Ganda Singh's *Guru Arjan's Martyrdom (Reinterpreted)* (Patiala, 1969) with H.R. Gupta, *History of the Sikhs* I, pp. 144–54.

99. Kirpal Singh's painting of the fifth Guru's ordeal (1973), however, shows a number of people in the chamber, viewing the horrifying proceedings. *Sikh Ajāibghar*, p. 17.

100. McLeod, for example, is very cautious in describing the death of Guru Arjan: 'The fifth Guru ... had in some manner incurred the displeasure of the Mughal authorities and in 1606 had died while in custody.' *ESC*, p. 3.

101. Surprisingly, Bhangu, whose *PrPP* deals repeatedly with Sikh martyrdom, only devotes one hemstitch to the fifth Guru's death:

Was Guru Arjan not thrown into the river? Was Tegh Bahadur's head not cut off?

This may be based on Kesar Singh Chhibar's *Bansāvalī-nāmā* (1769 CE):

[Guru Arjan] was tied up and thrown into the river.

PrPP, p. 433; P.S. Padam (ed.), *Bhāī Kesar Siṅgh Chhibbar krit Bansāvalī-nāmā Dasān Pātśāhīān kā* (Amrtisar, 1997), p. 85; and Ganda Singh, *Guru Arjan's Martyrdom*, p. 32. There is, of course, no reference to Guru Arjan's martyrdom in the *Bachitar Nāṭak*.

102. Interestingly, Paul Greenough notes that the Indian government not only kept the execution of Indira Gandhi's assassins private but their cremation as well. 'Why was it so hard for the Indian State to convict and do away with Prime Minister Indira Gandhi's assassins?' This paper was seen through the author's courtesy.

103. G.C. Narang, *Transformation of Sikhism* (Delhi, 1912), p. 95.

104. For an examination of these claims, see Chapter Five. The traditional narrative of Guru Arjan's death is found in Lakshman Singh, *Sikh Martyrs*, pp. 30–40. Another tradition holds that the cousin of Chandu Shah, the Hindu Bhagat Kahna, whose hymn Guru Arjan rejected for inclusion within the Adi Granth, proceeded to Lahore to complain against what he decried as the Guru's blasphemous book. Although he died on the way to the city, his case was taken up by his cousin. G.S. Chhabra, *Advanced History* I, p. 169.

105. Lakshman Singh, *Sikh Martyrs*, pp. 38–9.

106. In some accounts, Mian Mir asks the Guru if he can pray for the destruction of the Mughal empire. H.R. Gupta, *History of the Sikhs* I, p. 151.

107. See also Sunita Puri, *Advent*, p. 191.

108. J.P.S. Uberoi, *Religion, Civil Society and the State: A Study of Sikhism* (Delhi, 1996), p. 91.

109. Guru Arjan's *Āsā* 93, AG, p. 394. The tradition is noted by H.R. Gupta, *History of the Sikhs* I, p. 151. Gian Singh states that while Guru Arjan was bathing his battered body in the Ravi River, he was wholly absorbed in the recitation of Guru Nanak's Japji. See *PnP*, p. 117.

110. Guru Arjan's *Rāg bilāwalu* 79, AG, p. 819.

111. Whether he had voluntarily entered the river or was thrown in is a matter of controversy. This account closely follows that found in *SP* VII, pp. 2373–7.

112. For background see H.S. Gill, *A Phulkari From Bhatinda* (Patiala, 1977). The seventeenth-century caste make-up of rural Punjab is discussed in Chetan Singh, *Region and Empire: Panjab in the Seventeenth Century* (Delhi, 199 l), chapters 3 and 4.

113. *BG* 26:25:1, p. 419.

114. I.S. Gill (ed.), *Kavi Sohan ji Sri Gur-bilās Pātsāhi 6 Tipaṇiān Samet* (Patiala, 1969), pp. 149–58. The most famous dacoit to have joined the Guru's entourage and changed his lifestyle was Bidhi Chand Chhina.

115. Our sources often refer to a conversation between Guru Hargobind and Swami Ramdas Samrath, Shivaji's instructor, to demonstrate that Guru Hargobind continued to uphold the injunctions of Guru Nanak. For example, see Harbans Singh, *The Heritage of the Sikhs* (Delhi, 1985), p. 54.

116. Most texts agree that all the Sikhs killed in the battles between Guru Hargobind and the Mughals are considered martyrs. Bhajan Singh, *Sāde Śahīd*, pp. 27–41, for example.

117. Chhabra notes many traditions which indicate the Guru's compassion and altruism. *Advanced History* I, pp. 227–9.

118. Teja Singh and Ganda Singh, *A Short History*, p. 38, n. 2, state that the Guru's cell today bears a cenotaph commemorating this act.

119. Gopal Singh, *Sikh People*, pp. 237–9; and G.S. Chhabra, *Advanced History* I, p. 234.

120. Teja Singh, *Responsibility*, p. 42.

121. See, for example, the large number of articles devoted to the ninth Guru in the 1974–76 issues of *JSS*, *PPP*, *JRH* and *PPHC*.

122. In *Sri Gurbilās Pātsāhi 6*, p. 262, Guru Hargobind requests God to bestow courage on the infant to fight evil and establish righteousness.

123. Baba Gurditta was the son of Guru Hargobind's first wife, Damodari, while Tegh Bahadur was the son of his second wife, Nanaki.

124. A different interpretation is in Kirpal Singh, 'Guru Tegh Bahadur's Life at Baba Bakala and Anandpur', in G.S. Talib (ed.), *Guru Tegh Bahadur*, pp. 50–9. According to this account, Guru Tegh Bahadur spent twenty years at Bakala, from the death of his father in 1644 until he assumed the guruship in 1664. H.R. Gupta, *History of the Sikhs* I, pp. 184–5, places the Guru at Bakala between 1635 and 1656.

125. This is the standard interpretation of Tegh Bahadur's life prior to his guruship. H.R. Gupta, 'Guru Tegh Bahadur—A Biographical Study', in G.S. Talib (ed.), *Guru Tegh Bahadur*, pp. 3–24.

126. *TGK* I, pp. 667–8.

127. A Mina reading of this event, implying a cordial relationship between Guru Tegh Bahadur and the Minas, appears in the *bhatt vāhis*. Jeevan Deol, 'The Minās and Their Literature', in *JAOS* 118.2 (1998), p. 177.

128. H.R. Gupta, *History of the Sikhs* I, pp. 187–208.

129. The extant hukam-namas are in Fauja Singh (ed.), *Hukamnamas Shri Guru Tegh Bahadur Sahib [Punjabi-Hindi-English]* (Patiala, 1976).

130. J.S. Grewal, 'The Prophet of Assurance', in G.S. Talib (ed.), *Guru Tegh Bahadur*, pp. 75–80.

131. *TGK* I, pp. 720–3.
132. *TGK* I, pp. 745–7.
133. *TGK* I, pp. 745–7; 753–5.
134. Fauja Singh and G.S. Talib, *Guru Tegh Bahadur*, pp. 1–10.
135. According to Teja Singh, Guru Arjan's death was more an example of 'enlightened' rather than passive suffering. *Responsibility*, p. 38.
136. Lakshman Singh, *Sikh Martyrs*, pp. 41–50. S.S. Chawla, *Martyrdom of Guru Tegh Bahadur: Message for Mankind* (New Delhi, 1991), often prefaces chapters with hymns from the bani of Guru Nanak.
137. Chawla, *Martyrdom*, pp. 17–18.
138. The traditional sources utilized are the *Bhaṭṭ vāhis*, the diaries of the minstrels surrounding the Gurus' court; the *Pāndhā vāhis*, the diaries of Brahmans at major centres of Hindu pilgrimage; the literature of the gur-bilas genre, particularly the fifth canto of the *Bachitar Nāṭak*; and finally, the Persian chronicles in which the ninth Guru's life figures. To these may be added oral tradition. See Fauja Singh and G.S. Talib, *Guru Tegh Bahadur*, and Harbans Singh, *Heritage*, pp. 68–87.
139. *Bachitar Nāṭak* 5: 4–16, *DG*, pp. 53–4.
140. See J.S. Grewal, 'The Bachittar Natak', in his *From Guru Nanak to Maharaja Ranjit Singh* (Amrtisar, 1982), pp. 71–77; and S.S. Hans, *A Reconstruction*, pp. 227–34.
141. *Bachitar Nāṭak* 6:1–5, 29; *DG*, pp. 54–5, 57.
142. J.S. Grewal and S.S. Bal recognize the influence that his father's death had on the young Gobind in their *Guru Gobind Singh* (Chandigarh, 1966), pp. 41 ff. The ninth Guru is referred to in his role as father and pious pilgrim in the very brief seventh canto of the *Bachitar Nāṭak*. See *DG*, p. 59.
143. According to Surjit Hans, the passage implies that the martyrdom of the ninth Guru is proof of the legitimacy of the latter's guruship. S.S. Hans, *A Reconstruction*, p. 231.
144. Almost every text which deals with the martyrdom of the ninth Guru will allude to the *Bachitar Nāṭak* passage.
145. The use of Persian accounts dealing with the ninth Guru is very rare. When there are references to these sources, Sikh authors often represent them as 'distorted' views of Guru Tegh Bahadur's life. See Mona Kang, 'Concept of Martyrdom', pp. 81–2.
146. See the commentary attached to this hymn in the *Śabadārath Śrī Gurū Granth Sāhib Ji*, pp. 1427a–b. According to Hans, these shaloks may be subtitled 'Waiting for Martyrdom'. *A Reconstruction*, p. 226. McLeod makes clear that these shaloks are very popular for their poetic quality and because they are prominent in the *bhog* ceremony with which the Adi Granth concludes. *TSSS*, p. 54.
147. *Slok* 16, AG, p. 1427. For the connection with Guru Nanak's hymns see J.S. Grewal, 'The Prophet of Assurance', pp. 77–9.
148. Here, we also see the adherence to Guru Nanak's ideal of sacrificing one's life for righteousness.
149. According to tradition, having agreed to the qazi's request to perform a miracle, the Guru indicated that the executioner's blade would be unable to cut through his neck as long as a charmed message was hung around it. After the blade had fallen and the Guru's head was severed, the paper was removed from his neck and the message was read out as *sir diyā sirr na diyā*, 'I gave my head

but not my secret/honour'. It is quite plausible that this story has developed out of verse 5:14 of the *Bachitar Nāṭak*. Evidently, the same verse has prompted the anecdote dealing with the Guru's refusal to perform a miracle. See G.S. Chhabra, *Advanced History* I, p. 251.

150. Tegh Bahadur, *Slok* 33, AG, p. 1428:

Says Nanak, through devotion to Hari, my mind, you may attain the state of fearlessness.

151. Guru Nanak, *Vār malār* 19:1, AG, p. 1286:

Ignorant madmen confer caps of distinction on those who shamelessly accept them and deserve them not.

152. S.S. Chawla, *Martyrdom of Guru Tegh Bahadur*, p. 6. Also Fauja Singh, 'Guru Tegh Bahadur and Human Rights', pp. 38, 46. This phrase, *'nā ko hindū hai nā ko musalmān hai'*, occurs in the Puratan Janam-sakhi. *GNSR*, p. 12.

153. Nanak's *Āsā* 39, AG, p. 360.

154. Ganda Singh, 'The Martyrdom of Guru Tegh Bahadur', in *JSS* III:1 (Feb. 1976), p. 116.

155. P.S. Gill, *Guru Tegh Bahadur*, p. 76. Tradition maintains that the Khalsa was created in order that all Sikhs should henceforth spurn the now-corrupt masands, and give their offerings to their own sangat or directly to the Guru himself. Gopal Singh, *Sikh People*, p. 281.

156. *PrPP*, p. 42:

The *ṭopīs* on their heads sport rosaries of wool. The names they take are *Dās*. Such servility does not produce heroes who wield swords.

157. Many anecdotes emphasize this loyalty to the sixth Guru. See Gopal Singh, *Sikh People*, p. 235.

158. This story first appears in the *Siyar-ul-Mutā'khkhirīn*, according to John Malcolm's *Sketch of the Sikhs*, p. 81. Also Surjit Singh, '*Sikh-śahīd dī kaum*', in Surjit Singh (ed.), *Su Amrit Gur te Pāiā* (Jalandhar, 1991), p. 174.

159. As we have noted, the Sikh of the Khalsa is the ideal. That only these Sikhs had access to liberation in early Sikh literature is noted in Surjit Hans, 'Social Transformation and Early Sikh Literature', *JRH* 3 (1982), p. 11. Today, such Sikhs are known as *tiār bar tiār singh* or 'full-fledged Singhs'. See *Sikh Rahit Maryādā* (16th ed., Amritsar, 1989), p. 21.

160. Lakshman Singh, *Sikh Martyrs*, pp. 71–2. My emphasis.

161. For example, Kirpal Singh, 'Facts about Guru Gobind Singh's Martyrdom', in *Sikh Review* (Sept.–Oct. 1957), pp. 68–73; P.S. Gill's *Guru Tegh Bahadur*, p. 91; and Bhajan Singh, *Sāde Śahid*, pp. 84–7.

162. Teja Singh, *Responsibility*, p. 49.

163. Grewal and Bal, *Guru Gobind Singh*, p. 126.

164. Khushwant Singh, *A History of the Sikhs* I, p. 88. J.D. Cunningham's words to this purpose are also quoted frequently in our texts. See Cunningham's *History of the Sikhs*, p. 34.

165. Grewal and Bal, *Guru Gobind Singh*, p. 110.

166. Ibid., pp. 112–13.

167. Quoted from C.H. Loehlin, *The Granth of Guru Gobind Singh and the Khalsa Brotherhood* (Lucknow, 1971), p. 19.

168. G.S. Talib, *The Impact of Guru Gobind Singh on Indian Society* (Ludhiana, 1984), p. 28.

169. For *dharam yudh* see Chapter Five.

170. *Zafarnāmah* 1:22, *DG*, p. 1390.

171. J.D. Cunningham, *History of the Sikhs*, p. 66. In his various works on the tenth Guru, J.S. Grewal often elaborates upon this theme. Grewal and Bal, *Guru Gobind Singh*, p. 157.

172. For Udai Singh see Koer Singh, *Gurbilās Pātsāhī 10*, pp. 195-7.

173. H.R. Gupta, *History of the Sikhs* I, pp. 292-3.

174. Teja Singh and Ganda Singh, *A Short History*, pp. 69-70.

175. Lakshman Singh, *Short Sketch of the Life and Work of Guru Gobind Singh, the 10th and Last Guru of the Sikhs* (Lahore, 1909), pp. 109-11; and his *Sikh Martyrs*, p. 58.

176. H.R. Gupta, *History of the Sikhs* 1, p. 295; and EoS, p. 430.

177. Bhai Jivan Singh was the same Bhai Jaita who had brought the head of the ninth Guru to Gobind Singh. For Jivan Singh see J.D. Cunningham, *History of the Sikhs*, p. 71, n. 1; and *EoS*, p. 431. Of course, every warrior killed at Chamkaur is remembered as a martyr.

178. These Sikhs are remembered daily in the Ardas. Although the term *chali mukte* is also applied to those forty Sikhs who fought alongside the Guru in the *garhi* of Chamkaur, it is generally associated with the forty Sikhs who died at Mukatsar.

179. Compare Gopal Singh, *Sikh People*, pp. 355-6 with Ganda Singh's *Life of Banda Singh Bahadur* (Patiala, 1990). Lakshman Singh does not include Banda in his monograph.

180. Lakshman Singh, *Sikh Martyrs*, pp. 83-102, 111-21, 179-81, 195-7. The short domed structure bears a plaque noting that Gurbakhsh Singh took amrit from the hands of Mani Singh and died on this spot after engaging a thirty thousand-strong army. A martyry dedicated to both Bota Singh and Garja Singh stands within the precincts of Gurdwara Shahidganj Baba Dip Singh.

181. Gopal Singh, *Sikh People*, p. 352. A painting appears in *Sikh Ajāibghar*, p. 48. This narrative first appears in the *Muntakhab-i Lubāb* of Khafi Khan.

182. Lakshman Singh, *Sikh Martyrs*, pp. 103-10; 127-33; 134-8.

183. *Glimpses of Fatehgarh Sahib History (The Light House for the Forlorn)*, (Sirhind, 1950), pp. 20-2. According to a popular anecdote, Bibi Bhani's devotion prompted Guru Amar Das to allow her husband's male lineage to retain the Guruship. Her husband was the future Guru, Ram Das.

184. That is, the scene depicted in Kirpal Singh's painting, 'Sacrificing Family before Faith'. The bravery of the mothers is narrated in *Heroism of Sikh Women and the Martyrdom of a Sikh Youth*, pp. 7-20.

185. Lakshman Singh, *Sikh Martyrs*, pp. 63-4. Harpal Singh Tiwana's acclaimed play *Sirhind dī Dīwār* or 'The Wall of Sirhind' deals with the bricking up alive of the younger sons of the tenth Guru.

186. J.J.H. Gordon, *The Sikhs* (first pbd., 1883. Patiala, 1988), pp. 47-8.

187. *TGK* II, pp. 20-8.

188. Mona Kang applies this term to those killed in these two campaigns, 'Concept of Martyrdom', pp. 72, 108-13. Background on the *ghalūghāre* appears in *PnP*, pp. 775-89, 950-65; and *TGK* II, pp. 205-7.

189. Rajinder Singh, 'Heroic Tradition', in Fauja Singh (ed.), *The City of*

Amritsar: A Study of Historical, Cultural, Social and Economic Aspects (New Delhi, 1978), p. 169.

190. The now-demolished Gurdwara Shahidganj was also associated with the martyrs of the various holocausts. Ganda Singh, *History of the Gurdwara Shahidganj, Lahore, from its Origin to November 1935* (Amritsar, 1935). Also H.R. Gupta, *A History of the Sikhs* II, p. 187.

191. M. Tully and S. Jacob, *Amritsar: Mrs. Gandhi's Last Battle*, p. 53. In *EoS*, p. 588, we find that the misl led by Baba Dip Singh acquired the name *Sahid* only after its leader had secured a martyr's death.

192. *TGK* II, p. 198.

193. Two other traditions are noted in W.H. McLeod's *Popular Sikh Art*, pp. 38–9. Also see K.S. Zakhmi's *Bābā Dīp Siṅgh Jī Śahīd* (5th ed., Amritsar, 1992); *PnP*, pp. 910–25. A plaque at the Golden Temple precincts states that Dip Singh was killed in 1760.

194. Khushwant Singh, *A History of the Sikhs* I, pp. 145–6, for example. A recent article in the magazine *Punjab Monitor,* however, notes that Baba Dip Singh was probably able to move for some time after he had been decapitated. See B.S. Yadav, 'Can a Headless Body Move? The Mystery and Reality of a Strange Phenomenon' in the *Punjab Monitor* (July 1997), pp. 20–1.

195. On celebrations in honour of this martyr at this gurdwara, see Nahar Singh, 'Athārvī Sadī de Sikh Gabhrū', in Surjit Singh (ed.), *Su Amrit Gur te Pāīā,* p. 200. In June of 1997, the lamp was no longer in the Prakash Asthan of this gurdwara. There was, however, such a lamp on the small walkway surrounding the small martyry-gurdwara of Bota Singh and Garja Singh that is found within its precincts.

196. *Sikh Rahit Maryādā,* p. 11:

Except for the aforementioned ceremonies [of reading and closing the Guru Granth Sahib], practices such as the raising of incense or lamps around the scripture in the performance of *ārtī* ... are ones not sanctioned by Gurmat.

197. Because of the disturbances at the time, I was unable to visit this gurdwara. The reference comes from Ranjit Singh Bajwa.

198. Photos of both the hexagonal block and the shrine dedicated to this famous martyr are found in Patwant Singh's *The Golden Temple* (New Delhi, 1989), pp. 148–9.

199. Although *EoS*, p. 114, gives a brief history of the gurdwara, it does not mention its connection with Dip Singh. The information noted above is taken from a plaque placed at the entrance to the gurdwara compounds.

200. For the Nihangs see *MK*, p. 704.

201. The disturbance began in April, 1978 in Amritsar, spreading to Delhi in May. For the Nirankaris generally consult John Webster, *The Nirankari Sikhs* (Delhi, 1979), esp. pp. 32–5.

202. This prayer is taken from the personal diary of Pashaura Singh (Saturday, 27 May 1978), to whom I am indebted.

203. Nanak's *Slok vārān te vadhīk* 20, AG, p. 1412. This print, a reproduction of the 1992 original by the artist, Bodhraj, is in my collection. Zakhmi's narrative maintains that it was after reading this shalok that Dip Singh decided to immediately act. Zakhmi, *Bābā Dīp Siṅgh Śahīd,* pp. 95–6. This shalok also

appears on the plaque placed at the entrance to Gurdwara Talha Sahib mentioned above. McLeod has noted that Baba Dip Singh is depicted as obeying this command precisely. He also notes that allusions to this shalok are frequently heard today. See *Popular Sikh Art*, p. 132.

204. A.C. Banerjee, *Guru Nanak*, pp. 160–1 and I. Banerjee, *The Evolution of the Khalsa* I (Calcutta, 1975), p. 226. This hymn is also noted in connection with Guru Nanak's nomination of Lehana as Guru Angad. Trilochan Singh, *Guru Nanak: Founder of Sikhism (A Biography)* (Delhi, 1969), pp. 462–3.

205. A picture of the first page of the April 1925 issue of *Hindostān Ghadr* appears in Harish Puri's *Ghadr Movement: Ideology, Organisation and Strategy* (Amritsar, 1993), p. 280.

206. Harbans Singh describes post-1925 Sikh history in this way.

207. Muzaffar Alam's *The Crisis of Empire in Mughal North India: Awadh and the Punjab 1707–1748* (New Delhi, 1986), p. 154.

208. It appears, however, that recent 'standard' martyrologies do make room for the Namdhari martyrs. See Bhajan Singh, *Sāde Śahīd*, pp. 158–66. Also see *TSSS*, pp. 130–1.

209. B.S. Cheema and B.K. Mann, 'Concept of Martyrdom', p. 88; and Mona Kang, 'Concept of Martyrdom', p. 46.

210. Zakhmi, *Bābā Dip Singh Śahīd*, p. 95. This print is by Amolak Singh. As well, at Gurdwara Baba Dip Singh Shahidganj in Amritsar there is a plaque (which, during my visit in June 1997, was found in the kiosk set aside for worshippers' shoes) that narrates this story.

211. Kabir, *Mārū*, shalok 1, p. 1105. Although both verses may be interpreted in a yogic sense, such an interpretation is very rare indeed.

212. Kabir, *Gauṛī* 20(3) and *Goṇḍ* 2, AG, pp. 327, 870, for example. Namdev, *Bhairau* 10, AG, pp. 1165–6. These hymns are discussed in G.S. Talib, 'Martyrdom in Sikhism', pp. 194–6.

213. *GNSR*, p. 86.

214. Gurdit Singh, *Itihās Śrī Gurū Granth Sāhib (Bhagat Bāṇī Bhāg)* (Chandigarh, 1990).

215. Khushwant Singh, *A History of the Sikhs*, I, p. 107; and Ganda Singh, *Banda Singh Bahadur*, p. 69.

216. Annemarie Schimmel, *Mystical Dimensions of Islam* (Chapel Hill, 1975), chapters 2–3.

FOUR

Martyrdom in the Early Sikh Tradition[1]

Sevā harī gur thīn kurbān[2]

To become a sacrifice for the sake of the [Eternal] Guru is the [true]
service (*sevā*) of God.

According to a tradition we find in the early nineteenth-century
gur-bilas text attributed to the poet Sohan, *Gur-bilās Pātsāhī
6*, it was the sixth Guru who recognized the popularity of the
heroic tradition embodied in the tunes of the dhadhis. The *Gur-bilās
Pātsāhī 6* mentions that as the young Hargobind sat with both his
father, Guru Arjan, and the venerable Baba Buddha, he was told that

You [will] have to fight great battles. Contemplate with an undisturbed
mind the singing of the twenty-two ballads which we have recorded in the
[Adi] Granth. You should include heroic tunes at the beginning of those
ballads you like to hear most.[3]

This statement serves to complement the tradition mentioned
earlier that it was also the sixth Guru who built the Akal Takht and
instructed dhadhis to sing their martial songs in front of it in order
to infuse heroic traits into his newly transformed Sikhs.[4]

Pashaura Singh has recently claimed, however, that it was not Guru
Hargobind, but rather his father, Guru Arjan, who was responsible
for including heroic ballads in the scripture. This is a logical conclusion since according to tradition the fifth Master was clearly the
moving force behind the creation of a Sikh scripture. While compiling
the Adi Granth in the late sixteenth and early seventeenth centuries,
Guru Arjan recognized the popularity of the heroic var (ballad) among
the rural population of the Punjab and himself selected the heroic

dhunis (tunes) of these ballads at the beginning of the vars in different rag sections of the Adi Granth. This process of appropriation, we are told, was in order to attract this rural audience, particularly the Jat caste, to the Sikh faith. As Pashaura Singh makes clear, however, the fifth Guru selected such dhunis 'only for their musical directions, not for propagating the heroic stories behind them'.[5] This last point is a debatable one since the values which were made explicit in the heroic stories the tunes carried would have probably become associated with the Sikh faith by the inclusion of such melodies in the scripture, a possibility which Guru Arjan, an exceptionally gifted writer and compiler, could not have overlooked.[6] A statement of this nature certainly adds weight to the vigorously contested theory that the martial traditions of the Jats had a fundamental influence on the early formation of the Sikh tradition.[7]

Sources for the Execution of Guru Arjan and the Testimony of the Adi Granth

With this evidence at hand, one can well speculate that Guru Arjan appreciated these heroic values. He may have himself thus felt that both his defiance of Mughal authority (if such actually occurred) and his imminent death were heroic acts, perhaps those of the martyr. It is entirely possible, finally, that his Sikhs also understood such actions in this way. As we noted in the last chapter, Sikh tradition affirms all this as beyond doubt. Guru Arjan died the glorious death of the martyr, and his son, in response to this horrific ordeal, enjoined his Sikhs to bear arms to protect themselves and all those considered righteous. Such an understanding of the fifth Guru's demise, however, veers into the realm of conjecture as contemporary and near-contemporary sources for this event cannot substantiate the claims of tradition. There are three sources which allude to Guru Arjan's execution at the hands of the Mughal emperor, and these three form the base upon which the traditional interpretation has been erected. A critical examination of these demonstrates that many scholars of the Sikh tradition extrapolate far too much from them, filling in the numerous gaps in the narrative which these sources supply with popular understandings forged in later centuries.

The first is the *Dabistān-i Mazāhib*, or 'The School of Religions' (1645), a rather controversial text dealing with Indian religions, attributed to an unknown Persian Zoroastrian who toured India in the seventeenth century. The relevant passage seems to imply that Sikhs of the early to mid-seventeenth century were well aware of Guru Arjan's death at the hands of the Mughals, despite the lack of Sikh sources supporting this point.[8] The view this brief passage presents of Guru Arjan's death mimics that of the actual observer, reporting that the fifth Sikh Master 'gave up his life as a result of the heat of the sun, the severity of summer, and the tortures of the bailiffs' (*az tābash-i āftāb o shaddat-i garmā o āzar-i muhassalā jān dād*).[9] For many scholars this report, particularly 'the torture of the bailiffs', has been taken as an eyewitness account of the Guru's death, rather than second-hand information passed on to the author of the *Dabistān* almost forty years after the execution took place. The statement regarding the tortures to which the Guru was subjected may well have been part of mid-seventeenth-century oral tradition and may have, in fact, occurred as Jahangir notes in his memoirs (discussed below): that he had ordered Arjan to be 'punished [scil., tortured?] and executed' (*siyāsat o yāsā rasānand*).[10] Yet neither the *Dabistān* nor the emperor's orders are enough to verify beyond doubt that Guru Arjan was tortured during his imprisonment. We may assume from the references in the emperor's memoirs that some form of punishment was meted out to the Guru, but that these included the particular punishments narrated in the popular account cannot be substantiated.[11] Martyrologists are well aware of the fact that the more harsh the torture a martyr suffers, the more heroic is the martyrdom. In fact, even Sikh tradition is not altogether sure regarding the means of the Guru's death—whether it occurred by torture, execution, or drowning in the Ravi river. Until evidence closer to the event surfaces, demonstrating that torture was actually applied, we, as historians, must be sceptical about the claims of tradition. Ultimately, the account in the *Dabistān-i Mazāhib* cannot be verified.

A second source often used to reconstruct Guru Arjan's last days is a letter we find in the *Maktūbat-i Imām-i Rabbānī* of Shaikh Ahmad Sirhindi, a leading *pīr* of the Naqshbandi order of Sufis in the early seventeenth century.[12] In it, Sirhindi rejoices at the news of Guru Arjan's execution in 1606, referring to the Guru as the 'accursed infidel of Goindwal' (*kāfir-i la'īn gobind wāl*) whose 'execution ... very fortunately happened' (*kushtān ... bisyār khūb wāqi' shud*). For many scholars of the Sikh tradition, this jubilant tone is proof enough that Sirhindi's hand was evident in Jahangir's decision to imprison and subsequently execute Guru Arjan.[13] Yet again, the evidence does not support this conclusion. The Shaikh's infamous letter, for example, was not sent to Jahangir himself, as Khushwant Singh notes, but to the Governor of Punjab, Shaikh Bukhari, also known as Murtaza Khan.[14] More conclusively, Sirhindi wrote this letter well after the fact. One can only conclude from the available evidence that the Shaikh's role in the Guru's execution is again, conjectural.

The part Jahangir played in the fifth Guru's execution further supports this point. Emperor Jahangir's role in this death is, of course, pivotal and the evidence for this is beyond reproach, as it appears in the very memoirs of the emperor himself, the *Tūzuk-i Jahāngiri*. Here, there is no doubt that the fifth Guru was executed on Jahangir's orders. Jahangir's motive behind the execution, however, is still a matter of controversy amongst scholars. Was the emperor concerned at the growing Jat constituency of the Sikh Panth, the Jat *zāt* (sub-caste), a group which was known for its predilection towards violence in the early seventeenth century? Did the appropriation of imperial terminology to describe the Guru's situation—the Guru held a *darbār* ('court'), was considered a *sachchā pādśāh* or 'true king', and sat upon a *takhat* ('throne')—incite Jahangir to action against a religious leader whom he considered an upstart?[15] Both of these statements are speculatory and cannot be verified. According to Ganda Singh, Jahangir executed the Guru in order to assume the role of the 'Defender of Islam'. He had given a pledge to that effect to various Islamic clerics, particularly Sirhindi, in order to secure their support in his bid to ascend the throne of Mughal India during the last days of his father Akbar's life. The execution was believed, therefore, to have been 'prompted by some external agency of fanatical Mullas'.[16] This view is subject to controversy. In his memoirs and other contemporary seventeenth-century sources, there is no evidence suggesting that Jahangir was in any way influenced to act, directly or indirectly, by the *'ulamā* (state-supported judges, theologians and preachers), Naqshbandi Sufis, or other Islamic religious personnel at the Mughal court. Recent scholarship has shown, moreover, that Jahangir's personal religious predilections did not determine his state policies.[17] Specifically in regard to Ahmad Sirhindi, Jahangir notes in his *Tūzuk* that his relations with the Shaikh were cool at best, at times hostile, especially when the emperor had Sirhindi gaoled in the fort at Gwalior in 1619 so that his 'disturbed disposition and confused mind would calm down a little'.[18]

Jahangir's memoirs do note that the emperor was concerned with the growing popularity of the Sikh tradition and had for long chosen to act against 'this shop' (*in dokan*) which 'they [the Sikh Gurus] had kept warm for three to four generations' (*seh chahār pasht ... garam midāshtand*). This may certainly have played a part in the emperor's final decision, as Jahangir seems to have been hostile to popularly venerated religious figures.[19] Yet this hostility must not be exaggerated. The heated statement directly above was apparently prompted by Jahangir's concern with the later situation, that is the Guru's apparent support of Prince Khusrau. If Jahangir was, as Ganda Singh claims him to be, '[a man] with no fixed moral scruples, a debauche, always soaked in wine',[20] the concern over the Guru's activities at Goindwal would have probably precipitated much prompter action. The son of Akbar, it seems, has been much vilified in Sikh hagiography, for contemporary Persian accounts note (with some exaggeration perhaps) that Jahangir was an emperor known particularly for his just dealings with all the members of his vast empire.[21] The clear reason for giving the order of execution was Guru Arjan's supposed support of Prince Khusrau's rival claim to the throne, an alliance the emperor was bound to view disfavourably. Jahangir, it seems, ordered the Guru executed not for his faith or community, but for his apparent association with a rival. As Sajida Alvi notes, Jahangir was dealing with someone he believed to be 'a rebel who happened to be the leader of the Sikh community'. It is for this reason, she continues, that the emperor did not act against Arjan's followers and, we may add, that the apparent friendship between the sixth Guru and the emperor may have begun some years after 1606.[22] Jahangir's relations with other representatives of the Hindu tradition—Jahangir labels Guru Arjan a 'Hindu' in his memoirs—was, after all, a very positive and liberal one, particularly evinced by his reverence for the Vaishnava ascetic, Gosain Jadrup of Ujjain who, according to the emperor, possessed 'unusual grace, lofty understanding, exalted nature and a heart free from the attainments of the world'.[23]

What one can say about Guru Arjan's death, therefore, is very little. The only conclusion the evidence will support is that Guru Arjan acquired the enmity of the Mughal state by appearing to support the rival claim of Khusrau, was imprisoned (and perhaps beaten) by the emperor's minions, and subsequently died while in Mughal custody in Lahore. One's caution in accepting the claims of tradition are firmly based. Whether a saffron mark was placed on Khusrau's forehead by the Guru or not, and if so, whether this was a sign of support or not, is irrelevant as Jahangir clearly believed such an act occurred and that this was a pledge to Khusrau of Guru Arjan's allegiance.[24]

Yet the question still beckons. Did the Sikhs of Guru Arjan's period and afterwards understand the fifth Master's death as a martyrdom? To answer, let us approach the question of Guru Arjan's death from another perspective. Did there exist, within the early-seventeenth-century Sikh tradition, what Bowersock calls 'a conceptual system of posthumous recognition and anticipated reward'[25] which would accommodate such an example of courageous resistance to tyrannical authority and painful death? Was there, in other words, a concept of martyrdom at this point in Sikh history? For many traditional interpreters of Sikhism, this is beyond doubt as, they maintain, the idea of martyrdom was first developed by Guru Nanak and sustained by the following nine Gurus, especially Guru Arjan and Guru Tegh Bahadur. Yet despite this claim, it is near impossible to ascertain a concept of martyrdom during the period of the first nine Gurus (1469–1675). The problem lies in the source upon which all such claims rest, the Adi Granth. We have been privy to the numerous hymns which are marshalled to support the opinion that martyrdom has an early origin in Sikhism. Among the most popular is Guru Nanak's *Slok vārān te vadhīk* 20, mentioned earlier in connection with Baba Dip Singh.[26] Another hymn often cited in such support is the first Guru's *vadahansu alāhaṇīā* 2: 2–3:

O people! Death is not called bad if one knows how to die. Serve the Lord and your path will be an easy one. As you traverse this simple path you will obtain the fruit [of your efforts and God's grace] and achieve glory in the hereafter. If you take the gift [of the Name on your journey,] you will be absorbed in truth and your honour will be approved [by the Lord]. In the divine mansion you will find your place, and you shall win the Lord's pleasure and be joyful. O people! Death is not called bad if one knows how to die. [2

Blessed is the death of heroic men if their dying is approved of [by the immortal Lord]. Only these men may be called heroes who obtain true honour before the Court [of Akal Purakh]. Obtaining such honour at the Divine Court they depart [this world] with honour and do not suffer in the hereafter. This is the fruit they will obtain if they meditate on the Supreme One in whose service all fears are dissolved. How well You know that they ought not to speak aloud of [their separation from You] rather concealing [such pain] within.[27] The Lord himself knows these things intimately. Blessed is the death of heroic men if their dying is approved of [by the immortal Lord].[28]   [3

We know already that the refrain of stanza 3 is found on the statue of Udham Singh which stands before Gandhi Gate in Amritsar. Its intimate association with martyrdom in the Sikh tradition is, in other words, beyond doubt. For G.S. Talib, this hymn, particularly the refrains of stanzas 2 and 3, are 'truly a call to mankind not to shirk from sacrificing life, should a noble cause present itself'.[29] Yet the context in which we find this hymn does not support such a conclusion. The appropriate setting appears to be a funeral or a gathering lamenting those recently dead, as this set of hymns is subtitled *alāhaṇīān* or 'dirges', composed for the ceremonial mourning of the dead in the Punjab. Taken as a whole, the main concern of the shabads in *vaḍahansu alāhaṇīān* is to underscore both the transient nature of this world and of human existence. Noting that death is a natural part of life, the Guru states that a person's passing should not be mourned, especially if that person piously meditated on the divine name while alive. It is this person who is a 'hero' (*sūrā*) by Guru Nanak's account.[30] Talib interprets this hymn out of context when he claims that it underscores a notion of 'suffering undergone with a view to resisting evil in obedience to a movement of the soul ... of suffering borne in pursuit of some moral ideal'.[31] In other words, martyrdom. His interpretation, or perhaps interpolation, is clear in the following English translation he supplies of the two refrains:

> Folks! Revile not Death.
> Death is not an evil, should one know how *truly* to die.
> The death of heroic men is holy,
> Should they lay down their lives for a righteous cause.[32]

In another of his many translations of these two lines, Talib foot-notes the term 'heroic men' (*muṇsā sūre*), indicating within the note that '[t]his is, of course, martyrdom'.[33] Assuming that Talib understands martyrdom the way it is understood today, such a conclusion is by no means as obvious as our author contends.

Clearly, *vaḍahansu alāhaṇīān* 2: 2–3, as the full translation above indicates, as well as *slok vārāṇ te vadhīk* 20 and other hymns used to support an early Sikh tradition of martyrdom which were cited in Chapter Three, do not explicitly advocate sacrifice in the face of oppression and tyranny. Rather, it appears that these shabads were capable of engendering such action depending on the nature and extent of the oppression encountered. To put it differently, these hymns may have been appropriated in years preceding their composition to support an idea of selfless sacrifice with the hope of future reward, but nevertheless, it seems very unlikely that martyrdom is what the Bhatts, the Bhagats and the Sikh Gurus had in mind as they composed these shabads.

The Gur-bilas Literature

As we now know, the eighteenth-century evidence for martyrdom in the Sikh tradition is less opaque. Although material for this period is not abundant—Sikhs claim, for instance, that much written material was lost during these war-torn years[34]—what does exist allows us partially to reconstruct Sikh ideas regarding courageous death, sacrifice and martyrdom. It should be noted that the sparse written record of this 'heroic' period of Sikh history does not consist of written martyrologies or Martyr Acts. The Sikh tradition has no eighteenth-century hagiographer who recorded the lives and deaths of Sikh martyrs with the kind of loving detail we find in the janam-sakhis. Nor does the record include any authentic memorials noting the personal sufferings of Sikhs today labelled as martyrs. What we have, rather, is a type of hagiography that focuses attention on the mighty battles of the sixth and tenth Gurus, the supreme courage of the Sikhs, and their ultimate destiny in battling the forces of evil, forces clearly identified with Islam. This is the literature of the gur-bilas genre. Gur-bilas literature also draws one's focus to the eighteenth-century Khalsa's fascination with the goddess Durga or Chandi: the various buffalo sacrifices she is offered by the tenth Guru and his Khalsa, as well as her fundamental role in the militant order's foundation. Texts in the gur-bilas genre would include, amongst others, the *Bachitar Nāṭak*; Sainipati's *Gur-sobhā*; the texts attributed to Sukkha Singh and Koer Singh, both titled *Gur-bilās Pātśāhī 10*; as well as the *Gur-bilās Pātśāhī 6*, believed to be authored by Kavi Sohan.

Although the origins and date of the *Bachitar Nāṭak* provide scholars with a puzzling conundrum, there seems little doubt that this text is the archetype of the gur-bilas style. To it, therefore, may be ascribed a late-seventeenth- or early-eighteenth-century date. What we find in the *Bachitar Nāṭak* that concerns us specifically is the brief narrative recounting the execution of the ninth Sikh Master, Guru Tegh Bahadur. As we know, this event, like the execution of Guru

Arjan, is considered a martyrdom and marks a watershed in the history of the Sikh Panth. It is believed to have led to the creation of the Khalsa in 1699. Of course, the actual details of Guru Tegh Bahadur's execution are as shrouded in mystery as are those of Guru Arjan's death, hagiographic accounts filling in the few portions of the narrative we find in available contemporary and near-contemporary literature. We have, for example, competing Muslim and Sikh claims regarding the ninth Guru's activities and capture. Persian sources maintain that the Guru was a bandit who was justly executed for his role in rebellious activity,[35] while the Sikh narrative holds that Tegh Bahadur died in the attempt to secure the rights of all people, particularly the Brahmans of Kashmir, to practise their religion and don their religious symbols in good conscience.[36] One must, at this point, suspend judgement on these claims because of both the paucity of the available material and its questionable nature.

We noted earlier that other eighteenth-century texts within the gur-bilas genre allude to the passage of the *Bachitar Nāṭak* regarding Guru Tegh Bahadur's execution. This may confirm the early date of this work. The popularity of this passage, moreover, seems to indicate that a fascination with heroic sacrifice animated some members of the eighteenth-century Panth, at least those who produced the gur-bilas texts in question. We may presume that the authors of the gur-bilas works, like Seva Singh Kaushish after them, could be trusted to know what would captivate their audience and retain their interest. Sikh sources base their interpretation of the ninth Guru's death on the fifth canto of the *Bachitar Nāṭak*. It appears directly below.

It was for the protection of the sacred thread and frontal mark that Guru Tegh Bahadur performed a tremendous deed in the Dark Age. He gave his head for the sake of holy men and uttered not a sigh of regret.   [13

For the cause of righteousness he undertook this task, giving his head yet retaining his honour. The men of God do not perform the tricks of magicians!   [14

Breaking the earthen pitcher of his body on the head of the ruler of Delhi he left for God's abode. This was the feat of Tegh Bahadur, a deed that only he could perform.   [15

Lamentation covered the world at Tegh Bahadur's death. The world cried out in despair—yet from heaven came resounding shouts of victory.[37]   [16

This particular passage is the first in Sikh literature to aver that the 'great deed' (*mahi sākā*) of stoically sacrificing one's life for the 'purpose of righteousness' (*dharam het*) ensures one a spot in paradise. Whatever the circumstances of the ninth Guru's execution, it is justified to state that in the passage above we find something entirely new to the Sikh tradition. We may suppose that in the era prior to the writing of the *Bachitar Nāṭak,* principled and courageous persons provided examples of resistance to tyrannical authority and painful suffering before unjust persecutors. Although we cannot prove this definitively with regard to Guru Arjan, there were certainly Sikh warriors under Guru Hargobind's command who are believed to have died heroically in battle, perhaps supporting the claims of their Guru and the then nascent Panth.[38] But never before had such courage been absorbed into a conceptual system which rewarded the heroic sacrifice of one's life for a righteous cause with liberation. The *Bachitar Nāṭak* may provide the first example, in writing, of this concept but we may assume that it had been prevalent for some years before the production of this text.

It seems, also, that the *Bachitar Nāṭak* attributes to the martyr a more active type of death, one perhaps more fitting at the time that the text was believed to have been composed (between 1688 and 1699). This is, of course, the Sikh sant-sipahi who perishes on the battlefield defending all that is righteous. The particular Sikh in question is Guru Gobind Singh's own cousin, Sango Shah, who falls during the Battle of Bhangani (September 1688) after having killed the Muslim warrior, Najabat Khan. We find this reference in verse 23 of the eighth canto:

The heroic warrior Sango fell, but only after he had killed Najabat Khan. The world over mourned while victorious cries were heard in heaven.[39]

That this death represented the ideal demise of the time is reinforced by a passage we find in another significant work included within the Dasam Granth, the *Chaṇḍī Charitr* (Acts of [the goddess] Chandi), also attributed to Guru Gobind Singh:

O Lord of might, grant that I may not be deterred from performing righteous deeds. That I may fight with faith and without fear against my enemies, and win. The wisdom I require is the grace to sing your glory. When my end is near may I meet death on the battlefield.[40]

Recent interpretations of this passage are far more explicit in implying here the death of a martyr. Note, for example, the English translation of J.S. Grewal and S.S. Bal of the last sentence: 'When this mortal life comes to a close [m]ay I die with the joy and courage of a martyr.'[41] Of course, the word *śahīd* cannot be found in the original for reasons we noted earlier. Nevertheless, the interpretation is justified and is probably closer to the intent of the author than his original Braj terminology.[42] As we know, the early eighteenth century was a period in which Sikhs were pitted against an intractable foe they always described as Muslim. Islam and Muslims were the enemy, and the struggle against these was described in the Sikh literature of the period as virtuous and holy. One may, therefore, assume that fighting such an enemy (constantly described as 'Muslim', whether Mughal or Afghan) in battle would have been considered more than a mere accident of war, but a martyrdom.

One can certainly assume as much since Sikh literature of the period characterizes such battles as righteous ones. Within the many compositions attributed to Guru Gobind Singh in the Dasam Granth, heroic battles, be they the Guru's own as narrated in the *Bachitar Nāṭak* or the mythological battles of the goddess Chandi and the heroes Rama and Krishan, can all be read as battles fought to restore righteousness. In these the Eternal Guru participates, rescuing the innocent from tyrants and casting down the wicked. These are, in other words, dharam yudhs and it is probably the case that the warriors slain in these would have been considered martyrs by their contemporaries. Indeed, Christian knights who fell during the Crusades and Muslim warriors killed in *jihād* (struggle) are commonly referred to as martyrs in their respective religious traditions.[43] One is thus led to assume that martyrdom in the Sikh tradition develops in response to the complex social, religious and political pressures with which the Sikhs were confronted in the late seventeenth and first half of the eighteenth centuries.

It appears that the ideals of heroism, bravery and martyrdom recorded in the *Bachitar Nāṭak* (ideals which, we may assume, were also broadcast by the dhadhis of this period) were meant to be instilled in early eighteenth-century Sikhs. After all, Guru Gobind Singh is himself believed to have prepared many of the compositions we find in the Dasam Granth for just this reason.[44] The Guru appears to make this point in the *Kriṣanāvtār* (the Descent of Krishan), a work which was completed, according to tradition, just weeks before Guru Gobind Singh was about to engage in the Battle of Bhangani, vividly described in the *Bachitar Nāṭak*.[45] At line 2491, we find this verse:

The tenth story of Bhagaut has been written in the popular language for no reason other than that of [inspiring warriors to prepare themselves for] a *dharam juddh*.[46]

After the Guru's death in 1708, it does appear that the ballads of warfare in both poetry and song were still used to rouse martial fervour. Within Sainapati's early eighteenth-century *Sri Gur-sobhā,* one finds that

When the poet sings of battle all the warriors are filled with joy.[47]

The warriors to whom Sainapati refers here are members of the newly formed Khalsa, and it is to narrating both the divine and mundane glories of this elite group and its extraordinary founder that his text is devoted.[48]

There is no doubt that during the mid-eighteenth century, the dominant Sikh identity was that of the Khalsa.[49] Sainapati writes enthusiastically on this group of warriors in *Sri Gur-sobhā* despite the fact that during the period when his text was believed to have been composed (1711 CE), the Khalsa was still considered something of an innovation by the various other communities of Punjab, both Sikh and Hindu alike.[50] To Sainapati, however, the young Khalsa was no mere innovation. It was, rather, the very sangat of those Gurus who preceded the tenth Master.[51] For this poet, therefore, those Sikhs who abstained from the Khalsa's initiatory *khaṇde dā amrit* were considered nothing more than *be-mukh,* men and women who had turned away from the Eternal Guru.[52] The Khalsa Sainapati writes of is extraordinarily valiant: a group whose members personified the heroic ideals of martial prowess, bravery, sacrifice and martyrdom, willing to go to the extreme in order to ensure that righteousness prevailed. Although the poet does not use the words 'shahid' or 'shahidi', the concept of martyrdom is easily inferred in his text. According to Sainapati, for example,

[A Sikh's] fortunes were complete by laying down one's life (*prāṇ die hui*) as a Khalsa.[53]

Prāṇ deṇā, literally 'to give up one's breath', is a compound verb we today closely associate with the asceticism so prominent within the Hindu tradition. The notion of martyrdom in this passage, however, is easily inferred despite the terminology. By being killed in the thick of battle, a Khalsa Sikh's liberation from the cycle of existence ('completing one's fortunes', as it were) was assured.

The ideal of martyrdom is more explicit in a passage relating to Shahid Udai Singh, the brother of the famous Bachittar Singh:

[Guru Gobind Singh] (*kartār*) was overjoyed [to see] Udai Singh challenge [his enemies as he entered the battlefield]. 'The mission of life is fulfilled in this way,' he said, 'by [dying in the attempt to] destroy the enemies [of the Khalsa].'[54]

Here was a Khalsa Sikh consciously choosing to fulfil the maxims found in the poetry of the tenth Guru himself, particularly the final invocation to the Creator found in the *Chaṇḍī Charitr*,[55] deliberately opting to die fighting when desperate courage was required. Khalsa Sikhs who died in this way were guaranteed passage to paradise.[56]

Unlike Sainapati's text, later works in both the gur-bilas and rahit-nama genres would present a Khalsa much different from that envisioned by the reformers of the Singh Sabha.[57] Members of this late nineteenth-century society would not, of course, concede Sainapati's view that the tenth Guru was God himself (a view which runs contrary to a passage we find in the *Bachitar Nāṭak*[58]), but they would certainly agree with the vast majority of his insights into the eighteenth-century Khalsa.[59] The Khalsa we discover in works such as Sukha Singh's *Gur-bilās Pātśāhī 10* and Koer Singh's *Gur-bilās Pātśāhī 10* and, also, Santokh Singh's *Sūraj Prakāś*, is one very much unlike that we find recorded in the annals of Tat Khalsa Sikh history. The Khalsa's particular devotion to the goddess in these texts and its role within the mystical Sikh universe are examples of those features with which the Singh Sabha would most certainly disagree.[60] Nevertheless, alongside these apparently heterodox features was a Khalsa imbued with a tremendous martial prowess, bravery and the ability to sacrifice.[61] It was these ideals which still held true for members of this later group. In these gur-bilas texts, we have the basis of the traditions that would maintain that Sikhs initiated into the Khalsa were transformed from ordinary villagers into soldier-saints (sant-sipahi).[62]

Did the ideals of the gur-bilas literature manifest themselves amongst members of the eighteenth-century Panth? This is a very difficult question to answer because of the paucity of historical evidence. As we have seen, the testimony of popular Sikh tradition is all too clear. Sikhs of this period embodied these ideals to a person producing the martyrs celebrated by today's Panth. Yet the literary evidence suggests that very few of the distinguished martyrs of Sikhism can be traced back further than the early nineteenth century.

We have, for example, no reference to Taru Singh until Ratan Singh Bhangu's *Gur-Panth Prakāś* of 1841 (see Chapter Six). The same can be said for Mehtab Singh and Gurbakhsh Singh Nihang, whose heroic martyrdoms are also first found in Bhangu's text. One of those about whom we do hear prior to the nineteenth century is Mani Singh, the story of whose execution initially appears in Kesar Singh Chhibbar's *Bansāvalī-nāmā* (1769).[63] (Chhibbar's anti-Khalsa bias, though, does not present a particularly flattering picture of the tenth Guru's noted companion. It is here, for example, that we are told that Mani Singh wished to rearrange Guru Arjan's organization of the Adi Granth, a choice which drew strong protest from the Sarbat Khalsa). To be followed, of course, by Seva Singh's *Śahīd-bilās* circa 1802.[64] These traditions regarding eighteenth-century Sikh martyrdoms must not be discounted altogether, however. During the Sikh demolition of Gurdwara Shahidganj in Lahore in 1935, for example, the skulls and bones of a large number of people were, according to Ganda Singh, found in the foundation of the structure.[65] Although it is, of course, impossible to determine whether these were the remains of Sikh martyrs, the archaeological evidence does appear to support Ganda Singh's conclusion that the gurdwara 'was raised on the dead bodies of those martyred here and its walls were literally the Minars and Pyramids of the martyrs whose skeletons and bones have now been excavated'.[66] The one eighteenth-century Sikh considered a martyr and for whom we have the most written evidence is as well the most controversial, and that is Banda Bahadur.

The Life and Death of Banda Bahadur

The Tat Khalsa viewed Banda Bahadur very ambivalently. On the one hand, Gian Singh notes in his *Tavārikh Gurū Khālsā* that Banda 'violated Sikh principles' (*sikh asūlān de virudh kamm karan*) by establishing (amongst other things) a new Sikh *jaikārā* (battle-cry). We are told that this alteration prompted Mata Sundari, the widow of Guru Gobind Singh, to issue a hukam-nama urging all Sikhs to sever their ties with Banda. This, in turn, compelled Banda to establish the Bandai Khalsa, a group of Sikhs loyal to himself alone. Other members of the Khalsa who chose to abide by the Mata ji's dictum became known as the Tat Khalsa.[67] On the other hand, however, Banda and his followers were still understood as exceptionally brave Sikhs and, in the end, acknowledged as Sikhs who had sacrificed their lives in true Khalsa fashion. For the members of the late nineteenth-century Tat Khalsa, this heroism and ability to sacrifice stemmed from the compositions of the Adi Granth and was often recounted in eighteenth-century Sikh literature.

Yet despite the implicit claims of the Singh Sabha, much of the material regarding Banda Bahadur and his companions, particularly that which narrates their final days, is of a dubious nature. There were, alas, no stenographers present to record the last words of Banda and his Sikhs, nor did these men leave behind any authenticated journals or letters allowing us to capture their state of mind. What we find in particular are references to this event in the various Persian chronicles of the day, as well as one source which makes Banda's 'martyrdom' unique in the annals of early eighteenth-century Sikh history: a letter dated 10 March 1716 from John Surman and Edward Stephenson, British officers of the East India Company, recounting their alleged observation of the execution.[68]

Although Banda himself wrote two hukam-namas to the Sikh sangats scattered throughout India, indicating in one that he and his warriors had established the *Sat-jug* or Age of Truth (*sat-jug varatāiā hai*), these extant letters were written many years before his death and say nothing about Banda's desire or that of his warriors to fight to the end.[69] Contemporary Persian accounts deal principally with Banda's various incursions and depredations, sparing no effort to vilify him and the Khalsa Sikhs under his command.[70] Yet these also make a habit of noting Sikh bravery. Persian accounts that narrate the execution of Banda Bahadur and his men, for example, all agree on the stoic composure and cheerful countenances of these Sikhs as they were led through the streets of Delhi in irons to the *qatl-gāh* (place of execution) near the Qutb Minar. In the *'Ibarat-nāmah*, Muhammad Harisi, for example, notes that Banda's 'unfortunate men' (*bad-bakhtān*) appeared happy and contented with their fate as they were paraded in front of the jeering Muslim mobs lining the lanes and streets of Delhi in early March 1716. His account continues,

Not the slightest sign of disgrace or humility was to be discerned on their faces. In fact, most of them, [as they passed along] on [their] camels, were [seen] engaged in singing songs [scil., hymns?].[71]

No doubt this paints a scene of extraordinary heroism, yet one which must be tempered by the fact that Harisi, as well as other Persian authors writing about the Sikhs in this period, highlight Sikh bravery in order to underscore the courage and daring of their Mughal captors.[72] Such Sikh heroism is also noted in later Sikh accounts of the event. But for traditional historians of the Sikh Panth, this heroism is emphasized by the belief that these Sikhs could have easily avoided their painful and imminently fatal ordeals by choosing to convert to Islam.[73] This choice, of course, amplifies the courage of these Sikhs and makes the tale of their deaths far more edifying, to say the least.

Yet, that the choice to convert to Islam would have obviated the execution seems highly implausible. From the perspective of the Mughal authorities, Sikhs in this period were rebels, bandits and thieves. According to Kamran Khan, a chronicler attached to the Mughal court, for example, Sikhs of the Khalsa were a 'misguided, impious and detested community' (*firqeh-i zallah bad mazhabān-i la'in*), attempting to bring about the end of the Mughal regime in the Punjab.[74] Although Islamic legal precedent in regard to non-believers is clear in the *sharī'a,* which maintains that non-Muslims have the choice to be either converted, subjugated, or killed, it is highly unlikely that the execution of these captive Sikhs would have been stayed even had they abandoned their faith and converted to Islam.[75] These men were engaged in *fitnah* or rebellion, an act not tolerated by any ruler.[76] The defiance of imperial authority, whether from a Muslim, Hindu, or Sikh aspiring for political power (as Banda and the Sikhs following him apparently did), was thus mercilessly crushed.[77] This was politics pure and simple. In this light, the letter written by Surman and Stephenson is not as significant as some scholars posit.[78]

But by no means is this letter negligible. In this brief dispatch, we are told of the 'remarkable patience' with which the Sikh captives underwent their ordeal. We are also told that not 'one apostatized from his new-formed religion'. It is on the basis of this last statement in particular that Ganda Singh will claim that 'life was promised to any one who would renounce his faith, but they would not prove false to their Gurus ...'[79] Indeed, this letter does seem to indicate that the choice to convert to Islam was offered to at least some of the captive Sikhs. But by no means is this as clear as later historians of the Sikhs will assert. All that the letter says is that the captive Sikhs of Banda Bahadur did not apostatize from their faith. The difference between not apostatizing and being offered the choice to do so is a crucial one in this context.

However precarious this letter, it does mention the courage of the

Sikhs. And we may assume (based also upon constant Persian testimony) that such Sikh courage was beyond reproach. That their freedom to choose to be spared a painful death by conceding to their adversary's offer (if such was made) was not. From the qazi's or imam's point of view, the choice to convert may have been offered as a part of observed convention or etiquette rather than presenting the accused with a means of escaping his or her inevitable fate. This is, however, conjecture.

Even if they were offered the choice of conversion, why should these Sikhs convert to Islam? Ultimately it would prove fruitless, as it certainly did. The evidence suggests that the Sikhs being paraded through the streets of Delhi on that fateful day were no doubt aware of their upcoming end, and perhaps cognizant of the fact that conversion to Islam would have mattered naught. With this in mind, they may well have chosen to live their final moments heroically, remaining Khalsa Sikhs, and albeit unknowingly, give to their audience a scene of heroic resistance in the face of horrific punishment. That they may have drawn their inspiration from the ideals of Guru Tegh Bahadur and Guru Gobind Singh, from the hymns of the Adi Granth or Dasam Granth (if these were in circulation), from the value of dying as Khalsa Sikhs, which we find scattered throughout the *Bachitar Nāṭak, Gur-sobhā,* or (we may assume) within the compositions of the dhadhis, is nevertheless impossible to ascertain precisely.[80] We may only speculate that since the earliest gur-bilas literature indicates that martyrdom was an ideal in this period, the Sikhs executed in Delhi in 1716 and perhaps all contemporary Sikhs may have felt these deaths warranted the status of martyrdom.

British Accounts of Sikh Sacrifice and Martyrdom

In Ganda Singh's collection of early European observations on the Sikhs, it is clear that the heroic ideals narrated in the 10 March 1716 letter were also recognized by late eighteenth- and early ninteenth-century British observers.[81] Of course, we must approach these British accounts cautiously, for at the time these men and women were writing their observations, the Sikhs were quite new to the British eye. Although some of our writers were aware of Sikhs other than those of the Khalsa,[82] the vast majority wrote on the flamboyant Sikh soldiers of the misls and, afterwards, of the Khalsa army whom they admired for their martial prowess, skilful horsemanship and 'endurance of excessive fatigue'.[83] This should elicit little surprise since army spectacle had played such an important role in all aspects of life in England during the Georgian and Regency periods, the time during which many of these British and Scottish observers were raised. The heroic image of the soldier which was virtually manufactured by the songs, cheap books, magazines and newspapers of the periods seems to have been easily applied to the Sikh soldiers of the late eighteenth and early nineteenth centuries. In other words, such identities forged in Britain were effortlessly mapped onto Punjabi Sikhs.[84] It was this initial association and Sikh support of the British during the 1857 Rebellion that would eventually see Sikhs included in George McMunn's list of Indian 'martial races' and further caricatured in A.H. Bingley's *The Sikhs*.[85]

The English traveller, George Forster, was among the first Europeans to note in print the apparent pride Sikhs had in their traditions of martial skill, courage and sacrifice. He recorded these traditions in 1782 during his then-remarkable overland journey from Bengal to Russia.[86] Published posthumously in 1798, the eleventh letter in Forster's travelogue constantly refers to Sikh skill and endurance. He implies in the passage provided below the belief that it was the Sikh ability to bear all forms of persecution (including the death of their comrades) which eventually led to ultimate Sikh victory:

[The Sikhs] were driven from the sanctuary of their religion [i.e. Harimandir Sahib], and persecuted with a rage which seemed to keep pace with the increasing strength and inveterancy of their enemy; that they boldly seized on every hold which offered support; and, by an invincible perseverance, that they ultimately rose superior in a contest with the most potent prince of his age.[87]

That Forster took this statement from an oral tradition which was communicated to him seems highly likely, despite his partial reliance on an earlier account on the Sikhs written by A.L.H. Polier which, likewise, elaborates on Sikh martial prowess and endurance.[88] The understanding of the contemporary Sikh situation we find in the above passage would have been corroborated with Forster's visual observations in regard to Sikh mettle ('[men] who evinced ... an indefatigable intrepidity'). One may, therefore, assume that by the late eighteenth century, a segment of the Sikh Panth (particularly those involved with the misls) would have been aware of this interpretation of their history.

More than two decades after Forster had penned these words, John Malcolm found his way into the Punjab to join up with Lord Lake and the British Army, then pursuing the Marathas through Ranjit Singh's domains. Following in Forster's footsteps, Malcolm was certainly a product of the Georgian period on whom the army had had a significant influence in childhood.[89] Having carried this fascination with him overseas to India, he recorded in his *Sketch of the Sikhs* (first published in 1810 but based on his 1805 observations) many of his thoughts and observations in regard to Sikh martial ability. Although Malcolm notes that he received a good deal of his information verbally from Nirmala Sikhs, he does refer to various Punjabi and Persian texts which were available to him.[90] Quoting from a 'contemporary Muhammedan author', Malcolm states:

the Sikh horsemen were seen riding, at full gallop, towards 'their favourite shrine of devotion. They were often slain in making this attempt, and sometimes taken prisoners; but they used, on such occasions, to seek, instead of avoiding, the crown of martyrdom:['] and the same authority states that [']an instance was never known of a Sikh, taken in his way to Amritsar, consenting to abjure his faith.'[91]

Malcolm, like Forster, also notes Khalsa Sikh endurance,[92] an ability which would be further lauded forty-four years later in what would be at that time the most enthusiastic of European dissertations on the Khalsa—Joseph Cunningham's *History of the Sikhs,* first published in 1849.[93]

As Malcolm had been influenced by the general nineteenth-century conception of the army back in England, so, too, was Cunningham, who chose to enlist as a soldier despite what may well have been a promising academic career in mathematics at Cambridge University.[94] Eventually finding himself in the Punjab, Cunningham spent eight years among the Sikhs, years during which he cultivated a fondness for the tradition and its adherents. His book is a testament to this. He was the first to examine a wide range of Sikh material, including both the Adi Granth and Dasam Granth, the vars of Bhai Gurdas, and the rahit-nama literature. Cunningham's enthusiasm for the Sikhs would be to his disadvantage in later years, however. Divulging information in the ninth chapter of his book that was privy only to himself and the British commanders of the Sikh campaigns of the later 1840s, Cunningham was demoted and shuttled off to Bhopal. He died in Ambala two years after completing his *History.*[95]

That Sikh courage fascinated Cunningham is beyond doubt. His enthusiastic words in regard to the bravery Khalsa soldiers displayed during the Anglo–Sikh wars is, indeed, somewhat surprising for a man who was in all respects a formal adversary of the Sikhs.[96] In his narrative of eighteenth-century Sikh history, Cunningham notes the origin of Gurdwara Shahidganj in Lahore and its association with the martyrdom of Bhai Taru Singh. His brief passage on this martyr is worth reproducing.

... Bhai Taru Singh ... was required to cut his hair and to renounce his faith; but the old companion of Guru Gobind Singh would yield neither his conscience nor the symbol of his conviction, and his real or pretended answer is preserved to the present day. The hair, the scalp and the skull, said he, have a mutual connexion; the head of man is linked with life, and he was prepared to yield his breath with cheerfulness.[97]

We will see that the passage here closely resembles one we find in Bhangu's *Gur-panth Prakāś*, despite the fact that Cunningham was unaware of this manuscript's existence. Had Bhangu's text come within his view, it seems likely that he would have included it in one of the many appendices he provides with his second edition. From this, we may infer that either Bhangu's text was being disseminated through oral tradition, particularly dhadhi and katha; or more likely, that the oral tradition on which Bhangu based his narrative was still current and popular eight years after the manuscript's apparent completion.

Dhādhīs, Chroniclers and *Gurduāre*

That oral tradition was the primary means of dissemination in the early nineteenth century is a factor that we have already discussed. It seems doubtful that many inhabitants of village Punjab would have possessed the ability to read pre-colonial Punjabi, Braj, or English Sikh literature, let alone have had access to any of it.[98] They would, of course, have had access to many 'traditional Sikh intellectuals', gianis who would disseminate Sikh teachings in the form of katha and dhadhis who would sing the ballads on which, one may assume, many of our early nineteenth-century authors based their narratives. As dhadhis wandered from village to village, Sikh heroes, martyrs and a number of other popular warriors were brought to life. We must also keep in mind that during the period of the misldars, Khalsa soldiers would come into the villages to secure *rākhī* or money and goods given in return for the protection against those who would also claim to deserve such funds.[99] These warriors, most of whom would have been members of the Punjab peasantry, may have exercised a considerable romantic fascination in their fellow Punjabi peasants, a fascination recorded in various Sikh traditions.[100]

It seems that during Sikh rule and probably before, the number of dhadhis had increased. In a period when such stress was laid on courage and martial prowess, dhadhis would have certainly been in demand. This may be inferred from the particularly high number of people who, in the 1881 census, returned themselves as minstrels.[101] This high number may reflect the considerable amount of material available with which dhadhis could work. The army of the Lahore kingdom, for instance, had fought (and was still fighting) many battles on which the dhadhis could base their enthusiastic ballads. One may also assume, moreover, that the various powerful families of what was then the Punjab would have wished their 'historic and glorious' genealogies to be put to verse.[102] The famous Sikh kavishar or poet, Bir Singh, in an early nineteenth-century work narrating the battles of Guru Gobind Singh, for example, tells his audience,

How can the poet remain silent when his Guru has been victorious on the battlefield?[103]

Although the couplet alludes to early eighteenth-century battles, it is probably more a reflection of Bir Singh's contemporary situation, the time of the Lahore Darbar.

If one were unable to hear dhadhis performing in the village, one could see them perform at a gurdwara. There were, in fact, various dhadhi jathas affiliated with particular Sikh gurdwaras. As we noted earlier, the Golden Temple, within whose confines is the Akal Takht, was one such gurdwara. According to tradition, Abdul and Natha, the two most famous dhadhis of Guru Hargobind's period, regularly sang their martial ballads here.[104] At Harimandir Sahib, such special occasions as Diwali (the Festival of Lights) and Baisakhi (the New Year's day on which the Khalsa was created) were celebrated with much fervour. Ragi jathas performed kirtan and dhadhis sang to the crowds (many of whom had come on pilgrimage) within the precincts of the Sikh temple.[105] In the light of this tradition, one may assume that a number of gurdwaras associated with a particular Sikh Guru or martyr would have also had their own dhadhis.

Not only did the rural folk of the Punjab visit these pilgrimage centres and hear such martial ballads,[106] but we are also aware of the many times that the Sikh elite would venture out to such gurdwaras or martyries and grant its incumbents a stipend in the early nineteenth century. Sohan Lal Suri, in his extraordinary Persian chronicle of the Lahore Darbar, *'Umdat-ut-Tawārīkh,* notes Maharaja Ranjit Singh's visit to Gurdwara Shahidganj in Lahore, where he gave an Ardas of 125 rupees to Bhai Kahan Singh.[107] He further records that during a visit to the Golden Temple, Maharaja Sher Singh had donated 250 rupees to 'Shahid Bunga and Jhanda Bunga and secured everlasting felicity by going round that blessed place'.[108] In another Persian chronicle of the Lahore court, the author, Ganesh Das, would proudly assert that Amritsar possessed numerous places of worship among which were included 'the *samādhs* of *shahids* and *murids*'.[109]

What shahid actually means here, however, is a matter of speculation. Our British observers often interpret shahid to mean martyr, yet there are other European as well as Punjabi accounts which will note that the shahid indicates far more than this. It is to these narratives that we now turn.

Notes

1. Parts of this chapter have appeared in my 'Martyrdom and the Sikh Tradition', in *JAOS* 117.4 (1997), pp. 623–42.

2. Garja Singh (ed.), *Śahīd-bilās (Bhāī Manī Singh) krit Sevā Singh* (Ludhiana, 1961), p. 54 (herefter *Śahīd-bilās*).

3. I.S. Gill (ed.), *Kavi Sohan jī krit Srī Gur-bilās Pātśāhī 6 Tipaṇīān Samet* (Patiala, 1968), p. 90 (hereafter *Srī Gur-bilās Pātśāhī 6*).

4. Ibid., pp. 151–2, claims that Abdul and Natha were prominent dhadhis during Guru Hargobind's period.

5. Pashaura Singh, 'The Text and Meaning of the Adi Granth', (Ph.D. dissertation, University of Toronto, 1991), pp. 64–6.

6. The Adi Granth is a testament to Guru Arjan's skill with words, melodies and poetic measures.

7. *ESC,* p. 12. For criticism of the 'Jat theory' see Jagjit Singh, *The Sikh Revolution* (New Delhi, 1981), pp. 260–81.

8. See Chapter Three.

9. K. Isfandyar, *Dabistān-i Mazāhib* I (Tehran, 1362 H./1983 CE), p. 207.

10. The relevant Persian text is found in Ganda Singh, *Guru Arjan's Martyrdom (Re-interpreted)* (Patiala, 1969), p. 10.

11. Jerome Xavier's letter of 25 September 1606 is often cited to support this tradition. We are told here that Guru Arjan 'received kicks on his face on many occasions' and that after having 'suffered so many injuries, pains and insults ... the poor Guru died'. This letter, however, provides an account presented through secondary informants. *EEAS,* p. 185. According to J.S. Grewal, *The Sikhs of the Punjab,* p. 63, 'Bhai Gurdas admires the incredible equanimity of Guru Arjan under unbearable torture ...' The verse to which Grewal alludes appears in *vār* 24:

[Like] the deer [who remains intoxicated by the sound of the hunter's bell after capture], so, too, was the Guru wholly absorbed in the contemplation of the Word of God at the time of his distress. Nothing else came into his mind.

My translation of *vār* 24:23:3 is based on the textual commentary of Vir Singh, *BG*, pp. 386–7. His interpretation of pauri 23 is based on the understanding that it deals with the martyrdom of Guru Arjan.

12. Ahmad Sirhindi, *Maktūbat-i Imām-i Rabbānī* (Lucknow, 1889), letter 193.
13. Khushwant Singh, *A History of the Sikhs* (Princeton, 1963) I, pp. 59–60; and Ganda Singh, *Guru Arjan's Martyrdom*, pp. 16–19.
14. Khushwant Singh, *A History of the Sikhs* I, p. 59.
15. See *ESC*, pp. 12–13 and A.C. Banerjee, *Guru Nanak to Guru Gobind Singh* (New Delhi, 1978), pp. 123–5.
16. Ganda Singh continues: 'And this could be no other than the *Mujaddid* [that is, Shaikh Ahmad Sirhindi whose title was *mujaddid-i alf-i thānī* or Renewer of the Second Millenium] who worked upon the mind of Emperor Jahangir through his trusted friend and admirer Shaikh Farid Bukhari ...' *Guru Arjan's Martyrdom*, pp. 8; 14–15, 18, 35–40.
17. S.S. Alvi, 'Religion and State During the Reign of Mughal Emperor Jahangir (1605–27): Nonjuristical Perspectives', in *Studia Islamica* (1987), pp. 95–119.
18. Yohanan Friedmann, *Shaykh Ahmad Sirhindī: An Outline of His Thought and a Study of His Image in the Eyes of Posterity* (Montreal, 1971), pp. 83–5.
19. This is according to J.F. Richards, *The Mughal Empire* (Cambridge, 1993), p. 97.
20. Ganda Singh; *Guru Arjan's Martyrdom*, p. 14.
21. As noted in the *Intikhāb-i Jahāngīr Shāhī* as found in H.M. Elliot and John Dowson, *The History of India as Told by its Own Historians* VI (Calcutta, 1960), pp. 449–50. The one religious group which at times found itself the focus of the emperor's wrath was the Jain community. For the apparent psychological reasons behind the emperor's occasional hostility towards the Jains see E.B. Findly, 'Jahāngir's Vow of Non-Violence', *JAOS* 107 (1987), pp. 245–56.
22. Alvi, 'Religion and State', p. 113. Based, in large part, on the claim of the *Dabistān-i Mazāhib* I, p. 207 that

After [the Guruship of] Arjan Mal, [Guru] Hargobind claimed the succession and sat in the place of his father. [Once] joined to the victorious company (lit. stirrup) of [the Emperor] Jahangir [Hargobind] was not separated [from it],

most Sikh accounts agree that Guru Hargobind and Jahangir established some kind of friendship in the later years of the emperor's reign.
23. As quoted in Alvi, 'Religion and State', pp. 114–15.
24. Ganda Singh maintains that the story of the Guru placing a saffron mark upon Khusrau's forehead was the 'simple concoction of some conspirator's fertile imagination to exploit the Emperor's emotions against the Guru'. Ganda Singh, *Guru Arjan's Martyrdom*, p. 23. See also J.S. Grewal, *The Sikhs of the Punjab*, p. 63, n. 3.
25. G.W. Bowersock, *Martyrdom & Rome* (Cambridge, 1995), p. 5.
26. Guru Nanak's *Slok vārān te vadhīk* 20, AG, p. 1412.
27. An alternative reading of this sentence appears in Sahib Singh, *Srī Gurū Granth Sāhib Darpan* IV (Jalandhar, 1963), p. 425.
28. Guru Nanak, *Rāg vadahansu alāhaṇiān* 2:2–3, AG, pp. 579–80.

Martyrdom in the Early Sikh Tradition 139

29. G.S. Talib, 'The Concept and Tradition of Martyrdom in Sikhism', in
G.S. Talib (ed.), *Guru Tegh Bahadur: Background and Supreme Sacrifice* (Patiala,
1976), pp. 191–2.
30. Guru Nanak, *Rāg vaḍahansu alāhaṇīān* 1–2, AG, pp. 579–80. For more
on the hero in Guru Nanak's *bāṇī* see his *Japjī* 37, AG, p. 8:

There [with the Realm of Grace] reside mighty heroes whose hearts are filled to
the brim with the name of Ram.

31. G.S. Talib, 'The Basis and Development of Ethical Thought in Sikhism',
in L.M. Joshi (ed.), *Sikhism* (Patiala, 1980), pp. 86–130, esp. pp. 115–16.
32. G.S. Talib, 'The Concept and Tradition of Martyrdom', p. 192. The
emphasis appears in the original.
33. G.S. Talib, *Guru Nanak: His Personality and Vision* (Delhi, 1969), p. 232,
n. 1.
34. According to Sikh tradition, for example, the tenth Guru's writings along
with copies of the Damdama Bir of the Adi Granth were lost in the Sarsa River
as the Guru and his entourage attempted to cross it during a storm. Near this spot
today stands Gurdwara Parivar Vicchora Sahib Patshahi 10.
35. According to J.F. Richards, '[In Delhi] the qazi's court tried and convicted
the Sikh leader [Guru Tegh Bahadur] for blasphemy, sentenced him to death and
carried out the execution in November, 1675.' There is no evidence to support this
assertion. J.F. Richards, *The Mughal Empire*, p. 178. S.M. Latif's *History of the
Punjab: From the Remotest Antiquity to the Present Time* (New Delhi, 1989; 1st
edn, 1889), pp. 258–60, presents an alternative understanding of the ninth Guru's
execution.
36. For the Sikh narrative see Chapter Three.
37. *Bachitar Nāṭak* 5: 14–16, *DG*, pp. 53–4.
38. The earliest reference to Guru Hargobind's armed conflicts with the
Mughals appears in the *Dabistān-i Mazāhib* I, pp. 207–8. For a contemporary
understanding of these deaths see Chapter Three.
39. *Bachitar Nāṭak* 8:23, *DG*, p. 61. Both Kahn Singh Nabha and Randhir
Singh acknowledge Sango Shah's death as martyrdom, the latter subtitling the
above verse in his notes 'Sango Shah becomes a martyr' (*sangosāh sāhīd ho
jāndā hai*). See '*Sāhsangrām*', in *MK*, p. 176; and Randhir Singh (ed.), *Sabadārath
Dasam Granth Sāhib* I (Patiala, 1985), p. 78b, n. 34.
40. *Chandī Charitr* 231, *DG*, p. 99. According to R.S. Jaggi, the *Chandī
Charitr* was written some time before 1698 at Anandpur Sahib. See '*Chandī
Charitra*', in *EoS* I, pp. 433–4.
41. J.S. Grewal and S.S. Bal, *Guru Gobind Singh* (Chandigarh, 1967), p. 208,
n. 1. Also Mona Kang, 'Concept of Martyrdom', p. 54.
42. In 1805, perhaps with this passage from the *Chandī Charitr* in mind, John
Malcolm states in regard to the Dasam Granth that 'courage is, throughout this
work, placed above every other virtue; and Govind, like Muhammad, makes
martyrdom for the faith which he taught, the shortest and most certain road to
honour in this world, and eternal happiness in the future.' John Malcolm, *Sketch
of the Sikhs* (London, 1812), p. 190.
43. Colin Morris, 'Martyrs on the Field of Battle Before and During the First
Crusade', in Diana Wood (ed.), *Martyrs and Martyrologies* (Oxford, 1993),

pp. 93–104; and Mehdi Abidi and Gary Legenhausen (ed.), *Jihad and Sahadat: Struggle and Martyrdom in Islam* (Houston, 1986).

44. Nikky Singh maintains this point in regard to the various goddess compositions in the Dasam Granth in *The Feminine Principle in the Sikh Vision of the Transcendent* (Cambridge, 1993), pp. 118–49.

45. Grewal and Bal, *Guru Gobind Singh*, pp. 74–7.

46. *Krisanāvtār* 2491, *DG*, p. 570. See also Grewal and Bal, *Guru Gobind Singh*, p. 77:

The animated description, as also the prominent place given to the battle in the Natak, would suggest that in 1697 when he wrote his autobiography, he did regard it as part of the dharam yudh for which he was sent by God.

47. Ganda Singh (ed.), *Kavi Saināpati Rachit Sri Gur-sobhā* 13:10:554 (Patiala, 1988), p. 133 (hereafter *Gur-sobhā*). The numbers represent chapter, verse within the chapter, and finally verse within the entire text. For a brief biography of Sainapati see idem, pp. 1–10.

48. Background in S.S. Hans, *A Reconstruction of Sikh History from Sikh Literature* (Jalandhar, 1988), pp. 245–50.

49. Of course, the Khalsa about which Sainapati writes is not the present-day Khalsa. For a discussion of this eighteenth-century Khalsa see *WhS*, pp. 43–61; and J.S. Grewal's *The Sikhs of the Punjab*, pp. 95–8. For background on what the term 'dominant' implies here, see Harjot Oberoi, *Construction*, pp. 76, 81, 89.

50. For example, in *Gur-sobhā* 7:30:290, p. 100, we find the following statement:

On one side resides the Khalsa, on the other the world.

The fact that the Khalsa had yet to achieve the dominance it so clearly possesses in, for example, the rahit-nama of Chaupa Singh Chhibbar, written some time between 1740 and 1765 CE, supports the traditionally believed date of Sainapati's text to my mind. (For the dates of Chaupa Singh's text see *CSRn*, p. 20, n. 66.) Some scholars posit that *Gur-sobhā* was produced in 1747 CE. W.H. McLeod notes both views in his *The Sikhs: History, Religion and Society*, p. 98. Also see S.S. Hans, *A Reconstruction*, p. 246.

51. *Gur-sobhā* 5:11:127, p. 78.

52. Ibid., 5:54:170, p. 84.

53. Ibid., 9:7:344, p. 108.

54. Ibid., 12:3:472, p. 123.

55. *Chandi Charitr* 231, *DG*, p. 99.

56. *Gur-sobhā* 12:51:520, p. 128.

57. For the rahit-nama literature see W.H. McLeod, 'The Problem of the Panjabi Rahit-namas', in S.N. Mukherjee (ed.), *India, History and Thought: Essays in Honour of A.L. Basham* (Calcutta, 1982), pp. 103–26; and *CSRn*, pp. 9–12. For the gur-bilas see S.S. Hans, 'The *Gurbilās* in the Early Nineteenth Century', in *JRH* II (1981), pp. 43–56.

58. *Bachitar Nātak* 6:31, *DG*, p. 57.

59. In the statement regarding Udai Singh's bravery (12:3:472), for example, Sainapati appropriates the word *kartār* or 'creator' to describe Guru Gobind Singh. This term was usually used to designate Akal Purakh. Background on Sainapati's

understanding of the tenth Guru appears in S.S. Hans, *A Reconstruction*, pp. 246–7. Koer Singh also believes Guru Gobind Singh to be God. See S.S. Ashok (ed.), *Gur-bilās Pātsāhī 10 krit Kuir Siṅgh* (Patiala, 1969), pp. 68, 71, 79.

60. There are many passages within these texts which underscore Guru Gobind Singh's and his Khalsa's reverence towards the goddess. See, for example, G.K. Jaggi (ed.), *Gur-bilās Pātsāhī 10 Bhāī Sukkhā Siṅgh* (Patiala, 1989), pp. 150, 158; as well as Koer Singh's *Gur-bilas Pātsāhī 10*, pp. 103, 120.

61. Sukha Singh, *Gur-bilās Pātsāhī 10*, pp. 201, 335. Also Koer Singh, *Gur-bilās Pātsāhī 10*, pp. 72–100, which narrates the Battle of Bhangani.

62. For example, Sukha Singh's *Gur-bilās Pātsāhī 10*, 8:23, p. 127.

63. According to Garja Singh, Guru Gobind Singh sent a hukam-nama to Mani Singh and his sons, dated S. 1760 (1703 CE). A copy of the hukam-namā appears across page 71 in *Sahid-bilās*. Mani Singh also figures in the Bhaṭ Vahis. Of course, these make no reference to Mani Singh's ultimate fate. *Sahīd-bilās*, pp. 31, 42.

64. P.S. Padam (ed.), *Bhāī Kesar Siṅgh Chhibbar Krit: Bansāvalī-nāmā Dasān Pātsāhīān kā* (Amritsar, 1997), pp. 159–61. For the martyrdoms of Bhais Mati Das and Sati Das see idem, pp. 118–21.

65. Gurdwara Shahidganj occupied the site where it is believed that Taru Singh and Mani Singh, as well as many of the Sikh women and children captured during the *choṭṭā ghalūghārā*, obtained martyrdom. According to popular belief, it was a mosque prior to the Sikh occupation of Lahore in 1765. See Ganda Singh, *History of the Gurdwara Shahidganj Lahore from its Origins to November 1935* (Amritsar, 1935).

66. Ganda Singh, *Gurdwara Shahidganj*, p. 27.

67. *TGK* II, pp. 71–3. The account of Banda's fall from grace appears in *PrPP*, pp. 128–39. Bhangu's interpretation of Banda may be skewed as his grandfather, the famous Mehtab Singh, may have been personally involved in the factional dispute between the Bandai Khalsa and the Tatva Khalsa.

68. The letter appears in *EEAS*, p. 188.

69. Ganda Singh (ed.), *Hukam-nāme* (Patiala, 1985), pp. 192–5.

70. Gian Singh tells us that Banda massacred Muslims indiscriminately, desecrated their mausoleums, and even went so far as to exhume the bodies of long-dead Muslim saints to defile these. *TGK* II, pp. 20–8.

71. The Persian text is taken from Ganda Singh's *Life of Banda Singh Bahadur* (Patiala, 1990), p. 182, n. 7.

72. The bias in Persian chronicles dealing with the Sikhs is noted in J.S. Grewal, *Guru Tegh Bahadur and the Persian Chroniclers* (Amritsar, 1976), pp. 13–20.

73. Ganda Singh, *Banda Singh Bahadur*, p. 185.

74. As noted in Muzaffar Alam, *The Crisis of Empire in Mughal North India: Awadh and the Punjab, 1707–1748* (New Delhi, 1987), p. 154, n. 88.

75. It is now well known that during both the Delhi Sultanate and Mughal periods, non-Muslims were judged by their own customary law in terms of marriage and inheritance. For penal infractions, however, non-Muslims were sometimes subjected to Muslim penal law. Joseph Schacht, *An Introduction to Islamic Law* (Oxford, 1964), pp. 130–3. The tortures to which Banda and some of his Sikhs were allegedly subjected may have also been meted out to other rebels of the Mughal empire, whether Muslims or 'non-believers'.

76. For *fitna* see Andre Wink, *Land and Sovereignty in India: Agrarian Society and Politics under the Eighteenth-century Maratha Svarājya* (Cambridge, 1986), pp. 23–35.

77. I have yet to come across any mention of a non-Muslim rebel in India released on a pledge to convert to Islam. Although there were Sikhs who converted to Islam to avoid execution, these Sikhs were in no way connected to the conquests and subsequent depredations of Banda and his men. Rather, they were innocent men caught up in the general purge of the 'followers of Nanak', initiated by the Mughal authorities after 1712. This purge enjoined all Hindus (especially Khatris) within the Mughal bureaucracy to shave off their beards. Muzaffar Alam, *Crisis of Empire*, p. 154.

78. Regarding this letter, Ganda Singh claims that '[it] is of great historical value to the students and scholars of history'. *EEAS*, p. 187.

79. Ganda Singh, *Banda Singh Bahadur*, p. 185.

80. J.S. Grewal does note, however, that 'the political struggle of the Singhs can be appreciated ... also as an extrapolation of the pontificate of Guru Gobind Singh'. We may assume that some of Banda's Sikhs (if not Banda himself) drew inspiration from the life and message of their Guru. J.S. Grewal, *The Sikhs of the Punjab*, p. 82.

81. *EEAS*.

82. For example, George Forster in *A Journey From Bengal to England Through the Northern Part of India, Kashmire, Afghanistan and Persia, and into Russia by the Caspian-Sea* I (London, 1798), pp. 309–10, was the first to note the *khualasah* Sikh, the non-Khalsa adherent of Gurmat. Emily Eden mentions Nihangs in *Up the Country: Letters Written to her Sister from the Upper Provinces of India* (London, 1983), pp. 230–1.

83. Forster, *A Journey* I, p. 333.

84. See S.H. Myerly, ' "The Eye Must Entrap the Mind": Army Spectacle and Paradigm in Nineteenth-Century Britain', *Journal of Social History* (1992), pp. 105–31. Particularly during the Napoleonic wars, army spectacle was, according to Myerly, 'an enormously popular free entertainment for all classes of [British] society, at a time when many traditional recreations were being suppressed'.

85. George McMunn, *The Martial Races of India* (Edinburgh, 1912; reprint, London, 1933). According to Bingley, *The Sikhs* (Patiala, 1970), p. 126:

The Jat Sikhs have always been famous for their fine physique and are surpassed by no race in India for high-bred looks, smartness and soldierly bearing. The length of limb makes them excellent marchers, and their physical activity is developed by their active habits.

86. A brief account of Forster's life and writings appears in Leslie Stephen, et al. (ed.), *The Dictionary of National Biography* VII (Oxford, 1964), p. 454.

87. Forster, *A Journey* I, pp. 327; 303, 318, 320, 323, 333.

88. Polier's account is in *EEAS*, pp. 195–7.

89. That is, according to his biographer. See Rodney Pasley's *Send Malcolm! The Life of Major-General Sir John Malcolm* (London, 1982), pp. 1–20.

90. For example, Malcolm refers to the *Giān Ratnāvalī*, the 'Dasama Padshah ka Grant'h' and the 'Adi Grant'h'. Malcolm, *Sketch*, pp. 16, 31.

91. Malcolm, *Sketch*, p. 88. Malcolm's work was originally published in

1810. The author and text he quotes is probably Ghulam Hussain, *Siyar-ul Mutā'khkhirīn.*

92. Malcolm, *Sketch,* p. 141.

93. J.D. Cunningham, *History of the Sikhs* (1st edn, 1849. Delhi, 1990).

94. Apparently, Sir Walter Scott himself had procured the young Cunningham a cadetship. See 'Cunningham, Joseph Davey', in *The Dictionary of National Biography* V, pp. 314–16 and *History of the Sikhs,* pp. xi–xiii.

95. See H.L.O. Garrett's introduction to the revised 1915 edition of Cunningham's *History of the Sikhs,* pp. v–x. Also see J.S. Grewal's *From Guru Nanak to Maharaja Ranjit Singh* (Amritsar, 1982), pp. 169–72. Problems associated with having the book reprinted during the early twentieth century are explored in S.S. Bal, 'The First Edition of J.D. Cunningham's History of the Sikhs', in *PPHC* 11 (1976), pp. 54–65.

96. Cunningham, *History,* chapter 9.

97. Ibid., p. 84.

98. According to G.W. Leitner, however, children were instructed to read 'The Gurbilas (history of the first six Gurus and of the tenth Guru)' at a traditional Gurmukhi school. See his *History of Indigenous Education in the Punjab since Annexation in 1882* (1st edn, 1882. Lahore, 1991), p. 35.

99. For discussions on the nature of *rākhī* see Indu Banga, *Agrarian System of the Sikhs* (Delhi, 1978), pp. 27–8; J.S. Grewal, *Sikh Ideology, Polity and Social Order,* pp. 95–6; Bhagat Singh, *A History of Sikh Misals* (Patiala, 1993), pp. 45–51; and Veena Sachdeva, *Polity and Economy of the Punjab During the Late Eighteenth Century* (Delhi, 1993), pp. 91–3.

100. According to tradition, on returning to his village after having joined a misl, a Sikh was greeted by the village elders and given command of the entire village. Another tradition maintains that many Khalsa 'outlaws' of the eighteenth century were given shelter in the villages. Teja Singh and Ganda Singh, *A Short History of the Sikhs* (Patiala, 1989), pp. 112–13.

101. The figure was well over 250,000, according to D.S. Johal, 'Punjabi Literature: Late Eighteenth-Early Nineteenth Century', in *JRH* IV (1983), p. 24.

102. D.S. Johal, 'Institution of Marriage in Medieval Punjabi Literature', in *PHCP* 16 (1982), p. 195, states: 'Genealogists (*bhats*) and bards (*dums* and *dhadhis*) sung praises and recited histories of the ancestors of the guests [attending the wedding ceremony] as well as of the hosts.' Also see his 'Literary Evidence on Social Structure in the Punjab (1750–1850)', *JRH* I (1980), pp. 65–6.

103. The couplet appears in Bir Singh's *Bārā Māhā Gurū Gobind Siṅgh jī kī* in P.S. Padam (ed.), *Pañjābī Bārā Māhā* (Patiala, 1959), p. 142; as noted in D.S. Johal, 'Heroic Literature in Punjabi', p. 83. Johal notes that dhadhis were also known as kavishars. See his 'Literary Evidence on Social Structure', p. 66.

104. *Srī Gur-bilās Pātśāhī 6,* pp. 151–2. As this text was produced in the early nineteenth century, it probably reflects the concerns of this period rather than seventeenth-century ones. Surjit Hans, *A Reconstruction,* pp. 270–1. The functions of personnel at the Golden Temple are discussed in R.N. Cust, *Linguistic and Oriental Essays* I (London, 1880), p. 55. This account is based on his observations of 1862.

105. Madanjit Kaur, *The Golden Temple Past and Present* (Amritsar, 1983), p. 139.

106. D.S. Johal, 'Evidence on Religion in Punjabi Literature (Late 18th and Early 19th Centuries)', in *JRH* V (1984), pp. 27–39, esp. pp. 36–7, indicates that many rural Sikhs went on pilgrimage to such places.

107. This was by no means a single occurrence. Muhammad Latif's *Lahore: Its History, Architectural Remains and Antiquities* (Lahore, 1892) mentions that Ranjit Singh 'entertained a great reverence for this Place of Martyrs [*sic*]' and that the Maharaja had often visited the gurdwara and granted land for its maintenance. This is noted in Ganda Singh, *Gurdwara Shahidganj*, pp. 40–1.

108. Sohan Lal Suri, *An Outstanding Original Source of Panjab History, Umdat-ut-Tawarikh: Chronicle of the Reign of Maharaja Ranjit Singh 1831– 1839 A.D. Daftar III, Parts (I–V)* (New Delhi, 1961) [trans. V.S. Suri], p. 466. Also, his *An Outstanding Original Source of Panjab History Umdat-ut-Tawarikh: Chronicles of the Reigns of Maharaja Kharak Singh, Kanwar Nau Nihal Singh, Maharaja Sher Singh and Maharaja Dalip Singh, 1839–1845 A.D. Daftar IV* (Chandigarh, 1972), p. 168.

109. J.S. Grewal and Indu Banga's translation of Ganesh Das' *Chār Bāgh-i Panjāb* appears as *Early Nineteenth Century Panjab* (Amritsar, 1975), p. 133.

FIVE

The Shahid's Roles in a Mystical Universe

We have set out to the city of [the martyr] Ghazi [Miyan]—
to adorn our lives, to awaken our sleeping fate;
to tell him the tale of our woes,
to procure forgiveness for all of our sins—
we have set out to the city of [the martyr] Ghazi [Miyan].[1]

A
s we noted in the introduction, the term Sikhs use to describe
their martyrs is the Arabic word *shahīd*. That the contemporary
term in Punjabi Sikh culture retains much of its Islamic background is clear. In Kahn Singh Nabha's extraordinary encyclopaedia
of Sikh knowledge, *Gur-śabad Ratanākar Mahān Koś,* there are four
entries supplied for the term *śahīd*. The first two allude to the word's
meaning in the Qur'ān, ('evidence', 'testimony'), or the one who testifies (the 'witness').[2] The third entry is similar to definitions found in
the Hadith literature and Islamic theological texts, warriors who
have been killed while battling in a righteous war. Of course, it is
the Sikh warrior whom Kahn Singh has in mind as the term for
righteous war he appropriates is not jihad (Ar: 'struggle') but dharam
yudh.[3] And the last definition (particular to the Punjab and the Sikhs)
notes that the term once described a member of the Shahid misl, the
group believed to have been formed by Baba Dip Singh in the early
eighteenth century.

While the fourth entry is quite clear and needs no further elaboration, the first three of these definitions are not particularly specific.[4] What, for example, is classified as a dharam yudh? Moreover, to what kind of testimony do the first two entries refer? Let us use the above entries as a basis and turn to other martyr-related definitions in the *MK* in the attempt to make these definitions less vague.

In Chapter Three, we noted the many non-violent seventeenth- and eighteenth-century Sikhs who were captured by the Mughals and subsequently executed for choosing not to embrace Islam. It is clear that these men did not fall in battle. Can Kahn Singh's definition make room for these Sikhs? Yes it can, for just below his entry for shahid is the definition of *sahīdī* or martyrdom. Here, these non-violent Sikhs are clearly implied in the third sentence:

Shahidi: The act of sacrificing one's life for the purpose of dharam.[5]

We will have more to say about dharam later. For now, we are aware that this entry has much in common with Kahn Singh's third definition for shahid. The fact that this Sikh does not specifically die in battle, however, leads us to assume that the Sikhs who peacefully sought martyrdom are also covered by the first two categories of the shahid definition. Kahn Singh's entry for the famous Bhai Taru Singh, a Sikh who is believed to have calmly submitted himself to the executioner after having refused to convert to Islam, is a case in point. Briefly noting the history of this Sikh *dharam-vīr* and the events which led to his arrest, Kahn Singh then explains:

When [Taru Singh] refused to accept Islam [as his faith] the executioner scraped off the top of Bhai Sahib's skull—from which grew the sacred kes [of every true Sikh]—with a cobbler's knife. Despite this, Taru Singh ji kept on reciting [Guru Nanak's] Japu[ji] Sahib in a tranquil manner. He obtained martyrdom (*sahīdī pāī*) on 23 Assu S. 1802 [October 1745 CE].[6]

By describing his death as that of the shahid, Kahn Singh implies that Taru Singh is understood in the same way that many Muslim martyrs in post-Quranic Islamic understandings are apprehended, a witness to the greatest truth (in this case, the teachings of the Sikh Gurus), sealing his testimony with his blood. Other Sikhs in this category include Gurus Arjan and Tegh Bahadur; Bhais Mati Das, Sati Das and Dayal Das; the younger sahib-zade; Bhai Mani Singh; and many of the other Sikhs mentioned earlier.[7]

This brings us to the third entry noted above, the warrior who has fallen in a dharam yudh. We asked earlier what classifies as a dharam yudh in Kahn Singh's entry for shahid. Our author defines it as follows:

(1) A war which is fought while keeping the principles of dharam foremost [in one's mind and heart]. A war in which deception, betrayal and false-hoods are not used; (2) A war fought in order to protect the principles of dharam.[8]

Such a definition does not make the concept of dharam yudh any less vague. Clearly it is a war, but attempting to interpret what Kahn Singh means by the 'principles of dharam' is by no means effortless. Indeed, the word dharam is one which defies simple translation. Kahn Singh nevertheless makes the attempt. In his definition of dharam, he includes concepts such as 'pure principles' (*pavitr niyam*); religion/orthopraxy (*mazhabi/din*); customs and practices (*rivāz, rasam*); the 'embodiment of virtue' (*punyarūp*); duty (*faraz*); character (*śubhāv*); good works (*śubh karam*), and justice (*insāf*).[9] It may be that here, Kahn Singh is indicating the context-sensitive nature of dharam. For the most part, the Sikh understanding of dharam is quite similar to the dharma concept we find in the Hindu tradition. As A.K. Ramanujan has aptly demonstrated, within the Hindu tradition dharma is relative to each stage of life, to each class, to each given nature, and to whether one is in extremity or not.[10] But this point notwithstanding, what Kahn Singh implies in his entry for dharam is that the combination of all the ideas he includes collectively capture what it means. By noting these various nuances, we may come to an approximation with the English word righteousness, the term we will continue to use to denote dharam. It is in upholding righteousness, therefore, that the Sikhs who were believed martyred without resorting to the sword died. Kahn Singh implies, therefore, that a dharam yudh is a war which safeguards all those ideals that a community should treasure.

Battles such as that at Bhangani, then, would easily fit into Kahn Singh's definition of dharam yudh, despite the fact that the battle is not labelled as such in the *MK*.[11] As we saw in the third chapter, within Tat Khalsa historiography the Mughal empire of the eighteenth century was built upon bigotry and tyranny, a government whose policies and actions encouraged oppression. The many hill rajas with whom the sixth and the tenth Gurus fought are also understood in this light. All Sikhs who took up arms against these powers are thus shown to fight in an attempt to restore the righteousness the governors and minions of these regimes were attempting to subvert.[12] Clearly, Kahn Singh considers these battles dharam yudhs, as his entry for Chamkaur Sahib implies.[13]

In the definition of dharam yudh, however, there is much room for interpretation. Ranjit Singh's battles of territorial expansion, for example, are also understood as dharam yudhs since the Sikhs who fell in these campaigns are considered shahids. The most famous case in this regard is Akali Phula Singh, who was struck down while fighting in the Battle of Naushera (March 1823 CE) after he and his Akali jatha secured a miraculous victory for the heavily battered Khalsa.[14] Interestingly, Kahn Singh applies the term 'shahid' to the Sikh soldiers of the British army who fell while defending the fort of Saragarhi in the Samana Hills in 1897. Again, he does not specifically refer to this skirmish as a dharam yudh, yet the altercation would certainly fit his definition above as easily as the many battles of the eighteenth century.[15] For Kahn Singh, courageously fighting to the last man to maintain a government that ensured Sikhs the right to practise their faith in good conscience would be, one may assume, protecting the principles of righteousness. With this in mind, it comes as no surprise that the term 'shahid' is often applied to the Sikh soldiers killed in the various British and later Indo–Pakistani conflicts. Indeed, Kahn Singh was more than willing to fit the Sikhs of Saragarhi into his definition of shahid.[16]

To Kahn Singh, therefore, the Sikh shahid appears very much like the one defined in the introduction—a Sikh who dies heroically in the defence, maintenance, or establishment of dharam. A Sikh who, despite the threat of an imminent and painful death, continues to bear testimony to the truth, remaining steadfast in the determination to be true to the faith and ignoring the opportunity to be released from such a trial by abjuring his or her religion.[17]

Although Kahn Singh began compiling the *MK* in 1912 and had completed it as early as 1926, it was not until 1930 that the work was published.[18] By this time, thanks in large part to the overall success of the Gurdwara Reform Movement, the Singh Sabha interpretation of Sikh tradition had become by far the dominant view of the Sikhs and Sikhism. As a product of this movement's premier twentieth-century ideologue, the *MK* communicates Tat Khalsa ideals and aspirations. In his brief passage dealing with the eighteenth-century rahit-nama of Chaupa Singh Chhibbar, for example, Kahn Singh simply notes that the contemporary manuscript had been corrupted by ignorant Sikhs, a standard Tat Khalsa tactic in attempting to explain elements of the Sikh past which did not measure up to their interpretation of the tradition.[19] Despite his sympathy towards the more belligerent and extreme segments of the Panth, in particular the Panch Khalsa Diwan and its energetic secretary, Teja Singh, of Bhasaur, Kahn Singh's views on Sikh history and religion provide later historians of the Sikhs with the standard interpretation of the Sikh tradition.[20] A Tat Khalsa scholar of the highest calibre, Kahn Singh's works, particularly the *MK*, remain unsurpassed to this day. Indeed, when confronted with difficulties in producing his six-volume work on the Sikh religion, it was to Kahn Singh that M.A. Macauliffe would turn for both words of encouragement and words of criticism. One may assume that the 1909 publication is as much a product of Kahn Singh as it is of Macauliffe.[21]

It comes as no surprise, therefore, that in the attempt to seek a summary definition for the terms 'martyr' and 'martyrdom' in the Sikh tradition, it is often to the *MK* that later writers refer, under the assumption that it is this same definition unchanged throughout the years which has been widely understood amongst the Sikhs over the past five centuries.[22] This is, in other words, the only meaning that the Gurus, their contemporaries and post-eighteenth-century Sikhs applied to the term 'shahid'.

As we have already observed, the definition we find in the early twentieth century was also current in the period prior to the Tat Khalsa. So, too, were there Sikh authors before the mid-nineteenth century who interpreted the term 'shahid' primarily as a witness to the truth with one's life. In his much-neglected early nineteenth-century text, *Śahīd-bilās,* for example, Seva Singh Kaushish (who was, as we have seen, the first Sikh author to employ the word 'shahid' to describe Sikh martyrs) uses the term to denote just such a witness. In reference to the tenth Guru's mother and four sons, for example, he claims that:

The four sons of Guru Gobind Singh along with Mata [Gujari] died glorious deaths as martyrs. They departed this world filled with [complete] faith in the Guru.[23]

As we noted in the introduction, it is clear that the shahid which Seva Singh understood these semi-legendary figures to be is the martyr who gives his or her life for his or her faith. A near-contemporary text in which the term 'shahid' appears far more often than it does within Seva Singh's martyrology is Ratan Singh Bhangu's renowned *Gur-panth Prakās* (1841). We will have much more to say about Bhangu in the next chapter. For now, however, we can note that the numerous appearances of the term 'shahid' in *Gur-panth Prakās* also seem to advocate an understanding of the shahid similar to that of Seva Singh.

Yet in Bhangu's text, there are instances where the term 'shahid' implies far more than the pious witness to Sikhism's glory. Not only is it Guru Tegh Bahadur's martyrdom which leads to the decay of the Mughal empire—one of the principal statements for which J.S. Grewal credits Bhangu with evolving a 'metaphysics of martyrdom'[24]—but the famous Sikh martyr, Gurbakhsh Singh Nihang, is reincarnated as Maharaja Ranjit Singh, according to the text.[25] Such passages, then, allow us to question the character of the shahid permeating Bhangu's text. This is clearly required as within the majority of the literature produced in the nineteenth and early twentieth centuries in regard to the Punjab and its people, and in accounts which allegedly deal with contemporary Sikh participation in popular religion, it becomes clear that the term 'shahid' was and is far less exclusive than Kahn Singh's *MK* would suggest. As we will see, the category 'shahid' which we find in Kahn Singh's famous encyclopaedia, like many elements in what we today define as Sikhism, is a Singh Sabha construct.

A typical indication of this is that although Kahn Singh elaborates on how one becomes a shahid in the Sikh faith, he fails to mention how shahids are perceived by the general Sikh populace. He does state that memorials to Sikh martyrs exist, proudly noting at one point that *sikh de annat śahīd-gañj han*[26] (the Sikhs possess an infinite number of martyries). He also records that there are sacred days set aside in the Sikh calendar in memory of Sikh shahids, on which ritual feasts and the distribution of *karāh prasād* takes place in the langars of various gurdwara-martyries.[27] He does not, however, allude to what occurs during these festivals or the type of piety encountered at the various Sikh martyries. Of course, we may assume that the new austere, elite sub-culture which the Tat Khalsa represented would have perceived these Sikh martyrs as revered figures whose sacrifice for the Panth should be remembered and extolled. The large number of martyrologies issued under the auspices of the Singh Sabha and the CKD highlight this perception,[28] as does Kahn Singh's conspicuous silence in regard to popular martyrolatry, a form of piety with which the Tat Khalsa would have vehemently disagreed.[29] For the many Sikhs whose understanding of Sikhism the Tat Khalsa was attempting to dispel, however, shahids were understood as far more than the revered men and women of the Panth who had given their lives in the cause of righteousness. These Sikhs, who had invariably met an untimely and often violent, bloody death, had their place within the vast pantheon of benevolent and malign beings existing in the general framework of Indic culture.

The remainder of this chapter, therefore, will be concerned with what appears to be the popular nineteenth-century Sikh understanding of martyrs. We must pause here, however, to note that despite the Tat Khalsa's selective definition of the Punjabi term for martyr, there are many historians who suggest that the notion of the shahid, when applied to Sikhs, was imbued with a further nuance, an intent on the part of many Sikh shahids not shared by the martyrs of other religious traditions. According to G.S. Talib, for example, the term 'shahid' acquired a 'new and extended significance' under the Sikh Panth.[30] How he came to this conclusion is clear. Note, for example, the words of Mona Kang:

Sikhs had gone one step further [than the martyrs of other religious traditions in] that they died for principles which are universally acknowledged and applicable. The chief characteristics of these martyrdoms is that they [were] achieved not only for freedom of conscience or freedom of worship, but also for saving [the non-Muslim] communities [of India] from extinction. The martyrdom of the ninth Sikh Guru, Tegh Bahadur, stands alone unparalleled as a glorious example in this respect.[31]

Here, it is explicit that this conclusion is based on the contemporary understanding of the ninth Guru's martyrdom, the key point of which is in this regard the belief (one very common in later Sikh historiography) that the Guru died for the benefit of a community other than his own, the Hindu community of Kashmir.

Apart from the fact that 'principles' are constructs which are usually specific to their time and environment, there are two problems with the above interpretation of the Guru's martyrdom. The first is the fact that it underscores the Tat Khalsa view that the categories 'Sikh' and 'Hindu' were, before the Lahore kingdom, neither problematic nor ambiguous. These were categories, as far as the Tat Khalsa was concerned, which had possessed definite, clear-cut boundaries. Hindus of the period may well have crossed these boundaries from time to time, venerating the Sikh Gurus and undertaking pilgrimages to Harimandir Sahib or Goindwal, for example. Sikhs, however, would never venture into a terrain the Tat Khalsa labelled 'Hindu' and deemed superstitious, a terrain in which the worship of the numerous gods and goddesses of the Hindu pantheon or the propitiation of long-dead ancestors was common. As present-day scholars have aptly demonstrated, this interpretation is clearly a powerful myth, one firmly lodged within and perpetuated by the Tat Khalsa discourse.[32]

The second problem stems from the first. For this, we must refer to the earliest literature on the execution of the ninth Guru. Here, we find that the Tat Khalsa interpretation of the Guru's death is not borne out by written evidence, a fact to which one contemporary Sikh author seems to allude.[33] As we noted earlier, the first source to mention the martyrdom of Guru Tegh Bahadur is the text commonly attributed to his son, Guru Gobind Singh, the *Bachitar Nātak*. Inevitably, it is to this particular passage in the *Bachitar Nātak* that all historians refer when dealing with the ninth Guru's martyrdom. We present it directly below.

It was for the protection of the sacred thread and the frontal mark that [Guru Tegh Bahadur] performed a great deed in the Dark Age.[34]

Yet, as we examine this passage closely, we find no reason to maintain that the Guru died according to the contemporary Tat Khalsa understanding. The Tat Khalsa arrives at this interpretation through a simple syllogism. According to this view, the Guru sacrificed his life for the Hindu community because the items mentioned in the passage above and in all the earliest literature, the sacred thread (*janeū*) and frontal mark (*tilak*), were not recognized as religious emblems by the Sikhs but by the Hindus.[35] This notion is emphasized in English translations of the passage by including the pronoun 'their' before the terms to imply that these symbols had no part in the Guru's community.[36] To assume that the sacred thread and the frontal mark were not a part of the Sikh religious culture in which the author of the *Bachitar Nātak* was raised is an understanding clearly rooted in later Tat Khalsa thinking.[37]

What does the passage therefore imply? To answer this, we must note that the Dasam Granth in which the *Bachitar Nātak* appears has always been a very problematic text for those who follow the Tat Khalsa interpretation of Sikh tradition. Not only are the very origins of this text steeped in mystery, but to this day the controversy over whether the Dasam Granth shares the same status as the Adi Granth (that is as Guru Granth) continues to prevail.[38] With its massive sections devoted to the legends of Hindu gods and goddesses, along with its Puranic content and its folk tales, it takes considerable skill at interpretation and exegesis to bring it in line with later Tat Khalsa thought.[39] This endeavour is academic, however. As Harjot Oberoi's latest research maintains, the Dasam Granth is far more closely aligned with the thought of the Sanatan Sikh tradition, the tradition which the Tat Khalsa successfully displaced in the early to mid-twentieth century. This was a tradition which effortlessly mixed religious texts, theologies and social practices to form what Oberoi calls, after Levi-Strauss, a *bricolage:* an assembly of heterogeneous cultural elements and materials.[40] For Oberoi, the Dasam Granth becomes a paradigm for the entire religious culture of the Sanatan Sikhs, men and women who were as much at home in Haridwar as they were in Amritsar, who would sport janeus and unshorn hair, acknowledging both with a similar reverence. In other words, the text 'powerfully underwrote the diversity of religious identities singularly encompassed by Sanatan religious culture'.[41]

This incredible diversity is also a feature of the literature of the gur-bilas genre. Here, we not only find Sikhs propitiating the Devi, the special patron of the Khalsa, but we witness Guru Gobind Singh himself sacrificing 125,000 Sikhs to the goddess to ensure the creation of this elite, warrior band.[42] In the light of this, we may, therefore, assume that the sacred threads, weighing some 50 kilograms (which the Mughals seized), mentioned in the gur-bilas texts,[43] as well as the tilak and janeu we find in the Dasam Granth were indeed a part of the Sanatan and thus, Sikh *episteme* (Oberoi's term) of the eighteenth and nineteenth centuries. Strong support for this conclusion is found in the lengthiest of the gur-bilas texts, *Sri Gurpratāp Sūraj Granth* (commonly known as *Sūraj Prakāś*), completed in 1844 by the famous Nirmala Sikh scholar, Santokh Singh. Clearly placed within the Sanatan Sikh tradition, the version of the ninth Guru's martyrdom we find in *Sūraj Prakāś* has Guru Tegh Bahadur himself resoundingly state *dharam ham hindū* (ours is the Hindu faith).[44]

All this, of course, does not imply that the ninth Guru did not die the death of a martyr. The earliest evidence is clear on the fact that he did, and that he was understood to be a martyr by the Sikhs of the eighteenth century. The attempt above is simply to dispel the Tat

Khalsa notion that the community for which the Guru died was a different one from his own. It seems that the 'extended significance' of the term 'shahid' as it enters the Sikh fold, mentioned by G.S. Talib and implied in Kang's dissertation, is a Singh Sabha interpretation whose roots may be found in the thought of the European enlightenment, particularly the utilitarianism of the John Stewart Mill variety. As one may infer, this interpretation fits very well under the modern rubric of 'human rights', particularly when one considers that the current Singh Sabha understanding maintains that the Guru offered his life for another's right to practise a religion with which Guru Tegh Bahadur himself personally disagreed. The Tat Khalsa interpretation of the Guru's death underscores the inalienable right of all individuals to worship in good conscience, a belief (we are often told) very much in line with the charter of human rights designed by the United Nations.[45]

Sahīd-Parasti (Martyrolatry)

We may now return to the task of elaborating what the shahid signified in the Punjabi Sikh culture prior to the early twentieth century. For our purposes, the enduring silence we today detect in regard to Sikh participation in popular religion,[46] in which sahīd-parasti or sahīd-pūjā (martyrolatry) would certainly figure, ensures that our task will not be an easy one. Such difficulty is exacerbated by the nature of the majority of the sources we shall utilize. The primary accounts are records prepared by the British Government in India and its various officers, particularly ethnographies and travelogues among which we include the three-volume *Glossary of the Tribes and Castes of the Punjab and North-West Frontier Province*. All these texts produced by the agents of colonialism are, of course, very problematic, the last, in particular, belonging to a genre that Ronald Inden terms 'tomes of alphabetized empiricism'.[47] Despite such powerful claims, these texts are useful if read critically. As Oberoi cautions, one must view these through the 'hermeneutics of suspicion', a hypercritical reading of the text firmly fixed in scepticism.[48] Our second source must also be read critically. These are early nineteenth-century Gurmukhi texts. Though very few in number, these do allow us to buttress depictions of the shahid found in the various ethnographies.

Oberoi has demonstrated that diatribes against Sikh participation in popular religion which appear in many Singh Sabha tracts and newspapers also allow one to reconstruct nineteenth-century Sikh piety. Unfortunately, there exists no Singh Sabha tract which attempts to dismiss what was probably the common Sikh conception of the shahid in this period (that is, the shahid which appears in the ethnographic and Gurmukhi literature noted above). Such a deficiency should elicit little surprise as invectives against the shahid, in particular, would have been counterproductive to the Singh Sabha project. After all, shahids and shahidi were some of the confirmed features of pre–Singh Sabha Sikh tradition that, as we shall see, were profoundly utilized by the later reform movement. Singh Sabha intellectuals probably recognized that these features could be modified and amplified in certain respects.

We should finally note that the attempt to engage and interrogate the evident silences regarding Sikh participation in popular religion, in which we include martyrolatry, is met with a great degree of hostility from many Sikhs today,[49] a factor which is clearly stemming the course of further research into Sikhism in the Punjab and abroad. The partial reason for such distrust lies in the belief shared by many Sikhs that scholarship is just one other force utilized by the Government of India in the attempt to destabilize corporate Sikh identity.[50]

Despite this hostility, Oberoi has managed to skilfully re-weave the tapestry of pre–Singh Sabha Punjabi Sikh culture, presenting us with what may have been (and for many Sikhs may still be) the 'enchanted' or mystical Sikh universe, a cosmos in which dwell benign and malevolent deities, miracle saints, the spirits of ancestors, omens, charms and other elements that the enlightenment rationale of the Tat Khalsa was unable and unwilling to comprehend.[51] The sources into which Oberoi taps, however, only allow him to construct a composite picture of Sikh popular religion rather than a totally realistic one. Our sources also provide a composite rather than genuine picture of the shahid in this period. This is because understandings of this entity tend to differ from district to district, region to region, and perhaps even village to village. Nevertheless, we do perceive one sure commonality amongst the vast majority of these accounts dealing with the shahid—that in the nineteenth century, the beings labelled shahid were considered forces greater than the heroic warriors for the faith who sealed their testimony with their lives.

As the Punjab was primarily an agrarian society based on the production of peasant households from time immemorial to the nineteenth century, we may conclude that the Sikhism of this period was distinguished by the particular brand of religious experience found in peasant societies. Delineating all the features of this experience is a formidable task. Oberoi makes the attempt by outlining the four major characteristics of this religious tradition: the absence of scripture, the participation of those residing in the rural tract, a focus on pragmatic results, and the possession of its own cultural agents. He also notes that any pious peasant actually concerned with the ultimate reality laid out in scripture could emigrate to areas outside his or her locality and 'connect with any of the universal religions'.[52] What is relevant for our purpose is the third feature, the fact that peasant religion was not as concerned with explaining fundamental reality as with the pragmatic benefit which could be derived by manipulating this reality to the advantage of its constituents. This was a terrain where peasants would propitiate beings to ensure that the calamities they brought down would pass over them and reside elsewhere, where they sought the intercession of spirits in order to gain rewards in their day-to-day existence, and where a pilgrimage to the shrine of a miracle saint was undertaken to procure the saint's *baraka* or blessing, an elixir to lepers and other afflicted peasants, as well as a powerful ally against any form of disaster they may encounter.[53]

Among the most popular saints' shrines to which the pilgrimage traffic was directed in the Punjab were the sites of Sakhi Sarwar, Baba Farid Shakarganj, Khwaja Khizr and Gugga Pir. Of these saints, only Gugga Pir is affiliated with the so-called great tradition of Hinduism; the rest are usually referred to as Muslim pirs. Along with devotees from the members of the religions with which these saints were traditionally associated, they also counted among their votaries the adherents of the other two major traditions in the Punjab, Sikhs, and Muslims or Hindus, whatever the case be. In a world in which plague, famines and smallpox raged, and in which unexplainable behaviour was understood as the possession of malignant ghosts, peasants were not usually particular about whom they sought divine intercession from or to whom their worship was directed.[54]

It was not religious affiliation which attracted people to these shrines, but the various intercessionary, curative and preventative powers which the miracle saints and their shrines possessed. To ensure that one's passage into the next world would come easily, all one need do is walk through the door of Baba Farid's dargah in Pak

Pattan during the festival commemorating his death.[55] To avoid encountering snakes, one would worship Gugga Pir in the months of August and September, or travel to his shrine in Multan to seek cures for leprosy, blindness and barrenness. The shrine of Sakhi Sarwar was also sought out to cure many of these maladies. A visit to it, moreover, was encouraged if one wished to rid oneself of the malevolent spirits which often took possession of the human body.[56]

As the saints above are not particularly disposed to one group or another, so, too, are the martyrs of the Punjab who are sought out and venerated by all Punjabis, willing to aid any who venerate them.[57] Both Muslim and Sikh martyrs were venerated by all groups. The shrine of the Sikh martyr, Akali Phula Singh, in Naushera, for example, was an object of pilgrimage for Sikhs, Hindus and Muslims, despite the fact that the Akali Baba's fierce cruelty towards Muslims, in particular, was legendary at one point.[58] According to Denzil Ibbetson, furthermore, a shrine in Jalandhar district believed to have been erected in memory of Muslim martyrs was, in fact, the shrine of Sikhs who had died in battle.[59] Examples such as these were common in nineteenth-century Punjab. Indeed, the many shrines containing the bodies and relics of the ghazi-shahids (warrior-martyrs) believed killed in the battles following the early Muslim incursions into India were worshipped by the very people whom these warriors sought to destroy while alive.[60] The most renowned of these Muslim shahids is Sayyid Salar Masud Ghazi, popularly known as Ghazi Miyan and considered the first Muslim to achieve a martyr's death in India. According to tradition, this venerated soldier was the nephew of Mahmud of Ghazna and is often noted as one of the celebrated Panch Pirs, the five Muslim saints known throughout northern India.[61]

Ethnographies which mention Ghazi Miyan indicate that he was a historical person.[62] As with many sainted dead, however, there are numerous competing stories concerning his life and death which have been handed down by oral tradition. The standard narrative runs as follows. Ghazi Miyan was born in 1014 CE (401 H.) and began his military career in 1030 at the age of sixteen, by joining his uncle's expedition from Ghazna over the mountains into the Punjab. Having pushed his way through Lahore, Delhi and Meerut, the young Salar Masud finally halted in Awadh. In 1033 (423 H.), he received orders to storm the villages surrounding Bahraich in the north and proceeded to do so. Having set up camp here prior to the attack, he sat underneath a tree within sight of a temple dedicated to Mahadev as the god of the sun. It was here that the young soldier stated that he would settle in Bahraich after the idol was removed. The battle commenced and raged on for days. Although the forces of Islam would see victory, it would come at a terrible price. Pushed back to the edge of the Kosala river, a vast number of the young officer's faithful companions were killed. Nor was the valiant Masud spared during the melee. Caught by a powerful blow in 424 H. (1034 CE), the Ghazi's head was severed from his body. Miraculously, the head continued to roll along the ground for a considerable distance. Ensuring that the Ghazi's wishes were fulfilled, the surviving Muslim victors reunited head and trunk and buried him at the spot marked by the Hindu shrine to Mahadev.[63]

Although tradition is clear that as a human being, Ghazi Miyan sedulously attempted to kill those whom he considered idol-worshippers, his major tomb along with his many shrines throughout northern India (two of which stand in Gorakhpur and Bhadohi) are visited by as many Hindus as Muslims. Of course, the belief that the Ghazi's resting place was a site previously made sacred by a Hindu shrine seemed to ensure that the power of the shrine to Mahadev would now be parcelled out by the benevolent Ghazi. Indeed, we note that Shiva as Mahadev shared many of the attributes noted of Ghazi Miyan. Both powerful and wrathful, as well as generous and bountiful, these two beings were known to grant boons to their pious devotees.[64]

Such knowledge is noted in W.H. Sleeman's famous mid-nineteenth-century travelogue. In his conversations with various learned Hindus in Awadh (Oudh) at the end of 1849, Sleeman was told that God allowed Salar Masud and other Muslims to invade India as punishment for 'Hindu transgressions'. Sleeman's informants imply that Ghazi Miyan was the instrument of God's vengeance, and the Hindu offerings made at his shrine a form of propitiation to this divine scourge to ensure that such depredations never again transpired.[65] Sleeman knew that this was not necessarily the opinion of all Hindus. He notes, as well, a more popular interpretation for the shrine's sacred status.

The mass think that the old man [Ghazi Miyan] must still have a good deal of interest in heaven, which he may be induced to exercise in their favour, by suitable offerings and personal applications to his shrine.[66]

The time to propitiate Ghazi Miyan was during the rite which commemorates his death, known as the *biāh* (also *viāh*) or 'marriage', which at once suggests the great *'ūrs* festivals ('marriage [to God]') conducted at the dargahs of famous Sufi pirs throughout India and Central Asia on the traditional date of the Sufi's death.[67] At Ghazi Miyan's festival, which is annually celebrated throughout India in the month of Jeth (May–June), many groups approach the shrine carrying a standard of either red (the colour of brides) or green (the colour of Islam), possibly in the attempt to recreate the battle which had claimed the saint's life, according to one source.[68] Coming into contact with the shrine and the saint's baraka, the banners become sacralized. If the wish of the carrier was fulfilled, the banner remained at the shrine. If not, the banner was taken back to the village at which it originated to become an object of sacred power and, inevitably, one of veneration. At this festival during the nineteenth century and before, a long spear was paraded about on top of which was placed a wig representing the martyr's head.[69]

The belief that the Ghazi's head kept on rolling after being severed is an example of his *karāmat* or miraculous power, which may explain, as Sleeman notes, why both Muslims and Hindus revered the Ghazi. Through the veneration of martyrs like Ghazi Miyan, worshippers would attempt to harness in life the supernatural power which these martyrs exhibited in death. By coming into contact with the Ghazi's karamat, it was believed that the pious would be able to overcome both ailments and the many problems they encountered on an almost daily basis. To establish such contact, many pilgrims would suspend themselves from trees close to the shrine, tying ropes to their ankles, hands and necks.[70] One may assume that this form of self-mortification would demonstrate a heightened piety and thus assure those undergoing the rite of the saint's good fortune.

We are indeed fortunate to possess a few eyewitness accounts of the festival in Bahraich. Writing in the early twentieth century, sixty or so years after Sleeman's arduous journey, the missionary, N.L. Rockey, describes the biah with no small amount of disdain. Indicating that the festival was on the whole very lively and joyous ('little differing from the hilarity of Israel's festivals and the dancing of David before the ark ... even the phonograph was evident on the grounds!'), he pauses to note that

it was not a scene of unalloyed cheer. There was a sadder side. There were blind people there, and many with sore eyes and failing sight who crowded to the front, wild to touch the tomb, and, perchance, if 'God willed it', to receive their sight again. Passing around beyond the wall, shut without, and wading a ditch or pool that came from the great well within, I saw crowds of lepers and heard them shouting and wailing for cleansing. The sight was sickening, and so revolting that I will hardly go there again. My heart was sore at their disappointment. They had come weary miles on foot, some had perhaps fallen on the way. Legends have been told them in their misery that people had been healed through the virtue of the Sayyid Salar saint, so they had come.[71]

Despite Rockey's disparaging comments, the belief in the power of the Ghazi's shrine to heal afflictions is clear here.

In Islamic hagiography, the belief that such power stems from karamat is a common assumption. Here, there is often mention of the saint's ability to perform miracles, whether that saint is alive or dead.[72] For the moment, the key point on which we shall focus in the narrative of Ghazi Miyan is the theme of severing and dismemberment. A notion implied in the primary ethnography of Punjab of the late nineteenth century is important in this regard: the miraculous power the Ghazi and the majority of Muslim martyrs both exhibit and are willing to share among their devotees is, in fact, a form of *śakti*, the dynamic female power of the universe embodied in the goddess.[73] This point is well taken since martyrs like Akali Phula Singh and Ghazi Miyan and goddesses such as Kali and Durga are associated with blood-taking and violence, as well as with cleansing diseases and infirmities. These martyrs thus seem to tap into a tradition of goddess worship which is deeply rooted in the Hindu Puranas, particularly the text which appears in the *Markandeya Purāṇa*, the *Devī-māhātmya*, the stories of which are very common in popular Punjabi culture.[74] These stories, of course, are also a part of Sikh culture as we find versions of them in the Dasam Granth attributed to Guru Gobind Singh.

The major traditions we find coming together and expressed in the beheaded martyr are those of Kali, the blood-drinking form of the goddess; Durga, the slayer of the buffalo-demon, Mahisasur; and perhaps (as Richard Temple notes), the Hindu and Buddhist tantric goddess, Chinnamasta or Chinamunda (the one with severed head), whose iconography depicts a woman with her severed head in the left hand and a sword in her right, from whose neck gush forth streams of blood.[75] Such images of blood, terror, battle and the destruction of enemies are, in fact, common to the cults of both groups. The fact that devotees of various martyrs often sacrificed animals at the shrines of these shahids, for example, suggests similar pious offerings at temples of the goddess. When pleased in this manner, the goddess would offer the most generous of boons, a characteristic that martyrs in nineteenth-century Punjab certainly shared.[76] Interestingly enough, in the nineteenth century, one Sayyid-shahid known as Bhura, whose shrine is located at Bari in Kaithal, shared with the goddess Mansa Devi of village Mani Majra (about eight miles from Chandigarh) the honour of being the special saint of thieves.[77]

Such associations between martyrs and goddesses appear to have been common in the nineteenth century. According to one tradition, Baba Chuda of the Bhandari Khatri *zāt*, a headless martyr whose shrine is found in Batala, appropriated his name, Chuda, from the goddess Kali as Chamunda, the slayer of the demons Chanda and Munda.[78] Traditionally visited by Bhandari Khatris, this shrine commemorates the spot on which the lifeless corpse of the martyr fell. Legend notes that the head of this saint was severed in battle during the incursions of Nadir Shah some time in the mid-eighteenth century. It continues that his decapitated body went on fighting, sword in hand, through the streets of the town, falling a considerable time afterwards when the invading host was routed. The belief that he destroyed his enemies miraculously suggests the reason for the adoption of the goddess epithet.[79]

The belief that it was Ghazi Miyan's head which continued to travel, an inversion of the popular legend of the beheaded saint as we witness, for example, in the stories of Baba Chuda and Baba Dip Singh, is also encountered in the story of the martyr, Sar Prekarai Faqir.[80] According to tradition, as he was tending his cattle this saint was attacked by a gang of thieves. These men first beheaded the saint and then carried off his cattle. The story notes that the severed head of the martyr pursued his assailants for over a mile. Seeing the head, the raiders fled in terror and left the cattle behind. There now stand two shrines: one in which the saint's body resides and the other in which the head is placed. As the martyr was fond of cattle in his lifetime, those wishing to increase their herds make a pilgrimage to both sites. These worshippers drive small pegs into the ground and tie small pieces of rope around them, hoping that their herd will increase by as many cattle as they fix pegs.[81]

The fact that an individual shrine is dedicated to the various parts of this martyr's body and that the martyr's various members are endowed with the power to increase herds in this case highlights the strong association between the martyr and the goddess in Punjabi culture. The allusion is to the traditions regarding the various *śakti pīṭhās* (seats of power) scattered throughout India, that is, the spots at which parts of the Devi's body fell after she had been dismembered by the gods, a belief which has roots in the legend of the destruction of Daksa's fire sacrifice by the great Hindu god, Shiva. According to a medieval version of the legend, Daksa Prajapati, the father of the goddess Sati, was celebrating a great sacrifice to which he invited neither his daughter nor his son-in-law, Shiva. Finding that his daughter had come nevertheless, Daksa insulted her, a transgression which resulted in the goddess taking her own life. When news of his wife's death reached Shiva, he was incensed and quickly made his way to the site. Destroying the sacrifice and decapitating his father-in-law, Shiva picked up the body of his beloved Sati and wandered over the earth in a frenzied dance, with her corpse on his head (or shoulder). Wishing to rid Shiva of this destructive infatuation, the gods Brahma and Vishnu decided to enter the body of the goddess and gradually dismembered it through their power of yoga. The places where the *disjecta membra* fell became *pīṭhās* or holy seats of the mother goddess. For this reason, these places are alive with the presence of the goddess and infused with her powerful *śakti*, the active aspect of the divine.[82]

The spots at which are buried the various parts of martyrs such as Pir Zaki and Imam Badr-ud Din are also believed to be infused with power. Both of these martyrs have their heads and bodies interred in separate shrines. According to our ethnographers' native informants, Pir Zaki had had his head severed while battling the Mughals. Underneath the Yakki gate in Lahore, they continued, is buried his head, while his body is placed in a tomb believed to mark the spot at which he was killed.[83] According to tradition, Sayyid Badr-ud Din was decapitated by a Hindu Raja some time before the earliest Muslim incursions so that parts of the Sayyid's body could be placed within various sections of a castle's foundation. Such an act was believed to be auspicious and thus ensure the structure's and, by implication the kingdom's, continued life. Unfortunately, the Raja's astrologers were incorrect in this case. The kinsmen of the martyr arrived and fought against the Raja's soldiers to exact revenge for the cruel deed their king had perpetrated. The battle was heavily in favour of the

Raja by the sheer number of troops at his disposal. By the miraculous power of Badr-ud Din's shrines, however, whenever one of his kin fell in action ('drinking the cup of martyrdom'[84]), one of the enemy was mysteriously slain. Moreover, the soul of every slain Sayyid would come back as a grotesque warrior without hands and feet to slay his enemies.[85]

The belief that shrines to martyrs were noted for their power, particularly to ease the troubles of worshippers, is the theme of a legend associated with Ghazi Miyan, recorded in the early 1880s by the British ethnographer, Richard Temple. In this tale, we are not only made aware of the benevolence of Ghazi Miyan. We are also privy to the consequences that a worshipper who fails to fulfil his pledge to the martyr must face. In this case, the protagonist of the story, Hassan Ali the hakim (doctor), is made to pledge that he will tell no one that the saint had bestowed on him the ability to produce rupees from the soil. After a brief period of prosperity, he tells of his ability to a traveller and is subsequently deprived of all that he cherishes, eventually dying a broken man.[86]

Such a legend demonstrates a darker side to the benevolent Ghazi, a disposition well in keeping with the more malignant nature for which Muslim martyrs in northern India were well known.[87] Why martyrs were known as malevolent in nineteenth-century Punjab may stem from the notions inherent in the cult of the goddess: the shakti of the goddess heals and embalms, but at the same time, it is capricious and destructive, often carrying with it the very disease and affliction it may later cure. This is indeed a strong possibility. To this, however, must be added another notion, one whose roots are found in Punjabi folk tradition. The malevolence of the Muslim martyr in Punjab becomes quite clear when we examine how one attained the status of martyr.

We mentioned at the beginning of this chapter that Sikhs retain much of what the term 'shahid' signifies in Islam. As the Tat Khalsa interpretation of the term 'martyr' only acknowledges two major facets of the term (dying in a sacralized battle and sacrificing one's life for righteousness), so, too, does the Islamic interpretation we provide above. As we have witnessed in the example of Sar Prekarai Faqir, who was killed by thieves, however, there are other ways in which a person could become a martyr. We noted in the introduction T.W. Arnold's claim that the term 'shahid' was interpreted in many ways in early twentieth-century India.[88] The south Indian Muslim writer, Jafar Sharif, had taken this a step further by noting a number of deaths which awarded a person the status of martyr:

1, If a man expire in the act of reading the *Qoran*; 2, if in the act of praying; 3, if in the act of fasting; 4, if on the pilgrimage to Mecca; 5, if on a Friday ... 6, if in the defence of his religion; 7, if through religious meditation; 8, if he be executed for speaking the truth; 9, if he endure death by the hands of a tyrant or oppressor with patience and submission; 10, if killed in defending his own property; 11, if a woman die in labour or child-bed; 12, if murdered by robbers; 13, if devoured by tigers; 14, if killed by the kick of a horse; 15, if struck dead by lightning; 16, if burnt to death; 17, if buried under the ruins of a wall; 18, if drowned; 19, if killed by a fall from a precipice, or down a dry well or pit; 20, if he meet death by apoplexy, or stroke of the sun.[89]

To these may be added the belief that one became a martyr if, when killed or executed, the victim did not cry out while receiving the death-stroke, or if one was killed in an epidemic, in a foreign country, by dysentery or colic, or by pleurisy.[90] The enumerations here are not at all confined to Islam as practised in South Asia. In fact, many of the ways of attaining martyrdom mentioned here are also listed in various Arabic theological works (*kalām*) and legal dissertations (*fiqh*), as well as in the Hadith or Traditions regarding the Prophet Muhammad.[91] Today, furthermore, it is still common to refer to a Muslim who dies while on the Hajj or pilgrimage to Mecca as a shahid, a practice which prompts one Sikh author to declare that Sikhs do not accept the Muslim description of shahid.[92]

There are, moreover, shrines to martyrs who were not killed according to any of the criteria above. One version of the story of Pir Balawal Shah of Ferozepur, for example, maintains that during the time of Akbar, a group of thieves placed their booty under the saint's pillow as a pious offering. The owner of the stolen property, having eventually found Balawal Shah while the latter was still asleep, assumed that the pir was the culprit and killed him. As ordered by Miran Shah Nur, the corpse was buried in its blood-stained clothing where it lay, a ritual which clearly indicates a person's status as martyr. In Islamic tradition, only martyrs are so pure that they may be buried where they were killed and without the traditional, final washing of the corpse.[93]

Another example of a martyr killed in a manner unlike those in Sharif's list is that of Shadna Shahid, whose shrine may be found in Multan. According to tradition, this martyr met his death at ten months of age at the hand of his own mother when he had miraculously given evidence against her after she had unjustly accused the saint, Baha ud-din Zakariya, of forgoing his vows of chastity. Although the infant was brought back to life by the saint and eventually died a natural death, he is still considered a martyr. In the nineteenth century, this particular martyr was invoked by any person who wished something done quickly.[94]

In the light of these extensive criteria for attaining the status of shahid, one can understand why the Punjab countryside was literally dotted with the shrines of these beings in the late nineteenth century.[95] Such examples make clear the fact that the status of martyr was awarded to far more people than our later Sikh sources indicate. We must still, however, explain why martyrs were considered malevolent in nineteenth-century Punjab. Keeping in mind the ways one became a shahid, one need not search far for this answer, nor for the reason that Ghazi Miyan and his fellow Muslim martyrs were (and are) venerated by all Punjabis. The deaths martyrs suffered were in many ways similar to the deaths of those people whose spirits manifested themselves afterwards as the malevolent ghosts known in Punjabi folk culture as *birs, bhūts, baitāls, prets* and *churels*. These were, for the most part, sudden and often violent deaths.[96] The determinative difference between the shahid and these various other entities, of course, is the fact that shahids have a specific recognizable identity.

A pret is believed to be the spirit of a person who has died a violent death by suicide, accident, or execution. Already harmful at this stage, it wanders the space between heaven and earth for approximately a year, inflicting what damage it can on unsuspecting humans and their families. According to Punjabi folk tradition, after this initial period, it then manifests itself into the more harmful bhut, if male, or churel if female. There are, of course, many varieties of both spirits. If, for example, a male had died without the proper accompanying funeral ceremonies, then his state of malignancy increased dramatically. Often this type of bhut had lacked the male progeny necessary to perform the recommended funeral rites while still a human being. In this case, the bhut was termed a *gayāl*. To ensure that gayals would not harm the young sons of the village, a small shrine was erected into which both water of the Ganga and milk were poured. Lamps were also lit here and Brahmans fed to conciliate the malevolent spirit. Finally, mothers would dedicate a rupee to the ghost and hang it around the necks of their sons until they reached adulthood.[97]

The strong association of the *bhūt-gayāl* to the shahid is clear in the veneration of the Jat martyr, Ram Mal, commonly known as Buddha Shahid. According to tradition, Ram Mal was murdered by a group of Chima Jats into whose zat he had married through some connivance. After being severely wounded, he asked those who had attacked him for a drink of wine as a last request, but he died before it could be brought to him. For this reason, the saint is propitiated by Chima Jats by sprinkling wine over his shrine. The significant point is that this is done while a new mother goes through a rite known among the Chimas as *bhog bharnā*. The bhog bharnā enjoins the mother to avoid using collyrium, henna, perfume and dyed thread for some days after the child's birth. At the end of the period, on a Monday during the bright half of any month, all these items are then offered at the shrine of Buddha Shahid. Such an act seems to conciliate this martyr who died childless.[98]

Unless propitiated, it was believed that bhuts could cause a great degree of harm. Note, for example, the length to which Hindu and Muslim villagers went to ensure that the accidental death of a soldier would not see his spirit manifest itself to extract revenge from the people of the locale at which he died:

In [one] village an imperial trooper was once burnt alive by the shed in which he was sleeping catching fire, and it was thought well to propitiate him by a shrine, or his ghost might become troublesome. He was by religion a Musalmān; but he had been burnt and not buried, which seemed to make him a Hindu. After much discussion the latter opinion prevailed and a Hindu shrine with an eastern aspect now stands to his memory.[99]

As we can infer from this case, the type of shrine (rare in regard to bhuts) was considered highly significant, for when even slightly upset, these ghosts were believed to inflict terrible calamities. Indeed, these malevolent spirits were highly feared. In the nineteenth century, it was thought that at night, lonely herdsman could hear the cries of bhuts who had been killed in ancient battles during their human lifetime. We are told that for fear of these malevolent dead, Punjabis would very often avoid travelling during the evening, except in large parties.[100]

The churel is also a highly feared being. She is believed to be the spirit of a woman who had died while pregnant or within forty days of giving birth.[101] Always malignant, particularly towards the members of her own family, the churel is known to long for her dead child and to despise all other children. To ensure that a churel passes over her child, a mother would put a pinch of salt in the child's mouth after treating him or her to sweets. She would, moreover, instruct her children to say 'Narayan' (God) after they yawned, since churels were notorious for possessing a body by entering it through the open mouth.[102]

Finally, birs are in class similar to that of the bhut and the churel. These are the spirits of either males or females who had perished in battle, by accident, or by suicide. A very malignant village demon is the bir, who brings disease to both men and cattle unless propitiated.[103] A martyr who falls into this category is Kala Bir (also known as Kala Pir), another example of the headless warrior-martyr. Again, as the goddess Kali requires blood sacrifice, so, too, does this martyr. A black-and-white goat is offered to Kala Bir on special occasions at the small shrine which Sindhu Jats often built in their villages. During weddings, the bride and bridegroom are taken to the shrine to salaam, possibly to ensure either the birth of a child or that the child, when born, will not come under the gaze of this feared being.[104]

The parallels are plain and suggest that throughout the Punjab and the rest of India, shahids were both figures of tremendous power and a variety of malevolent ghosts which plagued the land.[105] This understanding is firmly buttressed in a rather controversial Sikh text known as the *Sau Sākhiān* (The One Hundred Testimonies).

Written in Gurmukhi script by an anonymous author, the *Sau Sākhiān* is believed to contain a series of sermons preached by Guru Gobind Singh just before his death. Internal evidence, however, demonstrates that this text was produced some time in the mid-nineteenth century.[106] It is the evidence presented within these sakhis that allows us to infer that Sikhs acknowledged the shahid in the nineteenth century as a being along the lines we have been examining above. In fact, the definition one finds in a text written in this period would have probably been equally shared among the adherents of all of the Punjab's religions. It is a very valuable source in the attempt to recreate pre–Singh Sabha martyrolatry among Punjabis since it gives the only sustained explanation of the martyr's role that I have come across in the mystical universe of nineteenth-century Punjab. The text does not specifically say how one becomes a martyr, possibly taking it for granted because the status could be applied to those who had suffered so many varieties of death,[107] but it does explain the function these beings fulfil, functions which are depicted in terms which clearly derive from Hindu, Islamic and Punjabi folk traditions. Here, for example, the connection between the malevolent and benign spirits of Punjabi folklore and shahids is made explicit. We are also told of the ability martyrs possess to intercede with the divine on behalf of the worshipper, a facet of Islamic tradition[108] as well as an element of Sikh martyrolatry we had noted previously in the contemporary Nihang Sikh prayer to Baba Dip Singh.[109] Moreover, as we also note in Baba Dip Singh's prayer, we are made privy to the power of the martyr to grant the wishes of all those who propitiate him. It is the twenty-fourth sakhi with which we are concerned. Its relevant portions appear below.

Once Sikhs asked [Guru Gobind Singh], 'O true king, to whom do we apply the name shahid? Disclose [to us] their works and [the nature of] the liberation they obtain.'

[The Guru] smiled and replied, 'You ask about secret things [my] Sikhs... [Those who are called shahids do] live in the world. [However,] they abide in the realm of Kuber, [the god of riches, as well as] in Bhuvlok, [the realm between the sun and the sky in which dwell the Munis and the Siddhas]. All that which the martyrs desire comes to pass. *Bhūts, prets, rakṣasas,* as well as humans, birds, serpents, *yakṣas, gandharvas* and *apasarases* are under their command. The messengers of Yama, the god of death, consult with them. Within the *Śāstras* [shahids] are referred to as *baitāl* and *vidyādhar,* beings who possess both malevolent and benevolent dispositions.[110] Their [particular] nature results [from the interplay] of the three constituent qualities of all matter, *sattva* (purity/virtue), *rajas* (passion), and *tamas* (darkness/dullness).[111]

Shahids are worshipped by their congregation and fulfil all the wishes of this group. It is [the shahids] who bestow both pain and pleasure. The gods, having entrusted them with [caring over] the realm of Bharat, departed for heaven. Whatever the gods receive it is through the hands of the shahids. Parmeshvar has placed them in [various] positions of power [and for this reason] there are all manner of shahids. Food, clothes and the means of transport are freely given by [the shahids]. They travel through all the rocky lands of deceit, yet never stray [from their appointed path]. They perceive the attractions (*tamāśā)* of Maya. As Raja Bipasachit[112] witnessed [these attractions] so too do they, and do not have to endure the transmigratory round.

The Guru protects them. He watches over them like a shepherd. These things [which I have stated] are the works [of the martyrs] and the knowledge of liberation [which they possess]... The sakhi is [now] complete. [Reflect on it and] say *Vāhigurū.*[113]

The views one finds expressed in this sakhi are reflected in Sikh participation in popular martyrolatry. Among Sikh and Hindu Jats in the nineteenth century, for example, a small masonry shrine or mound of earth termed *jaṭherā* (clan ancestor; elder) was built and dedicated to an ancestor who was either a shahid or a man of note. The bridegroom would circumambulate and bow his head before the shrine at the time of his wedding in order to be blessed by this being.[114]

That Sikhs venerated the martyrs of other religious faiths as well as their own is similarly confirmed in nineteenth-century sources. The Sikh worship of the Hindu Gugga Pir is by now very well documented. According to one version of the legend of Gugga, the saint was known as Mundlik, a headless martyr killed in battle with Muslim invaders, whose headless trunk continued to fight until it was eventually absorbed into the earth.[115] The Sikh fascination with the martyrs of Islam, moreover, was often encountered during the month of Muharram, commemorating the martyrdoms of 'Ali and his sons, Husayn and Hasan, the first of who (according to tradition) fell at the battle of Karbala (680 CE) in present-day Iraq.[116] In Shi'a Islam, these three men along with the Prophet's daughter, Fatima, are deemed the archetypal martyrs. For pious Shi'a Muslims, all martyrdoms and all suffering are only their own participation in the martyrdom of the Holy Family.[117] During '*āshūrā* or the tenth day of Muharram in the nineteenth century, Sikhs ('Nanak Panthis', according to our source) often engaged in the processional self-mortification for which the remembrance is noted.[118]

Such an analysis adds another dimension to the exceptional reverence that Sikhs accord Sikh martyrs. The piety towards Baba Dip Singh one sees at both Harimandir Sahib and Gurdwara Shahidganj Baba Dip Singh in Amritsar may be cited as an example. Such piety, moreover, is also directed towards those more recently 'martyred'. An article in the Amritsar edition of the *Indian Express* notes the concerns of the Punjab police regarding their attempts to take down and disallow the further construction of memorials to those young Sikh men killed in the contemporary crisis. It seems very likely that these 'memorials' were erected in order to secure a higher status for the families of the deceased within their respective villages. One cannot discount, however, the suspicion that these memorials were possibly shrines erected in part with a mind to propitiate those killed violently.[119]

These are elements of Sikh martyrolatry about which we do not hear in Tat Khalsa sources for the obvious reason that these would have been viewed as superstitions not sanctioned by the Adi Granth.

How the Tat Khalsa modified this concept and how they used this new understanding of the shahid in their programme of reform and revival is the subject of the following chapter.

Notes

1. A phrase from a folk song found in Tahir Mahmood, 'The Dargah of Salar Mas'ud Ghazi in Bahraich: Legend, Tradition and Reality', in Christian W. Troll (ed.), *Muslim Shrines in India* (New Delhi, 1992), p. 24.

2. *MK*, p. 139.

3. Ibid.

4. *MK*, p. 139, has a brief history of the Shahid misl.

5. *MK*, pp. 139–40.

6. *MK*, p. 588. Also see Savaran Singh, *Śahīdī Sākā: Bhāī Tārū Siṅgh ji* (Amritsar, 1997).

7. *MK*, pp. 80, 537, 588, 600, 631, 808, 944, 950–1.

8. *MK*, p. 186.

9. *MK*, p. 662.

10. A.K. Ramanujan, 'Is there an Indian way of thinking? An informal Essay', in McKim Marriot (ed.), *India Through Hindu Categories* (Delhi, 1990), pp. 41–58.

11. See *MK*, p. 927, for a description of the Battle of Bhangani. Kahn Singh refers to those who fell in this battle as shahids.

12. See both volumes of *TGK*.

13. *MK*, p. 455.

14. *MK*, p. 822. For background see K.S. Dhir, *Sikh Rāj de Vīr Nāik* (Patiala, 1984), pp. 58–70.

15. *MK*, p. 186.

16. Kahn Singh seems to be arguing in a circle here: as a dharam yudh produces martyrs, ergo, a war that produces martyrs must be a dharam yudh.

17. Also refer to Kahn Singh's *Gurmat Sudhākar* (Patiala, 1988), pp. 299–300.

18. Pritam Singh, *Bhāī Kānh Siṅgh Nābhā: Pichhokaṛ Rachnā te Mulaṅkaṇ* (Amritsar, 1989), pp. 33–4.

19. *MK*, p. 479. See also *CSRn*, pp. 12–13. For similar definitions inspired by Tat Khalsa 'reforms' see '*Bālā, Bhāī*' and '*Pañj Kakkār*', *MK*, pp. 791, 858.

20. Kahn Singh was also very sympathetic towards the Namdhari Sikhs, though he does not refer to those Namdharis who were executed by the British government in 1872 as shahids. Of course, *MK* was published while the British were still in power. See the eighth entry for '*Rām Siṅgh*' in *MK*, pp. 1033–4. For Kahn Singh's relationship with Teja Singh Bhasaur see N.G. Barrier, 'Sikh Politics and Religion: The Bhasaur Singh Sabha', in Indu Banga (ed.), *Five Punjabi Centuries: Polity, Economy, Society and Culture, c. 1500–1990* (Delhi, 1997), pp. 140–56. A biography of Kahn Singh appears in D.S. Vidiarathi, *Bhāī Kānh Siṅgh Nābhā: Jīvan te Rachnā* (Patiala, 1987), chapter 1.

21. M.A. Macauliffe, *The Sikh Religion: Its Gurus, Sacred Writings and Authors* I (Oxford, 1909), pp. xxix–xxx. The importance of the *MK* for historians is brought out in Teja Singh's foreword, *MK*, pp. chh–ñ.

22. For example Mona Kang, 'The Concept of Martyrdom in Sikhism and Sikh Martyrs up to the Eighteenth Century' (Ph.D thesis, Panjab University, Chandigarh, 1990), p. 46; Joyce Pettigrew, *The Sikhs of the Punjab: Unheard Voices of State and Guerilla Violence* (London, 1995); C.K. Mahmood, *Fighting for Faith and Nation: Dialogues with Sikh Militants* (Philadelphia, 1997); and J.P.S. Uberoi, *Religion, Civil Society and State: A Study of Sikhism* (New Delhi, 1995), to name a few.

23. Garja Singh (ed.), *Sahīd-bilās (Bhāī Manī Siṅgh) krit Sevā Siṅgh* (Ludhiana, 1961), p. 72.

24. J.S. Grewal, *Sikh Ideology, Polity and Social Order* (Delhi, 1996), p. 147. Bhangu also claims that as a result of Guru Tegh Bahadur's martyrdom,

The pirs and prophets of the Muslims were ejected from the court [of the Eternal Guru]. Expelled from paradise, they were then placed in a camp behind the [Heavenly] Court [and thus stripped of their power to intercede between the pious and the divine].

See *PrPP*, p. 39.

25. J.S. Sital (ed.), *Srī Gur-panth Prakāś krit Bhāī Ratan Siṅgh Bhaṅgū Sahīd* (Amritsar, 1994), pp. 511–25. Also see Grewal, *Sikh Ideology*, pp. 147–8.

26. In this entry, Kahn Singh names ten famous Sikh martyries. '*Sahīd-gañj*', in *MK*, p. 139. Also see '*Chamkaur Sāhib*' and '*Phūlā Siṅgh Akālī*', *MK*, pp. 455, 822.

27. '*Sahīdī Deg*', in *MK*, p. 140.

28. N.G. Barrier, *The Sikhs and Their Literature: A Guide to Books, Tracts & Periodicals (1849–1919)* (Delhi, 1970).

29. It should come as no surprise that Kahn Singh has no entry for 'martyrolatry' (*sahīd-pūjā* or *sahīd-parastī*). That such practices would not be recognized by the Tat Khalsa is implied in the later Sikh code of conduct. See, for example, section II of the code titled *gurmati dī rahiṇ* under entry '(s)' in *Sikh Rahit Maryādā*, p. 17.

30. G.S. Talib, 'The Concept and Tradition of Martyrdom in Sikhism', in G.S. Talib (ed.), *Guru Tegh Bahadur: Background and Supreme Sacrifice* (Patiala, 1976), pp. 179–80.

31. Mona Kang, 'Concept of Martyrdom', pp. 2–3. Another legend which underscores this facet of Sikh martyrdom regards those Sikh warriors who would go out against innumerable odds to rescue Hindu females from their Muslim captors. Trilok Singh, *Lahū Sahīdān dā* (Amritsar, 1989).

32. Harjot Oberoi, *The Construction of Religious Boundaries: Culture, Identity and Diversity in the Sikh Tradition* (New Delhi and Chicago, 1994). Also *WhS*, chapter 5. For the standard Singh Sabha interpretation of Sikh and Hindu categories prior to Ranjit Singh's empire, see Harbans Singh, 'Origin of the Singh Sabha', and Teja Singh, 'The Singh Sabha Movement', both of which appear in *PPP* VII:1 (1973), pp. 23–33, 34–49.

33. S.S. Chawla, *Martyrdom of Guru Tegh Bahadur: Message for Mankind* (New Delhi, 1991), p. 73.

34. *Bachitar Nāṭak* 5: 13, *DG*, p. 54.

35. Early literature would include Ganda Singh (ed.), *Kavi Saināpati Rachit Srī Gur Sobhā* (Patiala, 1988), p. 65; P.S. Padam (ed.), *Bhāī Kesar Siṅgh Chhibbar krit Bansāvalī-nāmā Dasān Pātśāhīān kā* (Amritsar, 1997), p. 120; G.K. Jaggi

(ed.), *Gurbilās Patśāhī 10 Sukkhā Siṅgh* (Patiala, 1989), p. 57; and S.S. Ashok (ed.), *Gurbilās Patśāhī 10 krit Kuir Siṅgh* (Patiala, 1968), p. 48.

36. In Gopal Singh (trans.), *Thus Spake the Tenth Master* (Patiala, 1978), pp. 88–89, the author supplies the words 'of the Hindus' in parentheses after 'sacred thread' and 'frontal mark'.

37. John Malcolm, *Sketch of the Sikhs* (London, 1812), pp. 67–8, notes that in the 'Penjábi narrative of B'hai Gúrú Dás B'halé, Guru Gobind Singh and his 'brave, but unfortunate [son], Ajit Singh' had not 'laid aside the *zunár*, or holy cord'. These, he claims, had been converted to sword belts. Furthermore, M.A. Macauliffe has Guru Hargobind claim that 'my seli shall be a sword-belt, and I shall wear my turban with a royal aigrette'. *The Sikh Religion* IV, p. 2.

38. See C.H. Loehlin, *The Granth of Guru Gobind Singh and the Khalsa Brotherhood* (Lucknow, 1971), pp. 9–10, for background. In the early nineteenth century, the Dasam Granth was as revered as the Adi Granth. Malcolm, *Sketch of the Sikhs*, pp. 120–1, makes this clear.

39. Randhir Singh (ed.), *Śabadārath Dasam Granth Sāhib*, 3 vols. (Patiala, 1985). M.A. Macauliffe, *The Sikh Religion* V, p. 83, supplies the typical Singh Sabha understanding of the Guru's desire to include this material in the Dasam Granth.

40. Oberoi, *Construction*, p. 137.

41. Ibid., p. 98.

42. Koer Singh's *Gur-bilās Pātśāhī 10*, p. 120.

43. Sukha Singh, *Gur-bilās Pātśāhī 10*, p. 57; Koer Singh, *Gur-bilās Pātśāhī 10*, p. 48.

44. *Sūraj Prakāś* XI, pp. 4468–9. Note Vir Singh's editorial comments to this statement. In a footnote (marked with an asterisk), Vir Singh explains that the Guru does not really mean that 'ours is the Hindu religion', despite the fact that the context clearly suggests this interpretation. The footnote shows Vir Singh at his best, as a Tat Khalsa hermeneute *par excellence*. For a brief comment on Vir Singh's editing policy in regard to Santokh Singh's classic gur-bilas text, see J.S. Neki, 'Bhai Vir Singh and Sikh Psyche', in *Khera: Journal of Religious Understanding* IX: 4 (1990), p. 88.

45. Oberoi, *Construction*, chapter 5. For Guru Tegh Bahadur and human rights see Fauja Singh, 'Guru Tegh Bahadur and Human Rights', in G.S. Talib (ed.), *Guru Tegh Bahadur* and Gurnam Singh, 'UN and Sikh Perspectives on Human Rights to Equality: A Comparative Study', in *JSS* XVI:2 (1989), pp. 75–84.

46. Debate on the nature of popular religion has been extensive in recent literature and need not detain us here. For the conceptual hazards it entails, see Peter Brown, *The Cult of Saints* (Chicago, 1981) and S.J. Tambiah, *Buddhism and the Spirit Cults in North-East Thailand* (Cambridge, 1970), pp. 367–77. Oberoi, *Construction*, pp. 138–41, maintains that such problems must be overcome in order to understand the Tat Khalsa project.

47. Ronald Inden, *Imagining India* (Oxford, 1990), pp. 58–9. Similar interpretations of such encyclopaedia-like accounts appear in Edward Said, *Orientalism* (New York, 1979), pp. 158–66. Contemporary literature dealing with the problems entailed in ethnography and travelogue is substantial. Some notable examples are James Clifford, *The Predicament of Culture: Twentieth-Century Ethnography, Literature and Art* (Harvard, 1988); Nicholas Thomas, *Colonialism's Culture:*

Anthropology, Travel and Government (Princeton, 1994); and B.S. Cohn, *Colonialism and its Forms of Knowledge: The British in India* (Princeton, 1996).

48. Oberoi, *Construction*, p. 145.

49. For example, G.S. Dhillon, *Researches in Sikh Religion and History* (Chandigarh, 1989), pp. 78–97, caustically claims that Harjot Oberoi's work, 'marked by descriptive profusion and meaningless rhetoric, betrays an obvious ignorance of the basic tenets of the Sikh faith'. In fact, nothing could be further from the truth.

50. V.A. Dusenbury, 'W.H. McLeod and his Sikh Critics: Knowledge/Power/ Representation'. Unpublished paper seen through the author's courtesy. W.H. McLeod, 'Cries of Outrage: History Versus Tradition in the Study of the Sikh Community', in *South Asia Research* 14:2 (Autumn, 1994), pp. 121–35; and Piar Singh, *Gatha Sri Adi Granth and the Controversy* (Grand Ledge, Michigan, 1996).

51. The 'enchanted universe' is noted in Oberoi's *Construction*, p. 141.

52. Ibid., pp. 142 ff.

53. *Baraka* is the Arabic term for 'blessing' (Punjabi: *barkat*). According to the *Encyclopaedia of Islām* I:2, p. 654, *baraka* is

a magic means of obtaining all sorts of good fortune, in particular the healing of diseases and infirmities, not only from God but also from holy men and objects which are supposed to possess the power of conferring blessings. By the mere touch these may be transferred to others.

54. For example M.A. Macauliffe, 'The Fair at Sakhi Sarvar', in *Calcutta Review* 60 (1875).

55. W. Crooke, *The Popular Religion and Folk-Lore of Northern India* I (Westminster, 1896), p. 215.

56. Oberoi, *Construction*, pp. 156–62. For legends of these saints see Richard Temple, *Legends of the Punjab* I (Patiala, 1988), pp. 91–7, 122–209. For contemporary Sikh worship of these saints see P.S. Jammu, 'Religion in a Malwa Village', in J.C.B. Webster (ed.), *Popular Religion in the Punjab Today* (Delhi, 1973), pp. 86–95.

57. The majority of saint-martyrs in the Punjab were Muslim. A significant exception is Gugga Pir who was, according to one account, a Chauhan Rajput who perished in battle with Mahmud of Ghazni. Crooke, *Popular Religion* I, pp. 211–58.

58. *Glossary* II, pp. 9–10.

59. Crooke, *Popular Religion* I, p. 201.

60. Examples of these shahids are Imam Nasir-ud-din and Sayyid Nimat Ullah Shahid. *Glossary* I, p. 13. Also, W. Crooke, 'Saints and Martyrs (Indian)', and T.W. Arnold, 'Saints and Martyrs (Muhammadan in India)', both of which appear in *The Encyclopaedia of Religion and Ethics* XI, pp. 60, 72, note the various *ganj-i shahīdān* or 'martyr-treasuries' which mark the spots at which Muslim warriors fell in battle against local fighters. We are told that both Hindus and Muslims would visit these places.

61. Crooke notes that the names of these five are subject to change, depending upon their locale. *Popular Religion* I, pp. 205–6. Also Aziz Ahmad, *An Intellectual History of Islam in India* (Edinburgh, 1969), pp. 48–9.

62. What follows is based primarily on what appears in both *The Gazetteer of the Province of Oudh* I (1st. pbd., 1877–8. New Delhi, 1985), pp. 112–13 (hereafter *Oudh*); W.H. Sleeman, *Journey Through the Kingdom of Oudh in 1849–50* I (London, 1858), pp. 48–9; and W. Crooke, *Popular Religion* I, pp. 207–8.

63. *Oudh* I, pp. 113–14. An alternative narrative which de-emphasizes the Ghazi's martial temperament appears in Tahir Mahmood, 'The Dargah of Sayyid Sala Mas'ud Ghazi in Bahraich', pp. 24–43.

64. *Oudh* I, p. 113, states that, according to tradition, the saint's head rests on the image of the sun, whose worship the martyr was attempting to eradicate. K.G.V. Schwerin briefly explores the idea that the martyr possessed the same powers as that of the sun in her 'Saint Worship in Indian Islam: The Legend of the Martyr Salar Masud Ghazi', in Imtiaz Ahmad (ed.), *Ritual and Religion among Muslims in India* (New Delhi, 1981), pp. 143–61.

65. Sleeman, *Journey* I, pp. 48–9.

66. Ibid., p. 49. This shrine has attracted attention since at least the thirteenth century. The Indo-Persian poet, Amir Khusrau (1253–1352 CE), alludes to its eminence in his *I'jāz-i Khusravi* II (Lucknow, 1896), p. 155:

On account of the fragrant grave of the soldier-martyr [Salar Masud] in the village of Bahara'ich all of India has taken on the scent of aloe's wood.

For a history of the pilgrimage traffic to Ghazi Miyan's dargah, see Iqtidar Husain Siddiqi,'A Note on the Dargah of Salar Mas'ud in Bahraich in the Light of Standard Historical Sources', in C.W. Troll (ed.), *Muslim Shrines in India*, pp. 44–7.

67. Schwerin refers to the Ghazi's sacred day as *'urs,* while T.W. Arnold claims that the festival is named *shadi* (also 'marriage'). Schwerin, 'Saint Worship in Indian Islam', p. 144 and Arnold, 'Saints and Martyrs (Muhammadan in India)', p. 72.

68. Schwerin, 'Saint Worship', p. 150. During Muharram, standards are carried to commemorate those who marched into battle with Husayn. A description appears in Jaffur Shurreef, *Qanoon-e Islam or the Customs of the Musalmans of India Comprising a Full and Exact Account of their various Rites and Ceremonies, From the Moment of Birth till the Hour of Death* [tr. G.A. Herklots] (Madras, 1895), pp. 115–16.

69. Crooke, *Popular Religion* I, p. 208.

70. J.H. Garcin de Tassy, *Memoire sur les Particularities de la Religion Musalmane dans l'Inde, d'apres les ouverage Hindustanis* (Paris, 1874), pp. 28–9; 77–85.

71. N.L. Rockey, 'Progress of Islam in Oudh', in *Moslem World* 3 (1913), p. 254. What Rockey found even sadder than the plight of these afflicted was the fact that over one half of the worshippers were not Muslims but Hindus.

72. A.J. Arberry (trans.), *Muslim Saints and Mystics: Episodes from the Tadhkirat al-Auliya' (Memorial of the Saints)* (London, 1990).

73. *Glossary* I, p. 14. Also Richard Temple, 'Folklore of the Headless Horseman in Northern India', *Calcutta Review* 77 (1883), pp. 158–83.

74. K.M. Erndl's *Victory to the Mother: The Hindu Goddess of Northwest India in Myth, Ritual and Symbol* (Oxford, 1993), pp. 135–52, deals, in part, with popular goddess worship in the Punjab. For the *Devimāhātmya* see Thomas

Coburn, *Encountering the Goddess: A Translation of the Devī-Māhātmya and a Study of its Interpretation* (Albany, 1991).

75. Temple, 'Folklore of the Headless Horseman', p. 174. For Chinnamasta/ Chinnamunda see E.A. Benard, *Chinnamasta: The Aweful Buddhist and Hindu Tantric Goddess* (Delhi, 1994). How the power of Muslim martyrs is expressed in terms which derive from the traditions of Hindu high gods and goddesses, as well as the fierce regional divinities of southern India, and how these martyrs annex such powers is examined in Susan Bayly's *Saints, Goddesses and Kings: Muslims and Christians in South Indian Society 1700–1900* (Cambridge, 1989), pp. 187–215. *Glossary* I, p. 14, also notes that many Muslim martyrs simply usurped the powers of the Hindu goddess.

76. K.M. Erndl, *Victory to the Mother*, p. 5. A martyr to whom sacrifice is offered is Mara Panga Shahid. This shrine, like the shrines of the goddess, is a resort for the infirm and afflicted. *Glossary* I, pp. 590–1. For other decapitated martyrs to whom sacrifices are offered, see *Glossary* I, pp. 402, 467. For descriptions of sacrifices to the goddess see *Glossary* I, pp. 330, 359–60.

77. This account occurs in Temple's 'Headless Horseman', p. 164. Apparently, according to both Crooke and Ibbetson, the term 'Sayyid' was a corruption of 'shahid'. *Glossary* I, p. 203; and Crooke, *Popular Religion* I, p. 201.

78. *Glossary* I, p. 326. Also Temple, 'Folklore of the Headless Horseman', p. 163. The story of Chamunda appears in David Kinsley, 'Blood and Death out of Place: Reflections on the Goddess Kālī', in J.S. Hawley and D.M. Wulff (ed.), *The Divine Consort: Rādhā and the Goddesses of India* (Berkeley, 1982), p. 145.

79. *Glossary* I, p. 326.

80. In Punjabi folklore, there are many other martyrs who continue to travel after decapitation. The *Sau Sakhīān,* for example, claims that many Sikh warriors kept on fighting after their heads were severed. G.S. Naiar (ed.), *Gur Ratan Māl Arthāt Sau Sākhī* (Patiala, 1985), p. 63. During the nineteenth century, moreover, Sada Singh, a disciple of Baba Dip Singh, is also credited with having battled while headless. Temple, 'Folklore of the Headless Horseman', pp. 159–60. For other decapitated saints see *Glossary* I, pp. 617, 621, 622.

81. *Glossary* I, pp. 587–8.

82. This legend and its variants may be found in most books which deal with goddess traditions in India. See, for example, W.D. O'Flaherty, *Asceticism and Eroticism in the Mythology of Śiva* (Oxford, 1973). The theme of dismemberment appears in the *Puruṣa-sūkta* hymn at Rig Veda 10:90. A thorough examination of dismemberment in Vedic religion is J.C. Heesterman, *The Inner Conflict of Tradition: Essays in Indian Ritual, Kingship and Society* (Chicago, 1985), pp. 45–58, 81–94.

83. *Glossary* I, p. 617.

84. 'Drinking the cup of martyrdom' is a standard formula in Persian historiography.

85. There is a similar legend of a Sayyid boy whose head was placed in the foundations of a structure in Panipat. In this case, the boy's headless corpse fought against his murderers alongside his kin until the former were all killed. *Glossary* I, pp. 327–8, 618. Stories of dismemberment are quite prevalent in the Punjab and its surrounding areas. Puran Bhagat as well as Mani Singh come to mind. Also, it is intriguing to note that there are two gurdwara-martyries in

honour of Guru Tegh Bahadur, one at which his body was burned (Gurdwara Rakabganj) and the other where his head was severed (Gurdwara Sis-ganj). According to popular belief, however, the head is not interred at the latter.

86. R.C. Temple, 'Folklore of the Headless Horseman', pp. 167–70.

87. Ibbetson claims all such martyrs were to be propitiated in order to avert the calamities these beings often delivered. *Glossary* I, p. 14. Tahir Mahmood says of contemporary visits to Baharaich:

Pilgrims religiously visit the dargah at every mela every year, believing that an unjustified absence even once will entail Ghazi Miyan's displeasure, to express which he might employ jinns [ghosts], evil spirits and thieves...

'The Dargah of Sayyid Salar Mas'ud Ghazi', p. 37.

88. T.W. Arnold, 'Saints and Martyrs (Muhammadan in India)', p. 72.

89. Jaffur Shurreef, *Qanoon-e Islam*, p. 48.

90. *Glossary* I, p. 13; and III, p. 399; A.J. Wensinck, *A Handbook of Early Muhammadan Tradition* (Leiden, 1927), pp. 146–8; and E.W. Lane, *Arabic-English Lexicon* 1:4 (London, 1872), p. 1610.

91. Wensinck's *Handbook* provides the type of martyrdom and the various Arabic texts in which it is elaborated.

92. Bhajan Singh, *Sāde Śahīd* (Amritsar, 1991), p. 10.

93. *Glossary* I, pp. 606–7. The rituals accompanying the burial of martyrs are noted in Wensinck's *Handbook*, p. 147.

94. *Glossary* I, p. 13. Compare this account of Shadna Shahid with the tale of Puran Bhagat as found in H.S. Gill, *Structures of Narrative in East and West* (New Delhi, 1989).

95. R.C. Temple, 'Headless Horseman', p. 164; *Glossary* I, p. 13; and T.W. Arnold, 'Saints and Martyrs (Muhammadan in India)', p. 73.

96. Crooke also mentions the *gārdevī* or river sprite, which is the malignant ghost of a person who met his death by suicide, violence, or accident and the Bhagaut, the troublesome spirit of a man killed by a tiger. The latter was another method of attaining martyrdom in nineteenth-century Punjab. Crooke, *Popular Religion* I, pp. 43, 267–9.

97. *Glossary* I, p. 202; and Crooke, *Popular Religion* I, pp. 234–5.

98. *Glossary* I, p. 14.

99. Ibid., p. 193. Dying by fire was also a way of attaining martyrdom.

100. Ibid., p. 208.

101. Ibid. I, p. 206. This type of death is also considered martyrdom.

102. Ibid., p. 204.

103. Other examples of *birs* appear in Crooke, *Popular Religion* I, pp. 62, 208, 254; and *Glossary* I, p. 213.

104. *Glossary* I, pp. 283, 402. The variety of *bir* that Kala Bir is known as is the *banbir* who, according to the *Glossary*, is the 'deified hero or champion of the olden times [*sic*]'. Ibid., p. 212.

105. In Ann Gold's *Fruitful Journeys: The Way of Rajasthani Pilgrims* (Oxford, 1989), pp. 40, 63–79, there is mention of the *jhūjhārī* which is either the spirit of a warrior or the spirit of an adult person which 'lingered after death was a mistake' (p. 64). Deaths which produced these beings ranged from drowning and snake bite to (in one case) tuberculosis. These beings continue to make themselves known to their descendants and insist on being worshipped.

106. Attar Singh dates the text to 1834 in his *Sakhee Book or the Description of Gooroo Gobind Singh's Religion and Doctrines, translated from Gooroo Mukhi into Hindi and afterwards into English* (Benares, 1873), p. vii. S.S. Kohli, *The Life and Ideals of Guru Gobind Singh (Based on Original Sources)* (New Delhi, 1986), p. v, contends that the text was, in fact, issued by the tenth Guru. The text on which I have relied is G.S. Naiar (ed.), *Gur Ratan Māl Arthāt Sau Sākhī* (Patiala, 1985).

107. Surprisingly, despite what today appears as the 'un-Sikh' content of the sakhi, the editor of the text, G.S. Naiar, notes that

The term shahid is applied to him who sacrifices his life in a dharam yudh.

The definition here is clearly similar to the one in the *MK. Gur Ratan Māl*, p. 165.

108. For the martyr as an intercessor in Islamic tradition see Wensinck, *Handbook*, p. 148.

109. See Chapter Three.

110. The various classes of malevolent spirits are very difficult to categorize.

111. These *guṇas* or strands of matter are explained in Ishvarakrishna's *Sāṅkhya Kārikās*. See W.T. DeBary, et al. (ed.), *Sources of Indian Tradition* I (New York, 1958), pp. 304–10.

112. This term is derived from the Sanskrit *bipaśchit*, or 'inspired', 'wise', 'learned in the Rig Veda'. For various characters in Hindu and Buddhist mythology named Bipaschit, see Vettam Mani's *Purāṇic Encyclopaedia* (Delhi, 1975), p. 857 and M. Monier-Williams, *A Sanskrit-English Dictionary* (Delhi, 1990), p. 972. It is also possible that this Bipaschit was simply named for the sake of the sakhi, 'King Wise'.

113. G.S. Naiar (ed.), *Gur Ratan Māl*, pp. 37–8.

114. *Glossary* II, p. 371; A.H. Bingley's *The Sikhs* (Patiala, 1970), p. 81.

115. *Glossary* I, pp. 183–5. The Sikh worship of Gugga Pir is found in Oberoi, *Construction*, pp. 160–2; as well as in P.S. Jammu, 'Religion in a Malwa Village', pp. 86–95.

116. L. Veccia Vaglieri, 'Ali B. Abi Ṭālib', in *The Encyclopaedia of Islam* I (Leiden, 1960), pp. 381–6 and idem, '(Al-) Ḥusayn B. Ali B. Abi Ṭālib', in *The Encyclopaedia of Islam* III:1 (Leiden, 1971), pp. 607–15.

117. Mahmud Ayoub, *Redemptive Suffering in Islam* (The Hague, 1978), p. 41.

118. The early nineteenth-century account from which this is taken is Mahommed Tippoo, 'Observations on the origin and ceremonies of the Mohurrum', in the *Madras Journal of Literature and Science* 9: 2 (1835), pp. 315–35, as noted in Susan Bayly's *Saints, Goddesses and Kings*, p. 142. That the 'Nanak Panthis' mentioned here were perhaps Udasi Sikhs is implied by the fact that these participants were smeared with ashes.

119. C.M. Singh, 'Police move against memorials to militants', in the *Indian Express*, 21 March 1993. According to the article, the memorials were in the form of '100-foot-tall nishan sahibs'.

SIX

The Game of Love
The Singh Sabha and
the Rhetoric of Martyrdom

A heart thrilling sermon on the martyrdom of the 'Sahib-zadas' makes converts in the family. It wakes up and resolves to follow in the footsteps of the departed Sikhs of the yore [sic] and give up old rites.[1]

On Thursday, 10 June 1909, at 5:30 in the morning in district Gujranwala, a Sikh named Lachman Singh was publicly executed by the government of British India before a crowd numbering in the thousands. The crime for which he was sentenced to the extreme penalty by the Sessions Court Judge of Sialkot was the murder of three Muslims who had, according to the accused, converted a Hindu *lambardār* (village headman) from his native faith to Islam.[2]

Although the act of conversion seems trivial today, in the Punjab of the early twentieth century, such acts mobilized large numbers of the disaffected group to which the newly converted had originally belonged.[3] Not only were conversions an obvious loss to the faith, but in a political system based on numbers, it also indicated a possible deprivation of the community's slight power and few privileges if such a trend continued. Conversions rarely led to the murder of the proselytizers or of those they had converted, but the vicious polemical tracts which these events often engendered are a testament to heightened feelings of anger and betrayal.[4] We must keep in mind, moreover, the tension in the political atmosphere brought about by the recent passage of the Morley–Minto reforms in 1909, which gave separate political representation to the Muslim peoples of India.[5] As the Sikhs were also a people separate from both the Hindu and Muslim (so proclaimed the Tat Khalsa), the various editorials in the two major Sikh newspapers of the early twentieth century called for a similar initiative on behalf of the 'sword-arm of British India', the Sikhs so that Sikh culture and religion may be further protected under the so-called benevolent British government.[6] That their appeals were met with a recurring silence may well have played a role in Lachman Singh's choice of action.

In regard to the individual himself, there is, unfortunately, very little information that survives. The space he has been allotted in the early twentieth-century history of the Sikhs is no more than a few newspaper articles, and these only concerned with the end of Lachman Singh's life. Although our second English article laments the fact that this man's life and career were not better known, it does note that Lachman Singh had actively participated in the attempt to enhance the overall status of the 'beloved Panth' vis-à-vis other religious communities in the Punjab during his short lifetime. As a result, it appears that he was very sympathetic to the Singh Sabha cause. The 26 June article paraphrases Lachman Singh to demonstrate his grave concern with the well-being of the Sikh Panth.

In the matter of the sustenance of [his wife and children], the Bhai ji said she was not to stretch her hand before the Panth so long as there was labour of the hardest description to be procured. The Panth was already sufficiently burdened with the expenses of upkeep of the various institutions, charitable and educational, all of which had yet to be perfected. It would, therefore, be exceedingly against the wishes of the Bhai ji that she should add to the burden by depending upon the community for the support of herself and children. If possible, she was to stint her meagre pittance and to contribute something, however little it might be, to the communal funds.[7]

The emphasis on the 'burdens' of the community indicates that Lachman Singh was well aware of the Singh Sabha's and CKD's efforts to improve the social and political situation of the Sikh Panth. Lachman Singh may have himself engaged in these efforts as it is certain that he was familiar with both the work and the writings of the Singh Sabha. In fact, it was reported that days prior to his hanging, Lachman Singh had specifically asked to see Bhais Lal Singh, Sohan Singh and Teja Singh,[8] highly visible members of the Singh Sabha movement. (It appears that it was to these men that Lachman Singh had confided.)[9]

That very little is stated about this man's previous life is probably just as well. It seems doubtful that these two newspapers, whose every issue reminded their readers of Sikh loyalty to the Crown, would have wished to incur the displeasure of the British by devoting numerous articles to a man accused of murder by a secular British court.[10] The reason for any reference at all to this individual (that his death was newsworthy notwithstanding) will become clear.

Although brief, the reports of Lachman Singh's execution are nevertheless highly revealing. The title of the 26 June report, 'A Sikh Martyr's End', is representative, making clear that the articles are not particularly concerned with the crime itself but with the events that followed Lachman Singh's sentencing.[11] In other words, these describe the words and actions of the accused and the statements of those with whom he had come into contact during his trial, brief incarceration and execution. The fact that he had committed murder is only briefly mentioned in all of the articles.[12] What we are told, rather, is that as soon as the 'Bhai ji' had entered the jailhouse, his passion for Sikhism had moved his fellow inmates to tears and that they 'had ceased to feel the discomforts of the place which, to them at any rate, had as it were been transformed into a veritable *Swarg* [heaven]'.[13] The tone of all four articles follow this type of style, that is, an enthusiastic martyrological style employing a rhetoric of martyrdom. It is within this framework that the attitudes and statements of these prisoners should be placed.

According to our English-language writer, as men and women visited Lachman Singh's cell, they were struck by the 'Bhai ji's beaming face' (a common literary device indicating the presence of God's light) and his 'Sikh-like fortitude in such an hour of trial'. Although notions such as 'Sikh-like' are somewhat vague and, indeed, quite open to interpretation, the article goes on to provide some substance to this rather shadowy term as evinced in the following observations recorded by our author. The writer notes that as Lachman Singh spoke to his wife just before his execution:

[his] tone ... was so steady, his bearing so manly and fearless, that the spectacle reminded the by standers of the cheerfulness with which the Sikh martyrs of yore accepted death by a variety of the most excruciating tortures without swerving a hair's breadth from the delicate path of Sikhism.[14]

'Sikh-like' should be thus read and interpreted here as martyr-like, or in this case, a fortitude similar to that we find in the narratives of Sikh martyrs which were very popular in the late nineteenth and early twentieth centuries.[15] There can be little doubt that the author's memory as well as the memories of other observers derive from Singh Sabha narratives of martyrdom or dhadhi compositions, or both, as the chance that any of the spectators had ever witnessed the executions of the 'Sikhs martyrs of yore' (a reference to seventeenth- and eighteenth-century Sikhs) is remote. The popularity of such tracts may have also influenced Lachman Singh's drastic actions. By 1909, Sikh writers inspired by the ideas of the Singh Sabha had published a large number of poems and accounts of how Sikhs had suffered under Muslim tyranny. His choice to kill three Muslims may well have been unconsciously derived from such narratives.[16]

Why such a reverential tone for a man who achieved death in so inglorious a manner? From what we have thus far understood in regard to the Sikh tradition of martyrdom, the death penalty for an act of cold-blooded murder qualifies for neither the status 'Bhai ji', nor for that of martyr. Are the writers simply embellishing the event with the language of martyrdom, a language which in this case focuses attention away from the murders that the accused had previously committed? As we progress through the reports and set these in their proper historical context, this seems very doubtful. Both the writers' use of this language and the connection they make between the 'Sikh martyrs of yore' and Lachman Singh were most likely unconscious ones and appear logical when the accused's actions during the days leading to and on the day of his execution are examined. As Clifford Geertz would claim, a 'thick description' is in order.[17]

We are told that while in jail, Lachman Singh would lovingly discourse on Sikhism, often buttressing his statements with hymns from the Adi Granth.[18] Seeing two clean-shaven fellow prisoners, he was, according to the English article, provided with an opportunity to address them (possibly indicating a desire that all Sikhs adhere to the Khalsa form propagated by the Tat Khalsa). As he preached to them, the article continues, 'he said that the sole purpose for which the Guru had founded the Khalsa was doing good to humanity'. Not for a moment did Lachman Singh's stalwart facade fall. When visited by his children, he remained steadfast, exhorting them to remain true to their faith even in the face of death: to die with one's 'faith in Sikhism intact', the article claims, 'was sure to make [one] acceptable in the eyes of the Guru'. He also told his children that they 'should not bear grudge to anybody [*sic*]'. One may surmise that the accused is here, in effect, forgiving his executor, the British government in

India.'For a Sikh,' Lachman Singh is reported to have said,'death loses all terrors.'

The article implies that he was fearless to the point that he could calmly propose how his body should be handled after it had lost life: 'He would like ... to have the skin stripped clean off the corpse and made into shoes for some of the Panthic workers whom he named.'[19] We are further told that as soon as Lachman Singh heard his sentence, he did not show the slightest sign of anxiety. Rather, the verdict delighted him and prompted him to continue preaching to those he met in jail on the importance of remaining firm in one's religious convictions.[20] We may assume that these as well as other words and actions left quite an impression on the many people who had visited Lachman Singh in jail.[21] So much so that on the day of his execution, people from the surrounding areas began to gather three hours prior to the event to take his *darśan* and to view his hanging. As Lachman Singh approached the gallows, the 'martyr' (as he was called by the people of Gujranwala, according to the articles[22]) was met with a 'lusty Jaikara of Sat Sri Akal'. 'On Thursday morning at 5-30 A.M. sharp,' continues the short 19 June piece,

Thousands of persons mustered strong outside the Jail compound to bid farewell to the brave man. Bhai Lachman Singh came out of the Jail smiling and in good cheer. He was throughout manly in his demeanour and enchanting *[sic]* Japji Sahib. He jumped at the scaffold most courageously and put the noose around his neck without the least sign of despair. He exhorted the audience to always care for their religion without which they could never attain salvation.[23]

To this may be added the statement of the 26 June article:

[the] last words of the Bhai ji on this earth were eagerly awaited by the spectators, when suddenly he burst into eloquence and exhorted the thousands that had assembled to witness his martyrdom to always remember death and strive to the utmost of their capacity to serve their country. He had hardly finished when the lever was pulled, the wooden floor parted and the Sikh was no more.[24]

One would assume that such odd behaviour would have enabled the accused to control the fear of his quickly approaching death. The articles make no hint of this whatsoever. It appears, rather, that the author accepts Lachman Singh's actions at face value, as behaviour 'naturally' belonging to the 'Sikh martyrs of yore'.[25] What these articles lead one to suspect is that Lachman Singh was acting out the role of the Sikh martyr, unconsciously adopting a particular pattern of behaviour which included what now appears to be a highly stylized series of actions and gestures, as well as a conventionalized language. In this light, it comes as no surprise that one of the hymns to which he would allude while incarcerated was Kabir's *Gauṛī rāg* 20 (3), a shabad often interpreted within Sikh martyrdom discourse:

Through the Eternal Word of the True Guru I have become privy to the mystery of death, the death which terrifies the entire world. How shall I die now that my whole being has come to terms with death? Those people who do not know Ram die over and over again. It is all of these people who talk incessantly of dying and death. Only those who die with the proper understanding become deathless. Kabir says, 'My whole being is in a state of bliss, my doubts are all gone, and I am in the most profound ecstasy.'[26]

Lachman Singh, it appears, no doubt thought of himself as a martyr, perhaps the first to the Singh Sabha cause of 'rejuvenating' the Sikh Panth, and acted out the drama of martyrdom accordingly.[27]

Although one cannot subject Lachman Singh to the same type of scrutiny to which the anthropologist, Victor Turner, subjects the famous Christian martyr, Thomas Becket,[28] the small space that Lachman Singh has been assigned does provide us with enough material to make for some very significant conclusions. In his analysis of Thomas Becket's last years, Turner suggests that the confrontation between this resolute Catholic archbishop and his executor, King Henry II of England, 'evince[s] the presence and activity of certain consciously recognised (though not consciously grasped) cultural models in the heads of the main actors'. Turner calls these models 'root paradigms'. The specific root paradigm to which Becket adheres, he notes, was 'the Christian root paradigm of martyrdom'.[29] That this paradigm had had a long history in the Christian tradition prior to Becket (d. 1170) is clearly taken for granted as the Christian saviour, Jesus, is himself believed to have died a martyr's death on the cross. The epistles of famous early Christian writers clearly show that many of the earliest Christians understood his death as such. These also note that such pious disciples were awed by this selfless and loving act (as they perceived it) and were thus inspired to practise, through a similar agonizing death and martyrdom, a profound *imitatio Christi*.[30]

We have thus far recognized that martyrdom was a part of the Sikh tradition prior to the rise of the Singh Sabha in 1873. That martyrdom had achieved the status of root paradigm in the Sikh tradition prior to the Sabha's height of influence is certainly possible. We see, for example, an emphasis on martyrdom and martyrs in Seva Singh's early nineteenth-century *Śahīd-bilās*, as well as in Ratan Singh Bhangu's mid-century *Gur-panth Prakāś*, not to mention the earlier gur-bilas literature. Santokh Singh's famous *Surāj Prakāś* (completed in 1844) has relatively fewer references to the martyr's death, but an admiration for such sacrifice is recognizable nevertheless.[31] Could this admiration have inspired those late nineteenth-century Sikhs before Lachman Singh who were believed, in retrospect, to have died the deaths of martyrs? Among these were Sikhs such as the Namdharis executed by the British in 1872, as well as the Sikh soldiers who fell at Saragarhi in 1897. That these men had this specific 'cultural model' in mind, and that other Sikhs of the mid- to late nineteenth century (and before) also came under the sway of such a root paradigm (if such there was), is impossible to determine with the lack of written evidence. There is, fortunately, written evidence in regard to Lachman Singh and this allows us to legitimately conclude that he (and his audience) did have such a root paradigm at his (and their) disposal.

What differentiates Lachman Singh's day from the period of the Namdhari or Saragarhi 'martyrs', of course, is the profound influence of the Singh Sabha. By virtue of his association with this group, we may surmise that Lachman Singh's behaviour was principally learned from the Tat Khalsa. We will note that it was through this group's tireless campaign of writing and preaching, in which we find a profound appropriation of a rhetoric of martyrdom, that the selfless sacrifice of one's life for a righteous cause became amplified, receiving a force and coherence which was hitherto unknown, perhaps allowing martyrdom to realize the status of root paradigm in the Sikh tradition of the early twentieth century. Whether such a status was achieved by the Singh Sabha or not, however, there can be no doubt that the basic importance of martyrdom in today's Sikh tradition can be traced back to this movement. In essence, then, Lachman Singh was following an unwritten script produced by the Singh Sabha which gave his performance (so to speak) a dignity, grace and a coherence that it might not have possessed otherwise.[32]

Many of the attitudes that Lachman Singh displayed clearly fit into the pattern we find in this script, a script governed in large part through the Sikh root paradigm of martyrdom. Lachman Singh appears to have taken courage from this cultural model while in jail, literally becoming an 'initiated defender' of the Singh Sabha.[33] His constant discourses on the glory of the Sikh tradition as espoused by the Sabha seem to bear this point out. By tapping into this paradigm, moreover, Lachman Singh may well have realized a peace and consistency which permitted him to remain firm during his incarceration and execution, and which also permitted him to exhibit a 'manly and fearless' bearing throughout the ordeal.

His actions also fit into this Singh Sabha script. His recitation of Guru Nanak's Japji Sahib as he was led to the gallows; courageously placing the noose around his own neck; the exhortation to the gathered crowd demonstrating the strength of his Sikh faith; and the joy he exhibits at his upcoming death; all these turn the dramatic spectacle of execution into a triumph of righteousness rather than the vindication of the government's moral right and authority. By this behaviour, Lachman Singh literally casts off the burden of the crime for which he had been condemned. It is, in large part, for these reasons that neither our writers nor the spectators dwell on the crimes this Sikh had committed.[34]

The reports of the execution seem to demonstrate that apart from Lachman Singh, there were many Sikhs who did, indeed, identify to varying degrees with the tradition of martyrdom which the Tat Khalsa had amplified and broadcast through their various publications and preaching tours in the late nineteenth and early twentieth centuries. As these people also possessed the same cultural model or root paradigm we recognize in Lachman Singh's actions, both our writers and the spectators easily tap into the tradition that Lachman Singh is reenacting and themselves unconsciously play their part in the drama. We recognize the audience's cooperation with their 'lusty Jaikara of Sat Sri Akal', for example, as well as the awe that Lachman Singh's fellow prisoners are alleged to have displayed as they heard him speak of his faith. Even Lachman Singh's jailers permitted him to meet with as many visitors as he wished. We are also cognizant of audience participation in the following statement:

When the body was taken to a neighbouring Gurdwara to be washed, many people bedecked the corpse of the departed Khalsa with flower garlands and chaplets while others profusely sprinkled Attar and rose-water. About two thousand people accompanied the bier to the crematorium where, after the cremation was over, it was resolved that some sort of memorial should be raised to commemorate the heroic end of the martyr. A noteworthy fact about the feelings of the citizens was that all the Hindu shops were closed on the day as a sign of mourning.[35]

In the light of the testimony of the spectators, we may, therefore, assume that the writers of these articles are not embellishing their respective pieces with a particular language so as to create a Sikh martyr, a technique of which some martyrologists certainly make use. Rather, it seems that Lachman Singh through his very actions had unconsciously made himself out to be the martyr and thus prompted both his audience and our authors to view him as such, as well as urged the latter to adopt a martyrological format in their articles.[36] Of course, since crimes do not figure in traditional martyr narratives of the Sikhs, it should come as no surprise that the reports fail to elaborate upon the actual murder of the three Muslims. Lachman Singh, therefore, becomes in this rhetoric a victim and a sacrifice rather than a murderer. Agency here is deleted.

That the audience so easily accommodated and participated in a scene which seems to have been taken directly from the narratives of a Sikh history prepared by the Singh Sabha appears to indicate that by the end of the first decade of the twentieth century, the ideas and ideals of the Tat Khalsa were finally being viewed as the standard or orthodox interpretation of the Sikh tradition.[37] It is worth noting in this context that it would be only four months after the execution of Lachman Singh, in October of 1909, that the Singh Sabha's foremost political body, the CKD, would score a resounding victory with the passage of the Anand Marriage Act. Although there were initially many problems associated in turning the 1908 proposition into law, the Act's final form does demonstrate the Panth's increasing reliance on those Sikh intellectuals whose thought was aligned with the Tat Khalsa, particularly in regard to proper Sikh practice and definitions.[38] Since Lachman Singh's crime was connected with the reform movement, we may infer that he received at least some of his inspiration from the Tat Khalsa attempt to 'reform' the Panth; in particular, the interpretation of the Sikh tradition that this reform had engendered, in which martyrdom was a key component.

Although the writers of the Lachman Singh report were prompted to utilize the language of martyrdom, it was by no means a rare usage. In fact, since the very dawn of the Sikh press in the late nineteenth century, the editors of Sikh newspapers discovered that their audiences were very willing to read or listen to the legends of Sikh martyrs. This was, of course, not a new phenomenon.[39] We noted in our second chapter that the music which dhadhis had played prior to the Singh Sabha and continued to play in the nineteenth and twentieth centuries was very popular throughout the land of the five rivers. One can assume that in a society primarily composed of rural peasants whose backs are bent in daily labour, the stories of those who keep their backs straight and defy the powers that be, despite the price they may have to pay, would no doubt appeal to romantic sensibilities.[40] The fact that Lachman Singh was able to adopt the role of the martyr and, especially, that the spectators were able to effortlessly interpret his actions as such implies, of course, that the image of the martyr modified, codified and made clear by the Tat Khalsa was, at least in 1909, a common one.

We have suggested in all that is written above that it was primarily the teachers, preachers, writers and various other personnel of the Singh Sabha who were responsible not only for the crowd's keen familiarity with the actions played out on that fateful morning of 10 June 1909, but in a sense, for the very actions themselves. The remains of this chapter will deal with this band of zealous, educated Sikhs and how they used and adapted the well-known legends of Sikh martyrs which predated the late-nineteenth-century movement to perpetuate their interpretation of Sikh religion, ritual and practice, and eventually allow this understanding to be viewed as the only interpretation of the Sikh tradition. Of course, the legends of martyrdom may well have inspired a great deal of reverence prior to the Singh Sabha, and may as well have encouraged many Sikhs to acts of rare daring and bravery.[41] The fact that the Tat Khalsa initially chose this theme of the many available in the early nineteenth-century Sikh tradition is indicative of both its popularity and its proximity to later Tat Khalsa interpretations.[42] In the process of constantly using these legends as a vehicle to carry and promote the Singh Sabha interpretation of the Sikh tradition, the legends of martyrdom themselves were modified and came to be seen—as a result of both this repeated use and modification—as far more integral to the Sikh faith than was previously the case. Logically, therefore, as the Tat Khalsa interpretation came to the forefront, so, too, did the primary vehicle with which it was intimately connected. Had these stories been as essential to the Sikh tradition found in the seventeenth and eighteenth centuries, there is no doubt that the author of the *Bachitar Nātak* would have relegated at least a small portion of his text to the martyrdom of the fifth Guru. Had martyrdom been as salient a feature of the tradition at this time as it would be in the nineteenth century, moreover, it seems likely that a word describing the concept would have been available.

The Tat Khalsa

The history of the Singh Sabha, as well as the answer as to how the Sikh community came to accept the Tat Khalsa interpretation of Sikh tradition as authentic, has been well discussed by Harjot Oberoi. Oberoi maintains that Singh Sabha intellectuals were influenced, in part, by western Orientalism and engaged European ideals of the period, such as humanism, liberal democracy and Enlightenment rationalism, in 'dialogic narrative', that is a 'polyphonic discourse based on tellings, retellings, or references to important cultural narratives'.[43] Through aggressive tactics such as 'eradication campaigns', polemics and the reconstitution of the sacred outlined in 'the manuals of *rites de passage*', linked with the armies of social change (communication and commercialization, respectively), Oberoi maintains that Tat Khalsa thinking gained ascendancy, displacing to a great extent the Sanatan Sikh discourse which had previously dominated Sikh imaginations.[44] The Tat Khalsa endeavour was strongly supported through their interest in both education, witnessed by the establishment of Khalsa College in 1892,[45] and in the Sikh soldiers of the Indian Army who, because they were seen as knowledgeable and experienced men in the eyes of their fellow Sikh villagers, spread the Tat Khalsa message.[46]

By the time of the Singh Sabhas, the Sikh faith was already a four-hundred-year-old tradition. Many of the reformers disliked elements of the contemporary faith, such as idolatry, 'Guru-dom' (a popular Tat Khalsa term), caste and the worship of popular saints, which, they felt, did not measure up to their new 'enlightened' rationale. They were exceptionally proud of the monotheistic religion enshrined within the Adi Granth, the stress on the equality of men and women, and the traditions of martial prowess, bravery and sacrifice.[47] Those practices they disliked they endeavoured to do away with altogether. The contemporary worship of both Gugga Pir and Sakhi Sarwar, for example, prompted Ditt Singh to write two pamphlets which were widely disseminated, condemning their worship as superstitious and against true Sikh principles.[48] Ditt Singh and other Tat Khalsa ideologues would also travel to areas notorious for popular festivities and quickly denounce such practices as un-Sikh, supporting their statements with hymns from the Adi Granth. After such meetings, we are told, many of the festival's participants would resolve to no longer engage in such activities.[49] Those features of the tradition for which the Tat Khalsa had an affinity, however, were applauded and appropriated to support their various modifications of the category, Sikh. In the process, these nineteenth-century features (which, nevertheless, did not always measure up to the standards of the Tat Khalsa) were themselves modified to promote Tat Khalsa concerns. One of those to which they were exceptionally partial was the heroic tradition which emphasizes sacrifice and martyrdom.

Vir Singh, Ratan Singh Bhangu, and the Transformation of *Sahīdī*

Very early in the history of the Tat Khalsa, therefore, the pre-Singh Sabha understandings of Sikh heroism, sacrifice and martyrdom came under the group's scrutiny. During the late nineteenth and early twentieth centuries, one of its most influential members, Bhai Vir Singh, would take up the task of 'editing' two of the more popular gur-bilas works in which such themes were found. Although these pre-Singh Sabha texts presented a Khalsa that was exceptionally heroic and willing to sacrifice itself, the reasons for such sacrifice were not always those of which the later Tat Khalsa was fond. When such early examples of martyrdom were noted by the Tat Khalsa, ideologues would alter the reason for the martyr's sacrifice and amplify what they understood the meaning of shahidi to represent.

This is best demonstrated in Vir Singh's 'editing' of Ratan Singh Bhangu's epic, *Gur-panth Prakāś* (History of the Guru's Panth), originally produced in 1841 (S. 1898) at the insistence of Sir David Ochterlony,[50] which our Tat Khalsa author renamed *Prāchīn Panth Prakāś* (the 'old' or 'former' history of the Panth) in the first 1914 printed edition in order that it not be confused with the *Panth Prakāś*, written by Gian Singh in 1880.[51] Of course, since the original text was produced to be recited and heard rather than read, some changes were necessary in the printed edition.[52] Yet, the extent of the changes undertaken by Vir Singh far exceed this need. In editing this text, it seems that Vir Singh both deleted anything he felt was contrary to his vision of Sikhism and added passages which supplemented his Tat Khalsa-aligned interpretation. While some of the modifications were subtle, others were quite obvious. In *Panth Prakāś*, for example, Gian Singh notes that he consulted the folios of Bhangu's manuscript while writing of the famous incident regarding Guru Gobind

Singh's veneration of the goddess Chandi.[53] In the Vir Singh edition of *Prāchīn Panth Prakāś*, this episode does not appear. And although Vir Singh does later write of Gian Singh's reference to Bhangu's passage in *Devī Pūjān Partal* (a text which endeavoured to put an end to the widespread belief that Guru Gobind Singh was a devotee of the goddess), he adds that he came across no such section in the manuscripts of *Gur-panth Prakāś* that he had consulted. A quick glance at any of the extant manuscripts will verify that this is not the case.[54] Another obvious addition to the original text is a suggestion that readers consult the *Purātan Janam-sākhī* to supplement the biography of Guru Nanak presented in *Prāchīn Panth Prakāś*. The *Purātan Janam-sākhī* is a manuscript discovered in the late nineteenth century (five decades after Bhangu completed his text) and published with additional janam-sakhi material in 1926, with Vir Singh himself as editor.[55]

It has been recently implied by Harinder Singh that Vir Singh wished to alter Bhangu's text so as to make it conform far more with the world that the early twentieth-century author presented in his three most famous and widely read historical novels, *Sundarī* (1898), *Bijai Singh* (1899), and *Satvant Kaur* (1899–1900).[56] These novels are highly idealistic works which present Sikhs and Sikhism very much within the Singh Sabha interpretation of the tradition: Sikhism as a unique, divine dispensation whose adherents were willing to sacrifice even their lives to ensure that the external insignia of all Khalsa Sikhs were retained; a community composed of men and women who were enthused by the martyrdoms of their fellow Sikhs, and sought a similar end for themselves.[57] Throughout these works, the Sikhs of Vir Singh's own day are often juxtaposed with the self-sacrificing, altruistic Sikh warriors of the eighteenth century, a technique which allows Vir Singh to provide scathing comments on late nineteenth- and early-twentieth-century Sikh practice and values.[58]

There is no doubt that Vir Singh's editing of Bhangu's text endeavours to carry out this transformation. During the period in which Bhangu composed his epic, for example, Sikhs were considered essentially Hindus, a fact that Bhangu acknowledged as easily as his contemporary, Santokh Singh. For Vir Singh, of course, this was unacceptable. Whenever Vir Singh felt that the term 'Hindu' was used in reference to what was obviously a Sikh, the editor would delete the former word and write in either 'Sikh' or 'Singh'. At times, moreover, the original word 'Sikh' would be replaced with 'Khalsa'.[59]

Furthermore, Vir Singh deleted passages which made the Sikhs appear anything less than the Tat Khalsa-inspired ideal he demonstrated in his novels. We have witnessed this in the omissions regarding the Sikh veneration of the goddess Chandi.[60] There are other examples. For instance, a Sikh who is a beggar in the original manuscript is eliminated from the printed text. As well, rather than create the Khalsa to partake in riots (*dange*) as mentioned in the original, Guru Gobind Singh creates this elite band of warriors to engage in glorious battle (*yudh*).[61] Among the most surprising revisions we find is in regard to the exploits of the famous Bhai Bidhi Chand. In the Vir Singh edition, the passage in which this noted Gursikh of the sixth Guru steals the royal horses, Gulbagh and Dilbagh, from the Lahore fort, for which he was glorified in both early-nineteenth-century song and legend, is omitted.[62] The fact that Vir Singh expunged the episode that alludes to Bidhi Chand's career as a thief appears to indicate that Vir Singh was unable to tolerate the inclusion of the slightest negative image of the Sikhs.

When Vir Singh confronts narratives of martyrdom in the original text, some of these also undergo a transformation. As mentioned above, the editor continues to present the episodes as glorious martyrdoms. He alters the focus of the martyrs, however, thereby altering their religious allegiance, and by implication, their identity. Where the extant manuscripts of Bhangu's epic show Sikhs happily sacrificing their lives for the Devi, for example, the version supplied by Vir Singh shows these same Sikhs sacrificing themselves for their Guru and for the benefit of the Panth.[63] Even Guru Gobind Singh is not spared in this regard. While he offers his four sons as a sacrifice to the goddess in the manuscripts, he is presented as sacrificing all he holds dear for the sake of the Panth in the printed version.[64]

These changes imply that for Vir Singh, the question of identity is paramount, requiring a much stronger stress than it does in Bhangu's version, the focus of which rests primarily upon the character's courage, sacrifice, commitment and ability to bear extreme hardship (including an often painful death), qualities of which valiant warriors are made. The notion of Sikh identity, particularly a Sikh identity that differed from a Hindu one, was simply not as fundamental an issue in the Punjab of 1840 as it was in the first decade of the twentieth century. It appears that Bhangu's principal concern in terms of Sikh identity was to demonstrate that Sikhs were not Muslims, an understanding that Sikh martyrs in the text ardently underscore. Vir Singh retains the stress on Sikh courage, sacrifice, and especially commitment, but he was keen to align Bhangu's heroes and martyrs to his own Tat Khalsa interpretation of the Sikh tradition, for such a representation in an 'old' (*prāchīn*) text would have strongly buttressed an interpretation of the Sikh tradition, which was very much at odds with the one presented, for example, by the so-called Sikh religious leader, Gurbakhsh Singh Bedi, at the 1910 Hindu Conference in Multan. At this conference, Bedi publicly proclaimed that Sikhs were Hindus.[65] In other words, Vir Singh reconstructs the categories 'Hindu', 'Sikh', 'Singh' and 'Khalsa' that we find in Bhangu's text to make these appear in line with early-twentieth-century understandings. In using and modifying the martyr legends to aid in and promote this reconstruction, thereby further underscoring the notion of a separate Sikh identity (recall that the idea of separate identity is inherent to the theme of martyrdom), Vir Singh recasts the category 'martyr' or 'shahid', denuding it of much of its early nineteenth-century content. As we noted earlier, this content was not congenial to the enlightenment rationale of the Tat Khalsa reformers. These men and women now become brave Khalsa Sikhs, truly worthy of the Panth's praise and reverence for their singular sacrifice on its behalf, not lives given in a sacrificial frenzy to the goddess, an act which would make these recently dead deserving of propitiation in 'Hindu' understandings.[66]

We must reiterate that the twentieth-century understanding of shahid was already in place by the time Vir Singh published this text. Of course, Vir Singh's own novels and articles contributed a great deal to this understanding. The fact that the original manuscripts of *Gur-panth Prakāś* can be placed beside the printed edition of this work, however, allows us a singular insight into the reconstruction of these categories, a reconstruction we can only infer in the martyrologies of earlier Tat Khalsa writers. As we shall see, this interpretation of the term was initially made standard by the most prolific Tat Khalsa writer of the late nineteenth century, Ditt Singh. In regard to martyrs, Vir Singh seems to rely heavily upon Ditt Singh's understandings of these pious Sikhs.

When we couple the emphasis on the respect and reverence for the noble sacrifice of the Sikh martyrs, found in Vir Singh's edition of *Prāchīn Panth Prakāś* and in every Singh Sabha martyrology predating 1914, with the resounding Tat Khalsa condemnations of the worship of demi-gods like Khwaja Khizr and Bhairon (again, led initially by Ditt Singh), we come to an understanding of how the category, shahid, was dramatically stripped to form the sparse definition we would later find in Kahn Singh's *Mahān Koś*.[67] We must keep in mind that although Sikh martyrs were noted as universal beings of power by the Sikhs in pre-Singh Sabha Punjab, they were not often associated with the martyrs and demi-gods of other traditions, such as Sakhi Sarvar, Gugga Pir, or Ghazi Miyan. In this respect, the Tat Khalsa found no need to cite Sikh martyrs in their attempt to rid the Panth of the so-called superstitious worship of such beings. As mentioned in the last chapter, such a citing would have been counter to Tat Khalsa goals.[68] Tat Khalsa objections to this form of worship were aimed at pirs and demi-gods, not at Sikh martyrs such as, for example, Baba Dip Singh.[69] By playing up the reverence for Sikh martyrs while condemning the worship of demigods and pirs, the Tat Khalsa successfully implanted in Sikh minds a definition of shahid which was shorn of much of its pre–Singh Sabha meaning.

In Bhangu's original, there is a martyr narrative where it seems that a specific Sikh, as opposed to Hindu, identity may be a question. Bhangu states that Taru Singh chose death over having the sacred kes shaved from his head. This is, however, an exception, but one which seems to demonstrate that the inherent element of identity in the theme of martyrdom that the Tat Khalsa would later exploit and mould to their purposes was present, albeit underplayed, in the early nineteenth century.[70] We must repeat, moreover, that the Khalsa Sikh who Bhangu has in mind is a Khalsa Sikh set within the Sanatan Sikh paradigm.

Despite the differences we have noted, there is a keen similarity between both Bhangu's original text and Vir Singh's later amended editions, particularly in respect to martyrdom. We may briefly pause to compare a passage which appears in the original with another that may have been added by Vir Singh or by another editor in the printed text.[71] Having finished narrating the martyrdom of Taru Singh, Bhangu tells his listeners that

Any person who hears the account of Taru Singh's [martyrdom] will no longer feel any suffering. As he approaches his last breath, Yama, the God of Death, will assail him not and he will die painlessly. This person will always observe the standards of the Sikh faith, ensuring that his sacred kes remain intact.[72]

One may assume that it is on the basis of this statement that Vir

Singh allegedly adds at the end of the entire text another *phalaśruti* passage, verses which tell the reader all the good that will result from the act of reading or hearing the text. According to Jit Singh Sital, this passage makes the benefit (*mahātam*) of reading and hearing the stories of Sikh martyrs apparent:[73]

In the same way that the Panth became manifest I have written this complete *Gur-panth Prakāś* [i.e. the text is historically accurate]. The enlightened mind who listens to this work will fight in battles and be unwilling to flee the battlefield. At the moment of death when he breathes his last, he will go to meet all the martyrs. He will mingle with all the martyrs in the same way that water blends with water.[74]

The similarity here is clear. Both phalashruti passages suggest that our authors do more than simply narrate historical events. It seems that they desire their readers to actually participate in history by exhorting them to mimic the characteristics personified by the martyrs on whom the text elaborates. In this regard, the texts of both *Gur-pànth Prakāś* and *Prāchīn Panth Prakāś* are martyrologies rather than histories, texts meant to inspire and enthuse Sikhs of the periods to which both our respective authors belonged.[75] All one need do is listen to these stories to be inspired to act as did the 'Sikhs of yore' (or so our authors believed). For both Bhangu and Vir Singh, there are compelling reasons to write in this fashion.

Let us first deal with Ratan Singh. We must recall that Bhangu is writing for both the territorially expanding British and the Sikhs during a period in which chaos (along with the Khalsa army) reigned.[76] One may thus assume that the sustained exposition on martyrdom and Sikh martyrs had two closely interconnected purposes. The first is obviously an exhortation to the Panth that Sikhs must prepare themselves for the inevitable conflict with the British. Bhangu notes that it was only through the sacrifices which past Sikhs had made that sovereignty became a reality and strongly implies that sacrifices of a similar calibre are urgently required if the Khalsa is to retain what it now possesses. He hopes to inspire Sikhs through the narratives of courageous martyrdom to once again make great sacrifices. All would belong to the Khalsa, notes Bhangu, if Sikhs are willing to offer their heads to the Guru.[77] To accomplish this, all Sikhs must aspire to be like the martyr, Mani Singh.[78] Such writing would have come easily to a man with a lineage as glorious as Ratan Singh's. As a descendant of the famous Shahid Mehtab Singh, the slayer of Massa Ranghar, we may assume that Bhangu had the force of conviction on his side.[79] Logically, Bhangu notes that martyr-doms like Mani Singh's are profound victories. We find these words, for example, in the original episode of Taru Singh's shahidi:

The more the Turks tortured [Taru] Singh the rosier a hue did the Singh's face take on. The more they starved him and kept him thirsty the more did he display contentment. The Singh's hope was set on life [in the next world] and his mind was not affected by the prospect of death [in this one]. In contentment and composure he bowed his head joyfully to the Guru's will.[80]

The victory over his oppressors reaches a crescendo as the torture comes to an end. A barber is first called in to shave Taru Singh's head and after repeated failures, the nawab (incensed at Taru Singh's repe-tition of 'Akal, Akal' while evading the barber) calls in a cobbler to perform the deed. The cobbler scalps Taru Singh with his adze, implying that the Sikh's kesas are still ultimately intact.[81] Would such victories over oppression lead to the defeat of the Mughal, Afghan, and by implication, future British aggressors? According to Bhangu, this belief is without question. It is the martyrdom of Guru Tegh Bahadur which, for Bhangu, marked the beginning of the decline of Mughal power.[82]

Such a statement has, one may infer, a double meaning in the light of the historical context in which the text was produced. And this double meaning leads to the second purpose of Bhangu's emphasis on martyrdom: a caution to his British benefactors. It is with this in mind that we must interpret much of what is written in the text. It should elicit no surprise that Bhangu underscores the unity of the Panth (a unity it sorely lacked in the 1840s[83]) and highlights the belief that those so-called Sikhs of the Malwa territory who had allied themselves with the British (an act which led to the signing of the Treaty of Lahore in 1809) were for him non-Sikhs. For Bhangu, the Sikh Panth exists in Majha alone.[84] The focus on martyrdom in this context dramatically demonstrates the length to which members of the Panth would go to ensure that the sovereignty which was handed down to them by Guru Nanak and granted by Guru Gobind Singh would remain inviolable. The focus also posits the inevitable victory of the Panth, a group encouraged by the deaths and sacrifices of their comrades. In a style characteristic of Bhangu, fierce enemies of the Panth narrate Sikh martial prowess, altruism, unity and the Sikh desire for martyrdom. A determined adversary of the Sikhs, Haribhagat Niranjania, speaks of Sikhs who give all they possess to their co-religionists to ensure that their Khalsa brothers do not go hungry and unclothed. He also refers to those Sikhs who travel to distant places to ensure that their comrades in the Punjab are supplied with funds to continue the struggle against the Afghans.[85] Asked by Nadir Shah to describe those men constantly raiding Punjab territory, Zakariya Khan answers in glowing language, focusing on the Sikh ability to bear all varieties of hardship, and their contempt for death. He closes with the following enthusiastic statement:

One [Sikh] battles like a hundred warriors. They are not afraid of death and their [fondest] desire remains to die for their faith. We are tired of killing them, but their numbers do not decrease.[86]

This is, of course, the type of warrior that any opposing army (as the British were to become) would certainly fear, a factor of which Bhangu was no doubt aware.

According to Vir Singh, this was also the type of warrior to which all early twentieth-century Sikhs should aspire. One could assume that Vir Singh completed the work and issued it in 1914 to inspire Sikhs to enlist for the First World War. As an avid journalist who wrote many articles for his aspiring newspaper, the *Khalsa Samachar*, Vir Singh would have certainly been aware of contemporary world events.[87] It is more likely, however, that the editor was following a maxim in his editing of Bhangu's original that he had enunciated a decade-and-a-half earlier in his novel, *Sundari*: 'In writing this book, our purpose is that by reading these accounts of bygone days, the Sikhs should become confirmed in their faith.'[88] Here, 'faith' means 'Tat Khalsa interpretation of Sikh tradition'.

The heroic ideals so fundamental to Vir Singh in the early twentieth century and to Bhangu in the mid-nineteenth were also recognized by early British observers. Bhangu was probably aware of this English fascination and may have written his *Gur-panth Prakas* with this in mind, a suggestion which at once raises the question of patronage.[89] Moreover, the emphasis on courage, sacrifice and martyrdom in both story and song was reflected particularly in the gurdwaras dedicated to Sikh shahids. Although the shahidi gallery we find at the Central Sikh Museum within the precincts of Harimandir Sahib is a mid-twentieth-century product, the Golden Temple itself has been associated with a long list of martyrs since well before it had become golden in the early nineteenth century. Two of the more famous martyrs are Basant Singh and his well-known companion,

Baba Gurbakhsh Singh Nihang, whose small, domed martyry, as we mentioned earlier, is placed behind the Akal Takht.[90] Furthermore, pilgrims circumambulating the parikarma will see the sign placed before the small Gurdwara *lāchī ber* or 'cardamom tree', noting that it was on this tree that the martyrs, Mehtab Singh and Sukha Singh, tied their horses before they went to kill Massa Ranghar in S. 1797 (1740 CE).[91] The most famous martyr of all those associated with the Darbar Sahib is the celebrated Baba Dip Singh.

Although the Sikhs of today trace Dip Singh's story back to Jahan Khan's desecration of Amritsar and the Harimandir in 1757 CE, there is no contemporary source on which they can base their statements. This is, of course, one of the major problems associated with the Dip Singh narrative, the lack of written evidence. Surprisingly, the first written account of the Dip Singh tradition is Gian Singh's famous *Panth Prakāś*, written in 1880, almost a century and a quarter after the supposed event.[92] This description in verse may be supplemented with the prose account found in the same author's *TGK*, which was written in instalments between 1891 and 1919.[93] As may be easily inferred, both these works were written during the period of the Singh Sabha and thus communicate many of the Sabha's ideals. In one pre–Singh Sabha work, however, there is a brief reference to the Dip Singh character. Although he is mentioned in Bhangu's *Gur-panth Prakāś*, the purpose of the narrative in which the martyr is included is to underscore the supernatural ability of Banda Bahadur, who cures Dip Singh of a toothache. It makes no reference whatsoever to the role Dip Singh and his companions would play in liberating Harimandir Sahib from its Afghan despoilers.[94] Richard Temple refers to Gian Singh's earlier account in an article noting the varieties of headless-warrior legends in northern India.[95] He also alludes to numerous other, competing stories of the Dip Singh legend in the late nineteenth century. One version of it, maintains Temple, has Dip Singh's ardent devotee, Sada Singh, continue to pursue the enemy host with both head and sword in hand, rather than the famous Jat sant-sipahi.[96]

That Temple would have chosen to present a lengthy portion of his article on Baba Dip Singh is probably indicative of the latter's popularity during the period in which the British ethnographer wrote. That this was the case finds some support in Rose's *Glossary*, which notes that this martyr and his companion, Sada Singh, had a strong cult following in the late nineteenth century.[97] This cult possibly went as far back as the late eighteenth century. During the Sikh kingdom

(1799–1839), for example, among the more popular subjects of mural art were, according to W.H. McLeod, 'Sikh martyrs to Muslim bigotry, notably the sons of Guru Gobind Singh and the eighteenth-century hero, Baba Dip Singh'.[98]

In the late nineteenth and early twentieth centuries, the popularity of the Baba Dip Singh tradition was certainly on the rise. Gian Singh was the first to write about him, but he was by no means the last. Giani Thakur Singh, who played a prominent role in Singh Sabha affairs, wrote several books on Sikh martyrs and was often a key speaker at the ritual proceedings organized by Sikh army units. He also produced a book on Dip Singh in the early twentieth century.[99] His brief *Gurū Siṅgh Sahīd-bilās* relates the standard narrative of Dip Singh in verse.[100] At this time, moreover, it appears that the Dip Singh legend was also spread among illiterate Sikhs since portraits of Dip Singh had become available. Although I have yet to find a Dip Singh portrait produced during the period of the Singh Sabha,[101] these prints certainly did (or do) exist because pictures of the famous martyr, along with other prominent Sikh Gurus, heroes and martyrs, were noted in the advertisement section of *The Khalsa Advocate*.[102] Bhai Amar Singh, whose Khalsa Agency of Lahore produced these prints, also advertised their sale at the back of the publications on Sikh martyrs and heroes produced by his company in the early twentieth century.[103]

By the time of these later developments, however, (developments which include the publication of Vir Singh's edition of *Prāchīn Panth Prakāś*) the rhetoric of martyrdom was already very prevalent in the Punjab. Previously, the new British government determined after the Rebellion of 1857 that Sikh martial bravery and Sikh loyalty to the Crown mystically flowed from the conspicuous Khalsa religion.[104] Their enforcement of a policy which enjoined all Sikhs inducted into the Indian Army to maintain the external Khalsa symbols was thus one force in enhancing the heroic idiom and, of course, in buttressing the Sikh self-image of themselves as a 'heroic and martial race'.[105] Another force, far more powerful, behind the prevalence of this idiom was the energetic writing of the famous Tat Khalsa polemicist, preacher and journalist, Giani Ditt Singh.

Ditt Singh and the Rhetoric of Martyrdom

To many of his modern biographers, Ditt Singh is the stuff of legend.

His name is often preceded by the adjective *anthakk* or 'tireless', and for good reason. Initially a Gulabdasi sadhu, Ditt Singh removed his ascetic's clothing, journeyed to Lahore and joined the Arya Samaj at the insistence of Jawahir Singh, the secretary of the Lahore Arya Samaj and then, after 1888, vice-president of the Lahore Singh Sabha. Later converting to the Tat Khalsa cause, Ditt Singh often voiced his opinion on matters of Sikh history, theology and doctrines during the meetings of the Lahore Singh Sabha. He toured the Punjab spreading his view of the Sikh tradition whenever possible, and established a strong reputation as a superb public speaker. After passing the Giani examination at the Oriental College, Ditt Singh was appointed a teacher in this same institution. When he turned to writing, he penned works which are hailed as the first of their type in the Punjabi language, and are often cited as the major influence in the later writings of Bhai Vir Singh.[106] Apart from books and tracts, Ditt Singh also liberally contributed articles dealing with Sikh history and reform to the *Khālsā Akhbār*, the organ of the Lahore Singh Sabha. He had eventually become the editor of this newspaper, succeeding Jhanda Singh Faridkoti. As Harjot Oberoi insightfully notes, 'One man can rarely change the course of history, but without Ditt Singh the [Lahore Singh] Sabha might have been a rather different body.'[107]

Like others in the Tat Khalsa, Ditt Singh worked to liberate ordinary Sikhs from those elements of contemporary Sikh tradition which he considered superstitions (*bharam*), abuses (*kurītīān*), fallacies (*vahim*) and 'hollow customs' (*phokīān rahu-rīt*). Ditt Singh felt that the observance of caste, idolatry and priesthood, the veneration of gurus apart from the Guru Granth Sahib, and the worship of popular saints were characteristics against which the Sikh Gurus had often spoken. At times, he directed his reforming zeal towards members of the Amritsar Singh Sabha who participated in many of the practices against which Ditt Singh spoke. The brief satirical play he wrote, entitled *Svapan Nāṭak* (Dream Play), for example, voiced a slightly veiled criticism of both the Sanatan Sabha's leadership and followers. Included as a supplement to the mid-April 1887 issue of the *Khālsā Akhbār*, the play was produced as a result of the Amritsar Singh Sabha's attempt (particularly on behalf of Baba Khem Singh Bedi, who was lampooned as the guru of Satan in the play) to have Gurmukh Singh excommunicated from the Sikh faith in March 1887.[108] As the play implies, the ideal Sikh identity was that of the Khalsa, and it was to this ideal that all Sikhs should aspire. Ditt Singh's memorable works, such as *Nakli Sikh Prabodh, Sultān Puāṛā* and *Guggā Gapauṛā*, show the futility of Sikhs indulging in what were considered non-Sikh activities, and implore adherents of the faith to do away with such practices so that the Khalsa may once again assume the form it had possessed during its Golden Age.[109]

Of course, the Golden Age to which Ditt Singh refers is not the period of the Lahore Kingdom under Maharaja Ranjit Singh, but rather, the 'dark' or 'heroic' age of persecution after the death of Guru Gobind Singh in 1708. As we have seen, this period is characterized as one in which members of the Khalsa were plagued by Muslim persecution, sustaining all types of horror to defend their faith and their gurdwaras, and to protect the oppressed, an ability which led to eventual Khalsa triumph. It was in recounting these heroic legends of Sikh martyrdom that Ditt Singh attempted to persuade Sikhs to adhere to the Tat Khalsa interpretation of Sikh tradition. This should by no means indicate that Ditt Singh saw these narratives as merely stories. To him, the events on which he wrote did indeed occur, events on which he would not impose his own ideas and interpretations (or so he thought). According to one of Ditt Singh's biographers, poetic licence had no place within the Giani ji's works on Sikh martyrs.[110]

We noted above that in editing *Gur-panth Prakāś,* Vir Singh recast the category, shahid. The precedent Vir Singh had followed, however, was probably set by Ditt Singh more than two decades before the publication of *Prāchīn Panth Prakāś.* It seems highly likely that the image of the shahid that Vir Singh had in mind while editing the text was the one provided in the many newspaper articles and eight martyrologies of Ditt Singh, an image, moreover, that Vir Singh enthusiastically presented in his three novels at the turn of the century. We must recall that by the time that Lachman Singh was executed in 1909 and *Prāchīn Panth Prakāś* appeared, the understanding of the Sikh martyr had been worked upon by the Tat Khalsa for at least three decades. The first to take this category and modify it to suit Tat Khalsa tastes was Ditt Singh.

Unlike Vir Singh's editing of Bhangu's text, Ditt Singh's martyrologies are far more explicit in the attempt to underscore the inherent element of identity. This seems logical in the light of the fact that these were the first Tat Khalsa publications of their sort. As many Tat Khalsa writers would after him, Ditt Singh correlated the present danger, with which he believed the nineteenth-century Panth was confronted, with the dangers of wholesale extermination that the Panth of the eighteenth century had faced. This time, however, both the enemies and the tools at their disposal were different. Rather than confront Afghans and Mughals, Sikhs were now placed before the Arya Samaj and its charismatic leader, Dayananda Saraswati, whose words and writings were modern-day cannons and swords. Ditt Singh attempted to make fast work of these adversaries in his famous *khaṇḍān-maṇḍān* text (polemic; lit., 'attacking and defending'), *Merā ate Sādhū Dayānand Jī Sambād*.[111] Another enemy they thought they faced, which would prove far more difficult to overcome, was the pride and arrogance of contemporary Sikhs, coupled with their ignorance of Sikh tradition. To defeat these, Ditt Singh had to make nineteenth-century Sikhs aware of their valorous past, a task he attempted to fulfil through his writings and his campaigning along with Gurmukh Singh for the creation of Tat Khalsa-inspired Sikh educational institutions, particularly the establishment of Khalsa College.[112]

We had mentioned in Chapter Two the logical reasons why the Tat Khalsa chose to use martyr legends as a vehicle to further their mandate. These legends were not only popular but possessed an inherent concern with identity. These stories, moreover, were a part of pre–Singh Sabha Sikh tradition that reinforced courage, sacrifice, and particularly, a strong commitment to the faith, themes that permeated the Adi Granth and which could thus easily be adapted to emphasize Tat Khalsa concerns. Characteristics such as these led to the eventual triumph of the Panth and could, according to the Tat Khalsa, once again prove to lead Sikhs to ultimate victory.

In his works on martyrs, therefore, Ditt Singh embedded a number of simple and forthright messages expressing his view of what the ideal Sikh of the late nineteenth century should be and should do. The ideal is, of course, the Sikh of the Khalsa, and all features related to this identity find their place in Ditt Singh's narratives of martyrdom. The initiatory nectar used at a Sikh's admission into the Khalsa, for example, becomes a potent elixir which enables one to overcome great difficulties and bear extreme hardship:

It is the power of the tenth Guru's amrit which blesses us. In this world He is your only protector for all time.[113]

and

The amrit of the tenth Guru has transformed us from sparrows into hawks. If you abandon it, then think: where will you fall?[114]

For Ditt Singh, Sikh martyrs of the eighteenth century possessed unblemished characters, preferring death to abandoning their principles. This belief prompted Ditt Singh to compare contemporary Sikhs with those of the past. Ditt Singh's version of Bhai Tara Singh's martyrdom, for example, critiques the contemporary practices and pride of the Khalsa Panth, juxtaposing these with the virtues of its eighteenth-century predecessor:

These very Singhs who sacrificed themselves while on the earth were exceptionally brave. Their task was the protection of righteousness, an act in whose execution they gave their heads cheerfully. Recalling [this heroic past] the Singhs of today are burdened with conceit and pride. But these Sikhs walk away from both righteousness and charity. It is they who forget Gurmat.[115]

Here, Ditt Singh is playing on notions of shame and honour (*izzat*) in the hope of recruiting future Sikh 'martyrs' who would commit themselves to the 'protection of righteousness' in the late nineteenth-century sense. That is, Sikhs who would both devote their lives (albeit less dramatically) to Panthic well-being and adopt the external symbols and the internal convictions that came to be associated with these insignia of past Sikhs. Ditt Singh is, in other words, inspiring Sikhs with martyrdoms of the Sikh past and simultaneously arousing guilt and tension and the urge to act on the two levels that Stanley Tambiah observes in the sermons of Jarnail Singh Bhindranwale: at the level of the interior lives of individuals and at the level of the Sikh collectivity.[116]

The most important of the five external insignia in Ditt Singh's martyrologies is the uncut hair (*kes*, one of the *pañj kakke*). Along the same lines we witnessed in the Bhai Taru Singh story supplied by Ratan Singh Bhangu, therefore, the Ditt Singh version of this martyrdom glorifies the martyr's desire to maintain his hair uncut. As in his Tara Singh narrative, however, Ditt Singh communicates a harsh moral judgement on the Sikhs of his day.

This warrior gave his life rather than have his hair cut. So long as the world endures he will be mentioned honourably. Despite being tempted by several varieties of greed, the warrior did not abandon his faith. He put his trust in the Guru and remained steadfastly brave. But the young [Sikhs] of nowadays spit on their shoulders [i.e. they are very proud] and sit in the upper storey [of their houses] cutting [and trimming] their own hair with scissors.[117]

Again we note the play on honour and shame. Put simply, Ditt Singh asks why contemporary Sikhs are unable to commit themselves to keeping their hair unshorn during this period of relative peace, when Sikhs of the eighteenth century suffered unutterable tortures and death to retain these religious symbols. Only a familiarity with Khalsa tradition, envisioned Ditt Singh, would inject these lax Sikhs with the piety of their ancestors. These martyrologies were an attempt to dramatically bring about that familiarity, demonstrating how contemporary Sikhs had abandoned the ideals for which their ancestors had given their lives. These texts therefore manifest, in the words of Kenneth Burke, a strategy to encompass the late nineteenth-century situation.

Ditt Singh was among the first to recognize the rhetorical potential which martyrdom possessed. In a society that highly prized the heroic ideal, the emphasis on sacrifice and martyrdom was to prove the most potent weapon in the Tat Khalsa arsenal. Alluding to the sacrifices their ancestors were believed to have made in defence of the Sikh Panth, Ditt Singh, in both his *Khālsā Akhbār* articles and his martyrologies, attempted to persuade Sikhs to act in a way similar to that of past Sikh martyrs, maintaining that it was altruistic Sikh warriors of this nature who were required to save the present-day Panth from a variety of evils. The Lachman Singh article we cited at the beginning of this chapter utilized the language of martyrdom. Likewise, Ditt Singh couched his stories in the 'rhetoric of martyrdom' or the 'idiom of martyrdom': a way of speaking which alluded to the legends of the brave men and women of the seventeenth- and eighteenth-century Panth in the attempt to influence contemporary Sikhs to alter their present practices and adopt patterns of behaviour their ancestors are believed to have gloriously displayed. Of course, this rhetoric was not restricted to the books narrating events from Sikh history or martyrologies. *Updeśaks* (teachers), *prachāraks* (preachers), newspaper editorials, appeals, handbills and various other Sikh publications also made use of the rhetoric in order to persuade Sikhs to adopt Tat Khalsa standards.

Newspapers, Tracts and Other Publications

To a certain extent, the martyr rhetoric apparent in Sikh newspapers and at various *divāns* (large assemblies at which gianis preached and, often, dhadhis sang) held throughout the Punjab helped keep heroic Sikh traditions alive. Since the oral traditions of pre-colonial Punjab were still circulating at this time,[118] particularly through the ballads of the dhadhis, such recognizable characteristics in print and at diwan gatherings must have enhanced the Tat Khalsa message.[119] Of course, one must be very careful when dealing with newspapers because by its very nature, this medium, particularly in its initial stages in northern India, mainly communicated the aspirations and views of those whom Oberoi calls the 'new elites' of Punjabi society.[120] In all but rare cases, these new elites were the ones who possessed the background to acquire the skills of writing and who had access to printing technology. (Ditt Singh was a rare case.) These views, moreover, were restricted to those who could read them. Or were they? N.G. Barrier points out that

The influence of these [newspapers] and related journals was significant. Individuals read material aloud in villages and copies circulated widely among students, the army and emigrant groups throughout the world.[121]

The related journals which spread throughout village Punjab noted here were those produced by the Khalsa Tract Society, founded in 1893 by Vir Singh. Although many of these tracts were published anonymously, the vast majority were written by Vir Singh himself.[122] These tracts covered a variety of subjects of concern to the Tat Khalsa and the Panth and thus provoked much discussion on what was considered ideal and less-than-ideal Sikh practice. Religion was, of course, the principal subject and within a tract, this topic was often presented in the form of a story or a conversation between two people.[123] Many tracts dealt with Sikh history. As these were penned by Vir Singh, a Tat Khalsa interpretation in which Sikh Gurus, heroes and martyrs dedicated their lives to righteousness and to ensuring that the symbols of the Khalsa remained inviolable was inevitable. Of course, not all KTS publications dealt with Sikh martyrs (one fourth, for example, presented the lives of the Gurus). However, many did, and the majority of these were in regard to the sons of Guru Gobind Singh. Two such were *Dharam het Balidān* (Sacrifices for the Sake of Righteousness), published in 1897, and *Sahīd-nāmā* (Martyrology), published in 1900.[124] Another, *Gulābī* (1903), like many of the anonymously published tracts, underscored Sikh martyrdom and heroism during Aurangzeb's reign.[125]

Because these tracts were inexpensive (approximately one pice to four annas each), they managed to find their way into the most remote village gurdwaras. According to N.G. Barrier, by 1911, over a million copies of these tracts, along with those issued by the Waziri-Hind Press, the Khalsa Handbill Society, the Sikh Book Club, the Panch Khalsa Agency and the Bhai Amar Singh Agency in Lahore, were in circulation.[126] With such statistics at our disposal, a report on the efficacy of the KTS published in *The Khalsa Advocate* that may at first seem exaggerated, takes on a new significance:

its publications have penetrated the most unpenetratable [*sic*] purdahs ... publications are widely read and circulated, and have succeeded in producing radical changes in the character of its reader...[127]

Morever, since in almost all cases Singh Sabhas and gurdwaras were under the same roof, all those who came to the gurdwara had access, through print or word of mouth, to the Tat Khalsa message.[128] These people may or may not have taken this message to heart (the newspapers indicate that many did), but when there were allusions to past Sikh sacrifices, they surely recognized the language in which the message was presented, and this in itself may have prompted a change.

Such changes did occur in some Sikhs who had read or heard the narratives found within these many publications Born in 1896 and raised within a 'Sikh milieu', Sohan Singh Josh emphasizes the inspiration he had gained as a result of reading his first Sikh martyrology:

Having learnt Punjabi, I began to read whatever came to my hand about the Gurus and their teachings. One day I came across a very sentimentally written pamphlet regarding the sacrifice of the two younger sons of Guru Gobind Singh. It was nightfall and I read the narration to the entire family. It told the story of Fateh Singh and Zorawar Singh who were bricked alive into a well in Sirhind. These young sons of Guru Gobind Singh were asked by the Qazi to embrace Islam in return for freedom, but they had refused to bow before the tyranny, and preferred death to surrendering to religious bigotry. As I read the episode, my voice was surcharged with emotion. Tears rolled down my parents' eyes and it was with much effort that I finished reading the pamphlet. This episode, and the sacrifices made by Guru Arjan Dev and Guru Tegh Bahadur influenced my life very much. In fact, these, to a great extent, moulded my character in those early years.[129]

Josh notes, moreover, that such writings led him to study more on Sikhism and Sikh history, and eventually encouraged him and a colleague to open in his village a library solely devoted to the dissemination of Sikh ideas.[130]

After the death of Ditt Singh in 1901, the force which came to dominate Singh Sabha affairs was the Chief Khalsa Diwan. Created in

1902 to bring the various Singh Sabhas together under one body, the CKD championed an interpretation of the Sikh tradition which was clearly inspired by members of the Tat Khalsa. Despite the fact that its leadership was dominated by men allied to the Khalsa Diwan of Amritsar, particularly Sunder Singh Majithian, the CKD ideology definitely stemmed from those of the Lahore society. The CKD, for example, required its members to be initiated Khalsa Sikhs, subscribe to the 5 Ks, consider the Guru Granth Sahib as both 'the physical embodiment of the ten Guru Sahiban' and their only Guru, and perform all rites and rituals according to Gurmat.[131] Moreover, it subscribed to the casteless ideology of the Tat Khalsa. Such policies, agreed to by members of both the Lahore and Amritsar constellations, allowed the CKD to virtually bring an end to the internal problems which had plagued the Singh Sabhas in the late nineteenth century.[132] For this reason, it was able to devote itself to both the pursuits of the earlier Singh Sabhas and Khalsa Diwan, particularly in regard to the spread of education, as well as pursue a far more expansive policy in regard to social, political and religious goals of the Panth. The CKD established a Khalsa Biradri (Khalsa Brotherhood) in 1908 to curtail the influence of caste and untouchability among Sikhs, for example. It also built widows' homes, orphanages, hospitals and other community-related services. At the same time, the CKD adopted a political programme of petitioning and constitutional means to gain advantages for the Sikh community from the British Government in the Punjab. Although often pejoratively described as 'loyalist', the CKD did mount opposition to British policies which harmed the Sikh community.[133] Finally, the CKD advocated the strength of the Punjabi language and attempted to implement a separate Sikh identity in the endeavour to underscore the belief that Sikhs were a separate social, religious and political entity.[134]

Expanding the Ditt Singh legacy and following in the wake of the *Khālsā Akhbār*, the two CKD newspapers, the *Khālsā Samāchār* (begun in 1899 by Vir Singh but allied to the CKD in 1902) and *The Khalsa Advocate* (begun in 1903), regularly appealed to the Sikh 'sense' of selfless sacrifice so that the present social and political situation of the Panth may be dramatically improved.[135] Both the *Khālsā Samāchār* and *The Khalsa Advocate* often contained articles which compared eighteenth-century Sikh martyrs with present-day Sikhs, a tactic developed by Ditt Singh and aimed at underscoring how Sikhs of the early twentieth century were not worthy of the title

'Sikh'.[136] The CKD newspapers embellished the martyr legends, more-over, in order to demonstrate that Golden Age Sikhs were martyred in the attempt to fulfil many of the eighteenth-century Panth's needs. The needs on which they focused, of course, were those which they felt the contemporary Panth possessed, but had trouble fulfilling. The need for castelessness, for all rites to follow *gur-rīti* (the Guru's traditions), and the necessity of educational and economic uplift were a few upon which they wrote.[137] By March of 1907, for example, the call for an 'All-India Sikh Educational Conference' had already been placed a number of times. The recurring silence had prompted one paper to proclaim that a conference of this nature was not really a new thing. According to the article, Sikhs of the eighteenth century gathered bi-annually despite the price that was placed upon their heads. It then states: 'It was in holding an "All-India Sikh Conference" that Bhai Mani Singh ... had his body cut up to pieces.'[138] The message here was straightforward and coherent: only through similar sacrifice will the necessities of today's Panth be fulfilled.

Noting the constant allusions to Sikh martyrs in the newspapers, one Sikh writes:

It does not require a prophet's vision to see that unless the Sikh people bestir themselves, they should cease harping upon the glorious deeds of their Gurus, their martyrs and their heroes, whose blood is coursing in their veins. For, where is the use, if we do not take a leaf out of their books?[139]

It was in the attempt to teach young Sikh boys just how to 'take a leaf out of their books' that the young Tara Singh (later Master Tara Singh) gave a lecture titled 'What Boys Can Do' at a meeting of the Karachi Singh Sabha. According to *The Khalsa Advocate*, Tara Singh requested young Sikhs to work for the uplift of the Panth by noting how young Sikhs in the past had dedicated their lives to this task. The newspaper notes that he 'illustrated [his lecture] by the heroic and Khalsa-like doings of Sikh boy-martyrs and their prototypes the darling sons of Sri Kalgidhar himself'.[140]

In these articles, the major concern is with educating Sikhs in Sikh history and religion. By no means were these the only examples of such articles. In an article dealing with district schools, *The Khalsa Advocate* reminds Sikhs of the sacrifices in days of old, and then indicates that Sikhs today should 'sacrifice' their time and wealth for the establishment and maintenance of Sikh schools which will act as 'feeders of the Khalsa College'.[141] Another article in the English organ of the Sikhs reports on education during the 'period of Sikh martyrdom'. Noting that Sikhs of the eighteenth century had found time to achieve 'rare literary attainments' and educate their young in religion while being 'harassed from place to place by official tyranny', the article questions its readers: 'Is it not a pity ... [that] such a nation should be left behind by every sister community in the race of education in these peaceful times?'[142] As well, the *Khālsā Samāchār,* in its regular column titled *benatī* (appeal), often requested Sikhs to devote their lives to the well-being of the Panth, noting that Panthic success had resulted from such sacrifice in the past.[143] In a characteristic use of the rhetoric of martyrdom, an article in *The Khalsa Advocate* dramatically underscores this belief:

If we find it ... hard to sacrifice our all for the regeneration of our Panth, as our illustrious ancestors did in the good old days, we are not called upon either to do anything of the kind. The only sacrifice *Panthsewa* demands of us [today] is a practical subordination, as far as it lies in our power, of our personal and individual interests to the higher and superior ones of the community as a whole. Done this much by a sufficiently large number of our brethren the Panth might once again reach the zenith of its glory which it had attained when fed most copiously by the blood of innumerable martyrs. But alas! even this much sacrifice ... has become rare like a black swan in this age of selfishness and self-interest.[144]

The idea here is clear that only those people who are willing to emulate their ancestors and sacrifice their lives for the benefit of the Panth may be called 'Sikh'.[145] Moreover, it is implied that only this will allow the Panth to thrive and survive.

References of this variety occurred frequently over the next decade through the agencies of the CKD. The secret report of the developments in Sikh politics during the years 1900–11, commissioned by the government and produced by David Petrie, the Assistant Director of Criminal Intelligence for the Government of India, notes that the itinerant preachers of the CKD often lectured on events of the eighteenth century, in which martyrdom strongly figured. For Petrie, such lectures were organized to encourage Sikhs to revolt against the British.[146] Petrie's conclusion for the period he was observing was baseless and need not concern us. What is important is that he notes the rhetoric employed by preachers.

The rhetoric of sacrifice and martyrdom utilized by the Tat Khalsa was spread far and wide under the auspices of the CKD. Through such activities as the staging of large diwans throughout the Punjab, sending preaching teams to areas where the Tat Khalsa message had yet to arrive, and promoting the publication of Sikh literature (the CKD raised funds for and aided in the administration of the KTS, for example), the CKD ensured that the Khalsa traditions of martial bravery, selfless sacrifice and martyrdom were kept alive and vibrant.[147] Of course, this rhetoric was utilized to ensure that the aims of the Tat Khalsa and CKD would be fulfilled. Even before the creation of the CKD, itinerant gianis whose thinking was aligned with that of the Tat Khalsa would travel to various towns and villages, where diwans were organized by their respective Singh Sabha, and give katha on proper Sikh practice, Sikh history and on what was required for the Panth to raise itself above its present educationally and politically backward predicament. Although such katha was rarely written down, some of these homilies survive due to the work of the many diligent members of the various Singh Sabhas scattered across the Punjab. Portions of the katha given by Bhai Teja Singh at the Rawalpindi Singh Sabha weekly diwan held on 3 December 1899, for example, are worth quoting in this context for they demonstrate how martyr rhetoric was used to help further Tat Khalsa goals. A letter sent to the *Khālsā Samāchār* by one *ṭahlīā* (servant) of the Sabha describes Teja Singh's homily:

Then Bhai Wahiguru Singh gave a homily from the Guru Granth Sahib. Afterwards, Bhai Teja Singh made apparent by means of description that we know from ancient history that the four sahib-zadas of the Lord of the Plume, [Guru Gobind Singh] Maharaj became martyrs with great joy for the sake of righteousness and, moreover, that several other young Singhs had smilingly given their lives in order to protect their religion. There are two main reasons for this. The first is that the power of the [tenth Guru's] amrit produced a strong impression in these children. The second is that during their childhood, instruction in Sikh dharam was available to these young Singhs. For these very reasons, as these young people grew older, so was their faith in the pristine [Sikh] dharam strengthened. Nowadays, it is our upcoming generation who are fallen (*patit*) from their faith. The reason for this is that instruction in the Sikh religion is not available to them while they are children. The cause of this unavailability is that their parents are both illiterate and, moreover, have not been administered amrit.[148]

Homilies such as these often saw the members of the audience take amrit and pass resolutions that aimed at building schools where instruction in the Sikh faith would be available. The author of the article notes that amrit was indeed administered to Sikhs during the occasion. Moreover, he claims that in this case, the Singh Sabha of Rawalpindi asked for aid for the upkeep of the two Khalsa schools and the one Khalsa boarding house it had already constructed.[149]

Like Ditt Singh, Teja Singh underscores the power of amrit in the katha above, implying that only those Sikhs who are given the elixir are capable of such extraordinary feats. The ceremony of pahul was portrayed in Singh Sabha literature as one that could dramatically transform the character of the individual from a weak, immoral person to a heroic, altruistic and virtuous warrior.[150] As we have seen, moreover, a connection between martyrdom and the ultimate aim of the Tat Khalsa and, later, the CKD is made here: the spread of education, modern western education combined with the precepts and ideals of Tat Khalsa Sikhism. The message here is one that Sikhs would hear numerous times over the years. An awareness of the traditions of the Khalsa (particularly those which stressed sacrifice and martyrdom) through education would inspire Sikh hearts and allow the Panth to again achieve the greatness it had once possessed. The many schools which the CKD helped erect not only provided students for Khalsa College and future sevadars, but also equipped the CKD with trained preachers, teachers and granthis.[151] Access to these schools was limited to Sikhs, preferably to those who had been administered amrit. Moreover, while in the school, students were only served rahit-prescribed jhatka meat. Their daily regimen included a considerable amount of time for prayers, and lessons in Sikh history and religion, along with courses in modern accounting and other such lessons. In effect, these provided an ideological and theological training ground, equipping students with the skills required both for government jobs and a vigorous and unique interpretation of Sikh tradition.[152] The use of martyr rhetoric to have these schools built and to keep them running occurs frequently throughout the two newspapers. Another article comparing contemporary Sikhs with their heroic ancestors, for example, attempts to influence Sikhs to establish a Khalsa school in Lahore:

The achievement [of opening a Khalsa school] requires, no doubt, a good deal of sacrifice on the part of those undertaking the task. But what is a Sikh without sacrifice? There was a time when the Sikhs sacrificed their wealth and riches, nay, even those near and dear to them to promote the cause of the Panth. Is it, now too much to expect a High School from the Sikhs of Lahore.[153]

To this may be added a paragraph from Teja Singh's paper, sent from England to the first Sikh Educational Conference of 1908:

I still believe that the sacred spirit of the Guru and the Sikh Martyrs, though greatly lying very much dormant in the Inheritors of their Renown, has not wholly died out. Where they shed streams of blood to pave the foundation structure of the Holy Guru Panth we need only direct the major portion of our energy and earnings to complete the sacred superstructure [i.e. educational institutions].[154]

Although all the articles thus far noted imply educating male students alone, the CKD's desire to educate female Sikhs was also very strong. Many reports appeared, for example, in regard to Takht Singh's Sikh Kanya Mahavidyala in Ferozepur and also, reports regarding the Guru Nanak's Girls' School in Quetta. An article on the topic of Sikhs and female education which employed the rhetoric of martyrdom and that is similar in tone and content to Teja Singh's homily above appeared in the 15 April 1910 edition of *The Khalsa Advocate*. The report narrates the reason why the daughter of Guru Amar Das, Bibi Bhani, was able to sacrifice all she did for the benefit of the Panth:

She [Bibi Bhani] sacrificed for the sake of her motherland no less than 5 generations of her children and grandchildren in the persons of Guru Arjan Dev, her son, who was tortured to death at Lahore for his firm convictions ... Guru Tegh Bahadur, her great grandson, whose martyrdom at Delhi in the noble cause is well known to you ... and her last children of the line, the four sons of our Saviour whose undaunted sacrifices have astonished and still astonish the whole world. Can anyone say that all this was not the effect of the home education which this noble lady received from her parents and imparted to her children?... Teach [young girls] the subjects that will bring them nearer to this ideal. Teach them what will produce ladies like Bibi Sundari [!] and Sharn Kaur of Sikh history and Rani Sahib Kaur of Patiala fame.[155]

This rhetoric does not seem to have been wasted on those who read or heard such articles. The number of Khalsa schools rose from a mere seven in 1908 to 200 by 1920.[156] Schools devoted to the education of Sikh girls also increased.[157] The dramatic increase in these schools during the most successful period of the CKD's existence (1902–20) appears to indicate that the rhetoric of martyrdom utilized in articles, tracts and katha did indeed inspire Sikhs to act so that the educational position of the Panth would improve. This rhetoric became the strategy to encompass the Panth's early-twentieth-century situation. Furthermore, the director of the educational department in the Punjab had noted the enthusiasm with which the Sikhs approached the opening of schools. In his report for 1914–15, he states: 'The activity shown by the Sikh community in starting new secondary schools has been particularly noticeable in recent years and several such schools are qualifying for recognition.'[158] The Lieutenant-Governor himself had buttressed these views: 'Wherever I go,' he wrote in 1920, 'I see the Khalsa schools well built and well founded which have been provided by the liberality of the Sikh Panth.'[159]

Of course, the schools noted here are those which survived. As articles and pamphlets of the period note, many schools had failed. As a result of these many failures, the newspapers report that a rumour began to circulate that Sikhs were very good when it came to beginning an educational project but were also notorious for abandoning it when its prospects began to look dim. To encourage Sikhs to remain with these projects, *The Khalsa Advocate* carried this article from a Sikh known only as 'H.S. from Rawalpindi'. The article, titled 'A Humble Request', was aimed at those members of the Panth who were finding out how difficult it was to sacrifice time and energy to the cause of Panthic welfare. The author asks these men and women to reflect on a number of points before making their decision to stop working for the benefit of the community. Three of the seven points on which he asks his readers to reflect are given below:

2) Have I or am I likely to face difficulties more trying than did the four beloved sons of Sri Guru Gobind Singh Ji? And if they did stick to their religion and performed their duty undergoing unbearable tortures at the hands of tyrants, is it not my duty to follow them?

3) If a child of seven years has set an example by sacrificing his life for his religion, am I not bound to follow that inspiring soul?

7) Did the Sikhs like Bhai Mani Singh Ji leave their Panthic works aside when they had to face not one but innumerable difficulties? If they did, so am I not, as a Sikh, bound to follow them?

In the final paragraph, he then tells his readers that without such sacrifice, 'a man's life in general and a Sikh's life in particular is fruitless ... It is the bound duty of a Sikh to serve his Panth, no matter to how much [or] little [an] extent he may do so.'[160] The equation here is clear: to be a true Sikh is to sacrifice one's all for the Panth.

Through the efforts of the CKD, the Tat Khalsa definition of

Sikhism as a religion unto itself with distinct rituals, a tradition conspicuous by the absence of Hindu influence, and a tradition in which bravery, sacrifice and martyrdom were prominent, was institutionalized. This is one of the key contributions of the CKD.[161] As we mentioned above, the vast number of Sikhs who turned out to support the legalization of the Sikh marriage ceremony, Anand karaj, demonstrates that for the Sikh Panth, the CKD had proven to be its representative and that the Tat Khalsa interpretation of Sikh tradition, with which the CKD was armed, was viewed as the dominant understanding of Sikhs and Sikhism. And thus, when Lachman Singh approached the gibbet in June of 1909, it was within this understanding that he was perceived. By this time, martyrdom was seen as fundamental to the Sikh tradition. The use of adjectives such as 'Sikh-like' would now imply 'martyr-like'. For the Sikhs gathered to view this spectacle, one may assume that this man represented the true Sikh sevadar against whom members of the Panth had been constantly juxtaposed over the last thirty years, a Sikh who took the rhetoric to heart and was willing to fulfil the demands of the CKD to sacrifice everything dear to him, including his life, to ensure that the Panth would benefit.

As we have noted, martyrdom was an integral feature of the Tat Khalsa interpretation of Sikh tradition. Here was a theme that emphasized those elements which the Singh Sabha admired most in past Khalsa Sikhs, characteristics that members of the society were attempting to recapture through the rhetoric of martyrdom: virtue, altruism, selflessness, heroism, and a commitment to the faith and its symbols that was simply unsurpassed. We have spent much time in this chapter elaborating on how the rhetoric influenced Sikhs to adopt a new outlook on education. The following chapter will demonstrate how the Tat Khalsa utilized the rhetoric to influence Sikhs to capture sacred space. This practice was continued under the successors of the Singh Sabha and the CKD, the Akali Dal. Under this group (1920–25), the rhetoric of martyrdom proved to be a very powerful motivating force in the attempt to liberate Sikh gurdwaras from an enemy considered all but intractable. Brave, fearless Khalsa Sikhs of the eighteenth century who were killed in the attempt to protect their faith and to protect innocents from Muslim bigotry became, in the twentieth century, brave, non-violent Khalsa Sikhs, sustaining all types of privations, including death, to protect the sanctity of their sacred shrines.

Notes

1. *The Khalsa Advocate*, 5 September 1908, p. 3.

2. The narrative of events which follows is based upon two articles which appeared in *The Khalsa Advocate*, 19 June 1909, p. 3; and 26 June 1909, p. 4; and two articles in the same issue of the *Khālsā Samāchār*, 24 June 1909, pp. 1, 2. Both *Khālsā Samāchār* articles mention that Lachman Singh killed these three Muslims 'in the zeal of his faith' *(āpane mazahbī jos̄ vich)* during a heated religious argument *(mazahbī jhagaṛe vich)*. Apparently, the report of Lachman Singh's execution first appeared in the newspaper, *Prem*, of Ferozepur.

3. Many articles in *The Khalsa Advocate* and *Khālsā Samāchār* decry the Arya Samaj ritual of conversion which involved, in regard to Sikhs, the shaving of 'kesas'.

4. N.G. Barrier, *The Sikhs and Their Literature: A Guide to Tracts, Books and Periodicals (1849–1919)* (Delhi, 1970), pp. 25–39. Polemic could indeed lead to murder. Pandit Lekh Ram of the Arya Samaj was assassinated in March 1897 for having slandered the Prophet Muhammad. Kenneth Jones, *Arya Dharm: Hindu Consciousness in 19th-Century Punjab* (Berkeley, 1976), pp. 193–202.

5. Background in Peter Hardy, *The Muslims of British India* (Cambridge, 1972), pp. 158–64. It is important to note that by 1904, disclosed employment circulars had made the British policy of bolstering Muslim numbers in the administration and other arenas common public knowledge, a fact which would have easily led to resentment by other communities in Punjab. Oberoi, *Construction*, p. 368.

6. For example, *The Khalsa Advocate*, 26 December 1908, pp. 2, 6–7. Also see 30 January 1909, p. 3; 6 February 1909, pp. 2–3, 7; and 13 February 1909, p. 7.

7. *The Khalsa Advocate*, 26 June 1909, p. 4.

8. That is Professor Teja Singh, who is neither the Teja Singh so prominent in Canadian affairs nor Principal Teja Singh.

9. *The Khalsa Advocate*, 26 June, 1909, p. 4. Bhai Lal Singh was an *updesak* who had established the Updeshak School in Gharjakh, Gujranwala, and Sohan Singh often contributed articles and poems to *The Khalsa Advocate*.

10. What the articles suggest is that Lachman Singh's three Muslim victims (Muslims being the traditional enemy of the Sikh Panth) were, in effect, directly responsible for Lachman Singh's 'sacrifice'. It should, therefore, elicit no surprise that not one of the copious resolutions passed throughout the years of Singh Sabha activity by the Singh Sabhas worldwide criticized the British government for the execution of this man.

11. The *Khālsā Samāchār*, 24 June 1909, p. 2, carried a similar title: '*Ik sikh dī sahīdī* or 'A Sikh's Martyrdom'.

12. *The Khalsa Advocate*, 26 June 1909, p. 4; 19 June, p. 3.

13. Ibid.

14. *The Khalsa Advocate*, 26 June, 1909, p. 4.

15. The numerous newspaper articles, pamphlets and books which dealt with the tradition were vast and widely available. See Barrier, *Literature*, pp. 135–6.

16. In many of these accounts, Khalsa Sikhs are especially noted as the protectors of the Hindu majority. Indeed, it is still common to hear Sikhs today say that all of India would be Muslim were it not for Guru Tegh Bahadur and

Guru Gobind Singh. One can, therefore, hypothesize that Lachman Singh may have perhaps felt that he was actually protecting the Hindu *lambardār*, and all Hindus by extension, from Islam in general and from the three Muslims he had killed in particular.

17. Clifford Geertz, 'Thick Description: Toward an Interpretive Theory of Culture', in his *Interpretation of Cultures* (New York, 1973), pp. 3–32.

18. *The Khalsa Advocate*, 26 June 1909, p. 4; and *Khālsā Samāchār*, 24 June, p. 2.

19. *The Khalsa Advocate*, 26 June 1909, p. 4; and *Khālsā Samāchār*, 24 June 1909, p. 2.

20. *Khālsā Samāchār*, 24 June 1909, p. 2.

21. It is difficult to determine exactly how many people came to visit Lachman Singh prior to his execution. *The Khalsa Advocate*, 26 June 1909, p. 4, notes that 'a regular concourse of humanity' and '[t]housands of persons' came 'to [feast] their eyes upon the beaming face of the Bhai ji for hours together'.

22. *The Khalsa Advocate*, 19 June 1909, p. 3:

His corpse was carried to the burning ghat in a grand procession by his co-religionists and the subject of his execution is a common talk amongst the people at Gujranwala who truly regard him as a martyr to the cause.

23. Ibid. *Khālsā Samāchār*, 24 June 1909, p. 2, tells us that he spoke while the noose was around his neck.

24. *The Khalsa Advocate*, 26 June 1909, p. 4.

25. Although our author earlier termed the belief that Lachman Singh was a martyr as 'inexplicable', he himself acknowledges Lachman Singh as such many times in his article.

26. Kabir, *Gaurī rāg* 20(3), AG, p. 327. An interpretation of this hymn through the lens of Sikh martyrdom is in Narain Singh, *Śahīdī* (Amritsar, 1997), pp. 1–2.

27. This assumption allows one to refute Dipankar Gupta's claim that it was unlikely that any Sikh felt that the Singh Sabhas were worth killing or dying for. Indeed, Lachman Singh appears to have himself killed and been killed in defence of the Singh Sabha. See Dipankar Gupta, *The Context of Ethnicity: Sikh Identity in a Comparative Perspective* (Delhi, 1996), p. 123.

28. Victor Turner, 'Religious Paradigms and Political Action: Thomas Beckett at the Council at Northampton', in his *Dramas, Fields and Metaphors: Symbolic Action in Human Society* (Ithaca, 1973), pp. 60–97.

29. Victor Turner, 'Religious Paradigms', pp. 64, 69. Turner defines 'root paradigm' on p. 64:

[root paradigms] have reference not only to the current state of social relationships existing or developing between actors, but also to the cultural goals, means, ideas, outlooks, currents of thought, patterns of belief, and so on, which enter into those relationships, interpret them and incline them to alliance or divisiveness. These root paradigms are not systems of univocal concepts, logically arrayed; they are not ... precision tools of thought. Nor are they stereotyped guidelines for ethical, esthetic, or conventional action. Indeed, they go beyond the cognitive and even the moral to the existential domain, and in so doing become clothed with allusiveness, implicitness and metaphor... Paradigms of this fundamental sort reach down to irreducible life stances of individuals, passing beneath conscious comprehension to a fiduciary hold on what they sense to be axiomatic values, matters literally of life and death.

30. Judith Perkins, *The Suffering Self: Pain and Narrative Representation in the Early Christian Era* (London, 1995), pp. 15–40, 189–90; and David Loades' introduction to Diana Wood (ed.), *Martyrs and Martyrologies* (Oxford, 1993), pp. xv–xviii.

31. Santokh Singh's text notes that Guru Arjan and Guru Tegh Bahadur died the heroic deaths of martyrs. *Suraj Prakās* VII, pp. 2374–7; XI, pp. 4470–7. That Santokh Singh recognized the appreciation for martyrdom is apparent in the following passage:

The condition of all warriors is thus: if he dies he goes to heaven, if he lives he is praised.

Suraj Prakās V, p. 1676.

32. According to Turner,

Such paradigms affect the form, timing and style of the behavior of those who bear them. Actors who are thus guided produce in their interaction behavior and generate social events which are non-random, but, on the contrary, structured to a degree that in some cultures provoke the notion of fate or destiny to account for the experienced regulation of human social affairs ... behavior which appears freely chosen resolves at length into a total pattern.

Turner, 'Religious Paradigms', p. 67.

33. Turner claims this of Becket. 'Religious Paradigms', p. 84.

34. J.R. Knott's *Discourses of Martyrdom in English Literature, 1563–1694* (Cambridge, 1993), particularly chapter 2, provided the inspiration for this portion of the chapter.

35. *The Khalsa Advocate*, 26 June 1909, p. 4. There is still no memorial to Lachman Singh.

36. Lachman Singh's actions may be interpreted in the light of Kenneth Burke's understanding of non-verbal rhetoric, as the accused is attempting to influence the audience for whom he is enacting this drama (an audience which includes himself). The term 'drama', as used by Burke, also fits the Lachman Singh episode very well. For Burke, as for others before him, drama confounds reality and the representation of reality. Drama is also highly formal or patterned, as well as rhetorical. Lachman Singh is attempting to persuade both himself and the audience that he is a Sikh martyr rather than a murderer. In Burke's terms, he has a wide appeal because his behaviour manifests a culturally held pattern or, as Turner notes, a root paradigm. As we noted in the introduction, Burke often uses this very term, 'drama', to describe his system of thought. Kenneth Burke, *Language as Symbolic Action: Essays on Life, Literature and Method* (Berkeley, 1966), p. 54; and *The Rhetoric of Religion* (Berkeley, 1970), pp. 40–1.

37. Barrier points out that Teja Singh of Bhasaur was harshly reprimanded by a large segment of the Panth for posing a view contrary to that of the CKD, thus implying that Tat Khalsa ideas (which the CKD propagated) were understood as orthodox. Barrier makes this same point by noting that Macauliffe's six-volume *The Sikh Religion* did not receive as enthusiastic a welcome as it would have a decade earlier. N.G. Barrier, 'In Search of Identity: Scholarship and Authority

among Sikhs in Nineteenth-century Punjab', in R.I. Crane (ed.), *Languages and Society in Modern India* (Delhi, 1981), pp. 11; 15.

38. For background on the Anand Marriage Act see R.S. Talwar, 'Anand Marriage Act', *PPP* II:2 (1968), pp. 400–10.

39. Barrier, 'In Search of Identity', p. 9.

40. For this phenomenon see E.J. Hobsbawm, *Bandits* (London, 1969). There is a fascinating similarity between the notions of the noble thief and the eighteenth-century Sikh martyr. Of course, I do not mean to imply that all rural folk in the Punjab were a single uniform mass with an unchanging folk culture.

41. See Chapter Five.

42. Of course, this was not the only theme on which the Tat Khalsa chose to write, but it is by far the most popular. Two other pre–Singh Sabha themes of which the Tat Khalsa would make use are the democratic element which runs throughout the Khalsa narrative and the theme of the equality of all humanity.

43. The quotation above belongs to Mikhail Bakhtin. Oberoi, *Construction*, pp. 277–9.

44. Oberoi, *Construction*, pp. 207–57; 304–80.

45. Ganda Singh, *A History of Khalsa College, Amritsar* (Amritsar, 1949), pp. 9, 29.

46. The Tat Khalsa relationship with the army may be traced to Ditt Singh, who authored a column titled *Jaṅgī Khabr* ('military news') in the *Khālsā Akhbār*. Often, this column instructed Sikh soldiers on what Ditt Singh felt was proper Sikh practice (*maryādā*). N.S. Kapur, *Giānī Ditt Siṅgh: Jīvan te Rachnā* (Patiala, 1987), p. 19. Later, the *Khālsā Samāchār* also published a regular column of the same title.

47. Oberoi, *Construction*, pp. 305–6.

48. Ditt Singh, *Gugga Gapaura te Sultān Puārā* (Amritsar, 1976). Oberoi, *Construction*, pp. 308–9, alludes to a report noting the far-reaching success of these pamphlets. Apparently, a group of twenty-five families descended from a woman who had piously worshipped Sakhi Sarwar, abandoned their reverence for the saint upon reading Ditt Singh's polemic and were administered *khaṇḍe dā amrit*. Oberoi's *Construction*, chapter 6, details the methods used by the Tat Khalsa to rid the Panth of many other contemporary features for which the group had no propensity.

49. *The Khalsa Advocate*, 21 March 1908, p. 4. Also, *Khālsā Samāchār*, 5 March 1900, pp. 3–5, reprimands Sikhs who participate in Holi, enjoining them rather to participate in Hola Mohalla.

50. See J.S. Sital (ed.), *Sri Gur-panth Prakāś krit Bhāī Ratan Siṅgh Bhaṅgū Sahīd* (Amritsar, 1984), p. 22; and *WhS*, p. 67, n. 18. The task was undertaken by Bhangu in order to give a Sikh perspective of Punjabi and Sikh history, a perspective that would be sorely lacking in Bute Shah's *Tawārikh-i Panjāb*. Bhangu states this fact at *PrPP*, p. 20:

[Bute Shah] the Maulvi is a Muslim. He would not praise the Sikhs.

51. The text published under the auspices of the SGPC in 1984 retains the original title. J.S. Sital (ed.), *Gur-panth Prakāś*. In all other respects, this version follows Vir Singh's edition precisely. The editing of Bhangu's text by Vir Singh is the subject of an essay by H.S. Chopra and Surjit Hans, 'The Editing of Panth

Prakash by Bhai Vir Singh', in *Punjab Journal of Politics* XII:1 (1988), pp. 51–62; which was expanded into the former author's two-volume doctoral dissertation, 'Bhai Vir Singh's Editing of Panth Prakash by Rattan Singh Bhangu', (Ph.D. dissertation, GNDU, 1990). From this point on, Bhangu's original text will be referred to as *Gur-panth Prakāś*, while Vir Singh's edited edition will retain the title *Prāchīn Panth Prakāś* (*PrPP*).

52. At one place, for example, Vir Singh changes the original verb 'tell' (*kaho*) to 'write' (*likho*). Vir Singh, moreover, deleted the obscenities within the original text. Chopra and Hans, 'The Editing of Panth Prakash', p. 61.

53. *PnP*, p. 79.

54. Vir Singh, *Devī Pūjān Partal* (Amritsar, 1963), pp. 65–6; as noted in Harinder Singh, 'Bhai Vir Singh's Editing' I, pp. xxv–xxvi. The manuscripts on which Harinder Singh bases his introduction are MS number 797 of Panjab University, Chandigarh; MS number 276 of GNDU; and an incomplete manuscript in possession of a private individual. Unfortunately, he does not supply their respective dates of completion. Vir Singh claims in the introduction to the second edition of *PrPP* that he lost the original manuscript on which he had based his printed edition and, moreover, that he had completed the many incomplete chaupais of the manuscript. *PrPP*, pp. 2, 3. Chopra and Hans' research may, therefore, simply be a case of one manuscript differing from another. Indeed, according to Jit Singh Sital, additions to the text of Bhangu's original work were supplied by one Gian Singh Longowal in 1867 and published in 1880. (This cannot account for the passage in the printed edition that makes reference to the Puratan janam-sakhi, however.) Sital (ed.), *Gur-panth Prakāś*, p. 583. Although the historian must suspend judgement, it seems highly unlikely that the manuscript Vir Singh initially consulted would differ so dramatically from the three surviving manuscripts on which the former two authors base many of their conclusions.

55. Vir Singh (ed.), *Purātan Janam Sakhī Srī Gurū Nānak Dev Jī* (7th edn, Amritsar, 1971). Also *EST*, pp. 16, 22–30. The reference to the janam-sakhi appears in *PrPP*, p. 27.

56. Harinder Singh, 'Bhai Vir Singh's Editing' I, p. xxvii.

57. Vir Singh, *Sundarī* (19th edn, New Delhi, 1989), p. 99, for example. Also see Vir Singh, *Bijai Siṅgh* (New Delhi, 1989); and *Satvant Kaur* (New Delhi, 1989). Passages from *Satvant Kaur* often appeared in the early issues of the *Khālsā Samāchār*.

58. For example, Vir Singh, *Sundarī*, p. 106 and *Bijai Siṅgh*, pp. 18, 156–7.

59. The original passage noting Bhangu's aim in writing text reads:

kabb hindūān jas kare bakhān
He would not praise the Hindus.

Harinder Singh, 'Bhai Vir Singh's Editing' I, p. xxx.

60. There is an episode omitted, for example, where Sikhs sacrifice a male buffalo to the goddess prior to battling with the army of Ahmad Shah Abdali. The text of this deleted passage is in Harinder Singh's 'Bhai Vir Singh's Editing' I, p. xxi, n. 109.

61. Harinder Singh, 'Bhai Vir Singh's Editing' I, pp. xxxix ff. Also *PrPP*, pp. 40, 47. In another passage, Vir Singh alters the term *luṭwārī* (looters) to *haṭhwārī* (obstinate ones) in describing the Sikhs. See Chopra and Hans, 'The Editing', p. 58. The amended passage appears at *PrPP*, p. 452.

62. Chopra and Hans, 'The Editing', p. 60. The traditional Bidhi Chand narrative appears in *Bhāī Bidhī Chand Jī Adutī Bahāduri* (Lahore, 1913) and Vasava Singh, *Daryā Ghoṛe* (Amritsar, 1916).

63. Harinder Singh, 'Bhai Vir Singh's Editing', I, pp. xxxiii–iv.

64. Ibid., p. xxxii.

65. The 4 November 1910 issue of *The Khalsa Advocate*, pp. 3 ff., contains a strong Tat Khalsa reaction to Bedi's speech:

Have [Bedi and the Arya Samaj] done anything to commemorate the memory of those Sikh martyrs who were killed in the attempt of rescuing [*sic*] the wives, the sisters and the daughters of the Hindus from the clutches of the tyrant Muslims? The answer will be in the decisive negative.

Also Barrier, *Literature*, p. xxxvii, n. 5.

66. David Kinsley, 'The Mahādevī', in his *Hindu Goddesses: Visions of the Divine Feminine in the Hindu Religious Tradition* (Berkeley, 1986), pp. 145–6.

67. *MK*, p. 139.

68. In many ways, as long as so-called superstitions were in favour of the Tat Khalsa interpretation of Sikh tradition, these were retained. For example, the Tat Khalsa advocated utilizing the Adi Granth to perform all those functions previously associated with exorcists, medical personnel and rural healers. Puran Singh's *Sardhā Pūran*, for instance, was a manual published in 1891 which contained 270 verses mainly from the Adi Granth (the manual was attributed to Guru Gobind Singh). Each verse was accorded a mantra-like quality in which repetition produced a desired wish or result. Oberoi, *Construction*, p. 318. Initially a product of the Tat Khalsa, S.S. Josh came out very strongly against using the hymns of the scripture in such 'superstitious' ways. S.S. Josh, *My Tryst with Secularism: An Autobiography* (New Delhi, 1991), p. 109.

69. The Tat Khalsa wrote nothing to either encourage or specifically condemn the worship of Sikh martyrs. As we have seen, however, they did write diatribes against the reverence of pirs and demi-gods.

70. *PrPP*, p. 290, has Taru Singh state that his kes is a part of his skull.

71. Sital claims that one Gian Singh Longowal, a resident of the village in which Bhangu's descendants lived in the nineteenth century, incorporated 'other stories'(*hor prasaṅg*) under the name *Panth Prakāś* in 1867, which was first published in 1880. See *Gur-panth Prakāś*, p. 583.

72. See *PrPP*, p. 302.

73. J.S. Sital (ed.), *Gur-panth Prakāś*, p. 32b. We should note that Sital assumes that this passage was written by Bhangu himself.

74. *PrPP*, p. 471.

75. Surjit Hans, 'Rattan Singh Bhangu's Purpose of Writing the Prachin Panth Prakash', in PHCP 9 (1975), pp. 75–82; and his 'Rattan Singh Bhangu's Method of Writing History', in PHCP 11 (1976), pp. 46–53. Vir Singh himself notes this mandate in the preface to *Sri Gurū Kalgidhar Chamatkār* (Amritsar, 1925). Also Kirpal Singh, 'Bhai Vir Singh's Portrayal of History', in PHCP 7 (1972), pp. 247–52.

76. A brief account of this period is in J.S. Grewal, *Sikhs of the Punjab*, pp. 119–127.

77. *PrPP*, p. 434.

78. *PrPP*, p. 227. Also p. 302 for a list of principal martyrs.

79. It is probably for this reason that the honorific 'Shahid' is placed at the end of Bhangu's full name.

80. *PrPP*, p. 287.

81. *PrPP*, pp. 290–1. Taru Singh does not die immediately after his scalping. According to Bhangu, Taru Singh prophesies that the nawab who was responsible for the desecration of his sacred kesas will be cursed. After Taru Singh is scalped, the governor is unable to pass urine. Eventually, the governor overcomes this malady only after he is hit on the head with the shoe of Taru Singh. Nevertheless, the nawab dies quickly afterwards. It is only after the nawab dies that Taru Singh gives up his life. See Sital (ed.), *Gur-panth Prakāś*, pp. 369–72; 82–3.

82. *PrPP*, p. 39:

It was at that time that the sovereignty [of the Mughals] in Delhi began to decline. It was at that time that the power of the Turks began to diminish.

83. W.L. M'Gregor's *The History of the Sikhs* II (Allahabad, 1979).

84. *PrPP*, p. 445: *huto panth tho mājhe māhi.* There are many instances in the text where Bhangu derides Malwa Sikhs and glorifies Majhails. After the tenth Guru tells Banda to enlist Majha Sikhs in his cause, for example, he states that Majhails are *oi sūran main hain ati sūre*, 'The heroes of heroes', and maintains that *ham main unamain bhed kicch nahin/ un main, ham oi hamre māhin*, 'There is no difference between me and them. I am in them and they are in me.' *PrPP*, p. 81.

85. *PrPP*, p. 269.

86. *PrPP*, p. 231.

87. An article in the *Khālsā Samāchār*, 20 November 1913, p. 4, pledged fierce Sikh support for the British war effort. Moreover, the KTS (ninety per cent of whose publications were written by Vir Singh) and various other agencies that published Sikh tracts and handbills had issued numerous publications which dealt with Sikh heroism, sacrifice and martyrdom in the early twentieth century and as the First World War was about to begin. According to N.G. Barrier, 'Sikh bravery and recruitment efforts during the First World War stimulated another round of tracts on this topic [i.e. sacrifice and martyrdom].' See his 'Vernacular Publishing and Sikh Public Life in the Punjab, 1880–1910', in Kenneth W. Jones (ed.), *Religious Controversy in British India: Dialogues in South Asian Languages* (New York, 1992), pp. 200–26, 284–9.

88. See Harbans Singh, *Bhai Vir Singh* (New Delhi, 1972), p. 44. See also Ganda Singh, 'Bhai Vir Singh and His Times', in G.S. Talib and Attar Singh (ed.), *Bhai Vir Singh: Life, Times & Works* (Chandigarh, 1973), pp. 19–37.

89. Recall that the text is written as a dialogue of sorts between both Bhangu and Captain Murray.

90. *PrPP*, pp. 414–20. For Basant Singh see *TGK* II, p. 199.

91. It was under this tree that Guru Arjan supervised the building of Harimandir Sahib.

92. *PnP*, p. 910.

93. *TGK* II, pp. 197–9.

94. See *PrPP*, p. 103. The fact that Bhangu does not provide a Dip Singh narrative is, to J.S. Sital, 'a matter of amazement'. Later, however, he identifies the character in the Dip Singh of *Gur-panth Prakāś* as the famous Baba Dip Singh Shahid. J.S. Sital (ed.), *Sri Gur-panth Prakāś*, pp. 32; 154, n. 2.

95. R.C. Temple, 'Folklore of the Headless Horseman in Northern India', *Calcutta Review* 77 (1883), pp. 159–61.

96. Ibid., p. 159:

The *misal* of which Karm Singh and Dharm Singh were leaders got their sobriquet of Shahīd or Martyr, as being the followers of Sadā Singh, the Martyr, who was so called because he fell fighting against the Musalmāns, and was said to have fought for a mile after his head was cut off.

Another version supplied provides a goddess theme, while a third is closer to the story we have today. There is, furthermore, a version which maintains that Sada Singh succeeded Dip Singh as head granthi of Damdama Sahib.

97. *Glossary* III, pp. 398–9.

98. W.H. McLeod, *Popular Sikh Art* (New Delhi, 1991), p. 14.

99. Giani Thakur Singh initiated Bhai Jodh Singh into the Khalsa.

100. Thakur Singh, *Gurū Siṅgh Śahīd-bilās* (Amritsar, 1903). Another of Thakur Singh's martyrologies is *Vaḍḍā Śahīd-bilās* (Amritsar, 1911).

101. McLeod's *Popular Sikh Art* does not mention these prints.

102. For advertisements of portraits of Dip Singh, Taru Singh, Phula Singh and Ranjit Singh, see *The Khalsa Advocate,* 30 June 1906, p. 8. The pictures were advertised in every issue of the English paper from 8 February 1908 until 27 June 1908.

103. Fortunately, Amar Singh has provided a miniature version of the portrait narrating the martyrdom of Bhai Taru Singh in *Anecdotes From Sikh History: Stirring Stories of the Heroism of Sikh Women and the Martyrdom of a Sikh Youth* (Lahore, 1906), p. 35.

104. See, for example, R.W. Falcon, *Handbook on the Sikhs for the Use of Regimental Officers* (Allahabad, 1896).

105. One must not make the mistake of exaggerating this point, however. As J.S. Grewal notes, this policy was also observed by Ranjit Singh, who 'gave revenue-free land to an individual for accepting pahul (initiatory water)'. See Grewal's review of Oberoi's *Construction* in *Khera: Journal of Religious Understanding* XV:1 (1995), p. 165.

106. N.S. Kapur, *Giānī Ditt Siṅgh*, pp. 1–23. Ditt Singh's influence on Vir Singh is noted on p. 45. Also G.S. Neki, *Siṅgh Sabhā Lahir de Usraīe* (Amritsar, 1985), pp. 33–7; and *EoS*, pp. 589–90.

107. *Construction*, p. 289.

108. The text of the hukam-nama issued against Gurmukh Singh in 1897 appears in Kapur, *Giānī Ditt Siṅgh*, pp. 43–4. See also the special supplement to the *Khālsā Akhbār*, 16 April 1887. Background on the events which led up to the production of the play may be read in Gurmukh Singh's own *My Attempted Excommunication from the Sikh Temple and the Khalsa Community at Faridkot in 1887* (Lahore, 1898).

109. Kapur, *Giānī Ditt Siṅgh*, pp. 15–19.

110. S.S. Ashok (ed.), *Giānī Ditt Siṅgh Rachnāvalī: Śahīdīān* (Patiala, 1977), p. 14.

111. Ditt Singh, *Merā ate Sādhū Dayānand Jī Sambād* (Lahore, 1900). Other polemics written by Ditt Singh against the Arya Samaj are noted in Barrier, 'Vernacular Publishing and Sikh Public Life', pp. 212–13. Also Kenneth Jones, *Arya Dharam*, chapter 5.

112. N.S. Kapur, *Giānī Ditt Siṅgh*, pp. 17–18; and G.S. Sidhu, *Pro. Gurmukh Siṅgh* (Patiala, 1989), pp. 21–2.

113. Ditt Singh, *Sikh Bacche dī Śahīdī* (Lahore, 1898), verse 105. Ashok (ed.), p. 21.

114. Ditt Singh, *Siṅghṇiān de Sidaq* (Lahore, n.d.), verse 137. Ashok (ed.), p. 287.

115. Ditt Singh, *Bhāī Tārā Siṅgh Vāinen dī Śahīdī* (Lahore, 1899), verses 400–1. Ashok (ed.), p. 86.

116. Stanley J. Tambiah, *Leveling Crowds: Ethnonationalist Conflicts and Collective Violence in South Asia* (Berkeley, 1996), p. 141.

117. Ditt Singh, *Bhāī Tārū Siṅgh dī Śahīdī* (Lahore, 1898), verses 341–2. Ashok (ed.), p. 210.

118. Oberoi, *Construction*, p. 264.

119. A large diwan is described in Harbans Singh, 'The Bakapur Diwan and Babu Teja Singh of Bhasaur', in *PPP* IX:ii, pp. 322–32. Also see *The Khalsa Advocate*, 21 September 1907.

120. Oberoi, *Construction*, pp. 279–95.

121. N.G. Barrier, 'The Singh Sabhas and the Evolution of Modern Sikhism, 1875–1925', in Robert D. Baird (ed.), *Religious Movements in Modern India* (Delhi, 1989), pp. 206–7. Also his 'Sikh Politics in British Punjab prior to the Gurdwara Reform Movement', in J.T. O'Connell, et al. (ed.), *Sikh History and Religion in the Twentieth Century*, pp. 176–77; and 'Punjab Politics and the Press: 1880–1910', in Barrier and Case (ed.), *Aspects of India* (Simla, 1985), pp. 118–33.

122. Harbans Singh's *Bhai Vir Singh*, p. 32, n. 1.

123. Although not a KTS publication, Kahn Singh's *Ham Hindū Nahīn* (Amritsar, 1899) is in the form of a dialogue between a Sikh and a Hindu.

124. Both these works were published anonymously. *Dharam het Balīdān* (Amritsar, 1897) and *Śahīd-nāmā* (Amritsar, 1900). Other martyrological tracts were *Sidaqī Śahīd Bhāī Maṇī Siṅghī* (Amritsar, 1899); *Vaḍḍā Ghalūghārā* (Amritsar, 1905); *Jīvan Britānt Bhāī Tārū Siṅgh Jī Śahīd* (Amritsar, 1912); and *Zaina dā Virlāp* (Amritsar, 1913). See also the various other tracts by the KTS in Barrier, *Literature*, pp. 135–6.

125. Barrier, 'Sikh Public Life in the Punjab', p. 210.

126. Ibid., p. 208. These societies also produced many martyrologies. An advertisement for three such tracts produced by the Khalsa Agency of Lahore appeared in the August and September 1908 issues of *The Khalsa Advocate*. Here, we see a Sikh soldier holding a standard over which a sign bearing the following words is superimposed: 'Pools of Blood or Church of Patriotism'. That the authors of these tracts were attempting to influence Sikhs is clear from the brief text descriptions within the advertisements. 'These narratives are written in a very high mood and cannot fail to inspire our young men with a desire of higher life by living nobly,' states the advertisement to Amar Singh's *Sketches from the Sikhs History*. *The Khalsa Advocate*, 4 July 1908, p. 7. Furthermore, N.G. Barrier also points out that as many as twenty thousand copies of tracts produced by the Khalsa Handbill Society were distributed in Punjabi villages free of charge. Barrier, *Literature*, p. xxxii.

127. *The Khalsa Advocate*, 23 March 1907, p. 5. Also Harbans Singh, *Bhai Vir Singh*, p. 31. Here, the author notes (with some exaggeration) that

A considerable circle of readers was established which awaited and devoured with eagerness each successive issue [of the KTS].

128. This was despite both the initial Sikh suspicion of the Singh Sabha and the fact that gurdwaras were in the hands of Udasi Sikhs. N.S. Kapur, *Giāni Ditt Singh*, p. 104.

129. S.S. Josh, *My Tryst with Secularism*, p. 7.

130. Ibid., pp. 7–9.

131. For the CKD see S.S. Narang, 'Chief Khalsa Diwan: A Study of Leadership, Ideology and Political Strategy' (Ph.D. dissertation, GNDU, 1989), chapter 3, pp. 59–122. The original pledge form (1906) and its revised version (1913), which all respective members were to endorse, appear on pages 65 and 66.·

132. The CKD retained the dominant position as the representative Sikh body until 1919. This was the criticism of Teja Singh Overseer of the Bhasaur Singh Sabha, who had formed his own Panch Khalsa Diwan to protest the CKD's conservative stance regarding proper Sikh interpretations, practices and rituals. S.S. Narang, 'The Chief Khalsa Diwan', chapter 3.

133. S.S. Narang, 'Chief Khalsa Diwan—An Analytical Study of its Perceptions', in Paul Wallace and Surendra Chopra (ed.), *Political Dynamics and Crisis in Punjab* (Amritsar, 1988), pp. 70–86.

134. S.S. Narang, 'Chief Khalsa Diwan: A Study of Leadership', chapter 3. Also N.G. Barrier, 'Sikh Politics in British Punjab prior to the Gurdwara Reform Movement', pp. 159-190. For the language question in the Punjab consult Paul R. Brass, *Language, Religion and Politics in North India* (Cambridge, 1974), pp. 277–336.

135. Joginder Singh, 'The *Khālsā Samāchār:* Some of its Major Concerns and Approach, 1899–1920', in PHCP 16 (1982), pp. 286–93. Joginder Singh emphasizes that the *Khālsā Samāchār* was concerned with the creation of Sikh schools that could disseminate Tat Khalsa ideals.

136. See the poem *'Purātan singh te asi'* (Sikhs of the Past and Us) in the *Khālsā Samāchār*, 6 April 1904, p. 9.

137. *The Khalsa Advocate*, 9 June 1906, p. 2; 29 September 1906, p. 5; and 5 September 1908, p. 3.

138. *The Khalsa Advocate*, 9 March 1907, p. 7.

139. *The Khalsa Advocate*, 11 March 1910, p. 4.

140. *The Khalsa Advocate*, 11 June 1908, p. 2. See also the *Khālsā Samāchār*, 5 February 1900, pp. 5–6. The *Khālsā Samāchār*, 15 January 1900, reports that Giani Thakur Singh also spoke of the four sahib-zade to students at the Khalsa Branch School, using as his source a book titled *Prasang Śahid Bilās*. Afterwards, the students read the story out to the gathered sangat.

141. *The Khalsa Advocate*, 1 June 1907, p. 5.

142. 'Education Among the Sikhs of Yore', in *The Khalsa Advocate*, 18 March 1910, p. 5.

143. There were many such appeals. See, for example, any 1903–5 issue of the *Khālsā Samāchār*.

144. *The Khalsa Advocate*, 13 July 1907, p. 3.

145. *The Khalsa Advocate*, 18 April 1908, p. 1, demonstrates how Mani Singh and Taru Singh followed Guru Ram Das' *Gauri ki vār* 22:1 (AG, p. 313), precisely remembering God despite the painful tortures they were undergoing.

146. D. Petrie, *Developments in Sikh Politics (1900–1911) (A Report)*,

[annotated by S. Nahar Singh] (Amritsar, n.d.), p. 32.

147. *The Khalsa Advocate,* 15 January 1905, p. 5, describes the large diwan held in Sindh and attended by CKD preachers. In this period, the number of tracts on martyrs dramatically increased. Barrier, *Literature.*

148. The *Khālsā Samāchār,* 11 December 1899, p. 7. Also see *The Khalsa Advocate,* 6 June 1908, p. 6. Here, the author follows the characteristic pattern set by Ditt Singh:

Oh, the race of martyrs that you know how infinitesimally small compared with the locust-numbered enemy our ancestors were! And yet they succeeded in ridding the country of tyranny and injustice. There was a day when the Sikh was considered a model of good resolution and perseverance. 'Grant me, O God! power that I may never refrain from good deeds,' prays the Saviour [Guru Gobind Singh]. A Sikh, therefore, must possess the unflinching courage to stick to virtue. Brethren, follow in wake of your forefathers and clear your nation of all ignorance and illiteracy. Let [*vidyā vichārī bhī paraupakārī* (Guru Nanak, *Āsā chaupad* 25(1), AG, p. 356)], meaning 'educationist is the great benefactor of his fellow-creatures', [*sic*] be your guiding motto and watchword.

149. Ibid., pp. 7–8.

150. Vir Singh's *Bijai Singh* underscores this feature of amrit. A note in the *Khālsā Samāchār,* 18 December 1899, p. 8, enjoins all Sikhs to read Vir Singh's *Bijai Singh* as 'it makes people cast off superstitions'. See Oberoi, *Construction,* p. 333 ff., for the emphasis on all Sikhs undergoing *khaṇḍe dī pāhul.* Also see '*amrit par vichār*' (Thoughts on amrit) in the *Khālsā Samāchār,* 23 April 1900, pp. 3–4.

151. Page 1 of a supplement to *The Khalsa Advocate,* 27 July 1907, details the history and financial accounts of the Khalsa Updeshak school in Gharjakh, Gujranwala, which was taken over by the Singh Sabha in 1903. In asking for donations, Ishar Singh (a CKD preacher) states, 'In [the] end we beg to appeal to those in whose veins surges the true blood of martyrdom [to give donations to the school] ... Bhai Mani Singh and Baba Dip Singh will also advise you thus.'

152. Texts which were taught in the Punjabi-language classes at various Singh Sabha-affiliated schools have yet to be examined by scholars. *The Khalsa Advocate,* 12 August 1910, p. 2, claims, for example:

In the fifth primary we had only to learn [*Nakalī Sikh Prabodh*] in reading the names of the parts of speech in grammar... We finished [*Nakalī Sikh Prabodh*] ten times in the first two months, with meanings. We had so much mastered the book that we could tell pages of the poetry by heart... In short, we read four books by B. Ditt Singh...

153. *The Khalsa Advocate,* 18 March 1910, p. 2.

154. *The Khalsa Advocate,* 2 May 1908, p. 4.

155. *The Khalsa Advocate,* 15 April 1910, p. 5.

156. Statistics taken from Amrit Walia, 'Achievements of the Sikh Education Conference', in PHCP 9 (1975), pp. 205–12.

157. Statistics taken from various articles in *The Khalsa Advocate,* 1903–10. There were girls' schools opened at Sialkot, Chunian, Koita, Amritsar, Farruka, Garli Yasin, Rawalpindi and Quetta.

158. Quoted in Narotam Singh, 'Chief Khalsa Diwan in the Field of Education', in *JSS* VII:1, 2 (1981), p. 123.

159. Ibid., p. 125.

160. *The Khalsa Advocate,* 4 January 1908, p. 3.

161. Barrier, 'The Sikhs and Punjab Politics, 1882–1922', in Paul Wallace and Surendra Chopra (ed.), *Political Dynamics and Crisis in Punjab* (Amritsar, 1988), pp. 502–41. Also his 'Sikh Politics in British Punjab Prior to the Gurdwara Reform Movement'; and Narotam Singh, 'Field of Education', pp. 118–29.

SEVEN

Playing the Game
The Movement for Gurdwara Reform

*je tuhāde andar bhāī manī. singh varagī kurbāni nahīn, je tuhāde
andar śahīd mahitāb singh jī varagī anakh nahin, je tuhāde sine
andar akālī phūlā singh varagā dil nahīn tān kiun nahin ailān kar
dende ki hun srī darbār sāhib sikhān dā nahin*[1]

If you cannot sacrifice like Bhai Mani Singh; if you do not possess
the self-respect of Shahid Mehtab Singh; if you cannot find within
your heart the courage of Akali Phula Singh, then why not simply
declare, 'Now, Sri Darbar Sahib (the Golden Temple) does not
belong to the Sikhs.'

In his seminal work on the Tat Khalsa and its attempt to purge the
Sikh Panth of diversity, Harjot Oberoi makes the following
summary statement as he approaches the end of his text:

By founding a string of publishing houses, cultural bodies, schools, colleges,
orphanages and clubs, the Tat Khalsa endeavoured to insert their definitions
of religion and community into the day-to-day life of Sikhs. Through this,
it became possible not only for a mass of people to experience themselves
as Sikhs in the fashion desired by the Tat Khalsa, but also for non-Sikhs to
visualize Sikhs as a distinct group. What had begun as a possibility turned
into a cultural reality, a social fact articulated at the level of everyday life.[2]

As erudite as this statement may be, there is nevertheless
one essential variable which can be added to the equation of the
dominance of the Tat Khalsa interpretation that was also vividly
articulated at the level of everyday life.

In the previous chapter, it was demonstrated that throughout the
cultural and educational institutions founded by the Tat Khalsa, a

common practice was to instil their interpretation of the Sikh tradition by utilizing a powerful rhetoric of martyrdom. We noted that the appeal to past Sikh martyrs greatly advanced the Tat Khalsa/CKD cause. As the Tat Khalsa's understanding of Sikhs and Sikhism came to be seen more and more as the only interpretation of the Sikh tradition, the rhetoric of martyrdom which often carried that interpretation across made martyrs and martyrdom seem a far more fundamental feature of the Sikh tradition than had been the case previously. And thus, when a large number of Sikhs actually took this rhetoric to heart during the Gurdwara Reform Movement between 1920–5, sacrificing both themselves and their property to protect Sikh sacred shrines, they became the 'supreme' exemplars of Tat Khalsa Sikhism, tapping into and embodying a tradition of martyrdom which had virtually saturated the Sikh environment for the last forty years. These valiant, non-violent men and women became the modern-day Mani Singhs and Mai Bhagos to both themselves and other Sikhs, as well as to most Indians engaged in the nationalist struggle. It is this, I believe, which provides the final variable, thereby completing Oberoi's equation: the personification of Tat Khalsa values, Sikhs who consciously imitated the 'Sikhs of yore'. The example provided by these Sikhs, in other words, sealed the dominance of the Tat Khalsa interpretation by providing a sustained and dramatically visible manifestation of Tat Khalsa Sikhism in action. One must, therefore, understand the Gurdwara Reform Movement not simply as a political or religious activity but as the stage upon which the ritual of martyrdom was played out. By taking a cue from the anthropologist, Clifford Geertz, one can say that the Gurdwara Reform Movement was not merely a spectacle to be watched, but a ritual to be enacted.[3] It was a grand, prolonged *rite de passage* for the Sikh Panth, whose most profound ritual component was martyrdom.

The Sikh vernacular press between 1920 and 1925, indeed during the entire period of the Singh Sabha, offered a particular self-understanding of the Sikhs, as a people 'through whose veins flowed the blood of martyrdom'.[4] The eager willingness of Sikhs to offer themselves as a sacrifice for recapturing the gurdwaras demonstrated the force that this image had in the actual lives of the Panth's members. The significance and distinction of the martyrs and potential martyrs of the Gurdwara Reform Movement suggests that martyrdom functioned in this period as a social ritual in the Sikh Panth. This understanding of martyrdom as social ritual is still quite cogent for today's Sikh community, as evinced by Joyce Pettigrew's maxim that Sikhs who were killed in the post-1984 period 'give substance to the insubstantial entity of the Panth'. Here, Pettigrew is underscoring the fact that martyrdom as social ritual works as most rituals do cross-culturally, that is to reinforce the bonds of the community. Since at least the time that Emile Durkheim published *The Elementary Forms of Religious Life* in 1912, rituals have been understood in this way, as the very means by which groups send collective messages to themselves, confirming their social substance and endorsing their world-view.[6] Geertz clearly acknowledges this point in his famous article, 'Religion as a Cultural System'. Yet, here it is Geertz's understanding of religious performances which should be of particular concern in any analysis of the Gurdwara Reform Movement:

Where for 'visitors' religious performances can, in the nature of the case, only be presentations of a particular religious perspective, and thus aesthetic-ally or scientifically dissected, for participants they are, in addition, enactments, materializations, realizations of it, not only models of what they believe, but also models *for* the believing of it. In these plastic dramas men attain their faith as they portray it.[7]

Martyrdom and the Gurdwara Reform Movement, in which martyrs and their families were so often presented for darshan, is especially consistent with this description.[8] To paraphrase Judith Perkins' fascinating study of early Christian self-representation, witnessing a martyrdom either in person or by report not only affirmed the Sikh self-understanding that to be a Sikh was to heroically suffer martyrdom, but also provided another instance.[9] The ritual of martyrdom as vividly and consistently enacted during the Gurdwara Reform Movement strengthened the social fabric of the Sikh community, a fabric whose principal weaver (at least in the early twentieth century) was the Tat Khalsa. It also functioned to affirm the understanding of the Sikh as martyr and the history of the Sikh Panth as one made up principally of martyrs.

All this was due in large part to the rhetoric of martyrdom adroitly employed by the Singh Sabha and its inheritors. Through this rhetoric, Sikhs (and non-Sikhs) were finally persuaded to see themselves as a community distinct from all others, a community known above all else for its ability to 'sacrifice for the sake of righteousness'. The rhetoric of martyrdom was thus an interpretive strategy (*à la* Kenneth Burke) as well as a 'technique of transcendence': soteriologically, it helped to bring Sikhs closer to Akal Purakh through their sacrifice (recall that the Arabic term *qurbān,* from which the Punjabi *kurbānī* or sacrifice is derived, means literally 'proximity'); sociologically, it aided in the creation of a sacred community whose members were raised above the members of all others.[10]

Most historical accounts of contemporary Sikh movements or the nationalist movement in India will doubtlessly mention the Gurdwara Reform Movement, also known as the Third Sikh War.[11] Sikh authors in particular are quick to note the legacy that present-day Sikh politicians have inherited from the movement, and its participants and leaders. This is, of course, a logical connection since the principal Sikh political organization of the late twentieth century retains the name and (so it is said) the spirit of this first Akali Dal or the 'Army of the Immortal [One]' which fought to liberate Sikh shrines from their supposedly corrupt, hereditary incumbents.[12] It has often been mentioned that the movement to reform gurdwaras stemmed directly from earlier Tat Khalsa attempts to define and control sacred Sikh space.[13] Despite such brief statements of this nature, however, contemporary accounts have not yet clearly established the links between the two movements.

Most authors dealing with the Gurdwara Reform Movement underscore the Akali debt to the Tat Khalsa.[14] It was the Tat Khalsa, after all, which began the campaign to cleanse gurdwaras of their present-day allegedly corrupt managers. In this chapter we shall examine why the Tat Khalsa is, in fact, indebted to the Akalis and their programme of gurdwara reform. There are texts which note that the Tat Khalsa interpretation of the tradition was worked into the very Sikh Gurdwaras Act of 1925, itself, particularly in its definition of the term 'Sikh'.[15] Nevertheless, these do not state that the movement was, in effect, the final stage in the Tat Khalsa attempt to dominate Sikh imaginations, an attempt begun in the 1870s. By 1925, thanks to the overwhelming success of the Gurdwara Reform Movement, the interpretation of Sikh tradition and history supplied by the Tat Khalsa was stubbornly entrenched. The 1920–5 movement ensured the dominance of the interpretation, a hegemony which today permeates the vast majority of texts that deal with the history and religion of the Sikhs. Although there are groups within the contemporary Sikh Panth, such as the Damdami Taksal and the Akhand Kirtani Jatha, which are often at odds with the SGPC, all three groups work within the paradigm formulated by the Singh Sabha and its inheritors, the

Shiromani Akali Dal, a paradigm whose limits were in place by 1925.[16] In this regard, the 1920–5 episode marks a watershed in Sikh history, one as significant (if not more so) as the initial reform impulse.

It is the use of the rhetoric of martyrdom that provides one of the largest planks in the bridge connecting the Singh Sabhas to the Gurdwara Reform Movement, and also provides, in part, the answer to why the Singh Sabha interpretation of Sikh tradition is by far the most prominent discourse articulated within the Sikh world of today. Isolating the rhetoric of martyrdom does a slight injustice to the total history and development of the Gurdwara Reform Movement. It is, however, a most important feature of the action as a whole and the concern of the present chapter. It thus deserves to be scrutinized in isolation. In doing so, references to other crucial elements will be made.

The Rules of the Game

Let us begin by noting that this chapter has been titled 'Playing the Game', for while the Tat Khalsa and the CKD described and set the rules of the 'game of love' about which Guru Nanak himself spoke (or so they believed), it was left to the SGPC and the Akalis to actually engage in the playing. We noted in our last chapter that it was probably the constant appeals to sacrifice, as did the 'Sikhs of yore', which pushed the community ahead in terms of education, thereby fulfilling, in part, the mandate of the CKD. Prior to 1919, the appeal to 'tender one's head' in the fulfilment of the CKD programme was, of course, a metaphor for sacrificing either time, money, or effort to it. In the years after 1919, such an appeal took on a dramatically vivid significance.

When the rhetoric of martyrdom was first utilized by the Sikhs of the Tat Khalsa in the late nineteenth century, the chance of a person dying or being killed in a manner similar to that of past Sikh martyrs was very remote indeed. The frequent catalogues of the various physical tortures that past Sikh martyrs had undergone were used as devices to heighten the heroism martyrs had displayed in the hope of inspiring contemporary Sikhs to commit their lives to 'improving' themselves (that is, to adopt Tat Khalsa standards), and also to improve the educational and political position of the Panth. It was mentioned in Chapter One that the Tat Khalsa and CKD may have developed the doctrine of the zinda-shahid as an attempt to come to terms with what may have been perceived as the end of martyrdom in the Sikh tradition. It, therefore, seemed highly unlikely that a Sikh would be decapitated, set aflame, or hacked limb from limb for adopting Tat Khalsa standards. This was particularly so in a society ruled by the 'benevolent British Sarkar' in which, according to many Sikh newspapers, tigers and goats drank at the same *ghat* (step). The worst that occurred in this period was that some Sikhs were ostracized by their relatives and neighbours for adopting Tat Khalsa rituals.[17]

All this was to change, however, after the massacres at Jallianwala Bagh in April 1919 and particularly Nankana Sahib in February 1921. By this time, the possibility of confronting such a terrifying and painful death had been dramatically realized by the hundreds of Sikhs who were the victims of both British and mahant excess, inflicted on a scale that would remain unprecedented until the Partition riots of 1947. The numerous descriptions of the tortures suffered by these hundreds were found in every newspaper in the Punjab and no doubt invoked the images of past Sikh martyrs about whom the Tat Khalsa had been speaking for the past four decades.[18] Rather than dissuade Sikhs from engaging in the movement to liberate gurdwaras for fear of a similar fate, such examples of horrific punishment and selfless suffering, and the emotional appeals that accompanied these, inspired Sikhs to leave their towns and villages *en masse* and make their way to the Akal Takht.[19] Here, Sikhs volunteered themselves for the Akali morchas and vowed to do all they could to aid the CSL and later, the SGPC and Shiromani Akali Dal, to oust 'evil' mahants such as Narain Das of Nankana Sahib from their positions as gurdwara *sarbrāh* (manager).

If Sikhs wished to 'play' in this attempt, however, they had to do so on the terms laid down by the Tat Khalsa, the CKD and later, the CSL, SGPC and Akali Dal. As we know from the case of the Lachman Singh execution of 1909, there were both individuals and groups which attempted to utilize the rhetoric of martyrdom to fulfil aims which, although in line with Tat Khalsa goals, nevertheless adopted standards and rules which were clearly outside the paradigm established by the Singh Sabha and its inheritors. The Sikhs intimately associated with the Ghadr movement during the First World War as well as the later Babbar Akalis (and perhaps Lachman Singh) were indeed inspired by the legends of Sikh martyrs and appealed to other Sikhs by alluding to the stories of these martyrs in their rhetoric and propaganda.[20]

The fact that the appeal of these groups was limited to a certain portion of the peasantry,[21] as well as their sheer lack of organization, ensured a speedy failure. Moreover, their adoption of an anti-loyalist and particularly violent campaign during the period when both the Singh Sabha and CKD sought British favour through loyal posturing led to both resounding official and Singh Sabha/CKD censure.[22] Although a small segment of the Tat Khalsa demonstrated some sympathy with the aim of these groups, the official policy was to distance itself from them. Both CKD ideologues and granthis of Harimandir Sahib, for example, loudly denounced 'revolutionary' Sikhs such as Ajit Singh and the Ghadrites. Like the Sikhs who returned to India on the ill-fated Komagata Maru, these men were labelled as *patit* or 'fallen' Sikhs, a denunciation that enjoined all true and loyal Sikhs to dissociate themselves from them.[23]

After the failure of the Ghadr Movement, many of the Sikh Ghadrites who had returned from North America helped put together a new movement in the 1920s. Formed in August 1922, the Babbar Akali Jatha was highly disillusioned with the non-violent campaign to liberate gurdwaras, initially drawn up by the CSL in collaboration with M.K. Gandhi and the Indian National Congress.[24] To answer the peasant demands that the Akali Dal was unable to address satisfactorily, the new group attempted to reorient the gurdwara movement, advocating terrorism, the violent overthrow of the British and the assassination of their *jholīchuks* or 'toady' collaborators.[25] Within their newspaper, the *Babbar Akālī Doāba* (which the Babbars printed on a mobile press to avoid detection), the Jatha utilized the rhetoric of martyrdom for this purpose. The issue of 20 October 1922, for example, constantly alluded to Bhai Mani Singh, imploring members of the Akali Dal and SGPC to adopt his selfless attitude in regard to the distribution of Panthic funds. Throughout the paper and in their political speeches, moreover, the Babbars often noted that according to the tenth Guru, the time to draw the sword against the British and their sycophants had come.[26]

The rules of their game were thus very much unlike those laid down by the Akali Dal and SGPC. The latter two groups demanded conservative militancy rather than the conservative reform of their predecessors, while the Babbar Akalis engaged in a clearly violent and bloody campaign of political assassination. A factor which certainly prolonged the life of the Babbars was the romantic image they cast.[27] Despite this Robin Hood-ish or, better yet, Jagga Daku-like appearance, however, the movement's appeal was limited only to a section of the Doaba peasantry.[28] In particular, it attracted entrenched soldiers who rightly felt that their war service was unappreciated by the British and those peasants most hard hit by colonial economics. The small size of the group, its lack of organization, and the fact that the SGPC and Akali Dal were by that time viewed by the majority of Punjabi Sikhs as the inheritors of the glorious tradition put forth by the Tat Khalsa dramatically decreased the Babbar Akali appeal over time. These factors, coupled with denunciations by the SGPC and Akali Dal, government propaganda and the harsh British measures adopted to suppress the violent movement, saw the quick arrest of the leading Babbars and subsequently, the movement's virtual dissolution.[29]

The Tat Khalsa, Chief Khalsa Diwan and Gurdwara Reform

Let us now turn to the game as devised by the Tat Khalsa and played out by the Akalis and SGPC. The attempt to define and control sacred space that initiated the Gurdwara Reform Movement began long before the British conquest of the Punjab. The simple facts that Guru Amar Das had constructed the Baoli Sahib in Goindwal and that Guru Ram Das chose to have Harimandir Sahib built demonstrated a need for a space set aside for congregational Sikh worship, a sacred space distinct from all other sacred (and mundane) spaces within the Punjab.[30] The tasks of Khalsa Sikhs in regard to the management of and etiquette within such space (initially called the dharamsala), as well as the character of its personnel, were firmly laid down in the rahit-nama literature, particularly the mid-eighteenth-century rahit-nama of Chaupa Singh Chhibbar.[31] Although there are no explicit statements in this work concerning the extent to which a Khalsa Sikh must go in order to protect this space, according to pre-Singh Sabha tradition, such duties clearly involved sacrificing one's life in order to ensure that the space would not be defiled.[32] In regard to Harimandir Sahib, for example, we see this tradition exemplified in the legends of Dip Singh and his companion, Gurbakhsh Singh Nihang; of Mehtab Singh and Sukha Singh, who killed the Muslim chief constable of Amritsar, Massa Ranghar, who had converted Harimandir into a dancing hall; and of Mansha Singh, who nightly swam across the sarovar to the Prakash Asthan in the eighteenth century in order to light the sacred *joti* or lamp lodged within the shrine.

The pre–Singh Sabha martyries within the precincts of Harimandir Sahib that commemorate the sacrifice of these extraordinary Khalsa Sikhs thus signify, if not a desire to directly control the space made sacred by the Gurus and defended by the martyrs, at least a need to rid it of those elements considered less than pious in the eighteenth century. These martyries, therefore, signify a necessity to ensure that the shrines remain undefiled.

During the period of the Singh Sabha, ensuring that these sacred spaces remained undefiled began to mean direct Tat Khalsa control of the sacred shrines. As martyrdom had been associated with the gurdwaras long before the Tat Khalsa came into existence, it was a rather effortless matter for them to incorporate the struggle to purify these shrines into the rhetoric of martyrdom. We mentioned in the last chapter that Tat Khalsa writers utilized the rhetoric to aid in fulfilling many of the needs which they felt that the contemporary Panth possessed. When it came to the present state of Sikh gurdwaras, Tat Khalsa newspapers made it abundantly clear that there were many such necessities. One need, they believed, was to convince Sikhs to abstain from the veneration of idols. Members of the Tat Khalsa fiercely maintained that the Gurus had clearly denounced such practices in the Adi Granth and that these must, therefore, be purged from the gurdwaras, all of which house the Eternal Guru, the Guru Granth Sahib. To the dismay of Sikh reformers, the parikarma of the Golden Temple, the bastion of Sikhism, was constantly thronged by brahman priests displaying the idols of Hindu gods and goddesses, a fact that had been often decried in the *Khālsā Akhbār* newspaper.[33]

Such sights prompted members of the newly formed CKD to pass resolutions requesting priests and pujaris to cease their performance of 'unsikhlike rites' and to likewise remove those elements deemed 'unsikhlike' from the precincts of the sacred shrine.[34] A CKD resolution of 15 September 1904, directed to the manager of the Golden Temple, Arur Singh, underscored the urgent need to fulfil this latter request in particular.[35] In May of 1905, Arur Singh finally agreed and ordered the removal of all idols from the precincts of the premier Sikh shrine.[36] The intense controversy which this move generated penetrated to all strata of Punjabi society. Members of the Arya Samaj, the Brahmo Samaj, and particularly those of the Singh Sabhas, leapt into the fray. The general public, moreover, especially the Sikh soldiers, demonstrated a passionate interest in the proceedings.[37]

Two particular positions eventually emerged over the action. The first supported Arur Singh, the second condemned him. The Tat Khalsa, of course, allied themselves with the manager, claiming (amongst other things) that when the temples were desecrated by those hostile to the Panth in the past, it was Sikh blood which was abundantly shed to preserve the sanctity of the gurdwaras, particularly Harimandir Sahib.[38] During the Gurdwara Reform Movement, one of the more oft-quoted statements was that there were far more skulls of Sikh martyrs in Harimandir Sahib than bricks.[39] In essence, editorials such as these attempted to underscore the belief that Sikhs died to rid the temples of all things considered 'non-Sikh'. To further highlight and justify such statements, articles on Sikh history were placed beside these editorials. The four-part article in the *Khālsā Samāchār*, for example, '*Srī darbār sāhib laī sikhān dīān kurbānīān*' (Sikh Sacrifices for the Sri Darbar Sahib), narrates the story of Sikhs, such as the previously mentioned Bhai Mansha Singh and others, who endangered themselves to bathe in the sarovar of Harimandir Sahib while the temple was occupied by Pathan soldiers.[40] Tacitly implied in this article was the idea that idols within the confines of the present-day temple complex were as harmful to contemporary Sikhs and Sikhism as the desecration of Harimandir was to the Sikhs of the 1700s. The narrative further suggested that all Sikhs should be willing to sacrifice themselves to manage the gurdwaras, thereby clearing the temples of all non-Sikh elements. In an attempt to do just this, the CKD requested the Punjab administration to grant it representative control of the Golden Temple in 1906.[41] No heed was paid to this request.

The request would take on a far more harsh tone a year later. On 29 July 1907, Bhai Harnam Singh, the Head Granthi of Harimandir Sahib, had died of natural causes. Noting that this sacred post was now vacant, both the *Khālsā Samāchār* and *The Khalsa Advocate* attempted to influence the 'British authorities' (presumably the Deputy Commissioner of Amritsar[42]) in a choice of successor. As Chaupa Singh Chhibbar had done 150 years before, the Tat Khalsa described the type of Sikh the Panth required to fill Harnam Singh's position. On 5 October 1907, *The Khalsa Advocate* noted that the successful candidate must be 'a really religious [Sikh] man ... who could adequately discharge the onerous duties of a spiritual leader'. It also requested the government 'to give due consideration to the opinion of the Sikh community' in the appointment and, further, it noted that representatives of the Panth had 'approached the authorities with whom the appointment rests ... to elect a fit man for the post'.[43] The next week, the same newspaper ran an article which detailed the history of appointing Head Granthis to the Darbar Sahib. To emphasize the importance of the post, the article noted the outcome of the first-ever dispute over the valued position between rival Sikh groups. According to tradition, both the Tattva Khalsa and the Bandai Khalsa of Banda Bahadur had fought for the position in the early eighteenth century, a dispute which was only resolved by the wife of Guru Gobind Singh, Mata Sundari, in favour of the former.[44] Excommunicating the great hero for his rash behaviour, the Mata Ji's choice for head granthi was the revered 'Martyr Mani Singh'. The article then notes:

Thus the very first Granthi ever appointed was Bhai Mani Singh of whose exemplary character no better proof can be found than the way he braved the glorious death of a religious martyr.[45]

The implication was straightforward: any Sikh proposed for this esteemed office must possess the qualities of a Sikh martyr in general and of this famous martyr in particular. The martyr had truly become the Sikh cultural ideal.

On 4 December 1907, the new Head Granthi of the Golden Temple was installed. Confirming the worst fears of the Tat Khalsa, the new appointee was not the Mani Singh Shahid that they had sought, but a 12-year-old boy who had previously been the *chelā* (disciple) of the deceased Harnam Singh.[46] Inevitably, such an act incensed many educated Sikhs. Numerous bitter letters were sent to the newspapers, reprimanding both the Panth and the CKD for allowing such an outrage by forgetting the lessons of the past, lessons dramatically taught through the selfless sacrifice and blood of their ancestors. Asking whether the Panth was aware of the 'enormity of the wrong done to them', one article comments on the situation, concluding with a strong rebuke:

Alas! the answer to this question, we fear, will be anything but cheering; for, the supineness which seems already to have overtaken the valiant Khalsa was never among the attributes of those who are not religiously dead and who have got the requisite moral courage to fight for and vindicate the rights which are as much theirs as the right to live. Fancy a nation counting over twenty two lakhs among its members, with a history to draw inspiration from, of the crusades of their ancestors who defended the holy Harimandir with as many heads as would cover the whole floor of the sacred precincts, and boasting to be living up to the traditions of these ancestors—fancy such a nation surrendering its most valuable rights without a word of protest![47]

Some months later, the same paper would note that the blame for the appointment lay not with the boy himself but with the Sikhs 'who embarrassed by mundane considerations, cannot pluck up the courage to take legal steps to save our temples and shrines from sacrilege'.[48]

Most of the young boy's actions in his capacity as Head Granthi prompted speedy criticism from members of the Tat Khalsa. The act of lowering the *Vaḍḍā Bābā*, the large, handwritten scripture housed on the second floor of the Prakash Asthan which is used to perform *akhaṇḍ paṭhs*, so that the child could conclude an unbroken reading of the scripture, for example, led the editor of *The Khalsa Advocate* to compose the following lines:

Alas! the *Holy Harimandir*, which was so dearly preserved with the blood of martyrs, should be so carelessly dealt with in these days of peace and law. Streams of blood once flowed to protect it against any contempt and disgrace; thousands of Sikhs sacrificed themselves for the sake of this Holiest of Holies. But nowadays, taking legal steps and pursuing peacefully against an encroachment upon its sanctity seems a burdensome task. Look upon this picture and upon that [of the heroic past].[49]

As this episode in Sikh history makes clear, the strong association between martyrs and sacred Sikh shrines that existed before the Singh Sabha movement was often elaborated by the group. Adopting a tactic developed by Ditt Singh, present-day Sikhs were compared to their heroic, selfless eighteenth-century brothers and sisters in the attempt to underscore the belief that contemporary Sikhs had ceased to care for the shrines for which their ancestors laid down their lives. In essence, the articles imply that the Bhai Mani Singh of the eighteenth-century Panth who guarded the shrine with his life, was now transformed by the present-day, faineant Panth into a child who was unable to even pronounce the shabads of the scripture correctly.[50] For this period, a harsher criticism of the Panth would be difficult to imagine.

While these letters and articles reprimanded the contemporary Panth for its listlessness and silence, and indirectly pressured Sikhs to adopt the behaviour of their ancestors to remedy the situation, they were also tacitly criticizing the British administration, which obliquely influenced the appointment of the Darbar Sahib's Head Granthi. One Sikh was far less tacit in his censure. In a letter signed only with the initials 'J.H.', the writer's utter frustration with the British authorities is dramatic:

The style in which I write is not elegant, but to me sincerity is better than grace. I write what I feel. The appointment of a minor as Head Granthi of the Golden Temple has disturbed the mind of many a devout Sikh and in penning these few lines I am not merely voicing my own individual feelings, but those of many others. We had expected something better from the powers that be. We used to hear that the Government thought twice before doing anything calculated to hurt the feelings of the Sikhs as a community; but alas! we have been painfully disillusioned. In matters mundane we shed our life-blood and others enjoyed the fruit. We attributed it to the policy of a wise Government and kept silent. But now we find that in matters religious also things are not allowed to be as they ought to... In the reform of our temples we expected help and not direct opposition; and this attitude of those in power has made the Sikhs to doubt the sincerity of the motives that have determined the present appointment and to seriously think whither they are drifting. These lines may excite derision ... but I care not for it. I am filled with a strong feeling of resentment [against the British administration in the Punjab] and cannot [help] giving vent to it.[51]

The only way to obviate such resentment, it was implied, was to entrust the management of Sikh gurdwaras to the Sikhs themselves.

These two years were not the first to see Sikhs appeal for control of the gurdwaras. In the mid-1880s, the Tat Khalsa had asked the administration on numerous occasions to allow Sikhs to manage temple affairs.[52] In the 1 January 1887 issue of the *Khālsā Akhbār*, the editorial points out elements with the contemporary management which were eliciting the concern of the Singh reformers:

We appeal before the Khalsa community and the government that the present committee for the management of the Golden Temple is neither based on the principles of the Khalsa Panth, nor on government legislation. If this committee was constituted on the basis of the Khalsa religion, then its membership would have been made up of only the Khalsa... It is rather ironic that the gurdwara belongs to the community but its management is presided over by a [Christian] deputy commissioner.[53]

For the Tat Khalsa, only Khalsa Sikhs who faithfully adhered to the Rahit had any right to be included in the management committee. To the British, this was to be avoided. Circumventing this Tat Khalsa request, however, was somewhat problematic because of Act XX of 1863 (the legislation to which the article referred). This Act enjoined the British administration to distance itself from the management of

Indian shrines and from interfering in the religious concerns of the faithful. The British repeatedly professed that they were indeed abiding by the dictates of this Act. In his address to the CKD in May 1909, for example, the Lieutenant-Governor of the Punjab, Sir Louis William Dane, in the light of the harsh criticism directed towards the government's approval of a minor's appointment as Head Granthi of the Golden Temple, expressed sympathy with the Tat Khalsa desire to correct abuses within the sacred Sikh gurdwaras. Sympathy was all he had to offer, however, for he reminded Sikhs 'that it is a most difficult thing for the Government to interfere in a matter of this sort' (i.e. a religious matter)', a direct allusion to Act XX.[54] Educated Sikhs were not so easily misled. The same article notes that despite these words, the administration did, indeed, have a hand in appointments. 'Let the interference [in Sikh religious matters] remain,' stated the article, 'but only let it be directed to the good of the [Sikh] community.'[55]

For the British administration, memories of the lost Sikh kingdom, the 1857 Mutiny and the 1872 Kuka incidents were not easily forgotten, memories which prompted them to be very suspect about allowing Sikhs complete control over a resource which they felt could strongly influence the Sikh community in any direction that the management so pleased. Within confidential reports, the Punjab government made clear that the Golden Temple should not be placed under Act XX because it was a special case, special because 'The Sikhs were a volatile people and problems at the Golden Temple could ignite them.'[56] The government, therefore, appointed the chief manager, who informed it of daily shrine proceedings, and the Deputy Commissioner of the Amritsar district was to approve of the manager and other members of the management committee.[57] This arrangement proved quite unsatisfactory, particularly due to the bitter conflicts which it engendered between the temple staff and the management over the distribution of offerings and the appointment of new personnel. These often turned into costly and lengthy court cases, the proceedings of which were regularly mentioned in various Sikh newspapers until 1925.[58] By this year, the British obviated the reasons for such trials for they agreed to transfer ownership of Sikh gurdwaras from their hereditary managers (the mahants) to a committee of Sikh representatives elected by the Panth, thus ending the Gurdwara Reform Movement.[59]

Although the actual history of gurdwara management prior to the annexation of Punjab in 1849 is an unclear one, Sikh tradition maintains that during the eighteenth century, Khalsa Sikhs were too busy upholding dharam, protecting the innocent and avoiding the authorities to effectively manage their temples. The task, therefore, fell to those Sikhs who were not as visible as those professing a Khalsa identity. These, according to tradition, were the celibate ascetics of the Udasi sect, a group established (so claimed the Udasis) by the son of the first Guru, Siri Chand.[60] Renowned for their piety and devotion, these Sikhs managed the temples according to the glorious standards of the Heroic Age.[61] During the Sikh kingdom, however, they succumbed to the temptations which land grants and other privileges gave rise to, thus evoking in later times a sharp response from the Singh Sabha reformers.[62] Casting off their ascetic's garb, they involved themselves in pursuits much more worldly. Adopting a lifestyle which may be termed anything but pious, a large number of hereditary mahants directed gurdwara income towards their own material gain.

It was mainly this misappropriation of funds which first attracted the attention of the Singh Sabhas, an abuse which was to form a regular Singh Sabha complaint. When the British annexed the Punjab, they inadvertently sowed the seeds of discord by reinforcing the mahant's position. By granting him title to the gurdwara's land, the mahant's legal claim to gurdwara property became recognized in British courts. The mahant now possessed the right to use the property in any way he saw fit and to seek protection for his doing so under the law of the land. As Sikh leaders had often told the British authorities, the mahants were the servants of the gurdwara, not the owners. Ownership of the institutions had been vested in the Panth by the Gurus themselves.[63]

To members of the Tat Khalsa, those mahants who styled themselves Udasis were not really Sikh but Hindu, since they declined initiation into the Khalsa. Rather than attempt to dissuade the reformers from this notion, the mahants themselves reinforced it by subscribing to all those characteristics of contemporary Sanatan Sikhism which the Tat Khalsa endeavoured to purge: they kept idols within the shrines, allowed Brahman priests to perform a number of rituals within the gurdwara's precincts, and went to great lengths to ensure that no outcaste Sikh would enter the gurdwara.[64] Over time, the Tat Khalsa found that it could effect some reform in the realm of ritual (the removal of idols from the Golden Temple being the prime example), but they could not oust a corrupt mahant through legal means. One should note that the law which protected the mahant was somewhat sympathetic to pious sangats and reformers since it did give them the right to contest the mahant's claim to gurdwara ownership. Unfortunately, in almost all cases, the resources required for such lengthy trials were vast and could only, in the end, be met by the mahant, who had temple coffers at his disposal. Legal cases of this sort were thus cut short in favour of the gurdwara incumbent.[65]

The implicit backing that the government bestowed on the mahants was made all the more apparent when first, the Tat Khalsa and then the CKD requested the administration to allow observant Khalsa Sikhs to themselves manage the Golden Temple in the late nineteenth and early twentieth centuries. Although this request was constantly ignored by the authorities, it was politely repeated within the newspapers for years, supported during critical events such as those of 1905 and 1907–8 by the letters of a number of angry Sikhs who demanded action be taken quickly.[66] The frequency of these letters allows one to infer that by this time, the ideology and practices of the Singh Sabha were beginning to be recognized as the sole authority in Sikh matters (to the educated urban elite anyway). In the light of this notion, the strong support the campaign to legalize Anand marriage received in 1909 should elicit no surprise.

The government's constant silence on this issue of management was broken in 1909 when the District Commissioner of Amritsar decided that members of the Tat Khalsa could be neither managers nor granthis at Harimandir Sahib.[67] Such policies were to prove disastrous for they were seen as government resistance to a popular demand. Although the idol controversy of 1905 was the first time that the idea of Sikh sacrifice for temple sanctity was vociferously proclaimed by the Tat Khalsa, we have seen that the connection between martyrs and gurdwaras goes back to the pre-Singh Sabha past. Here was an issue which could be powerfully represented in terms which stirred Sikh hearts. It was not just an issue which touched the hearts of urban, educated Sikhs who often wrote letters to the newspapers, but to an even larger extent, those of the rural community whose majority was made up of Jat Sikhs.

The Beginning: Gurdwara Rakabganj 1913–19

The causes of and the events leading up to the Gurdwara Reform

Movement have been well documented in numerous sources. These indicate that after the First World War, a number of new problems arose and that the gurdwara issue provided a focus for the distress caused by these problems. The increased pressure on Punjabi land cultivators since 1900, the ill treatment of Sikh migrants to North America, the inability of the CKD to procure adequate political representation for the Sikhs, the economic and social problems which followed the First World War, discontent over post–First World War army recruitment policy, Ghadr propaganda, the Rowlatt and Emergency Power Bills and the satyagraha these engendered, the Jallianwala Bagh massacre of 1919, and nationalist politics of the Congress variety all came together to create a highly charged atmosphere.[68] When the heroic traditions of sacrifice and martyrdom well known to all those raised in the Khalsa tradition were invoked in this environment, particularly in regard to liberating a sacred Sikh resource, large numbers of Sikhs acted without hesitation. The one group which was to supply the majority of Sikhs in the gurdwara endeavour was the Jat community, whose majority inhabited the vast rural tracts of the Punjab.

The seeds for their first action were planted in May of 1913, when the British government in India, in the attempt to lay out the initial street grid of their new capital city, bought some land belonging to Gurdwara Rakabganj in Delhi and demolished a wall attached to it so that a straight road could be laid to pass through the corner of the gurdwara to the new Viceregal palace.[69] Visiting the capital on 25–7 January 1914, Harchand Singh, the president of the Lyallpur Singh Sabha and an eminent person from that area, was incensed at the sight of the desecrated gurdwara. As soon as he returned to the Punjab, he not only helped organize protests against the British administration for defiling this most hallowed ground, but also began his Urdu weekly, the *Khālṣah Akhbār*, in order to dramatically illustrate his sense of outrage.[70] Nevertheless, these seeds so watered by Harchand Singh did not take root in the soil of 1914. The intervening World War and the issues mentioned above did, however, give them time to germinate and grow.

In his *The Akali Movement,* Mohinder Singh cites the Rakabganj episode as one which highlights the growing powerlessness of the CKD.[71] This statement deserves qualification. The Rakabganj issue, it is true, made far more apparent the CKD's unwillingness to adopt a new political strategy which could have compromised the Diwan in British eyes. Such an unwillingness was demonstrated during the canal agitations of 1907, when the CKD cautioned the Sikhs to remain loyal, branding the leading agitators Ajit Singh and Lala Lajpat Rai, as 'Arya Samajists' who were attempting to 'drive a wedge between the Sikhs and the British'.[72] In the same year, moreover, the CKD again demonstrated a reluctance to lead an agitation against the government for its comprehensive take-over of the management of Khalsa College, an act which had prompted Bhai Sundar Singh of Lyallpur to produce the widely distributed booklet, *Kī Khālsā Kālaj Sikhān ḍā hai?* (Does Khalsa College Belong to the Sikhs?), in 1909 criticizing both the CKD and the British authorities.[73]

These incidents, however, did not affect the whole Panth as the issues over Gurdwara Rakabganj appeared to. Although in regard to the Delhi gurdwara, letters from all over Punjab were received by the Chief Commissioner of Amritsar asking him to no longer view the CKD as a representative body of the Sikhs, events after 1914 would prove the CKD was still highly influential among its constituents.[74] The Gurdwara Rakabganj episode may well mark the beginning of the CKD's decline, but there was still some distance the institution had to travel before its power would be seriously depleted. The success of the CKD in recruiting Sikhs for the British war cause, their role in ensuring that the kirpan was exempted from the Arms Act in 1917, and the support they received in disowning the Ghadrites demonstrate, as N.G. Barrier has insightfully noted, that the CKD was perceived as an authority in both political and religious matters. It was only after the CKD failure to win adequate political represent-ation, as witnessed by the Government of India Act of 1919, and their support for the infamous General Reginald Dyer after the massacre at Jallianwala Bagh that its influence among Sikhs would be literally spent.[75]

It is significant, moreover, that the CKD management was mainly composed of upper-class conservatives such as Takhat Singh and Sundar Singh Majithia. Inevitably, this aristocratic class had their own social interests which did not coincide with either those of the new urban elites or the vast majority of Sikhs who were rural cultivators. As many men of this class before him, Sunder Singh Majithia, secretary of the CKD, was considered a 'natural leader' of his community by the British. From its first days as suzerain in the Punjab, the British government had ruled the province with the help of those identified as strong supporters of the colonial regime, men such as Baba Khem Singh Bedi, for whom there were reserved honours and appointments to local government positions. There were times of strain (in particular, the episode in which the former Maharaja of the Punjab, Dalip Singh, was supported by Thakur Singh Sandhanwalia of the Amritsar Singh Sabha in the former's attempt to return to the Punjab and claim his birthright in the late 1880s and early 1890s[76]), but on the whole, the arrangement worked very well for the British. These men were 'natural leaders' and the institutions which they often led or of which they were a part were perceived as pillars buttressing British power.

In the scurry to have resources allocated to both themselves and their respective communities, these 'natural leaders' began to compete for positions with other men styled as such by the government. Status was, indeed, significant and the more privileges a 'natural leader' possessed, the higher his status. To these aristocrats, the government was the source of justice and patronage. Often underscoring their own loyalty and attachment to the Crown, these men would simultaneously point out the seditious nature of their opponents.[77] This is the mantle that had been passed on to the CKD by the Singh Sabha. A prominent Sikh as conscious of high status as Majithia was well aware that his support of any form of agitation, a tactic the colonial powers were bound to find highly questionable, could seriously jeopardize his standing. It is perhaps for this reason that he chose to resign from his position in Khalsa College in November 1912 rather than contest the clearly discriminatory British policies in regard to the school.[78]

As the management of the CKD was made up of men belonging to this class, it continued the compromising and flexible political strategy which it had adopted from its very beginning, while perpetually proclaiming Sikh loyalty to the British government. When he first heard of the demolition of the wall in September 1913, therefore, Majithia wrote a letter to the Chief Commissioner of Delhi in order to find out the amount of land acquired and the mahant's arrangement for spending the money given in compensation.[79] Realizing that this issue could cause a great deal of resentment and could subsequently launch an agitation, the CKD petitioned the government to rebuild the wall and withdraw its proposal to straighten the road in March 1914.[80] By this time, however, Harchand Singh Lyallpuri had already begun to forcefully demand the wall's restoration. The government's unwillingness to entertain proposals in regard to the land and the wall prompted the CKD to utilize its resources and support the government's claim that the wall of Gurdwara Rakabganj which was demolished was not really part of the gurdwara complex.[81] In its support, Majithia published a pamphlet explaining the history of the gurdwara, the changes proposed by the government and the policy of the CKD.[82]

To contest the management's stand, Harchand Singh travelled to Jalandhar to attend the seventh annual Sikh Educational Conference in April 1914. When he asked to raise the issue of Gurdwara Rakabganj from the conference platform, he was flatly refused, an act which led to a disruption in the proceedings. According to one observer, Majithia stood up ('trembling like a man attacked unawares') and told the audience that Harchand Singh and his followers were the enemies of the Panth.[83] Unperturbed, Harchand Singh repeated his request while making his way towards the dais. CKD supporters, however, blocked his progress and forcibly expelled Lyallpuri from the conference. This act on the part of the CKD prompted the audience to cry out 'shame', 'shame'.[84]

Quickly following this unfortunate incident, the management of the CKD organized a meeting to deal with the Rakabganj issue. At the meeting held on 3 May 1914, Majithia's hand-picked supporters within the Diwan won the day, passing a series of resolutions which were to simply 'deal with the Rikabganj affair'.[85] There were many members of the new urban elite, however, who opposed the resolution, demanding that a direct agitation be launched. These members demonstrated their displeasure with it by breaking the windows in the hall at which the meeting was held. When on 30 May 1914, Harchand Singh convened a meeting in Lahore, many of these urban professionals joined in and passed a resolution demanding the restoration of the wall.[86]

All these activities motivated many Sikhs to denounce the CKD in both word and deed. One participant in the Rakabganj agitation reflected on the later Sikh perception of the CKD:

For all practical purposes, the Chief Khalsa Diwan had given a goodbye [to] the teachings of the Sikh Gurus... The Sikh Gurus had called [Sikhs together] to fight the rulers' tyranny and taught [them] to call a tyrant as such. But the leaders of the Chief Khalsa Diwan danced to the British rulers' tune instead, and did not want to come into conflict with the government.[87]

Indeed, to many eyes, the CKD constantly alluded to the heroic traditions of self-sacrifice and martyrdom, but would not sacrifice their loyalty to the British in order to have the wall rebuilt.[88] In effect, the British had proven themselves hostile to Sikh aspirations and the CKD was not willing to take the Sikhs into battle. This task would have to fall to the less conservative Sikhs of the new urban elites and their foot-soldiers as it were, the Sikhs of rural Punjab who were directly affected by harsh British policies and economic measures. Just when the movement was beginning to gain the support of the rural areas, however, the First World War broke out in August 1914, thus placing the movement on hold for the time being.

Blood and Gurdwaras

In 1919, the Rakabganj issue was revitalized and came to provide a channel for the expression of the discontent engendered by the various problems mentioned above. We must recall that by this time, the Tat Khalsa had made the gurdwaras 'Sikh corporate symbols par excellence'.[89] An attack on these was, therefore, not only perceived as an attack on the Sikh Panth, but also as an insult to the eternal Guru housed within each of these structures. According to Teja Singh, a staunch 'neo-Sikh' (the British label for Tat Khalsa Sikhs), who was writing at the height of the movement in 1922: 'To tell the truth, the freedom of their [Sikh] temples has always been the measure of the Sikh's freedom of prosperity.'[90] At a large meeting in Lahore's Bradlaugh Hall in October 1919, the newly formed Central Sikh League decided to put together a jatha or band of Sikhs to march to Delhi and reconstruct the wall. A prominent figure of the CSL, Sardul Singh Caveeshar, adopted a strategy here which was to prove enormously successful. In the columns of an up and coming Punjabi newspaper, the *Akālī*, a passionate appeal from Caveeshar was printed in early September 1920:

Sikh gurdvāriān nūn bachāvan vāste sau śahīdān dī loṛ[91]
Wanted: 100 martyrs to defend Sikh gurdwaras.[92]

The article continued:

If any irreligious officer stops you from serving your religious place, you should not turn from the service of the Guru even though your body is cut to pieces. You should not strike anyone who displays improper behaviour. But if someone violently stops you from serving at the temple of our beloved one, then you should not show your back. If someone shoots at us we will place our hands upon him and say, 'For the sake of God do not stop us, we are the protectors of the honour of our religion; we are called the *chādar* of India;[93] we are the guardians of the temple. Do not stop us from protecting our temple!' If some foolish black or white brother strikes his bayonet on our chests, we shall bare our chests before him and say, 'Baba ji, strike us, certainly strike us. But, for the sake of God, before dying, allow us to place one brick towards the rebuilding of the demolished temple of our beloved Guru.'

Khalsa ji! Today there remains to us only one way to set our misled officers [and] brothers onto the proper path [of understanding]. It is this: that we should suffer like Guru Arjan Sahib and convince these blunderers of their wrong-doing through our very own sacrifice.[94]

The response was overwhelming. Within a fortnight, seven hundred people, the vast majority Sikhs, replied to the request and offered themselves for the task. Some even sent their letters written in blood.[95] It was believed that this was the way that Sikhs of the Golden Age had protected the Panth from its Mughal and Afghan oppressors, and this would be the way that contemporary Sikhs would engage the now-inimical British government. Although the action would eventually become a professedly non-violent one (primarily due to Gandhi and the Congress[96]), the traditions of heroic selfless sacrifice were still very much apparent. The government eventually found a solution in early 1920 which obviated the need for the band of martyrs. It had the wall rebuilt, ignoring the new leaders of the Central Sikh League who demanded quick action, and upheld the CKD as the representative body of the Sikhs, thereby saving face. By that time, however, the die was cast. A note from Sohan Singh Josh, a Sikh who volunteered to join the *śahīdī jathā,* is highly revealing:

An issue which the resolutions, deputations and memorandums of the last seven to eight years could not solve was now settled within days when it was decided to make sacrifices... This was a great victory.[97]

In seeking to face the government, the new leaders utilized the rhetoric of martyrdom which the Singh Sabha had used for the last forty years, shifting it from an idiom of conservative reform to one of conservative militancy. In other words, while the reformers of the late nineteenth and early twentieth centuries appealed to Sikhs by alluding to the stories of their martyrs in order to inspire Sikhs to reform themselves and the Panth, they had never utilized the rhetoric to encourage Sikhs to forcefully confront a hostile political authority head on.[98] It was for this latter, militant reason that leaders of the

CSL and SGPC appropriated the idiom. Underlying the *Akālī* appeal in the epigraph which appears at the beginning of this chapter, for example, is the fact that Sikhs who choose to emulate the behaviour of these past martyrs will indeed confront an adversary as terrifying as those confronted in the seventeenth and eighteenth centuries, one who will subject their bodies to physical punishment, be it the blow of a lathi or confinement within a prison. It is this understanding which permeates Caveeshar's article in the *Akālī* of 2 September 1920. The article continues:

Rise up Khalsa and be vigilant in the protection of your religion. Now, the need is [to cultivate] within us the steadfastness of [both] Bhai Mani Singh and Bhai Taru Singh... Even if we are hacked limb from limb we shall not turn away from the service of our Guru.[99]

As the Sikhs to whom this appeal was directed were no doubt aware, these two martyrs kept their attention on the Eternal Guru and remained resolute as they were slowly dismembered.

The reasons for this shift from reform to militancy lie primarily in the prevailing circumstances of 1920 mentioned above, and also in the background of those Sikhs who led the Rakabganj agitation: landlords affected by British policies, like Harchand Singh and Teja Singh Samundari, and the new elites mentioned earlier, such as Sardul Singh Caveeshar and Tara Singh.[100] Many of these men broke away from the CKD in 1919 to form the Central Sikh League.

The failure of the Indian National Congress to grant Sikhs representation in the famous Lucknow Pact of December 1916 had worried many Sikh leaders about future Sikh participation in Punjab politics. The Pact between the Congress and the All-India Muslim League had drawn up a formula for future Muslim representation in provincial legislative councils, granted Muslims separate electorates, and given them a weightage of seats in all provincial councils which far exceeded their proportion of the population in Muslim minority provinces.[101] In the absence of a political body, the Sikhs had to express their concerns over the Pact through the loyal CKD. Over the next two years, memorandums were sent to the government, petitioning that Sikhs also be ensured their share of power in the provincial councils as well as in the civil administration of the country. In November 1917, the CKD met with and requested the Governor-General, Lord Chelmsford, to grant it the 'Lion's Share' or 30 per cent of the representation in the Punjab Council (a weightage clearly exceeding Sikh numbers in the province) in the light of both the incredible Sikh contribution to the British war effort and the Panth's 'unique' position as the previous ruler of the province. In the Montford Report, the claims of the Sikhs were conceded in theory: 'To the Sikhs ... and to them alone, we propose to extend the system already adopted in the case of the Muhammadans.'[102] When the Montagu-Chelmsford Report was published in 1919, however, Sikhs were to receive only 15 of the 93 seats in the Punjab Council, or 18 per cent, a little over half of their proposed representation. Although even this reduced figure was still proportionately higher than the Sikh population of Punjab, the concession was disappointing nevertheless and heightened Sikh anxiety at what was seen as the inevitable dissolution of the Sikh community and the Sikh faith. For many Sikh leaders, the motto which was often bandied about in this period was *sikh dharam khatre vich hai*, 'the Sikh religion is in danger'.[103]

To protect Sikh rights in future political councils, therefore, many members of the CKD gathered at Lahore on 30 March 1919 and announced the creation of a new political party, the Central Sikh League. Formally inaugurated during its first annual session at Amritsar, held from 27–30 December 1919, the CSL was patterned along the same lines as the Muslim League and opened branches throughout the towns and cities of the Punjab.[104] As the CSL was initially dominated by former members of the CKD, such as Jodh Singh, Gajjan Singh and Teja Singh (the Teja Singh who had spent much time in Britain and Canada), the first year of its operation saw the League adopt an approach along CKD lines: that is, the submission of cautiously worded resolutions and petitions to the British administration to take Sikh rights into consideration. This would soon end, however. In the light of the massacres at Budge Budge and Jallianwala Bagh, the declaration of martial law in the Punjab and the harsh treatment meted out to Punjabis (particularly the tainted findings of the Hunter Committee), the rising, less conservative members of the League gained strength and were able to displace the CKD-aligned leaders.[105] When the CSL then overwhelmingly resolved to throw its weight behind M.K. Gandhi and the Indian National Congress and espouse the policies of *swarāj*, 'self-rule' and *nāmilvartan* or non-cooperation at its second annual session in October 1920, many of the leaders elected in 1919 resigned.[106]

While the new leaders of the CSL did abandon the political programme of the CKD, they certainly did not forsake the religious dimension of the organization. In fact, they felt that it was because of this that they had to act, and displace the CKD, which itself had abandoned the very tenets of Sikhism. The Tat Khalsa interpretation of the Sikh tradition that the CKD had continued to articulate and had eventually institutionalized was something that the leaders of the CSL would not rebuke, for these new leaders had been raised and nurtured in the environment that Oberoi's statement at the beginning of this chapter underscores, an atmosphere in which the message of the Tat Khalsa was virtually everywhere, permeating all facets of 'everyday life'. Leaders of the CSL included Sikhs such as Kharak Singh (b. 1868), who had participated in the annual Sikh Educational Conference every year since 1912; Sardul Singh Caveeshar (b. 1886), who began the radical Sikh newspaper, the *Sikh Review,* in 1913; Harchand Singh of Lyallpur (b. 1887); and the three Jhabbal brothers, Amar Singh (b. 1892), Sarmukh Singh (b. 1895) and Jaswant Singh (b. 1898), all of whom studied at schools affiliated with the Tat Khalsa and all of whom would play a central role in organizing the Shiromani Akali Dal.[107] There were many others like them.

Tara Singh, for example, was born in 1885, just as the Singh Sabha began to spread its message. Unlike the other leaders, however, Tara Singh was born into a family of Hindu Khatris who revered the Sikh Gurus and the Guru Granth Sahib. After an early education in a village gurdwara school and then at the American Mission school in Rawalpindi, Tara Singh took amrit in 1902 and was persuaded to join Khalsa College, where he studied under the Panth's foremost theologian, Jodh Singh.[108] We noted in our last chapter Tara Singh's fascination with Sikh martyrs. In what may have well been an attempt to emulate these heroic Sikhs, the future Masterji had become involved in various agitations while at Khalsa College. In particular, in 1907, he led the student protest against the appointment of the paid British engineer who was to replace the Sikh engineer, Sardar Dharam Singh, who had donated his services without pay.

Another member who deserves separate notice is Kartar Singh Jhabbar. A Virk Jat, Kartar Singh was a student of the Gurmat Vidyala school in Gujranwala and, prior to his involvement in agitational politics, was employed as a CKD updeshak for the villages surrounding Lahore. His biographers state incidentally that it was due to Kartar Singh's forceful preaching that the membership of the Lahore Singh Sabha rose from 19 to 500 in just a few months.[109] It seems only logical, therefore, that the strategies and tactics to which these men and other leaders resorted would have been, in large part, informed by the message of the Singh Sabhas. Since men like Tara Singh, who actively participated in the Rakabganj movement, would become prominent Akali leaders,[110] it was inevitable that the Akali movement and the Singh Sabha ideology would become intimately connected, a fact which comes out in the wording of the 1925 Sikh Gurdwaras Act.[111]

The CSL was the first Sikh political body to call for an organized and sustained agitation to liberate all gurdwaras from the hands of their corrupt, British-backed custodians.[112] During a CSL diwan held at Tarn Taran in July 1920, Amar Singh Jhabbal asked Sikhs to come together to sacrifice themselves to liberate gurdwaras from their allegedly debased managers.[113] Although by this time, no formal title had been adopted to describe the voluntary Sikh bands which had vowed to take possession of the temples, these groups were informally referred to as Akali jathas, a term we shall examine later on. In many cases, those Sikhs who were enthused by the call of the CSL formed their own Akali jathas and began to oust gurdwara mahants from the shrines in their possession. The initial successes prompted more Sikhs to form or join Akali jathas and do the same. There were some problems with the procedures they had adopted, however. Initially, these disparate bands failed to coordinate their efforts. Moreover, once they had taken over a disputed gurdwara, they were unable to form appropriate management committees to deal with the meticulous, day-to-day running of the sacred institution.

In order to manage these shrines once they had come into the possession of the various Akali jathas, therefore, the CSL summoned a Sarbat Khalsa or a general assembly of Sikhs before the Akal Takht for the purpose of electing a representative body that would do just this, ensuring through its acceptance by the whole Panth that the new group would have the blessing of the eternal Guru. And thus, on 15 November 1920, the Shiromani Gurdwara Prabandhak Committee (SGPC) was formed. This committee was made up of 175 Sikhs. Although the majority were clearly 'radical', the leaders of the CSL chose to incorporate into the new SGPC the conservative 36-member Advisory Committee previously appointed by the government.[114] In appointing this committee, the government had not taken into consideration the views of the Sarbat Khalsa. Radical leaders of the CSL nevertheless incorporated the group in order to give the SGPC at least a limited legitimacy in the eyes of the authorities.

A few days after the formation of the SGPC, Master Mota Singh suggested the creation of a Gurdwara Sevak Dal (i.e., an army of those who would serve the gurdwaras), of 500 Sikh volunteers among whom would be included 100 paid workers. This group was to be always prepared to act against targeted gurdwara mahants at the call of the SGPC. This proposal was discussed by the leaders of the CSL and SGPC in front of the Akal Takht on 14 December 1920. At this time, it was declared that a central Dal or army would be formed, with Sarmukh Singh Jhabbal as Jathedar, to coordinate the activities and efforts of the scattered Akali jathas. This new body was termed the Akali Dal or the 'Army of the Immortal [One]' and would receive the prefix 'Shiromani' or 'exalted' in March 1922.[115] The relationship between this group and the SGPC, under whose control the latter was meant to function, was very close indeed. Hearing of a disputed gurdwara, the SGPC would summon Akali volunteers, who would then make their way to the particular shrine and attempt to liberate it from its present custodian. For some authors, the SGPC represented the brains behind the movement while the Akali Dal supplied the brawn.[116]

One essential point must be noted. Men such as Sarmukh Singh Jhabbal, Sardul Singh Caveeshar, Teja Singh Samundari and Kartar Singh Jhabbar, to name a few, were often affiliated to the CSL, the SGPC and the Akali Dal at one and the same time. As all three groups worked together for virtually the same aim, many of their key members had overlapping affiliations.[117] Therefore, when a reference is made to the leaders of the Gurdwara Reform Movement throughout this chapter, it is made bearing this in mind. In short, the leaders of the movement were men who could operate in their capacity as CSL, SGPC and Akali leaders simultaneously. This brings up another point. When the SGPC and Akali Dal came to dominate the Gurdwara Reform Movement, it seemed that the CSL was eclipsed. When we note that the members of the latter organization were, in fact, the leaders of the Akali Dal, however, we realize that such a conclusion is not particularly valid. As Sukhmani Bal implies, a victory of the Akali Dal was, in effect, a victory of the CSL.[118]

It is crucial to an understanding of the Gurdwara Reform Movement that scholars do not drain the activities of Akali leaders of all their symbolic content and interpret them simply as a means to achieve what appeared as a particularly political goal. This is an important point in the light of recent books and articles interpreting the Gurdwara Reform Movement. Many of these, relying principally upon English-language reports and the memorandums and proceedings of British officers engaged in fighting the so-called Third Sikh War, adopt (perhaps unknowingly) the bias of their sources.[119] While the rhetoric of martyrdom that leaders of the Gurdwara Reform Movement appropriated did serve a political and material aim, the references to Sikh martyrs were not simply 'rhetorical', that is, empty words without substance.[120] In most cases, people do not live their lives according to self-interest alone and individuals do seek purpose and meanings in their existence. Of course, political, economic and social concerns were very much evident. The up and coming leaders of the reform movement, however, were Sikhs (Tat Khalsa-influenced Sikhs at that) and carried with them all the meanings that such an identity embraced. The fact that there was no formal/legal definition of the 'Sikh' identity at this time was not a major concern of the Akali leaders since the issue of definition had been settled by the time the campaign began. When the initial call to form the SGPC was made in early November 1920, only Sikhs initiated into the Khalsa or amrit-dhari Sikhs who wore the Five Ks could be considered for membership. The following hukam-nama submitted to the *Akāli* by Dr Gurbakhsh Singh, *sevak* of the Akal Takht, and printed on 4 November 1920 makes this point lucidly:

HUKAM NAMA ISSUED BY SRI AKAL
TAKHT SAHIB, AMRITSAR JI

The assembled Khalsa ji has submitted [an order] that at nine o'clock in the morning on the first day of Magghar S. 1977, Nanak Shahi 451, both dates of which correspond to 15 November 1920, the entire Panth will gather before Sri Akal Takhat in assembly. At this time, the Panth will seriously engage in discussions to choose a representative Panthic Committee to manage the Darbar Sahib at Sri Amritsar and groups of other gurdwaras. For this reason, all [representatives of the] Gur-takhats, Gurdwara Khalsa jathas, Sikh Platoons, and the Princely Sikh armies should choose [representatives] from amongst themselves according to the criteria written below and send those Singhs who adopt these below-noted characteristics [to the Akal Takht on the appointed day]:

THE CRITERIA FOR A REPRESENTATIVE

(1) Should be an amrit-dhari Sikh; (2) should routinely recite the five *bāṇis*; (3) should sport the Five Ks according to [Sikh] rahit; (4) should rise during amrit-vela (the [second] quarter of the night, between 3 AM and 6 AM); (5) should contribute ten per cent of his total income to the welfare of the Sikh Panth.[121]

The hukam-nama continues by noting how many representatives each group may send. The various takhats are to send five each; every gurdwara (in the Punjab?) should send one; Khalsa jathas are enjoined to send five representatives per one hundred members; princely states are also asked to submit five; 'mixed' (*misī*) Sikh platoons and cavalry contingents to send two each, while 'complete' (*pūrā*) platoons and contingents are asked for five. Finally, Nihang jathas are requested to submit five representatives per hundred. Clearly, this would be a committee formed along Tat Khalsa lines as the majority of the prospective representatives would come from bodies that had been subjected to Singh Sabha interpretations for the last four decades, Khalsa jathas and the military in particular. Indeed, that this managing board would be made up of men, young and old, who had been thoroughly immersed in a Singh Sabha *weltanschauung* is further evinced by the fact that teachers and students were also encouraged to volunteer themselves from not only the Sikh university, Khalsa College (five members: one from the governing committee, two teachers, and two students), but from every major school and college whose curricukim was permeated by the Tat Khalsa interpretation of Sikh tradition: Guru Nanak College in Gujranwala, Akal College of Mastuana, as well as various high, middle and primary schools.[122] A note appended to the hukam-nama adds that all representatives should arrive at the meeting carrying their respective credentials.[123] In other words, what was required was proof that each member adhered to the five criteria noted above.

This type of scrutiny was, initially, quite common. At the inaugural meeting held a few weeks later, five Sikhs were appointed as *pañj piāre*, or Five Cherished Ones, and would ask those newly elected members how strictly they adhered to Sikh (i.e., Tat Khalsa) standards. If the five selected Sikhs felt that there was a shortcoming, the member was enjoined to overcome it and then given a penance in the form of some service to the gurdwara.[124] Moreover, when the first elections for the newly-formed SGPC were held in 1921, only Khalsa Sikhs over the age of 21 could vote.[125]

These leaders sincerely believed that Sikhs of old had heroically laid down their lives in defence of their sacred temples, and it was upon this conviction that they acted.[126] An eyewitness to many Akali morchas, who had spent some time with the leaders of the movement themselves, had this to say in regard to Teja Singh Samundari:

He struck me very frequently as I listened to the discussions [in the SGPC

Council of Action room] as possessing a critical knowledge of Sikh history and specially of the hard times in which the Khalsa had been hammered into beliefs and practices that had made the community what it is, and it was Samundri's greatest ambition to live up to the highest ideals and traditions which had come down to them [the Sikhs] from these hard times.[127]

Of course, Ruchi Ram Sahni is here implying that 1920–5 was also a 'hard time', in which the characteristics of eighteenth-century Sikhs which Teja Singh Samundri attempted to embody were essential for anyone who wished to free the gurdwaras from the allegedly notorious mahants and their all-powerful British backers.

Like Sahni, other leaders of the Gurdwara Reform Movement also understood their contemporary situation as one entailing a great deal of difficulty and which could only be obviated if Sikhs would emulate the martyrs of the seventeenth and eighteenth centuries by sacrificing all they could.[128] Often, they would characterize the movement in very familiar terms: a path 'sharper than a sword and straighter than a hair' or an alley on which one had to give one's head in order to travel. These were clear allusions to Guru Amar Das' *Anand* 14 and Guru Nanak's *Slok vārān te vadhīk* 20.[129] To procure support for travelling along this treacherous path and to inspire Sikhs to participate in the agitations, leaders of the reform movement referred virtually all contemporary incidents to the heroic past, underscoring, in particular, the sacrifice of eighteenth-century Sikhs for their temples. The tone of these articles was always optimistic. The *Akālī* of 19 August 1920, for example, reminded readers and listeners that

[It took only] one of the heroes of the tenth Lord to retrieve the Darbar Sahib from [the fiendish] Massa Ranghar.[130]

Here, we observe Akalis invoking old ideals in an idiom familiar to all those Sikhs raised in the Khalsa tradition put forth by the Tat Khalsa.

Martyrdom and the Nationalist Campaign

By the start of the Gurdwara Reform Movement, prospective Sikh shahids had been provided accounts outlining the proper actions and behaviour of past Sikh martyrs since the time they were children. These would become, as it were, models for their own sacrifices. As the SGPC had adopted the nationalist platform, they began to reinterpret the history of the Panth and the martyrdoms of past Sikhs in the light of the new ideas broadcast by the Indian National Congress and M.K. Gandhi. The eighteenth-century Khalsa became, for example, the first group to utilize non-cooperation in India, non-cooperating with all those who did not have the best intentions of the Khalsa at heart, be they Mughals, Afghans, Hindus, or other Sikhs. The martyrdoms of Guru Arjan and Guru Tegh Bahadur, moreover, became the first sustained examples of passive resistance in the subcontinent. This much is noted in the following article:

Peaceful non-cooperation is absolutely essential. Silently and peacefully offer [yourself as] a sacrifice for your religion according to the dictum 'Your Will, [o Lord,] is sweet to me'.[131] Do so with the fortitude and truthfullness [that] both Guru Arjan Dev ji Maharaj and Guru Tegh Bahadur ji [exhibited as they were martyred]. We are the progeny of great men and of a peaceful civilisation. Our dharma is noble indeed.[132]

Such examples helped to explain ideas such as *swarāj* (self-rule), *satyāgraha* (passive resistance), and *nāmilvartaṇ* (non-cooperation) to all Sikh participants in a language they could clearly understand. The 27 October 1920 issue of the *Akālī* contained a supplement (*zāmimā*) with the following explanation of some of these key Gandhian terms:

The first four True Kings, [that is] Sri Guru Nanak Dev ji to Satiguru Ram Das, preached unity amongst Hindus and Muslims which is the first step towards self-rule. Without taking such a step it is impossible to enjoy *swarāj*. Those who preach [such] unity in India engender a wave of love within the [country's] inhabitants and [in the process] teach the true lesson of beneficence and selfless service. This is the second step towards obtaining self-rule. Taking this [second step] to heart, the fifth and ninth Gurus taught the unadulterated lesson of genuine passive resistance after they had become distressed by the law of terror [unleashed throughout the land by the Mughals and their minions] and had seen the whole of India held tightly within the grip of torment. For dispelling terror and injustice from within the country, they sacrificed their lives while remaining thankful to the Creator's Will for nourishing true passive resistance [within them]. Hot sand was poured over [Guru Arjan] and he sat in boiling water, but he did not utter a sigh while fulfilling his mission. After [the martyrdom of Guru Arjan], the ninth True King, Sri Tegh Bahadur ji, also fulfilled [his mission according to] the precept, 'Having grasped one's hand (i.e., having given a pledge of aid), offer your head before letting go of that hand.'[133] In order to soothe the pain of India he offered passive resistance, which ought to be called the third step in obtaining self-rule. To this end, and to act upon this third step completely, he offered himself as a sacrifice in the town of Delhi.[134]

An article which appeared a week after the CSL had declared its intention of joining the Indian National Congress, moreover, highlights the Sikh interpretation of Congress tenets:

'Non-cooperation' is the special invention of the Khalsa. Satguru Arjan Dev ji was the first to offer passive resistance and [the first] to demonstrate the use of the principle of non-cooperation. Afterwards, this very tenet was put into practice by the wielder of the sword, Satguru Hargobind ji, [and then] by Sri Harikrishan ji, Sri Guru Tegh Bahadur ji and by the aigrette-donning father of all Sikhs [Guru Gobind Singh]. The martyred sons of [the tenth] Guru were the most conspicuous example of non-cooperation. Subsequently, the Khalsa [of the eighteenth century] would not co-operate with anyone [connected with] the Mughal emperor. During the reign of Farrukh Siyar [1713–19], the Khalsa accepted living in jungles and mountains, but they did not think to even dream of co-operating [with the government of the day]! Never was any Sikh in the employ of the Mughal emperor, nor did a single Sikh study in [Mughal-run] schools![135]

The last statement is probably an allusion to the fact that Khalsa College was run by a British management committee in 1920, a fact that was causing a great deal of unrest for both the faculty and students of the college. That such tactics and such sacrifices led to the eventual triumph of the eighteenth-century Khalsa was emphasized. That adopting such standards could once again lead to ultimate victory was often made explicit. As S.S. Caveeshar would write in December 1920 in regard to the 'victory' at Gurdwara Rakabganj:

The greatest of all things which the [Rakabganj] affair has proven is this: if you are true you stand on truth. And despite the enemy's sheer power, you will certainly be successful. The first door [one must open for] success, however, is sacrifice. The second, as well, is sacrifice and the third, too, is sacrifice. If you are prepared to sacrifice for the sake of truth, then in all matters you will be able to obtain victory.

Thus, Khalsa ji, if you want to tackle your remaining matters using the same technique appropriated in the Gurdwara Rakabganj affair, be prepared for all manners of sacrifice. See how the glory of the Khalsa increases [through sacrifice] and how the world is blessed (*bhalā*).[136]

In essence, these leaders wanted Sikhs of the twentieth century to participate in another heroic period of Sikh history as they, the leaders themselves, were participating. As the members of the Tat Khalsa and the CKD had done before them, leaders of the Akali movement would travel throughout the Punjab, holding diwans singing hymns, and speaking on the current problems in regard to the gurdwaras to procure support. Even when there were warrants out for their arrest,

speakers would continue to lecture in the villages, lecturing in one
while sleeping in another to avoid the authorities.[137] In their speeches
and appeals, these men were not the only ones alluding to past Sikh
martyrs. To add a dramatic element to the spectacle of the diwan,
dhadhis often accompanied the speakers and would sing of past
Sikh sacrifices and the legendary martial glory of the Sikhs. According to Ruchi Ram Sahni, 'The itinerant singing parties had now
become more active because they discovered that they met with
greater appreciation for their performance.'[138] Such displays certainly
made their mark. All accounts note that these diwans ('held in the
remotest parts of the province') were significant centres of recruitment as large numbers of Sikhs volunteered to undergo initiation
into the Khalsa and join the jathas. As one ardent Akali recruiter
and jatha participant had stated:

There were no dearth of people who came forward to get themselves
enlisted [that is initiated into the Khalsa, the prerequisite to morcha parti-
cipation]. The sacrifices of the Sikh Gurus inspired the Sikhs, and they
were once again ready to lay down their lives in the manner of the Sikhs
of the past who had made sacrifices to get the gurdwaras back from the
hands of the Moghuls.[139]

Purātan Jhākiān, Scenes from the Khalsa's Past

Leaders of the reform movement attempted to invest such spectacles
as the gurdwara morchas with the meaning that Josh notes above, that
is, to make the participants act 'in the manner of Sikhs of the past',
despite the fact that it was impossible for these leaders to truly know
how Sikhs of the sixteenth, seventeenth and eighteenth centuries
had acted. The only sources upon which they could base their conclusions were the histories and martyrologies produced by the Singh
Sabha, and this group's understanding of past Sikh literature, such
as the Dasam Granth and gur-bilas texts. Nevertheless, the way that
the second annual session of the CSL was described demonstrates a
conscious attempt to create an atmosphere believed to be reminiscent
of the diwans of the eighteenth-century Khalsa. Writing three weeks
before the session, the *Akāli* requests that the event should be a
purātan jhāki or a scene from the past, in other words, a meeting
structured along the same lines as meetings held in the eighteenth
century were believed to have been. It continues:

The Panth has joyfully heard the news that during the festival of Dusahira

on October 19, 20, 21, the Sikh League will hold its second annual meeting
in Lahore. At this time shall appear a scene from the Khalsa's [glorious]
past. In the past, when a Khalsa misl or dal sent a message [to another
misl or dal to gather] for the purpose of passing an essential gurmatta, a
vast number of Khalsa Sikhs endured marching a distance of hundreds of
kohs [1 koh=1.5 miles] through jungles and wild terrain to gather together
and pass gurmattas to benefit the welfare of the entire Panth. On some occasions, [diwans to pass gurmattas] were held at the Takht in Akal Bunga at
Darbar [Sahib]. On others, gurmattas were even passed in the marshes of
Kahnunvan.[140]

Indeed, it appears that such guidelines were carefully followed.
Rising during the 'ambrosial hour' on 20 October 1920, participants
and spectators began to sing shabads from the scripture, followed
by a religious diwan. This is, of course, a common feature of Sikh
religious meetings today. According to the *Akālī* reporter present, the
association between this meeting and meetings held in the heroic past
was clear:

On one side [of the hall], the daughters of Mata Sahib Kaur [the wife of
Guru Gobind Singh] were appearing. At this, our royal meeting, the
Singhnis present appeared to the Panth in the image of Mai Bhago. From
amongst them, Bibi Kartar Kaur ji (the wife of Bhai Randhir Singh ji[141])
was in the uniform of an Akali [of old]. It was said that she was in truth
the picture of a female Singh of ancient times.[142]

Similarly, on the first day of the November 1920 meeting organized
to form the SGPC the *Akālī* notes that the sight of the assembled
Sikhs appeared like a *purātan khālse dī jhākī*, 'a scene from [the
history of] the traditional [eighteenth-century] Khalsa'.[143]

As the Sikhs who participated in the movement were symbolically
identified with their heroic eighteenth-century brothers and sisters,
so, too, were the activities and personalities of the gurdwara mahants
compared to the previous, legendary enemies of the Panth. Reform
leaders enjoined Sikhs to see these men as evil and debased, thus
giving the Gurdwara Reform Movement the complexion of a battle
between the forces of all that was just and all that was corrupt,
battles which were found in virtually all Singh Sabha martyrologies,
Sikh histories and in the famous novels of Vir Singh.[144] A report in
the 23 February 1921 issue of the *Panch,* for example, two days
after the massacre at Nankana Sahib, refers to Mahant Narain Das
as the new Chandu Shah, the figure who, according to tradition, was
largely responsible for the arrest and execution of Guru Arjan:

In Sikh history, where in the past the name of the enemy Chandu [Shah] was written, in that very same place will now be written the name of the enemy and sinner Narain [Das].[145]

As the movement began, leaders broadcast that the mahants of Gurdwara Babe de Ber in Sialkot wasted temple funds in luxury, failed to take responsibility for gurdwara upkeep, were apostates who cut their hair and openly flouted Sikhism, as well as smoked and drank liquor within the confines of the sacred shrine. In popular martyr accounts, these were practices in which the Pathans and Afghans who had overrun the gurdwaras in the eighteenth century had often engaged—men such as, for example, the infamous Massa Ranghar.[146] The strategy which the reformers undertook to oust the custodians of Babe de Ber are in line with those adopted in the case of Gurdwara Rakabganj. When the government upheld the appointment of the grandson of the recently deceased mahant, the reformers contested the claim in court. High court fees saw the reformers' defeat which, in turn, evoked a strong response from the new leaders.

The reformers called for and assembled a Khalsa *sevak jathā*, a group of baptized Sikhs willing to sacrifice their lives in the service of the Panth. In October 1920, the sevak jatha led by Kharak Singh reached the shrine and removed the mahant. This was to characterize the strategy adopted in the majority of campaigns to seize gurdwaras throughout Punjab.

The Term *Akalī*

This strategy, however, was not yet complete. By setting the movement to reform the gurdwaras in the Akali paradigm, the reformers opened up a whole range of meanings. Fundamentally, the term 'Akali' refers to 'a follower of Akal [Purakh]'. Theologically, it characterizes the liberated person or the one who is beyond death. The term, according to tradition, first came into vogue during the period of Guru Gobind Singh to designate a militant order of Sikhs who showed no concern for death. These Sikhs are believed to have rigidly adhered to Khalsa precepts and forms, donning dark blue clothes, conical turbans and a variety of weapons. During the eighteenth century, these zealous devotees of the tenth Guru were the self-appointed guardians of the Sikh faith, reaching a position so prominent that Ranjit Singh himself considered them a threat in the early nineteenth century.[147]

In addition, as we now know, the major organ of the Gurdwara Reform Movement was also titled the *Akālī* (at least until October 1922[148]). The *Akālī's* deep bond with martyrdom in Sikhism began on the day of its very foundation, the shahidi gurpurab of Guru Arjan in May of 1920, a fact that was often noted in issues of the paper. In virtually every issue, the *Akālī's* advocacy of sacrifice for the sake of the gurdwaras and for the nationalist cause was made absolutely clear. The majority of articles, and particularly the poems which graced the first page, dealt with perceived British tyranny and the Singh Sabha-inspired Sikh history of sacrifice and martyrdom. A poem written by the editor of the *Akālī*, Sundar Singh, under his pen-name, *Mast Bhaurā* (the intoxicated black bee), was titled *Sikh dā faraz* (A Sikh's Duty) and was printed on page 1 of the 26 April 1922 issue, for example.[149] The third quatrain includes in its list of traditional Sikh martyrs Lacchman Singh, one of the earliest martyrs for the cause of gurdwara reform, killed at Nankana Sahib in February 1921.[150] The comparison would not have been lost on Sikh readers:

[A Sikh should] give his head for his religion, like Mati Das who was sacrificed on the wheel. [A Sikh should] cultivate the understanding of the heart of Mani Singh, who had his body cut up joint by joint like a bamboo. [A Sikh] should perform selfless service like Taru Singh, who was scalped with a cobbler's adze. [A Sikh] should become a martyr like Lacchman Singh and obtain freedom for truth and religion.[151]

Another feature of the paper emphasizing martyrdom was a phrase attributed to Guru Gobind Singh and found in *Khālsā Mahimā* of the Dasam Granth. This statement was superimposed above the title banner of every issue:

In my house (i.e., the Sikh Panth), I enthusiastically give my head [as a sacrifice]. This is the greatest of blessings.[152]

These allusions clearly indicate that the newspaper was attempting to establish an intimate identification between the Khalsa Sikhs participating in the Gurdwara Reform Movement and the heroic, altruistic Sikhs of the seventeenth and eighteenth centuries, Sikhs whose stories graced every page of the histories and martyrologies produced by the Singh Sabha.

This endeavour was also carried out by the leaders of the reform movement. By formally appropriating the name Akali Dal on 14 December 1920, for the organization to coordinate and control the various scattered Akali jathas, leaders attempted to form a direct link between contemporary Sikhs and the heroic selfless Sikhs of the past, thus, in a sense, fulfilling the forty-year desire of the Tat Khalsa.[153] Sikhs were now formally prepared to sacrifice like the 'Sikhs of yore'. Along with the name, present-day Akalis were made to undergo *khaṇḍe ki pāhul* and to adopt what were believed to be the external forms of their ancestors. Sword-length kirpans which eighteenth-century Akalis wore, for example, became hotly contested issues in the second decade of the twentieth century.[154] The turban also was initially dark blue, a colour which reform leaders felt symbolized militancy since it was believed to be the colour chosen by the Akalis of the seventeenth and eighteenth centuries. After the Nankana Sahib massacre in February 1921, however, leaders enjoined Sikhs to wear a black *pagaṛi* (turban), for black was, according to one contemporary Sikh, 'a grim sign of resolution to suffer all difficulties and sacrifices in the way of religion'.[155]

As one can infer from the fact that all prospective Akalis had to undergo the initiation of the double-edged sword, leaders of the Akali movement wished to control the behaviour of these participants as well as their external dress. We had noted in the previous chapter the supernatural abilities that the Tat Khalsa began to associate with the initiatory amrit, an ability particularly underscored in the widely read novels of Vir Singh.[156] Playing on these well-known beliefs, the leaders of the Gurdwara Reform Movement as well as other popular leaders of the nationalist movement would remind Sikhs of the legacy they must uphold after having received the nectar of the sword. In one lecture, Pandit Madan Mohan Malaviya, for example, had this to say:

In relation to the Sikh Gurus, it is said that they were brightly shining torches of patriotism. They risked their lives to abolish tyranny and injustice. O those of you who have tasted the amrit of Guru Gobind Singh! O sons of Mata Sahib Kaur! You must be prepared to abolish tyranny and protect dharma. Follow in the footsteps of your great men![157]

Indeed, leaders of the movement were sure that

The power of Guru Gobind Singh ji's amrit will certainly become manifest.[158]

The magical quality of amrit and the standard of behaviour the elixir was believed to engender were, as noted above, outlined in the novels of Vir Singh as well as the numerous martyrologies produced by the Singh Sabha. Every participant would have been familiar with these. In such popular accounts, it was deemed inevitable that all Sikhs initiated into the elite order through the amrit ceremony would be willing to sacrifice their lives to uphold dharam and the sanctity of their gurdwaras. In the attempt to ensure that individual Akalis would indeed live up to this standard, leaders requested that a group of five cherished ones be selected in each town to verify the character of those Sikhs wishing to join the jathas, in particular, their willingness to obey the rules of the SGPC and Akali Dal and make sacrifices.[159] For Sohan Singh Josh, an Akali came into the world 'to wage an unceasing war against slavery, tyranny, oppression, falsehood and evil. His chief object in life is to uphold and work for truth and justice. He would lay down his life rather than stoop to meanness and foul-play.'[160] In the article *'Akālī kaun han?'* (Who are the Akalis?), which appeared in the 11 May 1922 issue of the *Akālī*, we are told that

The name 'Akali' is bestowed upon those people within the Sikh Panth who clearly appear prepared to die for the sake of both religion and helping others and who are enthusiastically committed to sacrificing themselves [for these causes]. Whether one is a Namdhari, Nirmala, Nirankari, or Nihang Singh, any Sikh who is prepared to sacrifice for the protection of the glory of the places associated with the Sikh Gurus, for the freedom of the Sikh religion and for the independence of India, that Sikh is an Akali.[161]

All accounts of the Gurdwara Reform Movement confirm that the movement's leaders were very successful in persuading Sikhs to take amrit and follow the standards of behaviour noted in the *Akālī* article quoted directly above. As Teja Singh's quote regarding the black pagari implies, external symbols often reflect inner convictions. These inner convictions were to prove as conspicuous as their symbolic counterparts during the Akali campaigns.

Gurduāre Morche as Spectacle

Early in the gurdwara movement, leaders realized the power of the spectacle and attempted to thus control the events that people saw and the meaning these conveyed. At the inaugural meeting of the SGPC in late 1920, for example, the new leaders of the CSL made Sundar Singh Majithia humble himself in the presence of the gathered sangat as he joined the new gurdwara committee. In effect, Majithia's sheer humility demonstrated that the new radical members of the CSL were not only the legitimate heirs to the Tat Khalsa, displacing the now lacklustre CKD, but that control of the SGPC would be in their hands.[162] A similar tactic would be adopted in the first morcha to gain province-wide support, the agitation over the keys to the treasury of the Golden Temple, known simply as the *chabīān dā morchā*, the Keys Agitation.

After the custodians of the Akal Takht had abandoned the shrine in October 1920 because of the presence of outcaste Sikhs, the Golden Temple fell into the hands of the jatha led by Kartar Singh Jhabbar.[163] The keys of the *toṣākhānā* or treasury of the shrine, however, were still in the hands of the government-appointed manager, Sunder Singh Ramgarhia. In October 1921, a year after the Akal Takht had been abandoned by its former custodians, the SGPC requested Ramgarhia to place the keys in the charge of Kharak Singh, the committee's president. After hearing the news, the Deputy Commissioner of Amritsar ordered Ramgarhia to make the keys over to him, an act which began the first battle of what would be a four-year war.[164] Numerous leaders and other Akali Sikhs were arrested and given rigorous prison terms, acts which added to the movement's popularity. By January 1922, the government realized that the event was gaining ground and wished to settle the matter once and for all. Although the authorities had met the conditions of the Akalis and unconditionally released every person arrested in connection with the affair, the Akalis refused to pick the keys up themselves and instead, demanded that a government representative come to the Golden Temple and return the keys to Kharak Singh. For the occasion, a massive diwan was specially held in view of thousands of pilgrims. The event clearly underscored the power and the legitimacy of the new committee, as did the huge processions held throughout Amritsar, welcoming back the now-released agitators. The following article makes clear the joy of the leaders while once again elaborating an identification with the sacrifices of past Sikh martyrs and those martyred in the present attempt at gurdwara reform:

Congratulations brave borthers! You have kept the honour of our glorious tradition. You have made the following abundantly clear to this demon: 'How dare you look in the direction of the keys of the Sri Darbar Sahib?' Today you have protected the honour of both your great ancestors and the Guru Panth. The venerated Master of the Plume, Guru [Gobind Singh] ji, is very happy. Today Bhai Mani Singh, Baba Dip Singh, Bhai Mehtab Singh, Bhai Lacchman Singh, Sardar Dalip Singh[165] and several other martyrs are showering you with flowers from the Realm of Truth, *sach khaṇḍ.* Today the fame of your genuine zeal and national life is spreading throughout the world. The glorious feats and the high spirits of the Panth will be written in golden letters.[166]

A few months after the victory, the SGPC chose to hold Kar Sewa, that is, the cleaning and desilting of the sacred pool in the middle of which is situated the Golden Temple. This event, it seems, attempted to literally purify Harimandir from the effects and residue of its past mismanagement. The enormous success of the event emphasized the enthusiasm that Sikhs now had for gurdwara reform and for the SGPC and Akali Dal, which led the movement.[167]

This tide of enthusiasm would continue to swell in the months following the SGPC and Akali victory in the *chabīān dā morchā*, reaching a high point during the struggle at Guru ka Bagh. In fact, nothing could prepare the British administration for the overwhelming support Punjabis throughout the province gave to the Akalis at this time. About 12 miles from Amritsar, there are two gurdwaras erected in memory of the Guru martyrs, Guru Arjan and Guru Tegh Bahadur. Although the mahant of these had made arrangements to conform to Akali standards and allow representatives of the SGPC to manage the shrines, he was soon urged (according to Akali accounts) to rescind this agreement.[168] In order to cook the meals distributed within the langar, the Akalis would cut dry kikkar trees from the land adjoining the two gurdwaras. When five Sikhs had done just this on 8 August 1922, they were arrested and quickly convicted to six months' rigorous imprisonment. The SGPC felt this was a gross violation of Sikh rights since the land was part and parcel of the gurdwara property. Its reaction was to organize an agitation on a scale hitherto unseen in the Punjab.[169]

Every morning, prospective Akalis would bathe in the sarovar at Harimandir Sahib and then proceed to the Akal Takht, where they would take a solemn vow 'to go for sacrifice, and under all circumstances, to remain non-violent in word and deed'.[170] Following a short sermon in which Akalis were asked to recall the sacrifices of the Panth of old, the participants would join a jatha of approximately a hundred Akalis and would march in formation from Amritsar to Guru ka Bagh, singing shabads from the sacred scripture *en route*. According to Ruchi Ram Sahni, there was a distinct rivalry amongst members of the jathas to see who could sacrifice the most, acts clearly in line with the behaviour of Sikhs outlined in popular Sikh martyrologies.[171] Spectators would line the roads leading to the shrine

and offer the Akalis water or shower them with flower petals. Following the band closely was a train of ambulances.[172]

Along the way, the Akali jatha would have to pass various areas
where police attempting to bar their progress were stationed. In one
instance, an observer had this to say as the jatha approached their
adversaries in the village of Raja Sansi, approximately five miles
from Guru ka Bagh:

The sight was one of the most frightful witnessed in connection with the
Guru ka Bagh [morcha]. The Sikhs stood with folded hands singing hymns.
As soon as the Policemen came near, they [the Sikhs] sat down on the
ground with their heads bending forward, still singing, 'Wahiguru,
Wahiguru, Wahiguru Ji, Satnam, Satnam, Satnam Ji.' This they continued
till they all became unconscious or exhausted by [the] severe beatings. A
shower of lathis and kicks fell on them to the accompaniment of a drum,
which the police had brought with them and which now began to beat. It
was a frightful sight and was witnessed by several thousand persons who
also uttered prayerfully, 'Wahiguru, Wahiguru, Wahiguru Ji.' Soon, some
of the Akalis lay prostrate. The lathi blows continued descending vigorously
and quickly on those still sitting, till all lay down stretched on the ground.
Those that lifted up their heads received blows individually. They were
dragged and kicked, a few were lifted up by two or more Policemen and
thrown from a height of at least three feet into pits on either side of the
road.[173]

As Teja Singh and other authors note, such fierce beatings were faced
by the Akalis on a daily basis and not once was the oath of non-
violence broken.[174]

These morchas were indeed moments of high drama. Although
large numbers of Sikhs had come from every part of the Punjab to
help the Akalis in any way they could (thereby participating in the
movement), leaders of the movement continued to call people to
come forward to witness an episode from ancient Sikh history being
replayed. Sunder Singh Risaldar, the president of the SGPC, for
example, issued the following communique on 28 August 1922 at
the start of the Guru ka Bagh morcha:

At this hour of trial we expect of you nothing more than to come and
watch the ideally non-violent, spiritual struggle that is going on at Guru-
ka-Bagh to obviate the possibility of misrepresentation at the hands of the
clever government.[175]

There were also other reasons why Akali Dal and SGPC leaders like
Sundar Singh Majithia and his colleague, Teja Singh Samundari,

wished large numbers of spectators to view the sufferings at Guru ka Bagh. Ideally, these gave the Akalis as large a chance for self-display as possible.

Such witnessing was the most powerful factor in garnering support for the gurdwara cause. Chanting hymns as they marched in strict formation, sporting flowing beards, black turbans, *gatrās* or baldrics, belt straps over their right shoulders which held sheathed kirpans, and 'long shirts coming down to their knees', these men were believed to appear like the Akalis of old.[176] To ensure that the behaviour of these contemporary Akalis would, in fact, follow suit, leaders requested all volunteers (as we have noted) to take a vow before the Akal Takht. As a result, the individual was now responsible to Akal Purakh, not just to his fellow Akalis and the movement's leaders. It is significant to note that those Akalis who had captured gurdwaras without following this procedure were asked to give their prize back to the original custodians.[177]

Both the body of the Akali and his behaviour were familiar to all those who had been weaned on the stories of past Sikh martyrs. When the thousands of spectators who had lined the paths to Guru ka Bagh had witnessed the brutal assault upon these bodies and the non-violent behaviour strictly observed by the Akalis, the spectacle became reminiscent of eighteenth-century Sikh history, indeed, became identified with it. As Mani Singh had fearlessly suffered mutilation at the hands of the Mughals during the Golden Age (according to tradition), Akali Sikhs now bore as harsh a suffering at the hands of the British authorities and their constables. Even when beaten down and bloodied, Akalis would rise again in what was perceived as their fearless attempt to reach Guru ka Bagh. Inevitably, this act prompted the constables to inflict further blows.

Like Mani Singh, moreover, these men had the choice to have their beatings stopped. They chose, however, to remain true to their vow to the Eternal Guru, a choice of which, no doubt, the spectators were aware. In this instance, the body of the Akali became the vehicle by which the power and glory of Sikhism were affirmed. The beating these men received and continued to receive signified the strength of their faith rather than the need for public order, which the authorities had hoped the beating would underscore. The body of an Akali became, in effect, the canvas on which was painted an unshakable conviction in both the Guru and the SGPC. Each kick, each lathi blow and each bullet he suffered was a brush stroke adding colour to the canvas and further emphasizing the Akali's reverence towards the eternal Guru and the Panth. Such marks on the body and the apparent mercilessness with which these were inflicted also placed before the eyes of all spectators the debased nature of the opponent faced and the moral superiority of those who were the subject of their harsh attentions. The Sikh observers who reported these incidents make clear that spectators interpreted the events of the Guru ka Bagh morcha in this fashion.

. The ritual nature of both the Gurdwara Reform Movement and martyrdom explains many of the features described in the accounts of morchas like Guru ka Bagh, especially the ability to suffer and tolerate pain. As Judith Perkins notes, after Victor Turner, painful experiences are often associated with initiation rituals. Pain can be tolerated in such circumstances because it is understood to be a requirement of the initiation experience. To paraphrase Perkins, the thought-world of the Akali comprehended and made meaningful the pain which, in turn, made it bearable.[178] The *Akālī* would often print articles aimed to enhance this process of comprehension. A request from Principal Jodh Singh, which appeared in the *Akālī* of 18 March 1921, for example, noted that:

You must keep in mind and endure the memory of the [Nankana] martyrdoms. The Singhs who resolve to reform the gurdwaras cannot be frightened by such a test. I only have this request ... that you do not think to blame the apprehender. It is the Guru who is demanding this sacrifice from us. For good or for bad, this is our test. The more the sacrifice ... the more pure the Panth and the gurdwaras will become. We should, therefore, sweetly accept this new Will of God and not cast aside our principles. We should gladly endure the accusations and ridicule of our misled brothers, as well as the indecent remarks of a foreign or native brother. We should forget our own differences and become fearless, and inimical to none who exhibit an interest in our task to reform the temples. Guru Tegh Bahadur said that it is better to die than cast aside your dharma.[179]

The Akal Takht too, issued proclamations with this goal in mind, stating that Guru Gobind Singh would appear in the midst of the morchas and let lathi blows fall upon himself.[180] By keeping the notion or potential of martydom in mind, one may argue that the morchas took on the character of 'liminal' phenomena, as illustrated by Victor Turner in his study of cross-cultural *rites de passage*.[181] The evidence suggests that the Gurdwara Reform Movement was a *rite de passage*, the morchas becoming the liminal state 'in betwixt and between', in which its participants experienced 'anti-structural communitas' and its concomitant notion of 'flow'.[182] Communitas, according to Turner, is an elevated, consonant, transcending 'liminal' feeling that people experience in climactic phases of ritual. Because of its nature as inclusive, communitas makes for proselytization. In Turner's words: 'One wants to make the Others, We.'[183] All the evidence notes that the displays of the Akalis had made all participants, whether Sikhs in the crowd or marching in formation, adopt the standards of the Tat Khalsa. Indeed, the British authorities themselves noted that the Guru ka Bagh morcha had taken on the 'form of a holy pilgrimage', the *rite de passage par excellence*.[184] Although these remarks were based solely upon superficial observation, they certainly made a point. As pilgrims often do, Akalis had set themselves apart from all other Sikhs by donning a particular style of (sanctified) clothing, adhering to a stylized form of behaviour and taking vows before the Akal Takht, vows which were, we must add, followed exactly.[185] The Gurdwara Reform Movement and the morchas, in particular, in which martyrdom was a distinct possibility, became, as it were, initiation rituals into Tat Khalsa Sikhism. The communitas and 'flow' we find experienced during the morchas brought the imagined past and the present together in this liminal moment, making these 'ritually one', thus allowing the contemporary potential-martyr Akali and, by extension, the entire early twentieth-century Sikh community to become identified with, to indeed become the Sikh Panth of the heroic period. In other words, it became an imagined, homogeneous community, transcending both time and space.

The British were doubtlessly aware of the power of this spectacle. To decrease the time that a constable took to incapacitate an Akali, therefore, a manual was produced, showing spots on the body most vulnerable to the blows of a lathi.[186] Moreover, in the attempt to control the meaning of the spectacle, the British issued reports such as the following:

The Akalis displayed remarkable self-control, and in all sections of the Indian press, scarcely a word of commendation was given to the remarkable good temper and excellent discipline shown by the police in the discharge of their peculiarly unpleasant duty.[187]

Such reports may well have convinced some people. According to accounts of the Guru ka Bagh morcha, however, these statements were not only clearly insufficient but inaccurate. The police are alleged to have made a habit of oppressing inhabitants of the villages surrounding Guru ka Bagh. They are also alleged to have meted out particularly harsh treatment to all those Sikh soldiers and Sikh policemen who wore the black turban in sympathy with the Akalis and the Nankana martyrs.[188] According to Ruchi Ram Sahni, policemen who went into the villages in order to flush out and arrest those sympathetic to the movement (that is, those who wore black turbans) would, in fact, harass all villagers. According to some eyewitnesses, moreover, constables would continue to beat Akalis for some time after they had been rendered unconscious. After this, it was stated, some policemen would even rob the senseless bodies of these valiant Sikhs.[189] It is difficult to assess whether or not such claims are exaggerated. The constant denunciation of police brutality in the vernacular press of the Punjab, however, makes it seem that the constabulary was often given to excess.

In some cases, the British reports were not even enough to convince fellow Britons. The famous British clergyman, C.F. Andrews, was profoundly affected by the Akali display of selfless sacrifice, courage and non-violence. Throughout his eyewitness account of the Guru ka Bagh morcha, Andrews often highlights these Akali characteristics.

It was a strangely new experience to these men, to receive blows dealt against them ... and yet never to utter a word or strike a blow in return. The vow they had made to God [at the Akal Takht] was kept to the letter. I saw no act, nor look of defiance. It was a true martyrdom for them as they went forward, a true act of faith, a true deed of devotion to God. They remembered their Gurus how they had suffered, and they rejoiced to add their own sufferings to the treasury of their wonderful faith.[190]

Andrews was certainly not alone. Ruchi Ram Sahni was similarly affected.

I saw on these occasions the commonest men drawn directly from the lowest ranks of the community rising to great heights of idealism and acting the part of heroes ... I confess, till I saw some of the things with my own eyes, I did not believe all the recorded stories of the Sikh martyrs and their Gurus having gone through extraordinarily severe ordeals not only unflinchingly but with beaming faces and gladness in their hearts, because they were convinced that Akal Purakh expected such services of them. I wish to record my personal testimony of such sufferings borne with the inspiring words Wahi Guru, Wahi Guruji, on their lips...[191]

The Sikhs who partook in the struggles were clearly Akali in more than just name. In his observations, Sahni copies the Akali leaders themselves by comparing the present struggle to the struggles of the Golden Age.[192] The dialectic Sahni employs here is certainly worth noting: the Tat Khalsa interpretation of Sikh tradition in which martyrs play a fundamental role, the tradition that Akalis doubtlessly have in mind, is here legitimated by those very Akalis undergoing potential martyrdom. Indeed, the martyrdom ritual is both a model of and a model for Tat Khalsa Sikhism. As Teja Singh enthusiastically notes: 'Their [the Akalis'] gallantry reminds one of the days when the Khalsa existed solely for the purpose of defending the honour of men and women.'[193]

Addressing a massive crowd of Sikhs within the Nankana complex after the massacre there, Jodh Singh exhorted those assembled to 'bear the suffering like their forefathers as a sacrifice, without a reproach or curse'.[194] Teja Singh remarks that when Jodh Singh recalled the Sikh martyrs of the Sikh Ardas in this eulogy, 'it was as if a page of old Sikh history had been turned again'.[195] Those Sikhs killed at Nankana Sahib thus became 'holy martyrs', and to aid their families in years to come, a 'Martyrs' Fund' was established.[196] As far as the reformers were concerned, the identification with the Sikh martyrs of the past was now complete, in both word and deed. The support for the Akalis was indirectly noted in an article that appeared in *The Loyal Gazette*. Complaining that the CKD was unable to collect even a mere lakh of rupees (1 lakh=100,000) in ten years for the National Fund for Education, it then states that within three months of the Nankana massacre (6 July 1921), over 1.5 lakhs had been collected for the Nankana Shahidi Fund.[197]

The years after Nankana and Guru ka Bagh were to see Akalis offer their lives once again to preserve the sanctity of their gurdwaras. Although the Akali leaders waged the gurdwara campaigns in alliance with Gandhi and the Congress Party, the methods which they adopted were self-consciously Sikh. In fact, a number of features gave the morchas a distinctively Sikh appearance: gurmattas were passed by the assembled Panth which were binding on all Akalis, Akalis bathed in the sarovar prior to their departure, and the vast majority took oaths before the Akal Takht to abstain from violence and to avoid turning their backs until they had reached their destination. Often, the Jathedar of the Akal Takht would exhort the Akalis to remember their pledges and to recall the Panth's heroic traditions of selfless sacrifice.

In one such exhortation, made during the attempt to complete the disrupted akhand path at Jaito in 1924, the Jathedar constantly alluded to sacrifices in the past and referred to the Akalis about to march out as 'saintly martyrs', 'immortalized souls' and 'brave and saintly souls'.[198]

In *Lions of the Punjab,* Richard Fox points out that in organizing and coordinating protest, in recruiting to their cause and in discipline, the Akali leaders emulated patterns laid down by the British military.[199] This is true to some extent. Fox, however, greatly exaggerates his point when he reads two particular events in this light. The two incidents are somewhat similar since both regard the fulfilment of oaths taken at the Akal Takht. In the first instance, an Akali received a severe rebuke when he turned his head during the march to Guru ka Bagh, thus violating his vow to abstain from turning his back. At the second, an observer witnessed a jatha marching through fields deep with water rather than turning around after having missed the side road to the shrine.[200] To refer to these two incidents as examples of British military discipline is simply unacceptable.[201] The stress which Sikh tradition places on fulfilling a vow taken before the eternal Guru or Akal Takht, an emphasis which it traces to Baba Dip Singh and other Sikh martyrs, is one by which all Sikhs must abide. Violating such a vow is dishonourable as well as an insult to the eternal Guru.[202] It is thus principally in the light of Sikh tradition, amplified by the Tat Khalsa, that one must interpret these two incidents.

It is in this light, moreover, that one must view many of the activities of the Akalis until the passing of the Sikh Gurdwaras Act in 1925. The Akali reference to Guru Gobind Singh's hawk during the morchas, their singing hymns from the Adi Granth *en route* to the disputed temples, the looks of contentment on the faces of the severely beaten Akalis,[203] viewing the SGPC and the Akali Dal in the light of the Guru Panth doctrine—all these fit into the category of Tat Khalsa-enhanced Sikh tradition.[204] And all these played their respective parts in making the modern-day Akali as powerful and pious a signifier of the Sikh tradition as his eighteenth-century predecessor, to both himself and to those around him. An interpretation of this sort demonstrates, in part, why the vast majority of Akalis simply went back to the livelihood they previously had after the goal of the reform movement had been accomplished.[205]

In a recent essay, N.G. Barrier remarks that the Akalis 'in a sense ... completed the work of the Singh Sabhas by controlling the centres of Sikh power and orthodoxy, the shrines'.[206] Although this statement is correct, it demands far stronger emphasis. The Akalis did much more than complete the work of the Singh Sabhas. They became, in effect, the ultimate Singh Sabha propaganda since they exemplified, through their personal lives and in many cases, their deaths, the meaning of Sikhism as understood by the Tat Khalsa. It should elicit no surprise that almost seventy per cent of those considered Akalis were Jats. Not only was this proportionate to their numbers within the Panth, but as we have seen, the folklore and traditions of many in this group contain the ideals of heroism, bravery and martyrdom.

On a Jat and on other Sikhs nurtured in Khalsa traditions, both prior to and during the Singh Sabha period, the activities of the first Akalis would have had a profound effect. At the birthday celebrations of Guru Nanak in the November following the Nankana massacre, for example, 20,000 Sikhs of the 50,000 people present considered themselves Akalis and 12–15,000 belonged to jathas.[207] Fox also points out the mass enthusiasm for the Akali cause, highlighting the fact that British documents repeatedly mentioned the popular appeal of the protesters and the warm reception accorded to them in villages, followed by a number of initiations into the Khalsa.[208] With this, we are told, came the rigid adherence to Khalsa forms. It was probably under the influence of Akali actions and rhetoric, therefore, that these rural Sikhs became Akalis. Fox mentions, for example, that a large number of rural Sikhs encountered by recruiting diwans were not staunchly Khalsa Sikhs. 'If they had been', he states, 'jathas would not have required baptism for membership and the travelling diwans would not have performed so many baptisms.'[209]

Eyewitness accounts support such conclusions. Ruchi Ram Sahni constantly mentions the vast number of Sikhs—men, women and children—who accompanied the Akali jathas or lined the roads on which the jathas passed, sometimes showering them with flower petals.[210] The funerals of those Akalis who died while attempting to liberate the shrines were also vastly attended, often witnessing Sikhs resolving to continue the struggle. The funeral of Bhai Hazara Singh, the first Sikh killed in the Akali cause at Tarn Taran, for example, elicited such a response. To ensure the response would indeed be an enthusiastic one, Akalis had fastened a placard on the corpse of their fallen comrade, with the following familiar message:

My becoming a martyr will bear fruit if you will reform all of the gurdwaras.[211]

Bhagat Lakshman Singh managed to witness the funeral of two Akalis killed at Panja Sahib. He states:

Nearly the whole city [of Rawalpindi] was out. From the Gurdwara of the Singh Sabha to the end of the Bhabra Bazaar, for over a mile, one saw a sea of human faces. The roofs of all shops and balconies of houses on both sides of the bazaar were all full of women and children. All traffic was stopped. Only one body had arrived when I reached the bazaar. The vast crowd kept waiting for the other till late in the afternoon, in solemn quiet.[212]

This response, of course, was linked to the fact that the Akalis were very much in the public eye at the time. To Sikhs, however, there was another factor. Akalis had become the embodiment of the Tat Khalsa message, and the forceful maxim which Oberoi extends to Sikh holy men prior to the dominance of the Singh Sabha interpretation is also exceptionally relevant here: Tat Khalsa Sikhism was what Akalis did. They were Tat Khalsa Sikhism.[213]

Such a conclusion is supported in the formal Sikh prayer, Ardas, itself. Although the Ardas was standardized under the auspices of the SGPC in the *Sikh Rahit Maryādā* (published in 1950), there was an Ardas which predated the Singh Sabha movement. It is difficult to precisely define this version of the Ardas, but we do know that the modern text includes one prominent addition.[214] As early as 1922, Teja Singh states that a sentence referring to Akali sacrifices was added to the Ardas after the Nankana massacre.[215] The relevant portions of the modern text appear below, with the addition emphasized.

Those male and female Singhs who gave their heads for the faith; who were torn limb from limb, scalped, broken on the wheel and sawn asunder; *who sacrificed their lives for the protection of the sacred gurdwaras*, never abandoning their faith; and who zealously guarded the sacred kes of the true Sikh: O Khalsa, keep your attention on their merits and call on God, saying Wahiguru.[216]

Akalis were heroic and brave Khalsa Sikhs, sacrificing their lives in defence of the gurdwaras and the Panth, and for this they became the modern versions of the Sikh martyrs alluded to in the same paragraph of the Ardas: Bhai Mani Singh, Bhai Taru Singh, Bhai Mati Das and Bhai Subeg Singh.[217] The identification between the heroic Sikhs of the eighteenth century and the Akalis is complete and immortalized here. With this in mind, it is no wonder that leaders of the Akali movement chose to retain the name 'Akali Dal' for the new Sikh political party after 1925, and that Sikhs initially chose it as the representative of the Panth.

In a sense, therefore, the enormous devotion which Sikhs approaching the twenty-first century have towards the Tat Khalsa interpretation of Sikh tradition (whether they are cognizant of the popular tradition as a Tat Khalsa interpretation or not) is as much due to the Akalis of 1920–5 as to the late nineteenth-century reformers. The power of the reformers was that of ideas, but the power of the Akalis was putting such ideas into practice. Speaking, writing and touring were replaced by the ideals, enunciated therein: suffering, standing true to vows, and dying. The Tat Khalsa message had truly penetrated the very heart of the Punjab due, in large part, to the rhetoric of martyrdom.

Notes

1. '*Kī Srī Darbār Sāhib Sikhān dā hai?*' (Does the Sri Darbar Sahib belong to the Sikhs?) in the *Akālī*, 10 June 1920, p. 2.

2. Oberoi, *The Construction of Religious Boundaries: Culture, Identity and Diversity in the Sikh Tradition* (Delhi, 1994), pp. 417; 424.

3. Clifford Geertz, 'Religion as a Cultural System', in his *The Interpretation of Cultures* (New York, 1973), p. 116.

4. In the 1920s, both Sikh literacy and Sikh enrolment at CKD schools was higher than ever before. Statistics in Paul Brass, *Language, Religion and Politics in Northern India* (Cambridge, 1974), pp. 300–9. Also see Ian J. Kerr, 'Fox and the Lions: The Akali Movement Revisited' in J.T. O'Connell, et al. (ed.), *Sikh History and Religion in the Twentieth Century* (Toronto, 1987), p. 223 and n. 48.

5. Joyce Pettigrew, 'Betrayal and Nation-Building Among the Sikhs', *Journal of Commonwealth & Comparative Politics* XXIX: 1 (1991), p. 37.

6. Emile Durkheim, *The Elementary Forms of Religious Life* [trans. J.W. Swain] (New York, 1915).

7. Clifford Geertz, 'Religion as a Cultural System', pp. 113–14. Both Victor Turner's *Dramas, Fields and Metaphors: Symbolic Action in Human Society* (Ithaca, 1974), pp. 23–59, 166–230, and *From Ritual to Theatre: The Human Seriousness of Play* (New York, 1982), pp. 44–59 and 61–87, have also influenced my interpretation of the Gurdwara Reform Movement and martydom as ritual.

8. The *Akālī* newspaper often told its readers days in advance where the Akali diwans organized by the families of those martyred at Nankana Sahib would be held. See, for example, the three-part article, '*Sahīdī melā srī nankāṇā sāhib jī*', in the *Akālī*, 19 May 1922, p. 3; 21 May, p. 4, and 22 May, p. 3.

9. Judith Perkins, *The Suffering Self: Pain and Narrative Representation in the Early Christian Era* (New York, 1995), pp. 32–4.

10. Sandra Sizer, *Gospel Hymns and Social Religion: The Rhetoric of Nineteenth-Century Revivalism* (Philadelphia, 1978), p. 19, makes this claim about Revivalism rhetoric.

11. For example, R.G. Fox, *Lions of the Punjab: Culture in the Making* (Berkeley, 1984). The term 'Third Sikh War' was coined by S.S. Caveeshar.

12. For example, Mohinder Singh, 'Akali Struggle: Past and Present', in J.T. O'Connell, et al. (ed.), *Sikh History and Religion*, pp. 191–210.

13. Oberoi, *Construction*, pp. 320 ff. and N.G. Barrier, 'The Singh Sabhas and the Evolution of Modern Sikhism', in Robert D. Baird (ed.), *Religious Movements in Modern India* (Delhi, 1989) p. 213.

14. See any of the various publications of N.G. Barrier and Harjot Oberoi.

15. Rajiv Kapur, *Sikh Separatism: The Politics of Faith* (New Delhi, 1987), p. 187; and *WhS*, pp. 93–4. The Act itself is found in Kashmir Singh, *Law of Religious Institutions: Sikh Gurdwaras* (Amritsar, 1988), pp. 161–212.

16. The desire of these two groups to displace the SGPC is often traced back to the Sant Nirankari disturbances of April 1978.

17. For example, *The Khalsa Advocate*, 5 September 1908, p. 3.

18. For example, the *Pañjāb Darpan*, 24 February 1921; and *The Khalsa Advocate*, 25 February 1921. An emotional picture of the horrific events of 21 February 1921 are in *GRM*. For a comprehensive list of those martyred at Nankana Sahib see G.S. Shamsher, *Śahīdī Jīvan* (Nanakana Sahib, 1938).

19. One such appeal, for example, stated:

Sikh heroes! If this sacrifice affects your hearts, if those martyred in the name of religion enthuse you [to follow their example], then placing your own life on the palm of your hand in the name of faith take a resolution, make a promise, that Sri Nankana Sahib will [now remain] in the possession of the [Sikh] Panth, and will certainly continue to do so [forever]. Let no Udasi mahant stay in the service of any place of the Guru unless he surrenders the gurdwara to the Panth.

The *Panch*, 23 February 1921, as noted in Amarjit Kaur, 'The Nascent Sikh Politics' II (unpublished Ph.D. dissertation, GNDU, 1992), pp. 666–9.

20. For the Ghadr movement and its use of the rhetoric of martyrdom, see Harish Puri, *Ghadar Movement: Ideology, Organisation, Strategy* (Amritsar, 1993), pp. 139–41, 145, 211, 248. For the Babbar Akalis see below.

21. In some cases, not even this support was forthcoming. Thanks to the very good harvests of 1913–15, ghadr rhetoric literally fell on deaf ears.

22. Harish Puri, 'Singh Sabha and Ghadar Movements: Contending Political Orientations', in *Punjab Journal of Politics* VII:2 (1983), pp. 12–26.

23. Ibid. Also S.S. Narang, 'Chief Khalsa Diwan: A Study of Leadership, Ideology and Political Strategy' (unpublished Ph.D. dissertation, GNDU, 1989), pp. 101, 111. Background on the journey of the Komagata Maru is in Puri's *Ghadar Movement*, pp. 88–93. In a note in *The Khalsa Advocate*, 11 May 1904, p. 4, one Attar Singh of Bazazhoti queried whether Ajit Singh was a Sikh. In the following week's edition (18 May 1904, p. 4), Narain Singh replied, 'The man [Ajit Singh] is not a Sikh but the reverse of that ... an Arya Samajist. The word Singh must not mislead my brothers for it has long since ceased to be any test of a real Sikh.' Also see, the *Khālsā Samāchār*, 10 April 1907, pp. 1–2.

24. For background see Sukhmani Bal, *Politics of the Central Sikh League* (Delhi, 1990); and Amarjit Kaur, 'The Nascent Sikh Politics: 1919–21', II, pp. 449–601.

25. Mohinder Singh, *The Akali Struggle: A Retrospect* (New Delhi, 1988), pp. 119–32; and B.S. Nijjar, *History of the Babbar Akalis* (Jalandhar, 1987).

26. The passage often noted by the Babbars was from the *Zafar-nāmah* 1: 22, DG, p. 1690. Examples taken from S.B.C. Devalle and H.S. Oberoi's 'Sacred Shrines, Secular Protest and Peasant Participation: The Babbar Akalis Reconsidered', in *Punjab Journal of Politics* VII:2 (1983), pp. 53–4. Also, both Kamlesh Mohan, 'The Babbar Akalis: An Experiment in Terrorism', in *JRH* I (1980), pp. 142–74; and Mohinder Singh, *The Akali Struggle*, pp. 120–1.

27. Devalle and Oberoi, 'The Babbar Akalis Reconsidered', pp. 40, 55 ff. For an analysis of the role that this romantic image plays in the contemporary crisis in Punjabi Sikh society, see Dipankar Gupta's *The Context of Ethnicity: Sikh Identity in a Comparative Perspective* (Delhi, 1996), chapter 5.

28. The Doaba is the plains territory between the rivers Beas and Sutlej.

29. Mohinder Singh, *The Akali Struggle*, pp. 124, 130–31. Here, he also argues that Babbar Akali terrorism contributed to Akali bargaining power.

30. Background in *ESC*, pp. 8–9. For Harimandir see Madanjit Kaur, *The Golden Temple: Past and Present* (Amritsar, 1983), pp. 1–18.

31. *CSRn*, pp. 37–8.

32. *PrPP*, pp. 234–43. Also, John Malcolm, *Sketch of the Sikhs* (London, 1812), pp. 88–9.

33. *Khālsā Akhbār*, 12 February 1895, p. 5.

34. In particular, *Resolutions of Chief Khalsa Diwan: Proceedings Book*, 12 April 1903, as noted in Narang, 'Chief Khalsa Diwan', p. 88.

35. Narang, 'Chief Khalsa Diwan', p. 67.

36. There were no idols actually stationed within the Prakash Asthan of the Golden Temple. Brahman priests who visited the temples brought their idols (*ṭhākur*) with them every morning. They would place these on a small carpet that they had laid down by the edge of the parikarma for devotees to perform puja. This is described in various articles in *The Khalsa Advocate* from May to August 1905.

37. Oberoi, *Construction*, p. 323.

38. The other arguments which they used were that the Sikh Gurus condemned idolatry, and that it was Sikh wealth and labour which went into the building of the sacred temple. See *The Khalsa Advocate*, 20 May 1905, p. 1 and 1 July 1905, p. 2. In the 29 July 1905 issue, p. 5. A 'Sehijdhari Sikh' wrote: 'The blood spilled in defence of the Golden Temple was Sikh blood.' Also, the *Khālsā Samāchār*, 31 May 1905 to 23 August 1905. For the counter-arguments of the Arya Samaj, see the *Khālsā Samāchār*, 7 June 1905, p. 3; and *The Tribune*, 14 May 1905.

39. For example, the *Akālī*, 10 June 1920, p. 2:

darbār sāhib vich lagiān hoīān iṭṭān nālōn śahīd sikhān de sir bāhale lagge han

40. The *Khālsā Samāchār*, 31 May, p. 6; 7 June, pp. 4–5; 14 June 1905, p. 8; and 21 June 1905, p. 8.

41. This request appeared a number of times in both CKD newspapers. For example, *The Khalsa Advocate*, 27 October 1906, p. 5.

42. The many articles relating to the Head Granthi-ship never actually spell out which institution or which person was in charge of appointing gurdwara personnel.

43. *The Khalsa Advocate*, 5 October 1907, pp. 1–2.

44. *PrPP*, pp. 128–38. Also *TGK* II, pp. 71–3.

45. *The Khalsa Advocate*, 12 October 1907, p. 2.

46. The appointment of this boy had been rumoured for some months prior to

December 4. Members of the Tat Khalsa ignored it for they felt such an appointment would be ridiculous. *The Khalsa Advocate*, 5 October 1907, p. 1; and 26 October 1907, p. 2.

47. *The Khalsa Advocate*, 15 February 1908, pp. 1–2; and 21 December 1907, p. 3.

48. *The Khalsa Advocate*, 12 September 1908, p. 3.

49. *The Khalsa Advocate*, 29 February 1908, p. 4. Also, *The Khalsa Advocate*, 1 February 1908, p. 3 and 15 February 1908, p. 2.

50. *The Khalsa Advocate*, 22 February 1908, p. 1.

51. *The Khalsa Advocate*, 4 January 1908, p. 3. Also, 22 February 1908, p. 1; 2 May 1908. Many Sikhs also resented the judgement of the British courts that a band of Muslims who had set fire to and destroyed a gurdwara in the village of Udharwal had been found not guilty. Sikh opinion of the matter may be found in *The Khalsa Advocate*, 1 February 1908, p. 2.

52. *Khālsā Akhbār*, 4 September 1886, p. 7; 27 November 1886, pp. 4–5; 1 January 1887, pp. 3–5; and 8 January 1887, pp. 3–4, as noted in Oberoi, *Construction*, p. 327.

53. Quoted in Oberoi, *Construction*, pp. 326–7.

54. *The Khalsa Advocate*, 8 May 1909, p. 2.

55. Ibid.

56. I.J. Kerr, 'British Relationships with the Golden Temple, 1849–90', in *The Indian Economic and Social History Review* 21 (1984), pp. 143; and his 'The British and the Administration of the Golden Temple in 1859', in *PPP* X:2 (1976), pp. 306–21.

57. Kerr, 'British Relationships', p. 143.

58. For example, *The Khalsa Advocate*, 16 September 1905, pp. 5–6.

59. For background see Kapur, *Sikh Separatism*.

60. The traditional history of the Udasi panth appears in *PnP*, pp. 1269–83. The Tat Khalsa interpretation of the Udasis and their history, however, is quite different. While Gian Singh considers the Udasis a Panth in their own right, Teja Singh emphasizes: '[The Udasis] were no sect, but a class of missionaries, like the masands, sent out by the Gurus for the spread of Sikhism.' *GRM*, p. 216.

61. Master Tara Singh's speech in the Punjab Assembly on 7 May 1925 highlights this point. M.L. Ahluwalia (ed.), *Select Documents: Gurdwara Reform Movement 1919–1925, an Era of Congress-Akali Collaboration* (New Delhi, 1985), pp. 202 ff.

62. Such criticism of the personnel of Harimandir Sahib is in the *Khālsā Samāchār*, 18 December 1899, p. 2.

63. *GRM*, pp. 16–18, 92, 106.

64. Kapur, *Sikh Separatism*, p. 44. Also, *The Khalsa Advocate*, 5 August 1905, p. 2:

Most of the Sikh [village] Dharamsalas are in the hands of persons who belong to non-Sikh religions [Udasi mahants] and preach such doctrines as are quite inconsistent with the noble teachings of the Guru.

65. *GRM*, pp. 95–112, details many such court cases. Also *The Khalsa Advocate*, 5 May 1906, p. 2; and the *Akāli*, 17 April 1921. There were rare cases, however, in which the judge ruled in the sangat's favour. The process through which members of the congregation had to go was very tedious and time-

consuming. See, for example, the drawn out though successful case of the *sangat* versus the *mahant* of Akali Phula Singh's *samadh* in Naushehra, *GRM*, pp. 95-7.

66. *The Khalsa Advocate*, 2 February 1907, p. 4. Other issues in which such demands were made are 5 May 1906, p. 2; 7 July 1906, p. 3; 13 October 1906, p. 6; 10 November 1906, p. 5; 1 December 1906, p. 6. Singh Sabhas the world over sent in their resolutions supporting the Tat Khalsa.

67. *Khālsā Samāchār*, 26 August 1909, p. 2, as noted in Barrier, 'Sikh Politics in British Punjab prior to the Gurdwara Reform Movement', in J.T. O'Connell, et al. (ed.), *Sikh History and Religion*, p. 184.

68. *WhS*, pp. 89-90. A general background on the political economy of post-World War I India appears in B.R. Tomlinson, *The Political Economy of the Raj 1914-1947: The Economics of Decolonization in India* (London, 1979). Also, R.G. Fox, *Lions* and Rajiv Kapur, *Sikh Separatism*. Also see Barrier, 'The Punjab Disturbances of 1907: the Response of the British Government in India to Agrarian Unrest', in *Modern Asian Studies* I (1967), pp. 353-83; and Gobinder Singh's 'Compulsions of the Gurdwara Reform Movement: A New Perspective', in PHCP 16 (1982), pp. 345-54.

69. Mohinder Singh, *The Akali Movement* (New Delhi, 1978), pp. 16, 93-4.

70. Background on Harchand Singh is in Bal's *Central Sikh League*, pp. 32-3. According to Oberoi, Harchand Singh organized a series of diwans in February, protesting against the government action. See Oberoi, 'From Gurdwara Rakabganj to the Viceregal Palace: A Study of Religious Protest', in *PPP* XIV:1 (1980), p. 187. One of the pamphlets which Harchand Singh issued, condemning the government's actions, is in the CCOHP, B, 81 (5)/1914 in the Delhi Administration Archives.

71. Mohinder Singh, *The Akali Movement*, pp. 16, 93-4.

72. Background in N.G. Barrier, 'The Punjab Disturbances of 1907', pp. 353-83.

73. Sunder Singh, *Kī Khālsā Kālaj Sikhān dā hai?* (Lyallpur, 1909). See also *The Khalsa Advocate*, 14 August 1909, p. 2. An impassioned plea regarding the management of Khalsa College appeared in *The Khalsa Advocate*, 23 May 1908, p. 4:

For the last fifty years the Sikhs have been ungrudgingly shedding their blood for the maintenance of the British Raj ... other communities that are now favourites of the government have been merely *shouting* loyalty, while the silent Sikh has been *practising* loyalty.

74. Oberoi, 'Gurdwara Rakabganj', p. 189 and Barrier, 'Sikh Politics in British Punjab', pp. 185-90. According to CCOHP B, 81(7)/1914, letters were sent in from the Singh Sabha of Karachi, the Kirpal Singh Mission School, the Ambala Cantonment Singh Sabha and various other Sikh groups.

75. Barrier, 'Sikh Politics in British Punjab', pp. 185-90.

76. Ganda Singh (ed.), *Maharaja Duleep Singh Correspondence* (Patiala, 1972).

77. Barrier, 'Sikh Politics in British Punjab', p. 169.

78. Ganda Singh, *A History of Khalsa College Amritsar* (Amritsar, 1949).

79. As noted in Narang, 'Chief Khalsa Diwan', p. 112. The CKD's initial reaction to the events at Gurdwara Rakabganj appears in *The Khalsa Advocate*, 26 July 1913, p. 4. That the government was concerned with the CKD's (i.e., the

Sikh) attitude to the gurdwara wall is evinced by the record of this article found in the CCOHP, B, 81(5)/1914.

80. Narang, 'Chief Khalsa Diwan', pp. 112 ff.

81. For the British opinion, see Oberoi, 'Gurdwara Rikabganj', pp. 187–90. The Chief Commissioner considered the CKD a 'timid body'. Hailey to O'Dwyer in CCOHP, B, 81 (1)/1914.

82. Oberoi, 'Gurdwara Rakabganj', p. 189.

83. See S.S. Caveeshar, *The Sikh Studies* (Lahore, 1937), pp. 135–6.

84. Ibid. See also *The Tribune*, 19 April 1914.

85. Sangat Singh, *Freedom Movement in Delhi* (New Delhi, 1972), pp. 205–6, reproduces the six resolutions passed at this meeting.

86. Background in Narang, 'Chief Khalsa Diwan', p. 113 and Sangat Singh, *Freedom Movement*, pp. 198–220. The resolution passed by the CKD in its early May meeting is reproduced in *GRM*, pp. 54–5.

87. S.S. Josh, *My Tryst with Secularism* (New Delhi, 1991), p. 28.

88. Many felt that the CKD had betrayed Sikh interests. See Oberoi, 'Gurdwara Rikabganj', p. 189.

89. Oberoi, *Construction*, pp. 320–8.

90. *GRM*, pp. 12; 85. Also, Ruchi Ram Sahni's *Struggle for Reform in Sikh Shrines* (Amritsar, n.d.), p. 1.

91. This was the title of the piece. *Akālī,* 2 September 1920, p. 2. According to Caveeshar, the first time he made this call was at the CSL meeting in October 1919. See S.S. Caveeshar, '*Gurdwārā Rakābgañj dā Jhamelā*', in Ganda Singh (ed.), *Punjab: 1848–1960* (Ludhiana, 1962), p. 293. According to K.C. Gulati, *The Akalis Past and Present* (New Delhi, 1974), p. 26, the Punjabi *Akālī* begun in May 1920 was previously Harchand Singh's Urdu newspaper, the K̲h̲ālsāh Ak̲h̲bār. However, according to S.S. Bhatia, '*Akālī,* The', in *EoS*, p. 40, the paper was created by a friend of Harchand Singh, Sunder Singh Lyallpuri.

92. According to Trilochan Singh, the call for a jatha of martyrs was made as early as Baisakhi Day, 1914, by Randhir Singh. Trilochan Singh (ed.), *Autobiography of Bhai Sahib Randhir Singh* (Ludhiana, 1993), p. xxvi.

93. That is, the Sikhs are the protectors of the honour and self-respect of the country in the same way that the *chādar* protects the honour and self-respect of female Muslims. Guru Tegh Bahadur is still known as the *Hind dī chādar.*

94. *Akālī,* 2 September 1920, p. 2. S.S. Josh conveys the impact that Caveeshar's request had had on contemporary Sikhs:

The appeal touched the chords of my heart and I stood up and offered myself to be one of the volunteers.

Josh, *My Tryst*, pp. 20–1.

95. Oberoi, 'Gurdwara Rakabganj', p. 192. The report in the *Akālī,* 4 October 1920, p. 1, gives the number of respondents as 700–800. The respondents were not limited to those who could read the paper. According to a report in the *Akālī,* 10 September 1920, p. 4, a conference held in Jhabbal saw one Bhai Taihal Singh loudly read out Caveeshar's appeal for martyrs.

96. The Gurdwara Reform Movement's association with the Indian National Congress, Lala Lajpat Rai and M.K. Gandhi is strongly attested to in the newspaper of the movement, the *Akālī.* Virtually every issue had an article by either Gandhi,

Lajpat Rai, or other nationalist leaders. Articles in the *Akālī* called for Sikhs to adopt all sorts of Gandhian platforms, including the boycott of British manufactured goods and the wearing of home-spun cloth. See, for example, the *Akālī,* 25 September 1921, p. 1.

97. S.S. Josh, *Akālī Morchiān dā Itihās* (Delhi, 1991), p. 27.

98. In March 1907, however, Ajit Singh had used the rhetoric of martyrdom to motivate the Sikhs of Lyallpur who were affected by the proposed increase in canal rates to expand their agitation. See Narang, 'Chief Khalsa Diwan', pp. 101–2.

99. *Akālī,* 2 September 1920, p. 3.

100. *GRM,* p. 80.

101. Background in Peter Hardy, *The Muslims of British India* (Cambridge, 1972), p. 187.

102. Sahni, *Struggle,* pp. 46–7.

103. For example, in the SGPC's proceedings register, this motto appears on folio 12a. *Kārarvāīān Śromaṇī Gurdwārā Kamiṭī,* ms. no. S.H.R. 1793, Sikh History Reference Library, Khalsa College, Amritsar. It may also be found in numerous issues of the *Akālī.*

104. Bal, *Central Sikh League,* pp. 1–14.

105. The new membership consisted of members of 'the upper middle class' according to Bal, that is, the new urban, educated elite. See ibid, pp. 30–1. The Hunter Committee was put together in order to look into the causes of General Dyer's actions, which had led to the infamous massacre at Jallianwala Bagh. The committee placed the majority of blame on the 'open rebellion' plaguing the province during the month leading up to the incident. Its findings were published in May 1920.

106. An enthusiastic eyewitness account of the proceedings appears in Josh, *My Tryst,* pp. 21–2. According to a report found in the *Pañjāb Darpan,* 27 October 1920:

The largest number of delegates and visitors were inhabitants of the villages. They were so rambunctious that Bhai Kartar Singh Jhabbar and Bhai Teja Singh could keep them quiet only by singing out shabads from the Adi Granth.

Moreover, when the CKD representatives present at the meeting distributed pamphlets against non-cooperation, these were gathered up and burned as an effigy of both the CKD and Sunder Singh Majithia. See the *Akālī,* 25 October 1920, pp. 2–4.

107. Bal provides brief biographies of CSL leaders in her *Central Sikh League,* pp. 30–5.

108. Durlab Singh, *The Valiant Fighter: A Biographical Study of Master Tara Singh* (Lahore, 1942). According to his biographer, as a child, Tara Singh often listened to a giani who gave katha from Gian Singh's *Panth Prakāś.* Apparently, it had so affected his young mind that at the age of eight, he was determined to become a Sikh. Ibid, pp. 17–18. Also, Ganda Singh, *A History of Khalsa College,* pp. 65–71.

109. M.L. Peace and Rattan Kaur, *S. Kartar Singh Jhabbar: The Spearhead of the Akali Movement* (Jullundur, 1968), pp. 6, 8; and Narain Singh, *Jathedār Kartār Singh Jhabbar* (Amritsar, 1988), pp. 17–30.

110. During the Rakabganj episode, Tara Singh was chosen to be sent to England to present the Rakabganj case before the British Parliament. The trip was to be financed by the Maharaja of Nabha. Oberoi, 'Gurdwara Rakabganj', p. 190.

111. *WhS*, pp. 93–4. For the Act itself see Kashmir Singh, *Law of Religious Institutions: Sikh Gurdwaras* (Amritsar, 1989), pp. 161–212.

112. This call was broadcast in *The Tribune*, 28 January 1920.

113. Bal, *Central Sikh League*, p. 80, n. 3.

114. Background in Mohinder Singh, *The Akali Struggle*, pp. 94–6.

115. Ibid, pp. 110–18.

116. This impression is particularly clear throughout Sahni's *Struggle*. See also Rajiv Kapur, *Sikh Separatism*, pp. 124–7.

117. Piar Singh, *Tejā Siṅgh Samundarī* (Amritsar, 1975), pp. 68–81; and M.L. Peace, *Kartar Singh Jhabbar*, pp. 21–40.

118. Bal, *Central Sikh League*, pp. 79–127.

119. For example, Fox's *Lions* and Tai Yong Tan, 'Assuaging the Sikhs: Government Responses to the Akali Movement, 1920–5', in *Modern Asian Studies* 29:3 (1995), pp. 655–703. Although Tan notes that his essay looks at the movement from the 'standpoint of the Punjab government', he far too frequently interprets Sikh actions from that point of view alone. The article is, therefore, plagued with misunderstandings of the movement despite the fact that it provides new insight into the British response to the Akalis. One such misunderstanding, also found in Fox's *Lions* (p. 91 and n. 52), follows. Tan states that the British government's conciliatory attitude towards the Sikhs after the Nankana massacre 'was ... construed by the reformers as weakness ...' (p. 676). Not only have I not found any contemporary Sikh source to support this claim, but from the standpoint of the Akali leaders, labelling the British attitude as weakness would have been counter-productive. After all, the stronger the enemy, the more profound is the victory.

120. For example, Fox's *Lions*, p. 90; Rajiv Kapur's *Sikh Separatism*; and Tan's 'Assuaging the Sikhs'.

121. *Akāli*, 4 November 1920, p. 3.

122. I assume that all Sikh-run schools mentioned in the various newspapers of the Tat Khalsa and CKD were influenced by Sikh reformers.

123. The entire note is as follows:

In relation to this gathering, a written agreement with the applicant *sevak* should be signed. This announcement should endeavour to reach every place in which members of the Guru's Khalsa reside (islands and so on included). Every representative who wishes to be included in the committee ought to bring along a certificate from their respective organization.

124. *GRM*, pp. 165–6.

125. *GRM*, p. 163.

126. *GRM*, pp. 11–12. Also Khushwant Singh, *A History of the Sikhs* II, pp. 200–1.

127. Sahni, *Struggle*, p. 112. For Samundari see Piar Singh's *Tejā Siṅgh Samundarī*.

128. *Akāli* 16 July 1920, p. 2, notes that

Right in front of their eyes [the Sikhs] have the glorious life stories and the martyrdoms of both Bhai M[eh]tab Singh and Bhai Mani Singh.

And in the 18 April 1921 issue (p. 5), Bibi Jas Kaur, the wife of Variam Singh, tells prospective female *Akālaṇs:* 'Now is not the time to sleep as your brothers are in jail for the sake of [our] religion.' She continues,

At this time, the daughters of the Guru should appear in the image of Mai Bhago and proclaim to the world that the Singhnis, too, will march shoulder to shoulder with the Singhs.

129. *Akāli,* 6 November 1920, p. 2, and 5 September 1920, p. 2, for example.

130. *Akāli,* 19 August 1920, p. 2.

131. This alludes to Guru Arjan's *Āsā* 93, AG, p. 394.

132. *Akāli,* 6 November 1920, p. 2.

133. This is a stanza attributed to one Bhatt Chand, commemorating the martyrdom of Guru Tegh Bahadur. The entire quatrain appears in Lal Singh *'Guru Tegh Bahādur ji bāṇi te sāke vichi jivan darśan'*, in Satbir Singh (ed.), *Gurū Tegh Bahādur Simrti Granth* (Amritsar, 1975), p. 26. For other allusions to this poem, see the *Akāli,* 6 June 1920 and 18 March 1921.

134. *Akāli,* 27 October 1920 supplement, p. 2.

135. *Akāli,* 30 October 1920, pp. 2–3. Also, in the *Akāli,* 29 April 1922, p. 1, the poem *'Sikh itihās di lari'* (The chain of Sikh history) appears, explaining these Gandhian ideas in a similar fashion.

136. *Akāli,* 9 December 1920, p. 3.

137. S.S. Josh was one such speaker. During the Keys Affair, he would summon villagers by the beat of a drum, explain the government's stand on the issue of gurdwara management, and then shuttle off to another village. We may assume that such romanticized action certainly impressed Sikh villagers who had sheltered Josh wherever he went. See his *My Tryst,* pp. 38–40. Josh wrote about his particular type of *prachār* in the *Akāli,* 13 January 1922, p. 3.

138. Sahni, *Struggle,* p. 90.

139. Josh, *My Tryst,* pp. 26–7. Also Sahni, *Struggle,* p. 91.

140. *Akāli,* 29 September 1920, p. 2. The reference to Kahnunvan may be an allusion to Vir Singh's novel, *Sundari.* At one point in the story, Khalsa Sikhs gather in the marshes of Kahnunvan to pass a gurmatta. *Sundari,* pp. 78–9.

141. Randhir Singh was quite a famous figure amongst Akali and nationalist leaders in the 1920s as he had been one of the Sikhs implicated in the Lahore Conspiracy Case of 1915–16. He remained in prison until October 1930.

142. *Akāli,* 23 October 1920, p. 2. Today, it is still a common practice among Sikhs to refer to Guru Gobind Singh as the father of all initiated Khalsa Sikhs and the Guru's wife as their mother.

143. *Akāli,* 19 November 1920, p. 3.

144. In a letter to the Chief Secretary of the Punjab Government, Khazan Singh characterizes the mahants in this way. Khazan Singh, *Gleanings from the Indian History and the Morchas at Guru-ka-Bagh and Jaito* (New Delhi, 1974), p. 2.

145. As noted by Amarjit Kaur, 'The Nascent Sikh Politics II', pp. 666–9.

146. *GRM,* pp. 125–40.

147. For more background see *GRM,* pp. 443–8.

148. In October of 1922, the *Akāli,* which had run afoul of the administration many times by this point, had merged with the *Pradesi Khālsā* paper of Master Tara Singh and moved its operations from Lahore to Amritsar. The merger

prompted the editors to change the name from *Akāli* to *Akīli te Pardesī*. *EoS* I, p. 40.

149. Sundar Singh would be arrested a few weeks after the appearance of this issue on 5 May and sentenced to two-and-a-half years' imprisonment. See the *Akāli*, 19 May 1922, p. 1.

150. For Jathedar Lacchman Singh see S.S. Josh, *Akāli Morchiān dā Itihās*, pp. 64–72.

151. The *Akāli*, 26 April 1922, p. 1. The number of poems in the *Akāli* alluding to past Sikh sacrifices is vast.

152. *Khālsā Mahimā* 3, *DG*, p. 716. The words *nirbhau* (fearless) and *nirvair* (without enmity), epithets of Akal Purakh found in the *Mūl mantar*, also flanked the right and left side of the title on the first page of each issue.

153. Background in K.C. Gulati, *Akalis Past and Present*, p. 25; and Bal, *Central Sikh League*, p. 79.

154. Khazan Singh sent in a number of petitions filled with references to Sikh history and practice, condemning the maximum nine-inch length prescribed by law. Manjeet Singh, *Late S.S. Khazan Singh: A Pioneer in the Akali Movement. Vol I: Kirpan Episode* (New Delhi, 1975).

155. *GRM*, p. 449. For the Nankana Sahib massacre, see idem, pp. 212–50 and Josh, *Akāli Morchiān dā Itihās*, pp. 58–82.

156. For example, Vir Singh, *Bijai Siṅgh*, p. 6.

157. *Akāli*, 18 October 1920, p. 2.

158. *Akāli*, 6 November 1920, p. 2; also, 20 January 1922, p. 1.

159. The procedure is laid down in the *Akāli*, 2 April 1921, p. 2. As this article notes, there was some fear that the movement would be infiltrated by men affiliated with the Criminal Investigation Department (CID).

160. Josh, *My Tryst*, p. 85. Josh later retracts this statement in his autobiography, noting that Akalis were, after all, ordinary men with faults and drawbacks. He does note, however, why he initially felt that Akalis were altruistic warriors. Two of his reasons regard the selflessness with which Akalis came forward and the importance of martyrdom in Sikh history.

161. *Akāli*, 11 May 1922, p. 2.

162. *GRM*, pp. 166–8.

163. This famous incident is narrated in *GRM*, pp. 150 ff.

164. Akali reaction to the seizure appears in *Akāli*, 10 November 1921, p. 1; 11 November, p. 6; 13 November, p. 1.

165. Both these men were Nankana martyrs. See S.S. Josh, *Akāli Morchiān dā Itihās*, pp. 69–71.

166. *Akāli*, 21 January 1922, p. 2.

167. *GRM*, pp. 342–67. Also Sahni, *Struggle*, pp. 100–2.

168. In the *Akāli*, 28 August 1921, p. 3, Vairiam Singh states that the mahant of Guru ka Bagh and his disciples had agreed to take amrit in January 1921 after being confronted by an Akali jatha. After the massacre at Nanakana, however, the report claims that he apostatized and cast off his kirpan and kacchaihara. Many *Akāli* articles imply that this was characteristic mahant behaviour. Initially, mahants would comply with the demands of the Akali jathas. After some time, they would revert to their previous lifestyles.

169. *GRM*, pp. 396–452.

170. *GRM*, p. 403.
171. Sahni, *Struggle*, p. 107.
172. Ibid., pp. 105 ff.
173. *GRM*, pp. 409–10.
174. *GRM* supplies descriptions of many such beatings that non-violent Akalis suffered. For example, Gumtala Bridge (pp. 407–8), Chhina Bridge (pp. 407–14), and Guru ka Bagh itself (pp. 415–16). Also Sahni, *Struggle*, pp. 108–13.
175. As quoted in Sahni, *Struggle*, p. 128. Sahni notes that this communiqué was unique, for it was the only one he came across that was signed by the president of the SGPC rather than its secretary.
176. That these Sikhs appeared as eighteenth-century Khalsa Sikhs is noted in every account that deals with the Guru ka Bagh morcha. A photograph of one jatha is in Mohinder Singh's *The Akali Struggle*, p. iv.
177. *GRM*, pp. 312–13; and Kapur, *Sikh Separatism*, p. 142.
178. Judith Perkins, *The Suffering Self*, p. 34.
179. *Akālī,* 18 March 1921, as noted in Amarjit Kaur, 'The Nascent Sikh Politics', I, p. 89.
180. As noted in S.S. Dhillon, 'The Role of Symbols and Traditions in Akali Politics' (M. Phil dissertation, GNDU, 1986), p. 74. Likewise, *Akālī,* 19 May 1922, p. 3.
181. Victor Turner, *Dramas, Fields and Metaphors*, pp. 23–57, 166–298.
182. See Victor Turner, *From Ritual to Theatre*, pp. 44–59. According to Turner, there are six elements of the flow experience, all of which were exhibited during the gurdwara morchas: the merging of action and awareness, the centering of attention, the loss of ego, a complete control of one's action and environment, non-contradictory demands for action, seems to need no goals or rewards outside itself.
183. Ibid., p. 51.
184. Tai Yong Tan, 'Assuaging the Sikhs', p. 688.
185. According to Turner,

[pilgrimages are among] the processes through which religious paradigms are continually reinvested with vitality...which commit individuals unreservedly to the values of a particular faith in order to make not merely acceptable but glowing the hardships and unforeseen disasters of long journeys across several national frontiers.

With only some very minor modifications, this can describe the morchas of the Gurdwara Reform Movement. Victor Turner, *Dramas, Fields, and Metaphors*, p. 15.

186. *GRM*, p. 431. Teja Singh does not cite the actual manual but he does note that it was produced by the Superintendent of Police, Mr. MacPherson. He continues,

In [the booklet] we find laid down how the lathi is to be struck into the opponent's face, his belly, his throat, and even his 'fork'.

187. The report is reproduced in Sahni, *Struggle*, p. 172.
188. Compare this statement with those in Tan, 'Assuaging the Sikhs'.
189. All these apparent descriptions are found in Sahni, *Struggle*, pp. 137–8.

Also, *GRM*, p. 431:

The stray Sikhs found outside the Gurdwara Guru-ka-Bagh, or on the roads leading to it, were set upon, beaten and robbed. The robbing, as the beating, was carried on most publicly in the presence of hundreds, who can testify to these acts done by the forces of peace and order.

190. The entire account is reproduced in Sahni, *Struggle*, pp. 177–83.

191. Ibid., p. v.

192. Apparently Kartar Singh Jhabbar did more than just refer this struggle to those of the past. See, for example, the photo opposite page 72 in M.L. Peace and Rattan Kaur, *S. Kartar Singh Jhabbar.* Apparently, Jhabbar drew a line on the ground and asked those willing to sacrifice their lives for the gurdwaras to cross it in a manner very similar to the tradition ascribed to Baba Dip Singh. Ibid, p. 70.

193. *GRM*, p. 457. Also, S.S. Caveeshar in his *The Sikh Studies*, p. 180, speaking about the national campaign led by Gandhi and the Indian National Congress notes that:

We should compare our sacrifices with those of our ancestors, and if we find any difference, we should consider that difference to be the cause of the distance that still lies between us and the goal.

194. *GRM*, pp. 243–4.

195. Ibid.

196. *GRM*, p. 243.

197. As noted in Amarjit Kaur, 'The Nascent Sikh Politics' I, p. 329.

198. Ganda Singh (ed.), *Some Confidential Papers of the Akali Movement* (Amritsar, 1965), pp. 35–7. In this speech, the jathedar paraphrases Guru Nanak's *Slok vārān te vadhīk* 20. A description of the Jaito morchas is in Mohinder Singh, *The Akali Struggle*, pp. 73–80.

199. Fox, *Lions*, pp. 95–9.

200. The two incidents appear in Sahni, *Struggle*, pp. 143–4; also S.S. Caveeshar, *The Sikh Studies*, p. 202.

201. Fox, *Lions*, p. 95.

202. Harbans Singh, *The Heritage of the Sikhs* (Delhi, 1985), chapters VII–VIII.

203. C.F. Andrews mentions these in his account. Sahni, *Struggle*, pp. 176–83.

204. Kapur, *Sikh Separatism*, pp. 155, 179. Of course, the *Akāli* often mentioned that the SGPC was

The Central Gurdwara Management Committee chosen by the Guru Panth ...

and that

[I]ts order must be accepted as the supreme duty of each and every Sikh.

Akāli, 13 November 1921, p. 1; and 22 September 1921, p. 4. Other articles indicating that the Committee's authority stems from the doctrine of Guru Panth are legion, for example, 11 November 1921, p. 6.

205. Sahni, *Struggle*, p. 2. S.S. Josh notes that while in jail, imprisoned

Akalis would sing religious hymns and not national ones. *My Tryst*, pp. 50–1.

206. N.G. Barrier, 'The Singh Sabhas and the Evolution of Modern Sikhism', p. 213.

207. These figures are in Khushwant Singh, *A History of the Sikhs*, Vol. II, p. 201.

208. Fox, *Lions*, p. 94. Of course, virtually every issue of the *Akālī* tells us of individuals who had been administered amrit at various scattered diwans. The phrase that the *Akālī* often used to indicate the creation of Akalis and their taking of amrit was *kālī dastār sajāuṇī*, or 'to don the black turban'.

209. Ibid., p. 178.

210. Sahni, *Struggle*, pp. 105–6. Hindu and Muslim Punjabis did likewise.

211. *GRM*, pp. 207–8. The report of the attached placard appears in the *Vidyā*, 5 February 1921.

212. *BLSA*, p. 241.

213. Oberoi, *Construction*, pp. 116–17.

214. For *Sikh Rahit Maryādā* see *WhS*, pp. 94–7, 101. For references to the Ardas prior to the Singh Sabha, see *CSRn*, pp. 33, 34, 207.

215. *GRM*, pp. 243–4.

216. *Sikh Rahit Maryādā* (16th edn, Amritsar, 1989), p. 8.

217. For the stories of the martyrs to whom there are allusions within the Ardas, see Teja Singh, *Sikhism: Its Ideals and Institutions* (Bombay, 1964), pp. 122–3.

EIGHT

Post-1925
Conclusions

> Language functions more to *produce* a particular reality than to *represent* it. In this sense, neither Sikh nor Hindu identity can be treated as possessing an unchanging essence.[1]

The end of the Gurdwara Reform Movement would by no means see the end of the use of the rhetoric of martyrdom, nor of Akali and SGPC calls for sacrifice. In the attempt to involve Sikhs in the nationalist struggle for independence, such invitations were, at times, very successful. A respectable number of Akali Sikhs, for example, participated in the first phase of the Civil Disobedience movement of early 1930. By its end in March 1931, according to one estimate, the Sikhs had sent proportionately the largest number of volunteers to jail (some 3000 of the total 7000 arrested).[2] The second phase of civil disobedience also saw various Akali newspapers call for volunteers willing to sacrifice for India's independence, a call which saw many Sikhs once again court arrest and imprisonment.[3] Although many factors went into securing these Punjabi Sikh participants, one may assume that the use of the rhetoric of martyrdom by pro-Akali Sikhs certainly played a part in this endeavour. A glance at contemporary Sikh newspapers aligned with the Akalis will confirm this as beyond doubt.

The level of participation and commitment, however, would never again assume the levels it had reached during the gurdwara campaign. The Akalis who dominated the new Khalsa Darbar organization (which was established to oppose the Communal Award in September 1932), for example, would fall far short of their projected goal of amassing 100,000 Sikhs for a Shahidi Dal to oppose Ramsay

MacDonald's award.[4] Generally speaking, there were many reasons for this new Sikh attitude. Primary among these is the fact that Akali leaders (and other Sikh leaders) could rarely form a united front. Baba Kharak Singh and Master Tara Singh were initially at odds regarding the Indian National Congress and the Sikh role in this organization. The Central Sikh League also had its 'moderate' and 'extreme' wings, which did not often see eye to eye, while the CKD was still considered a pro-British organization. To complicate matters, during the late 1930s and early 1940s, numerous other Sikh parties had been established whose mandates often fundamentally differed from one another.[5] These Sikh politico-religious parties (and others), moreover, could not find a focus which affected all Sikhs as profoundly as that of the gurdwara. It was not until the spectre of Pakistan began to haunt the Punjab after 1940 that Sikhs would pay more heed to Akali calls. In May of 1940, for example, the Akali Dal would observe a Ghalughara Day in commemoration of the infamous massacres of the mid-eighteenth century by Muslim forces.[6] In this light, therefore, the participation in the nationalist struggle of the general Sikh population (particularly those rural Sikhs who engaged in the Gurdwara Reform Movement) was not as enthusiastic as during the period 1920–5. This is despite the fact that Sikh leaders such as Master Tara Singh and Baba Kharak Singh were in the forefront of the Independence movement in Punjab.[7] As Ruchi Ram Sahni stated, 'As soon as the duty [of protecting the gurdwaras] had been done, they [the Akalis] reverted to their usual daily avocations as ordinary householders.'[8]

Perhaps Sikhs of the rural areas were no longer willing to recognize the Akali Dal or the SGPC as organizations representing Sikh interests in general and their interests in particular. Richard Fox notes that after the Sikh Gurdwaras and Shrines Bill had become law in 1925, many of the morcha participants (those he calls 'Singh converts') did not benefit from the new situation in which Akali leaders found themselves. Fox supports this claim by noting that the economic plight of these participants was the same as it was in 1920 and that they were not given a major voice in the management of the gurdwaras which they had helped secure.[9] Fox clearly implies that these so-called Singh converts begrudged the Akali Dal and SGPC for the failure of these organizations to compensate participants in some form for their taking part in gurdwara agitations. This scenario seems unlikely as criticism of the Akali Dal or SGPC from these participants is not forthcoming. The Akali Dal and SGPC emphasis on morcha participation as sacrifice, martyrdom and *sevā* clearly indicated that involvement in the Gurdwara Reform Movement was a Sikh's duty to his Panth and to Akal Purakh. Sacrifice was, after all, just that: sacrifice. To seek any type of compensation for such action (despite the very well-known existence of the Akali Shahidi Fund) was tantamount to conceit. Sikhs were enjoined to participate as this would, moreover, ensure that the self-respect and honour of the Panth (and thus, their own individual self-respect and honour) would remain unblemished. Fox may well be right, therefore, in his cynical comment that these rural Sikhs 'made do by emphasizing that martyrdom was one element in their new orthodoxy'.[10] The attendant claim here, of course, is the new status that accrued to rural partici-pants as a result of their participation. This itself may have been a form of compensation.

After 1925, one could also argue that the call for martyrs was an old and tired one. Many Sikhs throughout Punjab had now sacrificed for forty years, and their material and political situation was not markedly different from the one of the 1870s (Panthic control over gurdwaras notwithstanding). Perhaps as a result, the term 'shahid' began to lose some of its emotional appeal. For the Akalis and SGPC, however, the word 'shahid' was still a profoundly emotive one. When in 1927, the Punjabi writer, S.S. Charan Singh, chose to affix the word 'shahid' to his name, for example, the *Pañjāb Darpan* newspaper took great umbrage. In its article, '*Śahīd pad dī be-izatī*' (Disgrac-ing of the word *śahīd*), the paper condemned the author's action in the strongest possible terms. The article states that the word 'shahid' is associated with a long list of glorious Sikh martyrs and that as a result, it has become a 'powerful' (*śaktī*) term prompting contempo-rary Sikhs to remain steadfast in their faith. It is a word, the article strongly implies, that must not be employed frivolously. Indeed, a word which makes 'every Sikh's hair stand on end'. It claims, however, that this *pavitr śabad* is being dishonoured in the presence of the Akal Takht itself by Charan Singh. It suggested the following solution:

It would be a good thing if Mr. Charan Singh would himself cease from appending this [most] hallowed word [shahid] to his name. Otherwise, the jathedar of the Akal Takhat ought to issue a hukam-nama which will declare that any man who will dishonour the term shahid [in this way] (and any newspaper that does likewise) [has gravely insulted the Sikh com-munity and] is [thus] fit for a penance (*tankhāhīā*) from the Sikh Panth.[11]

When issues over gurdwaras arose after 1925 and the rhetoric of martyrdom was employed in their light, Sikh participation in the Akali programme did increase. The firing on 6 May 1930 into Gurdwara Sisganj in Delhi, for example, saw the SGPC enter the Civil Disobedience movement alongside the Akali Dal and the CSL. It was on the spot that this temple occupies that the ninth Sikh Guru, Tegh Bahadur, was executed. Its desecration with government bullets and brickbats was, in the words of one Gurmukh Singh, an eyewitness to the events of that day, 'an insult ... [that the Sikhs] could hardly bear'.[12] The controversy over Gurdwara Shahidganj in Lahore in late 1935, moreover, saw a spate of articles in the *Pañjāb Darpan,* narrating the history of the Sikh martyrs associated with that gurdwara, particularly Bhai Tara Singh Van and Bhai Taru Singh.[13] The campaign to ensure that Gurdwara Shahidganj did not fall into the hands of the Muslim leaders of Lahore (all of whom claimed that the gurdwara was originally a mosque and demanded that it be returned to the Islamic community of Lahore) saw thousands of Akalis converging on that city. Although a few Muslims had lost their lives in the ensuing agitation for the return of the Shahidganj gurdwara and were immediately declared to be martyrs by their respective community leaders, the issue over this gurdwara (which has, according to one author, 'a special place in [the] Sikh imagination') was settled in favour of the Akalis and SGPC.[14]

After the Gurdwara Shahidganj affair was over, the gurdwaras ceased to be a major Sikh issue. Sikhs would be called upon by the Akali leaders many times over the next twelve years to volunteer themselves and sacrifice their lives, if necessary, for the nationalist cause, in particular to thwart the Muslim League's claim to Pakistan. After India's independence in 1947, this continued, with the use of the rhetoric of martyrdom to help collect Sikh support for the creation of a Punjabi-speaking state and to enjoin Sikhs to oppose Indira Gandhi's declaration of the Emergency, in which she assumed dictatorial powers in 1975.[15] Yet it was not until the Sant Nirankari dilemma of Baisakhi Day 1978 (which, in many ways, played a role in precipitating the recent crisis), however, that the martyr's appeal would once again elicit the kind of response seen in the early 1920s.[16] Indeed, the speeches of Jarnail Singh Bhindranwale clearly show that large numbers of Sikhs had volunteered themselves as *mar-jīvṛās*, men and women who resolved to sacrifice their lives to protect the Sikh religion, which they believed the Sant Nirankaris were threatening.[17]

I have, in the span of a few paragraphs, covered post-1925 events which would seem to require an extended, separate treatment. Although contemporary events in Punjab have been incorporated into my analysis of Sikh martyrdom as well, I have not directly focused upon these for any length. In the light of the topic at hand, the reason for this is uncomplicated: many of the rhetorical strategies used by post-gurdwara-campaign Akali and SGPC leaders and later, Sikh militants have their origins not in the contemporary events of their times, but in the rise and dominance of the Singh Sabha and the success of the Gurdwara Reform Movement. Amongst these men, we would include Master Tara Singh, Sant Fathe Singh, Gurcharan Singh Tohra and Harchand Singh Longowal, as well as Jarnail Singh Bhindranwale. In particular, of course, is the skilful use these men made of the rhetoric of martyrdom. It was a relatively easy task for these Sikh leaders to adapt this rhetoric to their present-day needs and thus stamp it with contemporaneity.

In the speeches of Jarnail Singh Bhindranwale, there were constant allusions and comparisons to the Sikh martyrs of the past. In a speech delivered in June of 1983, for example, Bhindranwale alluded to the martyrdoms of both Garja Singh and Bota Singh in order to counter-act the Indian government's claims that the disciples of Bhindranwale, a small segment of the Sikh Panth at best in 1983, could not accomplish a great deal.[18] Indeed, like the eighteenth-century Bota Singh, a single Sikh, Bhindranwale prophetically implies (perhaps referencing himself), could symbolically subvert the entire central government.

In her essay on Sikh militancy,[19] moreover, Veena Das underscores another rhetorical technique of which Bhindranwale and other militant Sikh leaders also made good use: incorporating into the rhetoric of martyrdom the language of the modern nation state, with the use of such terms as 'human rights', 'cultural rights', 'equal rights', 'minorities' and so on.[20] Such terminology permeates the now-departed Sant's many discourses. Alluding to a conversation he had had with a 'very well-known lawyer at the Supreme Court' of India, comparing Sikh and Hindu opposition to the Emergency of 1975, for example, Bhindranwale stated the following in a speech he gave in May 1983:

Now we[the Sikhs] are struggling on behalf of all Punjabis. We are not making demands. We are asking for our rights, only our rights. And we have to get our rights. It is not that we are not to get them and all this is idle talk. We have to get them even if it means we are cut up bit by bit. We have to get them under all circumstances.[21]

This, of course, reminds one of the inclusion of the vocabulary of the Gandhian programme of the early 1920s. As we noted, during the Gurdwara Reform Movement, the rhetoric of martyrdom was modified to include and define concepts such as satyagraha, non-cooperation, non-violence and swadeshi, among others.

Many scholars have noted that the rhetorical strategy of Bhindranwale was enormously successful in persuading Sikhs to take up arms against the 'Hindu' government of Indira Gandhi.[22] Weapons were adopted, in large part, to preserve Sikh self-respect and honour, casting off the shackles of 'Sikh slavery' (in the words of Bhindranwale) through violence and martyrdom. During the period of militancy in present-day Punjab, there were changes in the rhetorical strategy that was first used by Sikhs of the late nineteenth and early twentieth centuries. The most fundamental of these is the displacement of what the White Paper of the so-called Sikh Religious Parliament calls 'the narcotic cult of non-violence'.[23] In the rhetoric of Bhindranwale and other Sikh militants, non-violent means were the prerogative of 'Sikhs of the spinning wheel and the goat', and particularly of Hindus like M.K. Gandhi. These men were often characterized as effeminate or emasculated males in militant discourse. According to Bhindranwale, non-violent methods

are the techniques of the weak, not of a race that has never bowed its head before any injustice—a race whose history is written in the blood of its martyrs.[24]

In the words of Veena Das, the place that the Hindu occupies in this present-day rhetoric of martyrdom is that of the 'weak, effeminate and cunning' counterpart to the vigorously masculine Sikh. In other words, the Hindu is the negative Other of the Sikh.[25]

But despite the apparent modifications, we can easily observe that the rhetoric of martyrdom introduced by the Tat Khalsa and sustained by the SGPC and Akalis has remained intact. Like their Sikh predecessors, contemporary Sikh militants and their leaders use the legends of past martyrs to persuade Sikhs to act on the individual and the corporate level, simultaneously inspiring and shaming their Sikh audiences. At a speech delivered at the annual conference of the All-India Sikh Students' Federation (commemorating the two-year anniversary of the 'martyrdom' of eighteen Sikhs at Chowk Mehta, some twenty-five kilometres northeast of Amritsar) on 20 September 1983, for example, Bhindranwale made clear what was expected of the Sikh Panth in order to ensure that the principles of the Anandpur Sahib Resolution (first drafted in 1973) be implemented:

The birthplace of the Khalsa is Anandpur Sahib ... it is also the place where the Sacrificer of His Sons [an epithet of Guru Gobind Singh] gave His word to the Sikhs in return for the gift of amrit. [The Guru humbly requested,] 'Khalsa ji, give amrit to me as well.' Blessed was the Guru's Sikh... What fearlessness has he given to his Khalsa! The [spiritual] son [Daya Singh, the first Sikh to be administered amrit in 1699] told the Sacrificer of His Sons: 'My Beloved Father, you are welcome to take amrit ... but please tell us ... you gave us amrit in return for five heads ... What will you give us in return for the gift of amrit?' Blessed is the Sacrificer of his Sons ... [who] replied, 'Bhai Daya Singh ji ... If you give me the amrit of the double-edged sword and the steel bowl, the Timeless and Omnipresent One be my witness that I shall sacrifice all my family for you.' Khalsa ji, a resolution [i.e., the Anandpur Sahib Resolution] has been passed at the place where the Sacrificer of His Sons gave us his word, the promise to sacrifice his biological children for the sake of His spiritual ones. I ask all of us, particularly all the young men assembled here, to go over your faces with your hands. Have we entered Anandpur, our home? Are our beards intact? Have we got our kirpans? Do we remember the Guru's Word by heart? Do we abstain from alcohol? If a person has never entered his home, how will anyone allow him to fit it up with boards, lay chips in the floor and install windows? If you want the Anandpur Sahib Resolution, first enter your home, Anandpur. Take amrit, then you will certainly get [the Anandpur Sahib Resolution] implemented.[26]

In the process of appropriating such rhetoric, the image of the Sikh as the martyr and the Sikh community as a community of martyrs whose blood has sustained the Panth as well as the Indian nation persists.[27] In her analysis of Sikh militant discourse, Veena Das has insightfully pointed out the constant use of the images of *charkhī charhnā* and *khoprī utarvāuṇa*—broken on the wheel and scalped, respectively—in the oral discourse of militant Sikhs, images which sustain such powerful self-representations.[28] These are images which permeated the Tat Khalsa's rhetoric of martyrdom and which, as we noted in the first chapter, were used to describe the Sikh community in the early 1920s and earlier still, in the Sikh newspapers, publications and rhetoric of the day. Other similarities to the Singh Sabha's use of language are also easily detectable in the rhetoric of contemporary militants. The aforementioned White Paper, for example, claims that the preaching of non-violence, characterized as effeminate and identified with Hindus generally, has 'softened and conditioned [the Sikhs] during the last fifty years'.[29] Clearly, this is a technique often used during the period of the Singh Sabha, which also characterized Sikhs and Sikhism generally as 'softened', indeed, corrupted by the practice of so-called non-Sikh Hindu rites.

The long drawn-out struggle of the recent years has, of course, taken its toll on the Sikh understanding of the shahid. Written and oral evidence suggests that while some of these militants were ideologically driven and clearly wished to remedy the harsh situation which they believed faced the Sikhs of India (that Sikhs in India were denied their basic rights by virtue of their being Sikh), other militants were persuaded more by the profitable and romantic lifestyle that militancy afforded.[30] It was often the zeal of this latter group, their foolhardy actions, and especially the fact that they used their traditionally 'respectable' positions and their AK-47s to 'settle old scores' and bring a tragic and bloody end to old family feuds that led to large numbers of Punjabi villagers becoming disillusioned with militant goals and aspirations, villagers who at times had sheltered the militants from the police. Indeed, many of the less ideologically minded militants would often malign the very villagers who had helped them in the past, shamelessly demanding food, money and women.[31]

When men of this latter calibre were eventually killed in their battle with Indian government forces and declared shahids by their respective militant cells, the word, no doubt, began to lose the respect and reverence with which it was associated in the past. It appears, then, that the term today has become somewhat devalued. After all, in many gurdwaras in Punjab, it is not uncommon to see the pictures of many slain militants placed right beside those of the Sikh Panth's traditional martyrs.[32] Sikh authors are by no means ignorant of this turn of events. In an attempt to distinguish such militants (and soldier and dacoit and other such 'martyrs', presumably) from 'true' Sikh shahids, Narain Singh claims the following in his recent analysis of Sikh *śahīdī:*

> If you want to play the game of love
> Approach me with your head on the palm of your hand.

These are the wondrous miracles of the lovers of humanity. They who are seen dying with this faith have already obtained eternal life. It is, indeed, this type of death that one calls martyrdom, the foundation of which is within the very hymn [found] at the beginning [of this paragraph]. But the people of the world join every good thing with copies and forgeries and as a result, clearly discriminating a counterfeit [thing] from a genuine one becomes quite difficult. The lofty principle of martyrdom, as well, has become so confused. Young people are beginning to play the game of death for their own personal glory.

What, then, is genuine martyrdom? The entire world knows that Sikh history is the very history of martyrs, whose most glorious examples were Guru Arjan Dev ji and Guru Tegh Bahadur ji. Therefore, the correct understanding of an ideal martyrdom should be made in light of this hymn and according to the authentic examples of these two martyrs.[33]

For Narain Singh and others, the notions of martyr and martyrdom have been bandied about too frequently and applied far too indiscriminately in the years after 1978. He implies that the time has come to set the word aright again.

In this light, it appears that the techniques used by the Singh Sabha to broadcast their interpretation of Sikh tradition are being appropriated once again to clarify to Sikhs the 'proper' understandings of shahid and shahidi. On the back cover page of its 1996–7 catalogue of books, the famous Singh Brothers booksellers of Mai Sewa Bazaar, Amritsar, for example, have four small reproductions of Kirpal Singh's 'martyr art', below which appear the following statements:

What do your children know about these unparalleled events? With the reassuring support of the Guru's Word, these righteous men provided unique examples of sacrifice for living lives of honour and self-respect. If our children are ignorant of these great events, then instead of being motivated by our proud history, they may turn away and go astray from their rich heritage.[34]

No doubt the Singh Brothers are in the business of selling books and such statements may be interpreted merely as a marketing strategy. Much of this back cover, however, suggests the context in which the catalogue was produced, in which the word 'shahid' has been applied to the most violent and nefarious of militants.[35] It also suggests that the rhetoric of martyrdom, both today and during the time of the Singh Sabha, the Akalis and the SGPC, does much more than lay down the rules of a 'game of love'. It is, rather, a far more complicated game, whose participants are (to allude to a phrase of Clifford Geertz) involved in a much deeper play.[36] This is the game of self-respect, honour and status—all three of which are, of course, intimately interrelated in Punjabi Sikh culture.

This book has endeavoured to trace the concept of martyrdom throughout the history of the Sikh people. It is clear that a concept of martyrdom as a witness to the faith with one's life was in place in the nascent Khalsa Sikh tradition of the early eighteenth century. What remains unclear, however, is how salient a feature of this early Sikh tradition martyrdom was. The lack of a specific term for either the martyr or for martyrdom seems to indicate that these concepts (as these are now understood) had not yet achieved the status among the Sikh Panth, generally, and the Khalsa, in particular, which they today possess among the Sikh people and within the Sikh tradition. However, the concepts were indeed present. It is also clear that by the later eighteenth and early nineteenth centuries, the concept (whether prominent or not) had expanded, as a result of the Khalsa Sikh rise to power, to include the common description of the shahids found in Islamic texts and in the multi-faceted Sanatan or Sahaj-dhari Sikh tradition of the period, one of whose meanings was the shahid as a harmful or benevolent entity who required propitiation.

It was this understanding of the shahid that would confront the Singh Sabha. By appropriating the legends of martyrdom, this group, whose ideas we have seen were formed in part through dialogue with Western Orientalism, not only promoted their interpretation of the Sikh tradition but constructed the category 'shahid' afresh, gradually displacing understandings of it which would not hold up to their enlightened rationale. It is principally as a result of their use of language, in particular their formation of a rhetoric of martyrdom, that this concept came to be far more intimately associated with the Sikh tradition and the Sikh people than had been the case previously. As their interpretation of the Sikh tradition came to be a part of everyday life, so, too, did the rhetoric of martyrdom which they appropriated to persuade Sikhs enable martyrs and martyrdom to be seen as an essential part of that very tradition. The use of this rhetoric of martyrdom was continued by the SGPC and Akali Dal, their successors during the Gurdwara Reform Movement. This use was a major factor in encouraging Sikhs to engage their opponent *en masse*. During this campaign, these enthusiastic Sikhs provided a display of heroic, selfless suffering and martyrdom that made it appear as if the essence of the Sikh was, indeed, one of sacrifice and martyrdom, that made it appear as if another page of Sikh history had been turned.

This understanding of the Sikh character and of the history of the Sikhs is today's dominant interpretation and its questioning by scholars of the tradition leads to a great deal of Sikh resentment and mistrust. Questioned it must be, however, for an acceptance of contemporary Sikh claims regarding the Sikh tradition and the history of martyrdom within it will ensure that the extraordinary Singh Sabha effort to make martyrdom a far more fundamental feature of the Sikh faith will go unrecognized.

Notes

1. Veena Das, 'Time, Self and Community: Features of the Sikh Militant Discourse', in her *Critical Events: An Anthropological Perspective on Contemporary India* (Delhi, 1995), p. 121. Emphasis in the original.

2. J.S. Grewal, *The Akalis: A Short History* (Chandigarh, 1996), p. 78.

3. Ibid., p. 79.

4. Details in *The Tribune*, 30 July 1932.

5. At the second annual meeting of the Khalsa Darbar in 1933, Baba Kharak Singh and his supporters left the organization to form another. Although the CSL would merge with the Khalsa Darbar in 1934, the Darbar would split again in 1938. J.S. Grewal, *The Sikhs of the Punjab* (Cambridge, 1990), p. 170; and *The Akalis*, pp. 82–110. The post-1925 history of the CKD appears in S.S. Narang, 'Chief Khalsa Diwan: A Study of Leadership, Ideology and Political Strategy', (Unpublished Ph.D. dissertation, GNDU, Amritsar, 1989), pp. 162–87. The CSL's role in the nationalist campaign is noted in Sukhmani Bal, *Politics of the Central Sikh League* (Delhi, 1990), pp. 129–66.

6. Indu Banga, 'The Crisis of Sikh Politics, 1940–47', in J.T. O'Connell, et al. (ed.), *Sikh History and Religion in the Twentieth Century* (Toronto, 1988), pp. 240, 250; and Tan Tai Yong, 'Prelude to Partition: Sikh Responses to the Demand for Pakistan, 1940–47', in *International Journal of Punjab Studies* I:2 (1994), pp. 169, 170, 183, 188–9.

7. Scholarship dealing with the period 1925–40 focuses exclusively upon Akali leaders and politics. As a result, it is very difficult to fathom general Sikh participation despite the general impression that Sikhs contributed numerous sacrifices to procure Indian independence from Britain.

8. Sahni states this in reference to eighteenth-century Akalis, of course, but the implication that this applies to the Akalis of the Gurdwara Reform Movement is abundantly clear. Sahni, *Struggle for Reform in Sikh Shrines* (Amritsar, n.d.), p. 2.

9. R.G. Fox, *Lions of the Punjab: Culture in the Making* (Berkeley, 1987), p. 184.

10. Ibid.

11. *Pañjāb Darpan*, 20 August 1927, p. 4. A reply appears in 10 October 1927, p. 7. Despite the complaints, Charan Singh did not drop the term 'shahid' from his name.

12. *Report on the Firing into the Gurdwara Sis Ganj, Delhi on May 6, 1930* (Amritsar, n.d.), p. 26. This occurred during the *hartal* that was observed as a result of M.K. Gandhi's arrest in May 1930.

13. *Pañjāb Darpan*, 18 September 1935, p. 10; 3 October, pp. 6, 11, 12; 10 October, p. 7; 17 October, p. 7; 24 October, pp. 5, 7; 31 October, p. 7; 21 November, pp. 7, 13; 28 November, p. 7; 5 December, pp. 7, 11, 16; 19 December, p. 11.

14. Grewal, *The Akalis*, p. 89. During this affair, a small number of Sikhs were murdered by disgruntled Muslims in Lahore. Ganda Singh, *History of The Gurdwara Shahidganj, Lahore from its origins to November 1935* (Amritsar, 1935). The Muslim opinion of this event is in David Gilmartin's *Empire and Islam: Punjab and the Making of Pakistan* (Berkeley, 1988), pp. 99–103. The Muslim agitators were killed when police shot into the crowds in order to disperse them.

15. For the Punjab after 1947, see A.S. Sarhadi, *Punjabi Suba: The Story of*

txhe Struggle (Delhi, 1970) and Paul Brass, *Language, Religion and Politics in North India* (Cambridge, 1974), pp. 318–36. The Akalis and the Emergency are noted in Grewal, *The Akalis*, pp. 144–6. It is estimated that more than 40,000 Akalis were jailed during this campaign.

16. Grewal, *The Sikhs of Punjab*, pp. 215–18.

17. Bhindranwale's speech of May 1983 makes this claim (as translated into English by R.S. Sandhu of the Sikh Religious and Educational Trust of Dublin, Ohio). By this time, some 70,000 Sikhs had already volunteered to defend their faith from the Sant Nirankaris. Bhindranwale expected 100,000 to eventually sign up.

18. Bhindranwale speech, June 1983. Translated into English by R.S. Sandhu.

19. Das, 'Time, Self and Community', p. 128.

20. Bhindranwale sermon, 20 September 1983 and various sermons of May and June 1983, for example.

21. In the same sermon, Bhindranwale alludes to Guru Nanak's *Slok vārān te vadhik* 20.

22. Stanley Tambiah, *Leveling Crowds: Ethnonationalist Conflicts and Collective Violence in South Asia* (Berkeley, 1996), pp. 140–2 and Das, 'Time, Self and Community', pp. 118–36, for example.

23. *They Massacre Sikhs*, as noted in Das, 'Time, Self and Community', p. 126.

24. Ibid.

25. Ibid., pp. 122, 125–7.

26. Bhindranwale speech, 20 September 1983. Translated into English by R.S. Sandhu. The Anandpur Sahib Resolution which Bhindranwale had in mind was probably the one confirmed by the Akali Dal in 1982. It was in August 1982 that the leader of the Akali Dal, Harchand Singh Longowal, called upon Sikhs to engage in a *dharam yudh morchā* to persuade the government to adopt the principles of the resolution. Bhindranwale's speech was delivered with this backdrop. For the full text of the resolution, see *EoS*, pp. 133–41.

27. As with most Sikh leaders, Bhindranwale often alluded to the disproportionate number of Sikh sacrifices for Indian independence.

28. Das, 'Time, Self and Community', p. 122.

29. Ibid.

30. Joyce Pettigrew, 'The State and Local Groupings in the Sikh Rural Areas, Post-1984', in Gurharpal Singh, et al. (ed.), *Punjabi Identity: Continuity and Change* (Delhi, 1996), pp. 139–58; idem, *Sikhs of the Punjab: Unheard Voices of State and Guerrilla Violence* (London, 1995); and C.K. Mahmood, *Fighting for Faith and Nation: Dialogues with Sikh Militants* (Philadelphia, 1997). Various Sikh organizations worldwide have published numerous newspaper articles and pamphlets explaining the reasons why many Sikhs have taken to armed rebellion in India.

31. Although Pettigrew notes that many of those who demanded such items from Sikh villagers were really police informants or state-backed militant infiltrators, and that it was these men who tainted the image of the Sikh *khārkū*, her claims are based principally upon conversations with militants. Such conclusions are, therefore, suspect. Joyce Pettigrew, 'The State and Local Groupings in the Sikh Rural Areas'. The reasons for the failure of militancy in Punjab are also being examined (at the time of writing this book) by Harish Puri and Paramjit

Singh of GNDU, who are conducting interviews with villagers throughout Gurdaspur and Amritsar districts.

32. It appears that any Sikh who was killed by either the police or the militants in the period of strife is referred to as a shahid.

33. Narain Singh, *Sahīdī* (Amritsar, 1997), pp. 5–6.

34. *1996–97 Pustak Sūchī: Siṅgh Bradarz.* The four prints shown are Kirpal Singh's martyrdom of Mani Singh, the martyrdom of Subeg Singh and his son, Shahbaz Singh, on the wheel, the deaths of Sikhs at Panja Sahib during the Gurdwara Reform Movement, and the storming of the Golden Temple by the Afghan forces of Ahmad Shah Abdali.

35. Books on Sikh martyrs have increased markedly over the last ten years, moreover. Two authors who have written a number of martyrologies for the Singh Brothers of Amritsar are Giani Trilok Singh and Savaran Singh.

36. Clifford Geertz, 'Deep Play: Notes on the Balinese Cockfight', in his *The Interpretation of Cultures* (New York, 1973), pp. 412–53.

Index